Shorewords

Edited by Susan A. C. Rosen

Shorewords

A Collection of
American Women's
Coastal Writings

University of Virginia Press

Charlottesville

University of Virginia Press
© 2003 by the Rector and Visitors of the University of Virginia
All rights reserved
Printed in the United States of America on acid-free paper
First published 2003

9 8 7 6 5 4 3 2 1

Library of Congress Cataloging-in-Publication Data
Shorewords : a collection of American women's coastal
writings / edited by Susan A. C. Rosen.
    p.   cm.
  ISBN 0-8139-2233-x (cloth : alk. paper)
— ISBN 0-8139-2234-8 (pbk. : alk. paper)
    1. American literature—Women authors. 2. Seashore—
Literary collections. 3. Coasts—Literary collections.
I. Rosen, Susan A. C., 1956–
PS509.S35 S55 2003
810.8'032146—dc21

2003007375

Ships at a distance have every man's wish on board. For some they come in with the tide. For others they sail forever on the horizon, never out of sight, never landing until the Watcher turns his eyes away in resignation, his dreams mocked to death by Time. That is the life of men.

Now, women forget all those things they don't want to remember, and remember everything they don't want to forget. The dream is the truth. Then they act and do things accordingly.

—Zora Neale Hurston, *Their Eyes Were Watching God*

For my mother, who always returned to the shore

Contents

Observers and Naturalists Explore the Marginal World 119

Love and Desire in the Littoral Zone 171

Choosing the Coast 211

Working along the Shorelines 253

On the Edge: Madness, Illness, Seeking, and Healing 295

Preface

. . . .

I have just returned from a long walk on the winter beach. Not planning any particular course, I followed the shoreline east, passed by the homes of summer residents and a few year-round folks, passed the back of the small town of Montauk, New York, and I kept walking. I have been walking this shore most of my life, a geography of edges. Today's walk began with a dream. At some point in my sleep last night, I dreamed the sound of the waves had ceased. The rise and fall of the tide had stopped, and the ocean, flattened, had turned clear like a mountain lake so that I could see through to the bottom of the sea. Somehow the coast had reconfigured itself and was no more. A recurring dream, it tells me that I need to go walking along the edge of the Atlantic to let my mind shift freely from one thought to another.

On my walk, I encountered only two other people, both women. In the summer, this beach is filled with families and couples on honeymoons and groups of teenagers and surfers. But during the winter, despite the beauty of a winter beach, I find very few people to whom I can wave a friendly morning greeting. I have, however, been thinking about the beach world. For years I have been drawn to the stories of the sea and stories of the life that attaches itself to the sea, shoreline stories. When I was a child, I read great sea and travel stories, *Gulliver's Travels, Robinson Crusoe,* and *Kidnapped.* Later on I read *Moby-Dick, Two Years before the Mast,* and the *Old Man and the Sea,* plus many others. It didn't occur to me then that there were rarely women aboard these books, but later I wondered what stories the women might tell, so I went looking for them. The women's stories intrigued me. And as I wandered past Ditch Plains beach, a popular summer place for surfers, I realized that I am attached to women's stories because they connect so well to one another, each seems to complete another despite regional differences, and women often tell an alternative story to men's tales. One of the women I passed on my walk is familiar, and her particular story, although not written or published, can be found, in some version, in the works of women who write about the coast. She has been living in a wooden, two-room house in the

Hither Hills section of Montauk for over fifty years. Her little house sits tentatively on the top of a hill, and from her living room window she can see the ocean. For the last twenty years she has lived alone. Her husband died, and rather than return to the interior part of the United States where her children live, she stays on at the beach. It is a lonely world, a harsh one. What makes her stay? I'd say that she is caught in the littoral zone.

What is the world of the littoral? It is not, strictly speaking, the world of the vast, of the immense ocean, nor is it strictly a place enclosed, land locked; it is the space in between; it is the coast, a place that constantly reshapes itself. I often think of the coast in Gaston Bachelard's term of "intimate immensity." In *The Poetics of Space*, Bachelard warns that intimate immensity is not just the simple juxtaposition of land against sea but it is a place that inspires meditation and dreams. Weather, waves, and tides influence the intersection between land and sea here, and the force of the waves can transform the coastline in a few hours or sometimes just moments. Winter storms, hurricanes, and tidal currents can destroy a once wide beach in a day. The immediate and slow dramas of the coast inspire reflection. Rachel Carson in *The Edge of the Sea* says, "The edge of the sea is a strange and beautiful place. All through the long history of Earth it has been an area of unrest where waves have broken heavily against the land, where the tides have pressed forward over the continents, receded, and then returned. . . . Always the edge of the sea remains an elusive and indefinable boundary." Shores are the fastest changing environment on earth, and yet they remain constant within those changes, a place where one always hears the sound of surf against sand, rhythmic and true. The littoral is a place where, because of the many sets of oppositions—land/water, constancy/change, wilderness/built world, interior/exterior—intimate immensity might be found.

Coastlines vary physically and in the way we respond to them imaginatively. New England, bordered by an irregular coastline formed by the abrading action of glaciers, is known by scientists as a drowned coast, as is the coast of the Pacific Northwest, which was formed by volcanic action and the collision of tectonic plates. For the writer, a drowned coast might conjure up images dark and mysterious, a place of conflict and stubborn compromise. Or the writer may see hope, survival, potential. Both the northeast and northwest coasts of the United States are rocky and rugged; cliffs and trees hover close to the shore, giving the impression that only the most hardy species could survive in such an environment. Yet the protected bays and inlets may provide shelter or instead be the setting for quick and unexpected disaster, as Harriet Beecher Stowe imagines in *The Pearl of Orr's Island* when she writes, "the ship rose on a great wave clear out of the water, and the next second seemed to leap with a desperate plunge into the narrow passage; for a moment there was a shivering of the masts and the rigging, and she went down and was gone." Along the Atlantic shore south of New England, the coasts—commonly fronted by barrier islands—are broken up into a series of broad temperate bays and estuaries offering a greater sense of peace and survival, of birth and healing than their rugged counterpart of land or seascapes. The Gulf of Mexico, whose waves usually roll gently to shore, can turn unexpectedly violent during hurricane season, scattering human structures from their foundations. Beach dunes, barrier islands, rocky shore cliffs, tidal flats, salt marshes, mangrove swamps, deltas, and protected harbors all provide inspiration for writers.

The world of the littoral allows women writers to fully explore the conflicts, compromises, and transformations negotiated in an environment that is not simply a boundary or an edge but an active interaction between two worlds. Maritime literature and history have long been considered the province of seafaring men, while little critical consideration is given to the shoreline stories of women. There have been many collections of tales of storms at sea; great battles and great voyages; descriptions of boats, fishing, and soul searching; but the absence of women writers in these books is notable. Critically, women barely exist in the genre. Certainly male authors write about women, shore wives and lovers waiting for their sailors to return, bar prostitutes, mythic mermaids and silkies, mothers and daughters, but the women in the men's stories and lives are often peripheral. Is it true that women are just marginal in maritime literature? No, but much of what women have written has been written from the vantage point of the shore and has not found a place in the mainstream of maritime literature. Many women did set off to sea in the nineteenth century and even more in the latter part of the twentieth century to experience the adventures of the sea. Often they went disguised as men or, as was more common, they traveled with their seafaring husbands, as did Mary Brewster and Nancy Allen. The women who went to sea as captains' wives accompanied their husbands on a variety of voyages, trading goods, fishing, or whaling. Often these women kept diaries or journals recording their daily experiences. But many more women ended up living on the coast, set down on the shore to write from a littoral vantage point.

In this anthology, I bring together a selection of women authors who struggle to understand the littoral of female identity. Some of these writers feel trapped by the shore while others have chosen the shore to explore the tidal ebb and flow of their lives. After reading these selections, it becomes apparent there is not all that much distance between the men and women who write about the coast. While both genders concern themselves with issues of struggle and survival, of isolation and connection, and of abandonment, community, fear, joy, and self-revelation, the women's stories do differ in some fundamental ways, tackling these common themes from an alternative perspective. It is valuable to gather these women's stories simply because, taken together, these women create a chorus of coastal tales.

As I look at the selection of women writers collected here, eight thematic categories present themselves. There is a group of stories, a play, and poems that voice the frustrations, sorrows, and restrictions of being bound to the shore. In these works, women have often been left to maintain the domestic sphere while their husbands or lovers have gone to sea. A second group tells the experiences of growing up in a coastal environment, exploring, learning, and negotiating the shore as the authors gain an awareness and intimacy with place. Women have long been careful observers of the nature of the shore, and another set of these women's writings tells of passion and love and desire both lost and found in the in-between world of the coast. Many of the women writers whose works appear in this anthology have chosen the shore for a variety of reasons. One section of this anthology brings together stories of love and passion at the beach. Sometimes that love is wild and dramatic, mimicking the wildness of the ocean, and, at other times we see love and compromise, land and water. Some of these coastal women authors write about women who look for inspiration; other characters seek solace from an overly complex other world; some are fleeing from troubled relationships; and others are just drawn to a place where they can renew a sense of discovery and wonder. The shore, however, is also a place for hard work, a place to earn one's living. Women also write about working the shore; some work side by side with the men in their lives, while others tell the tales of those who have worked the shore all their lives. These second-hand observations of men who work the shore contain thoughtful observations about the nature of working along the coast. Many of the stories express great sorrow. Women often sought the shore when in emotional or physical pain, when their loved ones were ill or dying, or when they came to a point in their lives when they needed to find peace and healing. In the selections in On the Edge: Madness, Illness, Seeking, and Healing," the shore may offer the central characters paths to healing while at other times the shore forces the women to seek paths toward their sorrows. The last section of the anthology considers the women who go beyond the shoreline, those who, after standing along the edge for a while, decide to break free of the coast.

This anthology is admittedly selective and full of exclusions, as all anthologies inevitably are, but it earnestly works to add women's voices to maritime literature. Like most editors of anthologies, I have been compelled for practical reasons to abridge some of the selections. I hope that the final selection, a combination of established, award-winning writers with less well-known authors, brings together works that will take you to the shore.

I would gratefully like to acknowledge the following colleagues, friends, and family for their generous help and support. Ian Marshall for his suggestion that I begin this project and his encouragement along the way. Jim Papa for providing conversation, debate, and insight into coastal literature. Kent Ryden for reading an early draft and offering advice for improvement. Diane Freedman for her meticulous reading of the final draft. Melody Graulich for her pertinent comments and her excellent essay "Opening Windows toward the Sea: Harmony and Reconciliation in American Women's Sea Literature." The many ASLE folks who made suggestions via cyberspace: Bill Atwill, Pamela Banting, Brian Bartlett, Bill Doyle, John Gamber, Mark Hoyer, Alex Hunt, Richard Hunt, Paul Lindholdt, Walter Minot, Carter Neal, Bernard Quetchenbach, Jim Stebbings, Allison Wallace, Fran Zauhar. I would also like to thank Boyd Zenner for her persistence and kindness; Ellen Satrom and Toni Mortimer for their editorial guidance; Kath Sanders, a most reliable reader and critic; Jane Kleinman, my summer shore-walking companion; Lil at the Wagon in Montauk; the Sanibel Island librarians; Vicki Jacobs for meandering through the California Surf Museum with me; and Stephanie Berger, Kathleen Krivack, and Rebecca Kajs for their friendship and support throughout this project. And special love and thanks to Perry, Sara, and Jake.

Caught in the Ecotone

As I leave my house early this June morning to go wander along the beach with Kali, my dog, I first notice my across-the-way neighbor's house. It is a small house with only three rooms, no basement, and a one-car garage. The house tilts slightly, as though years of bearing up against the wind have gently tipped it away from the ocean. I think about my other neighbors. Most of the houses in this section of Hither Hills in Montauk, New York, have been here for more than thirty years, and some of the houses, like the one directly across from mine, have been here for more than fifty. These are not the large and elegant summer-boom houses; instead, they are the ones mostly inhabited by year-round residents, many by single women. When I get to talking to Marge, the neighbor two houses down, she reminds me that she has been widowed for seven years now, that she misses her husband, her dog, her daughter, and her son. She takes her time talking with me and petting Kali. "Come back soon," she says, more to Kali than to me, I think. I look at her solid A-frame house and remember when her husband and son were framing it. I watched them build that house, hard work, careful work. Her son has long since moved away. Yet she stays here by the coast, as do many of the other now-single women in this coastal neighborhood. These very real women who work in town or raise money for the library or donate time to the lighthouse call up the stories of fictional women, some of whom have chosen to live on the coast and others who have been trapped in the ecotone.

An ecotone is a point of abrupt change, a place where two or more ecosystems interact, as, for example, prairie-forest junctions or intertidal zones on a seacoast. However, for the writer, coasts can be more than physical zones; sometimes they are actual or metaphoric ecotones. Women writers have long been found in the ecotone. The writings of women such as Harriet Beecher Stowe, Susan Glaspell, and Tess Gallagher consider the lives of women bound to the shore while their husbands/lovers/fathers/brothers go to sea. In these authors' works, the shore is not simply a boundary or an edge; it assumes the existence of an active interaction between two or more ecosystems, land and sea, resulting in an area that has qualities nonexistent in either of the adjacent ecosystems. Often the flora and fauna fight hard to adjust to the merging of environments; some species may not survive, and, sometimes, the flora and fauna become bound to the ecotone, like the women who wait ashore for their men to return from faraway adventures at sea. Susan Glaspell's one-act play *The Outside* takes place both inside an old but protective boathouse and outside on the shore facing the sea, where great danger is ever present. The boat-house is actually an abandoned lifesaving station and provides a setting where issues of life and death merge. The main female character of the play, Mrs. Patrick, has been abandoned to the shore. After her husband's drowning she no longer belongs to the interior landscape of the city where she once lived, nor can she join her husband in the sea. Although not physically dead, her emotional state resides somewhere between life and death, reflective of the physical place she inhabits. Glaspell's protagonist pays close attention to the shore grasses, trees, and vines. Near the end of the play Mrs. Patrick, in despair and exhaustion, says of her littoral world that it is "The edge of life. Where life trails off to dwarfed things not worth a name." Glaspell's sensitiv-ity to women who have been left behind in an environment that entraps them is only one aspect of what makes this play so compelling.

Sometimes, ecotones are populated by more kinds of birds, animals, or plants than can be found in their neighboring communities. They are brim-ming with life and creativity, and the species found there are tenacious and strong. But, as Tess Gallagher points out in "The Woman Who Raised Goats," the new species created in an ecotone must fight for its place. In this poem, a woman recalls how she had wanted the same life choices as her father and brothers, all fishermen. The old men of the town laugh her back into her home, where she begins to develop odder and odder behaviors. She does not, however, forget her desire for the sea, and she spends her days watching the harbor. It is not unusual to find these women watching the sea from behind a window, where their visions are always framed and limited. The narrator in "The Woman Who Raised Goats" is a new species, one who grows up on the coast and is therefore suited to a coastal life but, for all her tenacity, because of societal traditions remains trapped.

In *The Pearl of Orr's Island*, Harriet Beecher Stowe presents two charac-ters—mother and daughter—whose lives are bound to the shore. Both women are portrayed as frail, stereotypically feminine, and unable to stand up to the rugged life of the New England coast. Under no circumstances can ei-ther of these women go beyond their domestic activities. The mother, Naomi, is compared to a fragile April wildflower who clings to the mossy New En-gland granite: She is not a part of the regular and rough landscape. She col-lapses at the very moment her husband's ship crashes in the harbor and lives just long enough to give birth. The daughter, Mara, is also trapped in interior space. She "sits at the open window that looked forth toward the ocean." And, like her mother, Mara will not live long enough to fulfill the community's wish that she live into maturity in her mother's place.

The women caught here on the coast can no more leave the shore than can the sea grass. Many are not suited to the place they find themselves inhabiting; they cannot survive or thrive. Other women do survive the narrow boundaries of the littoral, becoming acclimated to the terrain, but as some of these coastal women writers tell us, society is not yet ready to accept these new and aggressive female species. I think about these women—the ones who are trapped, the ones who are strong, the ones who have found themselves to be someone new—as I continue on my walk down the hill from my house toward the shore.

Naomi

On the road to the Kennebec, below the town of Bath, in the State of Maine, might have been seen, on a certain autumnal afternoon, a one-horse wagon, in which two persons were sitting. One was an old man, with the peculiarly hard but expressive physiognomy which characterizes the seafaring population of the New England shores. A clear blue eye, evidently practiced in habits of keen observation, white hair, bronzed, weather-beaten cheeks, and a face deeply lined with the furrows of shrewd thought and anxious care, were points of the portrait that made themselves felt at a glance.

By his side sat a young woman of two-and-twenty, of a marked and peculiar personal appearance. Her hair was black, and smoothly parted on a broad forehead, to which a pair of penciled dark eyebrows gave a striking and definite outline. Beneath, lay a pair of large black eyes, remarkable for tremulous expression of melancholy and timidity. The cheek was white and bloodless as a snowberry, though with the clear and perfect oval of good health; the mouth was delicately formed, with a certain sad quiet in its lines, which indicated a habitually repressed and sensitive nature.

The dress of this young person, as often happens in New England, was, in refinement and even elegance, a marked contrast to that of her male companion and to the humble vehicle in which she rode. There was not only the most fastidious neatness, but a delicacy in the choice of colors, an indication of elegant tastes in the whole arrangement, and the quietest suggestion in the world of an acquaintance with the usages of fashion, which struck one oddly in those wild and dreary surroundings. On the whole, she impressed one like those fragile wild-flowers which in April cast their fluttering shadows from the mossy crevices of the old New England granite,—an existence in which colorless delicacy is united to a sort of elastic hardihood of life, fit for the rocky soil and harsh winds it is born to encounter.

The scenery of the road along which the two were riding was wild and bare. Only savins and mulleins, with their dark pyramids or white spires of velvet leaves, diversified the sandy wayside; but out at sea was a wide sweep of blue, reaching far to the open ocean, which lay rolling, tossing, and breaking into white caps of foam in the bright sunshine. For two or three days a northeast storm had been raging, and the sea was in all the commotion which such a general upturning creates.

The two travelers reached a point of elevated land, where they paused a moment, and the man drew up the jogging, stiff-jointed old farm-horse, and raised himself upon his feet to look out at the prospect.

There might be seen in the distance the blue Kennebec sweeping out toward the ocean through its picturesque rocky shores, decked with cedars and other dusky evergreens, which were illuminated by the orange and flame-colored trees of Indian summer. Here and there scarlet creepers swung long trailing garlands over the faces of the dark rock, and fringes of goldenrod above swayed with the brisk blowing wind that was driving the blue waters seaward, in face of the up-coming ocean tide,—a conflict which caused them to rise in great foam-crested waves. There are two channels into this river from the open sea, navigable for ships which are coming in to the city of Bath; one is broad and shallow, the other narrow and deep, and these are divided by a steep ledge of rocks.

Where the spectators of this scene were sitting, they could see in the distance a ship borne with tremendous force by the rising tide into the mouth of the river, and encountering a northwest wind which had succeeded the gale, as northwest winds often do on this coast. The ship, from what might be observed in the distance, seemed struggling to make the wider channel, but was constantly driven off by the baffling force of the wind.

"There she is, Naomi," said the old fisherman, eagerly, to his companion, "coming right in." The young woman was one of the sort that never start, and never exclaim, but with all deeper emotions grow still. The color slowly mounted into her cheek, her lips parted, and her eyes dilated with a wide, bright expression; her breathing came in thick gasps, but she said nothing.

The old fisherman stood up in the wagon, his coarse, butternut-colored coat-flaps fluttering and snapping in the breeze, while his interest seemed to be so intense in the efforts of the ship that he made involuntary and eager movements as if to direct her course. A moment passed, and his keen, practiced eye discovered a change in her movements, for he cried out involuntarily,—

"*Don't* take the narrow channel to-day!" and a moment after, "O Lord! O Lord! have mercy,—there they go! Look! look! look!"

And, in fact, the ship rose on a great wave clear out of the water, and the next second seemed to leap with a desperate plunge into the narrow passage;

Caught in the Ecotone

for a moment there was a shivering of the masts and the rigging, and she went down and was gone.

"They're split to pieces!" cried the fisherman. "Oh, my poor girl—my poor girl—they're gone! O Lord have mercy!"

The woman lifted up no voice, but, as one who has been shot through the heart falls with no cry, she fell back,—a mist rose up over her great mournful eyes,—she had fainted.

The story of this wreck of a home-bound ship just entering the harbor is yet told in many a family on this coast. A few hours after, the unfortunate crew were washed ashore in all the joyous holiday rig in which they had attired themselves that morning to go to their sisters, wives, and mothers.

This is the first scene in our story.

Mara

Down near the end of Orr's Island, facing the open ocean, stands a brown house of the kind that the natives call "lean-to," or "linter,"—one of those large, comfortable structures, barren in the ideal, but rich in the practical, which the workingman of New England can always command. The waters of the ocean came up within a rod of this house, and the sound of its moaning waves was even now filling the clear autumn starlight. Evidently something was going on within, for candles fluttered and winked from window to window, like fireflies in a dark meadow, and sounds as of quick footsteps, and the flutter of brushing garments, might be heard.

Something unusual is certainly going on within the dwelling of Zephaniah Pennel to-night.

Let us enter the dark front-door. We feel our way to the right, where a solitary ray of light comes from the chink of a half-opened door. Here is the front room of the house, set apart as its place of especial social hilarity and sanctity,—the "best room," with its low studded walls, white dimity window-curtains, rag carpet, and polished wood chairs. It is now lit by the dim gleam of a solitary tallow candle, which seems in the gloom to make only a feeble circle of light around itself, leaving all the rest of the apartment in shadow.

In the centre of the room, stretched upon a table, and covered partially by a sea-cloak, lies the body of a man of twenty-five,—lies, too, evidently as one of whom it is written, "He shall return to his house no more, neither shall his place know him any more." A splendid manhood has suddenly been called to forsake that lifeless form, leaving it, like a deserted palace, beautiful in its desolation. The hair, dripping with the salt wave, curled in glossy abundance on the finely-formed head; the flat, broad brow; the closed eye, with its long black lashes; the firm, manly mouth; the strongly-moulded chin,—all, all were sealed with that seal which is never to be broken till the great resurrection day.

He was lying in a full suit of broadcloth, with a white vest and smart blue neck-tie, fastened with a pin, in which was some braided hair under a crystal. All his clothing, as well as his hair, was saturated with sea-water, which trickled from time to time, and struck with a leaden and dropping sound into a sullen pool which lay under the table.

This was the body of James Lincoln, ship-master of the brig Flying Scud, who that morning had dressed himself gayly in his state-room to go on shore and meet his wife,—singing and jesting as he did so.

This is all that you have to learn in the room below; but as we stand there, we hear a trampling of feet in the apartment above,—the quick yet careful opening and shutting of doors,—and voices come and go about the house, and whisper consultations on the stairs. Now comes the roll of wheels, and the Doctor's gig drives up to the door; and, as he goes creaking up with his heavy boots, we will follow and gain admission to the dimly-lighted chamber.

Two gossips are sitting in earnest, whispering conversation over a small bundle done up in an old flannel petticoat. To them the doctor is about to address himself cheerily, but is repelled by sundry signs and sounds which warn him not to speak. Moderating his heavy boots as well as he is able to a pace of quiet, he advances for a moment and the petticoat is unfolded for him to glance at its contents; while a low, eager, whispered conversation, attended with much head-shaking, warns him that his first duty is with somebody behind the checked curtains of a bed in the farther corner of the room. He steps on tiptoe, and draws the curtain; and there, with closed eye, and cheek as white as wintry snow, lies the same face over which passed the shadow of death when that ill-fated ship went down.

This woman was wife to him who lies below, and within the hour has been made mother to a frail little human existence, which the storm of a great anguish has driven untimely on the shores of life,—a precious pearl cast up from the past eternity upon the wet wave-ribbed sand of the present. Now, weary with her moanings, and beaten out with the wrench of a double anguish, she lies with closed eyes in that passive apathy which precedes deeper shadows and longer rest.

Over against her, on the other side of the bed, sits an aged woman in an attitude of deep dejection, and the old man we saw with her in the morning is standing with an anxious, awestruck face at the foot of the bed.

The doctor feels the pulse of the woman, or rather lays an inquiring finger where the slightest thread of vital current is scarcely throbbing, and shakes his head mournfully. The touch of his hand rouses her,—her large wild, melancholy eyes fix themselves on him with an inquiring glance, then she shivers and moans—

"Oh, Doctor, Doctor!—Jamie, Jamie!"

"Come, come!" said the doctor, "cheer up, my girl, you've got a fine little daughter,—the Lord mingles mercies with his afflictions."

Her eyes closed, her head moved with a mournful but decided dissent.

A moment after she spoke in the sad old words of the Hebrew Scripture,—

"Call her not Naomi; call her Mara; for the Almighty hath dealt very bitterly with me."

And as she spoke, there passed over her face the sharp frost of the last winter; but even as it passed there broke out a smile, as if a flower had been thrown down from Paradise, and she said,—

"Not my will, but thy will," and so was gone.

Aunt Roxy and Aunt Ruey were soon left alone in the chamber of death.

"She'll make a beautiful corpse," said Aunt Roxy, surveying the still, white form contemplatively, with her head in an artistic attitude.

"She was a pretty girl," said Aunt Ruey; "dear me, what a Providence! I 'member the wedd'n down in that lower room, and what a handsome couple they were."

"They were lovely and pleasant in their lives, and in their deaths they were not divided," add Aunt Roxy, sententiously.

"What was it she said, did ye hear?" said Aunt Ruey.

"She called the baby 'Mary.'"

"Ah! sure enough, her mother's name afore her. What a still, softly-spoken thing she always was!"

"A pity the poor baby didn't go with her," said Aunt Roxy; "seven-months' children are so hard to raise."

"'Tis a pity," said the other.

But babies will live, and all the more when everybody says that it is a pity they should. Life goes on an inexorably in this world as death. It was ordered by THE WILL above that out of these two graves should spring one frail, trembling autumn flower,—the "Mara" whose poor little roots first struck deep in the salt, bitter waters of our mortal life.

Rebecca Harding Davis

Out of the Sea

A raw, gusty afternoon: one of the last dragging breaths of a nor'easter, which swept, in the beginning of November, from the Atlantic coast to the base of the Alleghenies. It lasted a week, and brought the winter,—for autumn had lingered unusually late that year; the fat bottom lands of Pennsylvania, yet green, deadened into swamps, as it passed over them: summery, gay bits of lakes among the hills glazed over with muddy ice; the forests had been kept warm between the western mountains, and held thus late even their summer's strength and darker autumn tints, but the fierce ploughing winds of this storm and its cutting sleet left them a mass of broken boughs and rotted leaves. In fact, the sun had loitered so long, with a friendly look back-turned into these inland States, that people forgot that the summer had gone, and skies and air and fields were merry making together, when they lent their color and vitality to these few bleak days, and then suddenly found that they had entertained winter unawares.

Down the lee coast of New Jersey, however, where the sea and wind spend the year making ready for their winter's work of shipwreck, this storm, though grayer and colder there than elsewhere, toned into the days and nights as a something entirely matter-of-course and consonant. In summer it would have been at home there. Its aspect was different, also, as I said. But little rain fell here; the wind lashed the ocean into fury along the coast, and then rolled in long, melancholy howls into the stretches of barren sand and interminable pine forests; the horizon contracted, though at all times it is narrower than anywhere else, the dome of the sky wider,—clouds and atmosphere forming the scenery, and the land but a round, flat standing-place: but now the sun went out; the air grew livid, as though death were coming through it; solid masses of gray, wet mist moved, slower than the wind, from point to point, like gigantic ghosts gathering to the call of the murderous sea.

"Yonder go the shades of Ossian's heroes," said Mary Defourchet to her companion, pointing through the darkening air.

They were driving carefully in an old-fashioned gig, in one of the lulls of the storm, along the edge of a pine wood, early in the afternoon. The old Doctor,—for it was MacAulay, (Dennis,) from over in Monmouth County, she was with,—the old man did not answer, having enough to do to guide his mare, the sleet drove so in his eyes. Besides, he was gruffer than usual this afternoon, looking with the trained eyes of an old waterdog out to the yellow line of the sea to the north. Miss Defourchet pulled the oil-skin cloth closer about her knees, and held her tongue; she relished the excitement of this fierce fighting the wind, though; it suited the nervous tension which her mind had undergone lately.

It was a queer, lonesome country, this lee coast,—never so solitary as now, perhaps; older than the rest of the world, she fancied,—so many of Nature's voices, both bird and vegetable, had been entirely lost out of it: no wonder it had grown unfruitful, and older and dumber and sad, listening for ages to the unremorseful, cruel cries of the sea; these dead bodies, too, washed up every year on its beaches, must haunt it, though it was not guilty. She began to say something of this to Doctor Dennis, tired of being silent.

"Your country seems to me always to shut itself out from the world," she said; "from the time I enter that desolate region on its border of dwarf oaks and gloomy fires of the charcoal-burners, I think of the old leper and his cry of 'Unclean! unclean!'"

MacAulay glanced anxiously at her, trying to keep pace with her meaning.

"It's a lonesome place enough," he said, slowly. "There be but the two or three farm-keepers; and the places go from father to son, father to son. The linen and carpet-mats in that house you're now in come down from the times before Washington. Stay-at-home, quiet people,—only the men that follow the water, in each generation. There be but little to be made from these flats of white sand. Yes, quiet enough: the beasts of prey aren't scaret out of these pine forests yet. I heard the cry of a panther the other night only, coming from Tom's River: close by the road it was: sharp and sorrowful like a lost child.— As for ghosts," he continued, after a thoughtful pause, "I don't know any that would have reason for walking, without it was Captain Kidd. His treasure's buried along-shore here."

"Ay?" said Mary, looking up shrewdly into his face.

"Yes," he answered, shaking his head slowly, and measuring his whip with one eye. "Along here, many's the Spanish half-dollar I've picked up myself among the kelp. They do say they're from a galleon that went ashore come next August thirty years ago, but I don't know that."

"And the people in the hamlet?" questioned Mary, nodding to a group of scattered, low-roofed houses.

"Clam-fishers, the maist o' them, There be quite a many wrackers, but they live farther on, towards Barnegat. But a wrack draws them, like buzzards to a carcass."

Miss Defourchet's black eye kindled, as if at the prospect of a good tragedy.

"Did you ever see a wreck going down?" she asked, eagerly.

"Yes,"—shutting his grim lip tighter.

"That emigrant ship last fall? Seven hundred and thirty souls lost, they told me."

"I was not here to know, thank God," shortly.

"It would be a sensation for a life-time,"—cuddling back into her seat, with no hopes of a story from the old Doctor.

MacAulay sat up stiffer, his stern gray eye scanning the ocean-line again as the mare turned into the more open plains of sand sloping down to the sea. It was up-hill work with him, talking to this young lady. He was afraid of a woman who had lectured in public, nursed in the hospitals, whose blood seemed always at fever heat, and whose aesthetic taste could seek the point of view from which to observe a calamity so horrible as the emigrant ship going down with her load of lives. "She's been fed on books too much," he thought. "It's the trouble with young women nowadays." On the other hand, for himself, he had lost sight of the current of present knowledges,—he was aware of that, finding how few topics in common there were between them; but it troubled the self-reliant old fellow but little. Since he left Yale, where he and this girl's uncle, Doctor Bowdler, had been chums together, he had lived in this out-of-the-way corner of the world, and many of the rough ways of speaking and action of the people had clung to him, as their red mud to his shoes. As he grew older, he did not care to brush either off.

Miss Defourchet had been a weight on his mind for a week or more. Her guardian, Doctor Bowdler, had sent her down to board in one of the farm-houses. "The sea-air will do her good, physically," he said in a note to his old chum, with whom he had always kept up a lingering intercourse; "she's been over-worked lately,—sick soldiers, you know. Mary went into the war *con amore*, like all women, or other happy people who are blind of one eye. Besides, she is to be married about Christmas, and before she begins life in earnest it would do her good to face something real. Nothing like living by the sea, and with those homely, thorough-blood Quakers, for bringing people to their simple, natural selves. By the way, you have heard of Dr. Birkenshead, whom she marries? though he is a surgeon,—not exactly in your profession. A surprisingly young man to have gained his reputation. I'm glad Mary marries a man of so much mark; she has pulled alone so long, she needs a master."

So MacAulay had taken pains to drive the young lady out, as to-day, and took a general fatherly sort of charge of her, for his old friend's sake.

Doctor Bowdler had frankly told his niece his reasons for wishing her to go down to the sea-shore. They nettled her more than she chose to show. She was over thirty, an eager humanitarian, had taught the freedmen at Port Royal, gone to Gettysburg and Antietam with sanitary stores,—surely, she did not need to be told that she had yet to begin life in earnest! But she was not sorry for the chance to rest and think. After she married she would be taken from the quiet Quaker society in Philadelphia, in which she always had moved, to one that would put her personal and mental powers to a sharp proof; for Birkenshead, by right of his professional fame, and a curiously attractive personal eccentricity, had gradually become the nucleus of one of the best and most brilliant circles in the country, men and women alike distinguished for their wit and skill in extracting the finest tones from life while they lived. The quiet Quaker girl was secretly on her mettle,—secretly, too, a little afraid. The truth was, she knew Doctor Birkenshead only in the glare of public life; her love for him was, as yet, only a delicate intellectual appreciation that gave her a keen delight. She was anxious that in his own world he should not be ashamed of her. She was glad he was to share this breathing-space with her; they could see each other unmasked. Doctor Bowdler and he were coming down from New York on Ben Van Note's lumber-schooner. It was due yesterday, but had not yet arrived.

"You are sure," MacAulay said to her, as they rode along, "that they will come with Ben?"

"Quite sure. They preferred it to the cars for the novelty of the thing, and the storm lulled the day they were to sail. Could the schooner make this inlet in a sea like that?"

Doctor Dennis, stooping to arrange the harness, pretended not to hear her.

"Ben, at least," he thought, "knows that to near the bar to-day means death."

"One would think," he added aloud, "that Dick Bowdler's gray hairs and thirty years of preaching would have sobered his love of adventure. He was a foolhardy chap at college."

Miss Defourchet's glance grew troubled, as she looked out at the gathering gloom and the crisp bits of yellow foam blown up to the carriage wheels. Doctor Dennis turned the mare's head, thus hiding the sea from them; but its cry sounded for miles inland to-day,—an awful, inarticulate roar. All else was solemn silence. The great salt marshes rolled away on one side of the road, lush and rank,—one solitary dead tree rising from them, with a fish-hawk's uncouth nest lumbering its black trunk; they were still as the grave; even the ill-boding bird was gone long ago, and kept no more its lonely vigil on the dead limb over wind and wave. She glanced uneasily from side to side: high up on the beach lay fragments of old wrecks; burnt spars of vessels drifted ashore to tell, in their dumb way, of captain and crew washed, in one quick moment, by this muddy water of the Atlantic, into that sea far off whence no voyager has come back to bring tidings. Land and sea seemed to her to hint at this thing,— this awful sea, cold and dark beyond. What did the dark mystery in the cry of the surf mean but that? That was the only sound. The heavy silence grew intolerable to her: it forboded evil. The cold, yellow light of day lingered long. Over-head, cloud after cloud rose from the far watery horizon, and drove swiftly and silently inland, bellying dark as it went, carrying the storm. As the horse's hoofs struck hard on the beach, a bird rose out of the marsh and trailed through the air, its long legs dragging behind it, and a blaze of light feathers on its breast catching a dull glow in the fading evening.

"The blue heron flies low," said the Doctor. "That means a heavier storm. It scents a wreck as keenly as a Barnegat pirate."

"It is fishing, maybe?" said Mary, trying to rouse herself.

"It's no canny fisher that," shaking his head. "The fish you'd find in its nest come from the deep waters, where heron never flew. Well, they do say," in answer to her look of inquiry, "that on stormy nights it sits on the beach with a phosphoric light under its wings, and so draws them to shore."

"How soon will the storm be on us? after a pause.

"In not less than two hours. Keep your heart up, child. Ben Van Note is no fool. He'd keep clear of Squan Beach as he would of hell's mouth, such a night as this is going to be. Your friends are all safe. We'll drive home as soon as we've been at the store to see if the mail's brought you a letter."

He tucked in his hairy overcoat about his long legs, and tried to talk cheerfully as they drove along, seeing how pale she was.

"The store" for these two counties was a large, one-roomed frame building on the edge of the great pine woods, painted bright pink, with a wooden blue lady, the old figure-head of some sloop, over the door. The stoop outside was filled with hogsheads and boxes; inside was the usual stock of calicoes, china-ware, molasses-barrels, and books; the post-office, a high desk, on which lay a half dozen letters. By the dingy little windows, on which the rain was now beating sharply, four or five dirty sailors and clam-diggers were gathered, lounging on the counter and kegs, while one read a newspaper aloud slowly. They stopped to look at Miss Defourchet, when she came in, and waited by the door for the Doctor. The gloomy air and forlorn-looking shop contrasted and threw into bright relief her pretty, delicate little figure, and the dainty carriage-dress she wore. All the daylight that was in the store seemed at once to cling to and caress the rare beauty of the small face, with its eager blue eyes and dark brown curls. There was one woman in the store, sitting on a beer-cask, a small, sharp-set old wife, who drew her muddy shoes up under her petticoats out of Mary's way, but did not look at her. Miss Defourchet belonged to a family to whom the ease that money gives and a certain epicu-reanism of taste were natural. She stood there wondering, not unkindly, what these poor creatures did with their lives, and their dull, cloddish days; what would they know of the keen pains, the pleasures, the ambitions, or loves, that ennobled wealthier souls?

"This be yer papper, Doctor," said one; "but we've not just yet finished it."

"All right, boys; Jem Dexter can leave it to-night, as he goes by. Any mail for me, Joe? But you're waiting, Mother Phebe?"—turning with a sudden gentleness to the old woman near Mary.

"Yes, I be. But it don't matter. Joseph, serve the Doctor,"—beating a tattoo on the counter with her restless hands.

The Doctor did not turn to take his letters, however, nor seem to heed the wind which was rising fitfully each moment without, but leaned leisurely on the counter.

"Did you expect a letter to-day?"—in the same subdued voice.

She gave a scared look at the men by the window, and then in a whisper,—

"From my son, Derrick,—yes. The folks here take Derrick for a joke,—an' me. But I'm expectin'. He said he'd come, thee sees?"

"So he did."

"Well, there's none from Derrick to-day, Mother Phebe," said the burly storekeeper, taking his stubby pipe out of his mouth.

She caught her breath.

"Thee looked carefully, Joseph?"

He nodded. She began to unbutton a patched cotton umbrella,—her lips moving as people's do sometimes in the beginning of second childhood.

"I'll go home, then. I'll be back mail-day, Wednesday, Joseph. Four days that is,—Wednesday."

"Lookee here now, Gran!" positively, laying down the pipe to give effect to his words; "you're killin' yerself, you are. Keep a-trottin' here all winter, an' what sort of a report of yerself'll yer make to Derrick by spring? When that 'ere letter comes, if come it do, I've said I'd put on my cut an' run up with it. See there!"—pulling out her thin calico skirt before the Doctor,—"soaked, she is."

"Thee's kind, Joseph, but thee don't know,"—drawing her frock back with a certain dignity. "When my boy's handwrite comes, I must be here. I learned writin' on purpose that I might read it first,"—turning to Mary.

"How long has your boy been gone?" asked Miss Defourchet, heedless of Joseph's warning "Hush-h!"

"Twenty years, come February," eagerly volunteered one or two voices by the window. "She's never heerd a word in that time, an' she never misses a mail-day, but she's expectin'," added one, with a coarse laugh.

"None o' that, Sam Venners," said Joe, sharply. "If so be as Dirk said he'd come, be it half-a-hunder' years, he'll stan' to 't. I knowed Dirk. Many's the clam we toed out o' th' inlet yonner. He's not the sort to hang round, gnawin' out the old folk's meat-pot, as some I cud name. He"—

"I'll go, if thee'll let me apast," said the old woman, humbly curtsying to the men, who now jammed up the doorway.

"It's a cussed shame, Venners," said Joe, when she was out. "Why can't yer humor the old gran a bit? She's the chicken-heartedest woman ever I knowed," explanatory to Miss Defourchet, "an' there ten years she's been mad-like, waitin' for that hang-dog son of hers to come back."

Mary followed her out on the stoop, where she stood, her ragged green umbrella up, her sharp little face turned anxiously to the far sea-line.

"Bad! bad!" she muttered, looking at Mary.

"The storm? Yes. But you ought not to be out in such weather," kindly putting her furred hand on the skinny arm.

The woman smiled,—a sweet, good-humored smile it was, in spite of her meagre, hungry old face.

"Why, look there, young woman,"—pulling up her sleeve, and showing the knotted tendons and thick muscles of her arm. "I'm pretty tough, thee sees. There's not a boatman in Ocean County could pull an oar with me when I was a gell, an' I'm tough yet,"—hooking her sleeve again.

The smile haunted Miss Defourchet; where had she seen it before?

"Was Derrick strongly built?"—idly wishing to recall it.

"Thee's a stranger; maybe thee has met my boy?"—turning on her sharply. "No, that's silly,"—the sad vagueness coming back into the faded eyes. After a pause,—"Derrick, thee said? He was short, the lad was,—but with legs and arms as tender and supple as a wild-cat's. I loss much of my strength when he was born; it was wonderful, for a woman, before; I giv it to him. I'm glad of that! I thank God that I giv it to him!"—her voice sinking, and growing wilder and faster. "Why! why!"

Mary took her hand, half-scared, looking in at the store-door, wishing Doctor Dennis would come.

The old woman tottered and sat down on the lower rung of a ladder standing there. Mary could see now how the long sickness of the hope deferred had touched the poor creature's brain, gentle and loving at first. She pushed the wet yellow sun-bonnet back from the gray hair; she thought she had never seen such unutterable pathos or tragedy as in this little cramped figure, and this old face, turned forever watching to the sea.

"Thee does n't know; how should thee?—gently, but not looking at her. "Thee never had a son; an' when thee has, it will be born in wedlock. Thee's rich, an' well taught. I was jess a clam-fisher, an' knowed nothin' but my baby. His father was a gentleman: come in spring, an' gone in th' fall, an' that was the last of him. That hurt a bit, but I had Derrick. *Oh, Derrick! Derrick!*— whispering, rocking herself to and fro as if she held a baby, cooing over the uncouth name with an awful longing and tenderness in the sound.

Miss Defourchet was silent. Something in all this awed her; she did not understand it.

"I mind," she wandered on, "when the day's work was done, I'd hold him in my arms,—so,—and his sleepy little face would turn up to mine. I seemed to begin to loss him after he was a baby,"—with an old, worn sigh. "He went with other boys. The Weirs and Hallets took him up; they were town-bred people, an' he soon got other notions from mine, an' talked of things I'd heerd nothin' of. I was very proud of my Derrick; but I knowed I'd loss him all the same. I did washin' an' ironin' by nights to keep him dressed like the others,—an' kep' myself out o' their way, not to shame him with his mother."

"And was he ashamed of you?" said Mary, her face growing hot.

"Thee did not know my little boy,"—the old woman stood up, drawing herself to her full height. "His wee body was too full of pluck an' good love to be shamed by his mother. I mind the day I come on them suddint, by the bridge, where they were standin', him an' two o' the Hallets. I was carryin' a basket of herrings. The Hallets they flushed up, an' looked at him to see what he'd do; for they never named his mother to him, I heerd. The road was deep with mud; an' as I stood a bit to balance myself, keepin' my head turned from him, before I knew aught, my boy had me in his arms, an' carried me t' other side. I'm not a heavy weight, thee sees, but his face was all aglow with the laugh.

"'There you are, dear,' he says, puttin' me down, the wind blowin' his brown hair."

"One of the Hallets brought my basket over then, an' touched his hat as if

I'd been a lady. That was the last time my boy had his arms about me: next week he went away. That night I heerd him in his room in the loft, here an' there, here an' there, as if he could n't sleep, an' so for many nights, comin' down in the mornin' with his eyes red an' swollen, but full of the laugh an' joke as always. The Hallets were with him constant, those days. Judge Hallet, their father, were goin' across seas, Derrick said. So one night, I'd got his tea ready, an' were waitin' for him by the fire, knittin',—when he come in an' stood by the mantel-shelf, lookin' down at me, steady. He had on his Sunday suit of blue, Jim Devines giv him.

"'Where be yer other clothes, my son?' I said."

"'They're not clean,' says he. 'I've been haulin' marl for Springer this week. He paid me to-night; the money's in the kitchen-cupboard.'"

"I looked up at that, for it was work I'd never put him to."

"'It'll buy thee new shoes,' said I."

"'I did it for you, mother,' he says, suddint, puttin' his hand over his eyes. 'I wish things were different with you.'"

"'Yes, Derrick.'"

"I went on with my knittin'; for I never talked much to him, for the shame of my bad words, since he'd learned better. But I wondered what he meant; for wages was high that winter, an' I was doin' well."

"'If ever,' he says, speakin' low an' faster, 'if ever I do anything that gives you pain, you'll know it was for love of you I did it. Not for myself, God knows! To make things different for you.'"

"'Yes, Derrick,' I says, knittin' on, for I did n't understan' thin. Afterwards I did. The room was dark, an' it were dead quiet for a bit; then the lad moved to the door."

"'Where be thee goin', Derrick?' I said."

"He come back an' leaned on my chair."

"'Let me tell you when I come back,' he said. You'll wait for me?' stoopin' down an' kissin' me."

"I noticed that, for he did not like to kiss,—Derrick. An' his lips were hot an' dry."

"'Yes, I'll wait my son,' I said. 'Thee'll not be gone long?'"

"He did not answer that, but kissed me again, an' went out quickly."

"I sat an' waited long that night, an' searched till mornin'. There's been a many nights an' days since, but I've never found him. The Hallets all went that night, an' I heerd Derrick went as waiter-boy, so's to get across seas. It's twenty years now. But I think he'll come,"—looking up with a laugh.

Miss Defourchet started; where had she known this woman? The sudden flicker of a smile, followed by a quick contraction of the eyelids and mouth, was peculiar and curiously sensitive and sad; somewhere, in a picture maybe, she had seen the same.

Doctor Dennis, who had waited purposely, came out now on the stoop. Miss Defourchet looked up. The darkness had gathered while they stood there; the pine woods, close at the right, began to lower distant and shapeless; now and then the wind flapped a raw dash of rain in their faces, and then was suddenly still. Behind them, two or three tallow candles, just lighted in the store, sputtered dismal circles of dingy glare in the damp fog; in front, a vague slope of wet night, in which she knew lay the road and the salt marches; and far beyond, distinct, the sea-line next the sky, a great yellow phosphorescent belt, apparently higher than their heads. Nearer, unseen, the night-tide was sent in: it came with a regular muffled throb that shook the ground. Doctor Dennis went down, and groped about his horse, adjusting the harness.

"The poor beast is soaked to the marrow: it's a dull night: d' ye hear how full the air is of noises?"

"It be the sea makin' ready," said Joe, in a whisper, as if it were a sentient thing and could hear. He touched the old woman on the arm and beckoned her inside to one of the candles.

"There be a scrap of a letter come for you; but keep quiet. Ben Van Note's scrawl of a handwrite, think."

The letters were large enough,—printed, in fact: she read it but once.

"Your Dirk come Aboord the Chief at New York. I knowed him by a mark on his wrist—the time jim hallet cut him you mind. he is aged and Differentt name. I kep close. we sail today and Ill Breng him Ashor tomorrer nite plese God. be on Handd."

She folded the letter, crease by crease, and put it quietly in her pocket. Joe watched her curiously.

"D' Ben say when the Chief ud run in?"

"To-night."

"Bah-h! there be n't a vessel within miles of this coast, without a gale drives 'm in."

She did not seem to hear him: was feeling her wet petticoats and sleeves. She would shame Derrick, after all, with this patched, muddy frock! She had worked so long to buy the black silk gown and white neckercher that was folded in the bureau-drawer to wear the day he'd come back!

"When he come back!"

Then, for the first time, she realized what she was thinking about. *Coming to-night!*

Presently Miss Defourchet went to her where she was sitting on a box in the dark and rain.

"Are you sick?" she said, putting her hand out.

"Oh, no, dear!" softly, putting the fingers in her own, close to her breast, crying and sobbing quietly. "Thee hand be a'most as soft as a baby's foot," after a while, fancying the little chap was creeping into her bosom again, thumping with his fat feet and fists as he used to do. Her very blood used to grow wild and hot when he did that, she loved him so. And her heart to-night was just as warm and light as then. He was coming back, her boy: maybe he was poor and sick, a worn-out man; but in a few hours he would be here, and lay his tired head on her breast and be a baby again.

Joe went down to the Doctor with a lantern.

"Van Note meant to run the Chief to-night,"—in an anxious, inquiring whisper.

"He's not an idiot!"

"No,—but, bein' near, the wind may drive 'em on the bar. Look yonder."

"See that, too, Joe?" said bow-legged Phil, from Tom's River, who was up that night.

"That yellow line has never been in the sky since the night the James Frazier—*Ach-h! it's come!*"

He had stooped to help Doctor Dennis with his harness, but now fell forward, clapping his hands to his ears. A terrible darkness swept over them; the whole air was filled with a fierce, risping crackle; then came a sharp concussion, that seemed to tear the earth asunder. Miss Defourchet cried aloud: no one answered her. In a few moments the darkness slowly lifted, leaving the old yellow lights and fogs on sea and land. The men stood motionless as when the tornado passed, Doctor Dennis leaning on his old mare, having thrown one arm about her as if to protect her, his stern face awed.

"There's where it went," said Joe, coolly, drawing his hands from his pockets, and pointing to a black gap in the pine woods. "The best farms in this Jersey country lie back o' that. I told you there was death in the pot, but I didn't think it ud 'a' come this fashion."

"When will the storm be on us?" asked Mary, trembling.

Joe laughed sardonically.

"Have n't ye hed enough of it?"

"There will be no rain after a gust like that," said MacAulay. "I'll try and get you home now. It has done its worst. It will take years to wipe out the woe this night has worked."

The wind had fallen into a dead silence, frightened at itself. And now the

Caught in the Ecotone

sudden, awful thunder of the sea broke on them, shaking the sandy soil on which they stood.

"Thank God that Van Note is so trusty a sailor as you say!" said Mary, buttoning her furs closer to her throat. "They're back in a safe harbor, I doubt not."

Joe and Doctor Dennis exchanged significant glances as they stood by the mare, and then looked again out to sea.

"Best get her home," said Joe, in a whisper.

Doctor Dennis nodded, and they made haste to bring the gig up to the horse-block.

Old Phebe Trull had been standing stirless since the gust passed. She drew a long breath when Mary touched her, telling her to come home with them.

"That was a sharp blow. I'm an old Barnegat woman, an' I've known no such cutters as that. But he'll come. I'm expectin' my boy to-night, young woman. I'm goin' to the beach now to wait for him,—for Derrick."

In spite of the queer old face peering out from the yellow sun-bonnet, with its flabby wrinkles and nut-cracker jaws, there was a fine, delicate meaning in the smile with which she waved her hand down to the stormy beach.

"What's that?" said Doctor Dennis, starting up, and holding his hand behind his ear. His sandy face grew pale.

"I heard nothing," said Mary.

The next moment she caught a dull thud in the watery distance, as if some pulse of the night had throbbed feverishly.

Bow-legged Phil started to his feet.

"It's the gun of the Chief! Van Note's goin' down!" he cried, with a horrible oath, and hobbled off, followed by the other men.

"His little brother Benny be on her," said Joe. "May God have mercy on their souls!"

He had climbed like a cat to the rafters, and thrown down two or three cables and anchors, and, putting them over his shoulder, started soberly for the beach, stopping to look at Miss Defourchet, crouched on the floor of the store.

"You'd best see after her, Doctor. Ropes is all we can do for 'em. No boat ud live in that sea, goin' out."

Going down through the clammy fog, his feet sinking in the marsh with the weight he carried, he could see red lights in the mist, gathering towards shore.

"It's the wrackers goin' down to be ready for mornin'."

And in a few moment stood beside them a half-dozen brawny men, with their legs and chests bare. The beach on which they stood glared white in the yellow light, giving the effect of a landscape in Polar seas. One or two solitary headlands loomed gloomily up, covered with snow. In front, the waters at the edge of the sea broke at their feet in long, solemn, monotonous swells, that reverberated like thunder,—a death-song for the work going on in the chaos beyond.

"Thar's no use doin' anything out thar," said one of the men, nodding gloomily to a black speck in the foaming hell. "She be on the bar this ten minutes, an' she's a mean-built craft, that Chief."

"Could n't a boat run from the inlet?" timidly ventured an eager, blue-eyed little fellow.

"No, Snap," said Joe, letting his anchor fall, and clearing his throat. "Well, there be the end of old Ben, hey? Be yer never tired, yer cruel devil?" turning with a sudden fierceness to the sly foam creeping lazily about his feet.

There was a long silence.

"Bowlegs tried it, but his scow stud still, an' the breakers came atop as if it war a clam-shell. He war n't five yards from shore. His Ben's aboard."

Another peal of a gun from the schooner broke through the dark and storm.

"God! I be sick o' sittin' on shor', an' watchin' men drownin' like rats on a raft," said Joe, wiping the foam from his thick lips, and trotting up and down the sand, keeping his back to the vessel.

Some of the men sat down, their hands clasped about their knees, looking gravely out.

"What cud we do, Joey?" said one. "Thar be Hannah an' the children; we kin give Hannah a lift. But as for Ben it's no use thinkin' about Ben no more."

The little clam-digger Snap was kindling a fire out of the old half-burnt wrecks of vessels.

"It's too late to give 'em warnin'," he said; "but it'll let 'em see we're watchin' 'em at the last. One ud like friends at the last."

The fire lighted up the shore, throwing long bars of hot, greenish flame up the fog.

"Who be them, Joe? whispered a wrecker, as two dim figures came through the marsh.

"She hev a sweetheart aboord. Don't watch her."

The men got up, and moved away, leaving Miss Defourchet alone with Doctor Dennis. She stood so quiet, her eyes glued on the dull, shaking shadow yonder on the bar, that he thought she did not care. Two figures came round from the inlet to where the water shoaled, pulling a narrow skiff.

"Hillo!" shouted Doctor Dennis. "Be you mad?"

Caught in the Ecotone

The stouter of the figures hobbled up. It was Bowlegs. His voice was deadened in the cold of the fog, but he wiped the hot sweat from his face.

"In God's name, be thar none of ye ull bear a hand with me? Ud ye sit here an' see 'em drown? Benny's thar,—my Ben."

Joe shook his head.

"My best friend be there," said the old Doctor. "But what can ye do? Your boat will be paper in that sea, Phil."

"That's so," droned out one or two of the wreckers, dully nodding.

"Curses on ye for cowards, then!" cried Bowlegs, as he plunged into the surf, and righted his boat. "Look who's my mate, shame on ye!"

His mate shoved the skiff out with an oar into the seething breakers, turning to do it, and showed them, by the far-reaching fire-light, old Phebe Trull, stripped to her red woollen chemise and flannel petticoat, her yellow, muscular arms and chest bare. Her peaked old face was set, and her faded blue eye aflame. She did not hear the cry of horror from the wreckers.

"Ye've a better pull than any white-liver of 'em, from Tom's to Barnegat," gasped Bowlegs, struggling against the surf.

She was wrestling for life with Death itself; but the quiet, tender smile did not leave her face.

"My God! If I cud pull as when I was a gell!" she muttered. "Derrick, I'm comin'! I'm comin', boy!"

The salt spray wet their little fire of logs, beside which Snap sat crying,—put it out at last, leaving a heap of black cinders. The night fell heavier and cold; boat and schooner alike were long lost and gone in outer darkness. As they wandered up and down, chilled and hopeless, they could not see each other's faces,—only the patch of white sand at their feet. When they shouted, no gun or cry answered them again. All was silence, save the awful beat of the surf upon the shore, going on forever with its count, count of the hours until the time when the sea shall at last give up its dead.

Ben Van Note did not run the Chief near the shore purposely; but the fog was dense, and Ben was a better sailor than pilot. He took the wheel himself about an hour before they struck,—the two or three other men at their work on the deck with haggard, anxious faces, and silent: it is not the manner of these Jersey coast-men to chatter in heavy weather.

Philbrick, Doctor Bowdler's boy, lounged beside Ben, twisting a greasy lantern: "a town-bred fellow," Ben said; "put him in mind of young, rank cheese."

"You'd best keep a sharp eye, Van Note," he said; this is a dirty bit of water, and you've two great men aboard: one patcher of the body, t' other of the soul."

"I vally my own neck more than either," growled Ben, and after a while forced himself to add, "*He's* no backbone, the little fellow with your master, I mean."

"Umph!" superciliously. "I'd like to see the 'little fellow' making neat bits out of that carcass of yours! His dainty white fingers carve off a fellow's legs and arms. Caring no more than if they were painting flowers. He is a neat flower-painter, Dr. Birkenshead; moulds in clay, too."

He stared as Van Note burst into a coarse guffaw.

"Flower-painter, eh? Well, well, young man. You'd best go below. It's dirtier water than you think."

Doctors Bowdler and Birkenshead were down in the little cabin, reading by the dull light of a coal-oil lamp. When the vessel began to toss so furiously, the elder man rose and paced fussily to and fro, rubbing his fingers through his iron-gray hair. His companion was too much engrossed by his paper to heed him. He had a small, elegantly shaped figure,—the famous surgeon,—a dark face, drawn by a few heavy lines; looking at it, you felt, that, in spite of his womanish delicacies of habit, which lay open to all, never apologized for, he was a man whom you could not approach familiarly, though he were your brother born. He stopped reading presently, slowly folding the newspaper straight, and laying it down.

"That is a delicious blunder of the Administration," with a little gurgling laugh of thorough relish. "You remember La Rochefoucauld's aphorism, 'One is never so easily deceived as when one seeks to deceive others'?"

Doctor Bowdler looked uncomfortable.

"A selfish French Philister, La Rochefoucauld!" he blurted out. "I feel as if I had been steeped in meanness and vulgarity all my life, when I read him."

"He knew men," said the other, coolly, resetting a pocket set of chessmen on the board where they had been playing,—"Frenchmen," shortly.

"Doctor Birkenshead," after a pause, "you appear to have no sympathies with either side, in this struggle for the nation's life. You neither attack nor defend our government."

"In plain English, I have no patriotism? Well, to be honest, I don't comprehend how any earnest seeker for the truth can have. If my country had truth, so far she nourishes me, and I am grateful; if not,—why, the air is no purer nor the government more worthy of reverence because I chanced to be born here."

"Why, Sir," said the Doctor, stopping short and growing red, "you could apply such an argument as that to a man's feeling for his wife or child or mother!"

Caught in the Ecotone

"So you could," looking closely at the queen to see the carving.

Doctor Bowdler looked at him searchingly, and then began his angry walk again in silence. What was the use in answering? No wonder a man who talked in that way was famed in this country and in Europe for his coolness and skill in cutting up living bodies. And yet—remorsefully, looking furtively at him—Birkenshead was not a hard fellow, after all. There was that pauper-hospital of his; and he had known him to turn sick when operating on children, and damn the people who brought them to him.

Doctor Bowdler was a little in dread of this future husband of his niece, feeling there was a great gulf between them intellectually, the surgeon having the rare power in a line of life of which he knew nothing. Besides, he could not understand him,—not his homely, keen little face even. The eyes held their own thought, and never answered yours; but on the mouth there was a forlorn depression sometimes, like that of a man, who, in spite of his fame, felt himself alone and neglected. It rested there now, as he idly fingered the chess-men.

"Mary will kiss it away in time, maybe,"—doubting, as he said it, whether Mary did not come nearer the man's head than his heart. He stopped, looking out of the hole by the ladder that served the purpose of a window.

"It grows blacker every minute. I shall begin to repent tempting you on such a harebrained expedition, Doctor."

"No. This Van Note seem a cautious sailor enough," carelessly.

"Yes. He's on his own ground, too. We ought to run into Squan Inlet by morning. Did you speak?"

Birkenshead shook his head; the Doctor noticed, however, that his hand had suddenly stopped moving the chess-men; he rested his chin in the other.

"Some case he has left worries him," he thought. "He's not the man to relish this wild-goose chase of mine. It's bad enough for Mary to jar against his quiet tastes with her reforming whims, without my"—

"I would regret bringing you here," he said aloud, "if I did not think you would find a novelty in this shore and people. This coast is hardly 'canny,' as MacAulay would say. It came, literally, out of the sea. Sometime, ages ago, it belonged to the bed of the ocean, and it never has reconciled itself to the life of the land; its Flora is different from that of the boundaries; if you dig a few feet into its marl, you find layers of shells belonging to deep soundings, sharks' teeth and bones, and the like. The people, too, have a 'marvelously fishy and ancient smell.'"

The little man at the table suddenly rose, pushing the chessmen from him. What is there to wonder at?—with a hoarse, unnatural laugh. "That's

Nature. You cannot make fat pastures out of sea-sand, any more than a thorough-blood *gentilhomme* out of a clam-digger. The shark's teeth will show, do what you will." He pulled at his whiskers nervously, went to the window, motioning Doctor Bowdler roughly aside. "Let me see what the night is doing."

The old gentleman stared in a grave surprise. What had he said to startle Birkenshead so utterly out of himself? The color had left his face at the first mention of this beach; his very voice was changed, coarse and thick, as if some other man had broken out through him. At that moment, while Doctor Bowdler stood feebly adjusting his watch-chain, and eyeing his companion's back, like one who has found a panther in a domestic cat, and knows not when he will spring, the tornado struck the ocean a few feet from their side, cleaving a path for itself into deep watery walls. There was an instant's reeling and intense darkness, then the old Doctor tried to gather himself up, bruised and sick, from the companion-way, where he had been thrown.

"Better lie still," said Birkenshead, in the gentle voice with which he was used to calm a patient.

The old gentleman managed to sit up on the floor. By the dull glare of the cabin-lantern he could see the surgeon sitting on the lower rung of the ladder, leaning forward, holding his head in his hands.

"Strike a light, can't you, Birkenshead? What has happened? Bah! this is horrible! I have swallowed the sea-water! Hear it swash against the sides of the boat! Is the boat going to pieces?"

"And there met us 'a tempestuous wind called Euroclydon,'" said Birkenshead, looking up with a curious smile.

"Did there?"—rubbing his shoulder. "I've kept clear of the sea so far, and I think in future—Hark! what's that? as through the darkness and the thunderous surge of the water, the short, fierce calls of men on board, came a low shivering crack, distinct as a human whisper. "What is it Birkenshead?" impatiently, when the other made no answer.

"The schooner has struck the bar. She is going to pieces."

The words recalled the old servant of Christ from his insane fright to himself.

"That means death! does it not?"

"Yes."

The two men stood silent,—Doctor Bowdler with his head bent and eyes closed. He looked up presently.

"Let us go on deck now and see what we can do,"—turning cheerfully.

"No, there are too many there already."

There was an old tin life-preserver hanging on a hook by the door; the surgeon climbed up to get it, and began buckling it about the old man in spite of his remonstrances. The timbers groaned and strained, the boat trembled like some great beast in its death-agony, settled heavily, and then the beams on one side of them parted. They stood on a shelving plank floor, snapped off two feet from them, the yellow sky overhead, and the breakers crunching their footing away.

"O God!" cried Bowdler, when he looked out at the sea. He was not a brave man; and he could not see it, when he looked; there was but a horror of great darkness, a thunder of sound, and a chilly creeping of salt-water up his legs, as if the great monster licked his victim with his lifeless tongue. Straight in front of them, at the very edge of the horizon, he thought the little clam-digger's fire opened a tunnel of greenish light into the night, "dull and melancholy as a scene in Hades." They saw the men sitting around the blaze with their hands clasped about their knees, the woman's figure alone, and watching.

"Mary!" cried the old man, in the shrill extremity of his agony.

His companion shivered.

"Take this from me, boy!" cried Doctor Bowdler, trying to tear off the life-preserver. "It's a chance. I've neither wife nor child to care if I live or die. You're young; life's beginning for you. I've done it. Ugh! this water is deadly cold. Take it, I say."

"No," said the other, quietly restraining him.

"Can you swim?"

"In this sea?"—with a half-smile, and a glance at the tossing breakers.

"You'll swim? Promise me you'll swim! And if I come to shore and see Mary?"

Birkenshead had regained the reticent tone habitual to him.

"Tell her, I wish I had loved her better. She will understand. I see the use of love in this last hour."

"Is there anyone else?"

"There used to be some one. Twenty years ago I said I would come, and I'm coming now."

"I don't hear you."

Birkenshead laughed at his own thought, whatever it was. The devil who had tempted him might have found in the laugh an outcry more bitter than any agony of common men.

The planks beneath their feet sank inch by inch. They were shut off from the larboard side of the vessel. For a time they had heard the oaths and cries from the other men, but now all was silent.

"There is no help coming from shore,"—(the old man's voice was weakening,)—"and this footing is giving way."

"Yes, it's going. Lash your arms to me by your braces, Doctor. I can help you for a few moments."

So saying, Birkenshead tore off his own coat and waistcoat; but as he turned, the coming breaker dashed over their heads, he heard a faint gasp, and when his eyes were clear of the salt, he saw the old man's gray hair in the midst of a sinking wave.

"I wish I could have saved him," he said,—then made his way as best he could by feet and hands to a bulk of timber standing out of the water, and sitting down there, clutched his hands about his knees, very much as he used to when he was a clam-digger and watched the other boys bringing in their hauls.

"Twenty years ago I said I'd come, and I'm coming," he went on repeating.

Derrick Trull was no coward, as boy or man, but he made no effort to save himself; the slimy water washed him about like a wet rag. He was alone now, if never before in those twenty years; his world of beautiful, cultured, graceful words and sights and deeds was not here, it was utterly gone out; there was no God here, that he thought of; he was quite alone: so, in sight of this lee coast, the old love in that life dead years ago roused, and the mean crime dragged on through every day since gnawed all the manliness and courage out of him.

She would be asleep now, old Phebe Trull,—in the room off the brick kitchen, her wan limbs curled under her check nightgown, her pipe and noggin of tea on the oven-shelf; he could smell the damp, musty odor of the slopsink near by. What if he could reach shore? What if he were to steal up to her bed and waken her?

"It's Derrick, back, mother," he would say. How the old creature would skirl and cry over her son Derrick!—Derrick! he hated the name. It belonged to that time of degradation and stinting and foulness.

Doctor Birkenshead lifted himself up. Pish! The old fish-wife had long since forgotten her scapegrace son,—thought him dead. *He was dead.* He wondered—and this while every swash of salt-water brought death closer to his lips—if Miss Defourchet had seen "Mother Phebe." Doubtless she had, and had made a sketch of her to show him;—but no, she was not a picturesque pauper,—vulgar, simply. The water came up closer; the cold of it, and the extremity of peril, or maybe, this old gnawing at the heart, more virulent than either, soon drew the strength out of his body: close study and high living had made the joints less supple than Derrick Trull's: he lay there limp and unable,—his brain alert, but fickle. It put the watery death out of sight, and brought his familiar every-day life about him: the dissecting-room; curious cases that had puzzled him; drawing-rooms, beautiful women; he sang airs from the operas, sad, broken little snatches, in a deep, mellow voice finely trained,—fragments of a litany to the Virgin. Birkenshead's love of beauty was a hungry monomania; his brain was filled with memories of the pictures of the Ideal Mother and her Son. One by one they came to him now, the holy woman-type which for ages supplied to the world that tenderness and pity which the Church had stripped from God. Even in his delirium the man of fastidious instincts knew this was what he craved; even now he remembered other living mothers he had known, delicate, nobly born women, looking on their babes with eyes full of all gracious and pure thoughts. With the sharp contrast of a dream came the old clam-digger, barefoot in the mud, her basket of soiled clothes on her shoulder,—her son Derrick, a vulgar lad, aping gentility, behind her. Closer and closer came the waters; a shark's gray hide glittered a few feet from him. Death, sure of his prey, nibbled and played with it; in a little while he lay supine and unconscious.

Reason came back to him like an electric shock; for all the parts of Dr. Birkenshead's organization were instinctive, nervous, like a woman's. When it came, the transient delirium had passed; he was his cool, observant self. He lay on the wet floor of a yawl skiff, his head resting on a man's leg; the man was rowing with even, powerful strokes, and he could feel rather than see in the darkness a figure steering. He was saved. His heart burned with a sudden glorious glow of joy, and genial, boyish zest of life,—one of the excesses of his nature. He tried to speak, but his tongue was stiff, his throat dry; he could have caressed the man's slimy sleeve that touched his cheek, he was so glad to live. The boatman was in no humor for caresses; he drew his labored breath sharply, fighting the waves, rasping out a sullen oath when they baffled him. The little surgeon had tact enough to keep silent; he did not care to talk either. Life rose before him a splendid possibility, as never before. From the silent figure at the helm came neither word nor motion. Presently a bleak morning wind mingled with the fierce, incessant nor'easter; the three in the yawl, all sea-bred, knew the difference.

"Night ull break soon," said Bowlegs.

It did break in an hour or two into a ghastly gray dawn, bitter cold,—the slanting bars of sharp light from beyond the sea-line falling on the bare coast, on a headland of which moved some black, uneasy figures.

"Th' wrackers be thar."

There was no answer.

"Starboard! Hoy, Mother Phebe!"

She swayed her arms round, her head still fallen on her breast. Doctor Birkenshead, from his half-shut eyes, could see beside him the half-naked, withered old body, in its dripping flannel clothes. God! it had come, then, the time to choose! It was she who had saved him! She was here,—alive!

"Mother!" he cried, trying to rise.

But the word died in his dry throat; his body, stiff and icy cold, refused to move.

"What ails ye?" growled the man, looking at her. "Be ye giv' out so near land? We've had a jolly seinin' together," laughing savagely, "ef we did miss the fish we went for, an' brought in this herrin'."

"Thee little brother's safe, Bowlegs," said the old woman, in a feeble far-off voice. "My boy ull bring him to shore."

The boatman gulped back his breath; it sounded like a cry, but he laughed it down.

"You think yer Derrick ull make shore, eh? Well, I don't think that ar way o' Ben. Ben's gone under. It's not often the water gets a ten-year-older like that. I raised him. It was I sent him with Van Note this run. That makes it pleasanter now!" The words were grating out stern and sharp.

"Thee knows Derrick said he'd come," the woman said simply.

She stooped with an effort, after a while, and, thrusting her hand under Doctor Birkenshead's shirt, felt his chest.

"It's a mere patchin' of a body. He's warm yet. Maybe," looking closely into the face, "he'd have seen my boy aboord, an' could say which way he tuk. A drop of raw liquor ull bring him round."

Phil glanced contemptuously at the surgeon's fine linen, and the diamond *solitaire* on the small, white hand.

"It's not likely that chap ud know the deck-hands. It's the man Doctor Dennis was expectin'."

"Ay?" vaguely.

She kept her hand on the feebly beating heart, chafing it. He lay there, looking straight in her eyes; in hers—dull with love and waiting of a life—there was no instinct of recognition. The kind, simple, blue eyes, that had watched his baby limbs grow and strengthen in her arms! How gray the hair was! but its bit of curl was in it yet. The same dear old face that he used to hurry home at night to see! Nobody had loved him but this woman,—never; if he could but struggle up and get his head on her breast! How he used to lie there when he was a big boy, listening to the same old stories night after night,—the same old stories! Something homely and warm and true was waking in him to-night that had been dead for years and years; this was no matter of æsthetics or taste, it was real, *real*. He wondered if people felt in this way who had homes, or those simple folk who loved the Lord.

Inch by inch, with hard, slow pulls, they were gaining shore. Mary Defourchet was there. If he came to her as the clam-digger's bastard son, owning the lie he had practiced half his life,—what then? He had fought hard for his place in the world, for the ease and culture of his life,—most of all, for the society of thorough-bred and refined men, his own kindred. What would they say to Derrick Trull, and the mother he had kept smothered up so long? All this with his eyes fixed on hers. The cost was counted. It was to give up wife and place and fame,—all he had earned. It had not been cheaply earned. All Doctor Birkenshead's habits and intellect, the million nervous whims of a sensitive man, rebelled against the sacrifice. Nothing to battle them down but—what?

"Be ye hurt, Mother Phebe? What d' yer hold yer breath for?"

She evaded him with a sickly smile.

"We're gainin', Bowlegs. It's but a few minutes till we make shore. He'll be there, if—if he be ever to come."

"Yes, Gran," with a look of pity.

The wind stood still; it held its breath, as though with her it waited. The man strained against the tide till the veins in his brawny neck stood out purple. On the bald shore, the dim figures gathered in a cluster, eagerly watching. Old Phebe leaned forward, shading her eyes with her hand, peering from misty headland to headland with bated breath. A faint cheer reached them from land.

"Does thee know the voices, Bowlegs?"—in a dry whisper.

"It be the wreckers."

"Oh!—Derrick," after a pause, "would be too weak to cheer; he'd be worn with the swimmin'. Thee must listen sharp. Did they cry my name out? as if there was some'ut for me?"

"No, Mother," gruffly. "But don't ye lose heart after twenty years waitin'."

"I'll not."

As he pulled, the boatman looked over at her steadily.

"I never knowed what this was for ye, till now I've loss Ben," he said, gently. "It's as if you'd been lossin' him every day these twenty years."

She did not hear him; her eyes, straining, scanned the shore; she seemed to grow blind as they came nearer; passed her wet sleeve over them again and again.

"Thee look for me, Bowlegs," she said, weakly.

The yawl grated on the shallow waters of the bar; the crowd rushed down to the edge of the shore, the black figures coming out distinct now, half a dozen of the wreckers going into the surf and dragging the boat up on the beach. She turned her head out to sea, catching his arm with both hands.

"Be there any strange face to shore? Thee did n't know him. A little face, full o' th' laugh an' joke, an' brown curls blown by the wind."

"The salt's in my eyes. I can't rightly see, Mother, Phebe."

The surgeon saw Doctor Bowdler waiting, pale and haggard, his fat little arms outstretched: the sea had spared him by some whim, then. When the men lifted him out, another familiar face looked down on him: it was Mary. She had run into the surf with them, and held his head in her arms.

"I love you! I love you!" she sobbed, kissing his hand.

"There be a fire up by the bathing houses, an' hot coffee," said old Doctor Dennis, with a kindly, shrewd glance at the famous surgeon. "Miss Defourchet and Snap made it for you. *She* knew."

Birkenshead, keeping her hand, turned to the forlorn figure standing shivering alone, holding both palms pressed to her temples, her gray hair and clothes dripping.

"Thee don't tell me that he's here, Bowlegs," she said. "There might be some things the wrackers hes found up in the bathin'-houses. There might,—in the bathin'-houses. It's the last day,—it's twenty year"—

Doctor Birkenshead looked down at the beautiful flushed face pressed close to his side, then pushed it slowly from him. He went over to where the old woman stood, and kneeled beside her in the sand, drawing her down to him.

"Mother," he said, "it's Derrick, mother. Don't you know your boy?"

With the words the boy's true spirit seemed to come back to him,—Derrick Trull again, who went with such a hot, indignant heart to win money and place for the old mother at home. He buried his head in her knees, as she crouched over him, silent, passing her hands quickly and lightly over his face.

"God forgive me!" he cried. "Take my head in your arms, mother, as you used to do. Nobody has loved me as you did. Mother! mother!"

Phebe Trull did not speak one word. She drew her son's head close into her trembling old arms, and held it there motionless. It was an old way she had of caressing him.

Doctor Dennis drew the eager, wondering crowd away from them.

"I don't understand," said Doctor Bowdler, excitedly.

"I do," said his niece, and sitting down in the sand, looked out steadfastly to sea.—

Bow-legged Phil drove the anchor into the beach, and pulled it idly out again.

"I've some'ut here for you, Phil," said Joe, gravely. "The water washed it up."

The fellow's teeth chattered as he took it.

"Well, ye know what it is?" fiercely. "Only a bit of Scotch cap,"—holding it up on his fist. "I bought it down at Port Monmouth, Saturday, for him. I was a-goin' to take him home this week up to the old folks in Connecticut. I kin take *that* instead, an' tell 'em whar our Benny is."

"That's so, said Joe, his eye twinkling as he looked over Phil's shoulder. A fat little hand slapped the said shoulder, and "Hillo, Bowlegs!" came in a small shout in his ear. Phil turned, looked at the boy from head to foot, gulped down one or two heavy breaths.

"Hi! you young vagabond, you!" he said, and went suddenly back to his anchor, keeping his head down on his breast for a long while.—

He had piled up the sand at her back to make her a seat while they waited for the wagons. Now he sat on her skirts, holding her hands to warm them. He had almost forgotten Mary and the Doctor. Nature or instinct, call it what you will, some subtle whim of blood called love, brought the old clam-digger neared to him than all the rest of the world. He held the bony fingers tight, looked for an old ring she used to wear, tried to joke to bring out the flicker of a smile on her mouth, leaned near to catch her breath. He remembered how curiously sweet it used to be, like new milk.

The dawn opened clear and dark blue; the sun yet waited below the stormy sea. Though they sat there a long while, she was strangely quiet,—did not seem much afraid of him as she used to be when he began to rise above her,— held his hand, with a bright, contented face, and said little else than "My Boy! my boy! under her breath. Her eyes followed every movement of his face with an insatiate hunger; yet the hesitation and quiet in her motions and voice were unnatural. He asked her once or twice if she were ill.

"Wait a bit, an' I'll tell thee, Derrick," she said. "Thee must remember I'm not as young as I was then," with a smile. "Thee must speak fast, my son. I'd like to hear of thee gran' home, if thee's willin'."

He told her, as he would to please a child, of the place and fame and wealth he had won; but it had not the effect he expected. Before he had finished, the look in her eyes grew vague and distant. Some thought in the poor clam-digger's soul made these things but of little moment. She interrupted him.

"There be one yonner that loves my boy. I'd like to speak a word to her before—Call her, Derrick."

He rose and beckoned to Miss Defourchet. When she came near, and saw the old woman's face, she hurried, and, stooping down quickly, took her head in her arms.

"Derrick has come back to you," she said. "Will you let him bring me with him to call you mother?"

"Mary?"

She did not look at him. Old Phebe pushed her back with a searching look.

"Is it true love you'll give my boy?"

"I'll try." In a lower voice,—"I never loved him so well as when he came back to you."

The old woman was silent a long time.

"Thee's right. It was good for Derrick to come back to me. I don't know what that big world be like where thee an' Derrick's been. The sea keeps talkin' of it, I used to think; it's kep' moanin' with the cries of it. But the true love at home be worth it all. I knowed that always. I kep' it for my boy. He went from it, but it brought him back. Out of the sea it brought him back."

He knew this was not his mother's usual habit of speech. Some great truth seemed coming closer to the old fish-wife, lifting her forever out of her baser self. She leaned on the girl beside her, knowing her, in spite of blood and education, to be no truer woman than herself. The inscrutable meaning of the eyes deepened. The fine, sad smile came on the face, and grew fixed there. She was glad he had come,—that was all. Mary was a woman; her insight was quicker.

"Where are you hurt?" she said softly.

"Hush! don't fret the boy. It was pullin' last night, think. I'm not as strong as when I was a gell."

They sat there, watching the dawn break into morning. Over the sea the sky opened into deeps of silence and light. The surf rolled in, in long, low grand breakers, like riders to a battle-field, tossing back their gleaming white plumes of spray when they touched the shore. But the wind lulled as though something more solemn waited on the land than the sea's rage or the quiet of the clouds.

"Does thee mind, Derrick," said his mother, with a low laugh, "how thee used to play with this curl ahint my ear? When thee was a bit baby, thee begun it. I've kep' it ever since. It be right gray now."

"Yes, mother."

He had crept closer to her now. In the last half-hour his eyes had grown clearer. He dared not look away from her. Joe and Bowlegs had drawn near, and Doctor Bowdler. They stood silent, with their hats off. Doctor Bowdler felt her pulse, but her son did not touch it. His own hand was cold and clammy; his heart sick with a nameless dread. Was he, then, just too late?

"Yes, I did. I kep' it for thee, Derrick. I always knowed thee'd come,"—in a lower voice. "There's that dress, too. I'd like thee to 've seen me in that; but"—

"Take her hands in yours," whispered Mary.

"Is it thee, my son?"—with a smile. After a long pause,—"I kep' it, an' I kep' true love for thee, Derrick. God brought thee back for' t I think. It be the best, after all. He'll bring thee to me for 't at th' last, my boy,—my boy!"

As the faint voice lingered and died upon the words, the morning sun shone out in clear, calm glory over the still figures on the beach. The others had crept away, and left the three alone with God and His great angel, in whose vast presence there is no life save Love, no future save Love's wide eternity.

Susan Glaspell

. . . .

The Outside

Captain (of "The Bars" Life-Saving Station)

Bradford (a Life-Saver)

Tony (a Portuguese Life-Saver)

Mrs. Patrick (who lives in the abandoned Station)

Allie Mayo (who works for her)

SCENE: *A room in a house which was once a life-saving station. Since ceasing to be that it has taken on no other character, except that of a place which no one cares either to preserve or change. It is painted the life-saving grey, but has not the life-saving freshness. This is one end of what was the big boat room, and at the ceiling is seen a part of the framework from which the boat once swung. About two thirds of the back wall is open, because of the big sliding door, of the type of barn door, and through this open door are seen the sand dunes, and beyond them the woods. At one point the line where the woods and dunes meet stands out clearly and there are indicated the rude things, vine, bushes, which form the outer uneven rim of the woods—the only things that grow in the sand. At another point a sand-hill is menacing the woods. This old life-saving station is at a point where the sea curves, so through the open door the sea is also seen. (The station is located on the outside shore of Cape Cod, at the point, near the tip of the Cape, where it makes that final curve which forms the Provincetown Harbor.) The dunes are hills and strange forms of sand on which, in places, grows the stiff beach grass— struggle; dogged growing against odds. At right of this big sliding door is a drift of sand and the top of buried beach grass is seen on this. There is a door left, and at right of big sliding door is a slanting wall. Door in this is ajar at rise of curtain, and through this door* BRADFORD *and* TONY, *life-savers, are seen bending over a man's body, attempting to restore respiration. The captain of the life-savers comes into view outside the big open door, at left; he appears to have been hurrying, peers in, sees the men, goes quickly to them.*

CAPTAIN: I'll take this now, boys.

BRADFORD: No need for anybody to take it, Capt'n. He was dead when we picked him up.

CAPTAIN: Dannie Sears was dead when we picked him up. But we brought him back. I'll go on awhile.

(The two men who have been bending over the body rise, stretch to relax, and come into the room.)

BRADFORD: *(pushing back his arms and putting his hands on his chest)* Work, —tryin' to put life in the dead.

CAPTAIN: Where'd you find him, Joe?

BRADFORD: In front of this house. Not forty feet out.

CAPTAIN: What'd you bring him up here for?

(He speaks in an abstracted way, as if the working part of his mind is on something else, and in the muffled voice of one bending over.)

BRADFORD: *(with a sheepish little laugh)* Force of habit, I guess. We brought so many of 'em back up here. *(looks around the room)* And then it was kind of unfriendly down where he was—the wind spittn' the sea onto you till he'd have no way of known' he was ashore.

TONY: Lucky I was not sooner or later as I walk by from my watch.

BRADFORD: You have accommodating ways, Tony. No sooner or later. I wouldn't say it of many Portagees. But the sea *(calling it in to the* CAPTAIN*)* is friendly as a kitten alongside the women that live *here*. Allie Mayo—they're *both* crazy—had that door open *(moving his head toward the big sliding door)* sweepin' out, and when we come along she backs off and stands lookin' at us, *lookin'*—Lord, I just wanted to get him somewhere else. So I kicked this door open with my foot *(jerking his hand toward the room where the* CAPTAIN *is seen bending over the man)* and got him *away. (under his voice)* If he did have any notion of comin' back to life, he wouldn't a come if he'd seen her. *(more genially)* I wouldn't.

CAPTAIN: You know who he is, Joe?

BRADFORD: I never saw him before.

CAPTAIN: Mitchell telephoned from High Head that a dory came ashore there.

BRADFORD: Last night wasn't the *best* night for a dory. *(to* TONY, *boastfully)* Not that I couldn't 'a' stayed in one. Some men can stay in a dory and some can't. *(going to the inner door)* That boy's dead, Capt'n.

CAPTAIN: Then I'm not doing him any harm.

BRADFORD: *(going over and shaking the frame where the boat once swung)* This the first time you ever been in this place, ain't it, Tony?

TONY: I never was here before.

BRADFORD: Well, *I* was here before. *(a laugh)* And the old man—*(nodding toward the* CAPTAIN*)* he lived here for twenty-seven years. Lord, the things that happened *here*. There've been dead ones carried through *that* door. *(pointing to the outside door)* Lord—the ones I've carried. I carried in Bill Collins, and Lou Harvey and—huh! 'sall over now. You ain't seen no *wrecks*. Don't ever think you have. I was here the night the Jennie Snow was out there. *(pointing to the sea)* There was a *wreck*. We got the boat that stood here *(again shaking the frame)* down that bank. *(goes to the door and looks out)* Lord, how'd we ever do it? The sand has put his place on the blink all right. And then when it gets too God-for-saken for a life-savin' station, a lady takes it for a summer residence—and then spends the winter. She's a cheerful one.

TONY: A woman—she makes things pretty. This not like a place where a woman live. On the floor there is nothing—on the wall there is nothing. Things—*(trying to express it with his hands)* do not hang on other things.

BRADFORD: *(imitating* TONY's *gesture)* No—things do not hang on other things. In my opinion the woman's crazy—sittin' over there on the sand—*(a gesture towards the dunes)* what's she *lookin'* at? There ain't nothin' to *see*.

And I know the woman that works for her's crazy—Allie Mayo. She's a Provincetown girl. She was all right once, but—

(MRS. PATRICK *comes in from the hall at the right. She is a "city woman," a sophisticated person who has been caught into something as unlike the old life as the dunes are unlike a meadow. At the moment she is excited and angry.*)

MRS. PATRICK: You have no right here. This isn't the life-saving station any more. Just because it used to be—I don't see why you should think—This is my house! And—I want my house to myself!

CAPTAIN: (*putting his head through the door. One arm of the man he is working with is raised, and the hand reaches through the doorway*) Well I must say, lady, I would think that any house could be a life-saving station when the sea had sent a man to it.

MRS. PATRICK: (*who has turned away so she cannot see the hand*) I don't want him here! I—(*defiant, yet choking*) I must have my house to myself!

CAPTAIN: You'll get your house to yourself when I've made up my mind there's no more life in this man. A good many lives have been saved in this house, Mrs. Patrick—I believe that's your name—and if there's any chance of bringing one more back from the dead, the fact that you own the house ain't goin' to make a damn bit of difference to me!

MRS. PATRICK: (*in a thin wild way*) I must have my house to myself.

CAPTAIN: Hell with such a woman!

(*Moves the man he is working with and slams the door shut. As the CAPTAIN says, "And if there's any chance of bringing one more back from the dead," ALLIE MAYO has appeared outside the wide door which gives on to the dunes, a bleak woman, who at first seems little more than a part of the sand before which she stands. But as she listens to this conflict one suspects in her that peculiar intensity of twisted things which grow in unfavoring places.*)

MRS. PATRICK: I—I don't want them here! I must—(*But suddenly she retreats, and is gone.*)

BRADFORD: Well, I couldn't say, Allie Mayo, that you work for any too kind-hearted a lady. What's the matter with the woman? Does she want folks to die? Appears to break her all up to see somebody trying to save a life. What d'you work for such a fish for? A crazy fish—that's what I call the woman. I've seen her—day after day—settin' over there where the dunes meet the woods, just sittin' there, lookin'. (*suddenly thinking of it*) I believe she *likes* to see the sand slippin' down on the woods. Pleases her to see somethin' gettin' buried, I guess.

(ALLIE MAYO, *who has stepped inside the door and moved half across the room, toward the corridor at the right, is arrested by this last—stands a moment as if seeing through something, then slowly on, and out.*)

BRADFORD: Some coffee'd taste good. But coffee in this house? Oh no. It might make somebody feel better. *(opening the door that was slammed shut)* Want me now, Capt'n?

CAPTAIN: No.

BRADFORD: Oh, that boy's dead, Capt'n.

CAPTAIN: *(snarling)* Dannie Sears was dead too. Shut that door. I don't want to hear that woman's voice again, ever.

(*Closing the door and sitting on a bench built into that corner between the big sliding door and the room where the* CAPTAIN *is.*)

BRADFORD: They're a cheerful pair of women—livin' in this cheerful place— a place that life savers had to turn over to the sand—huh! This Patrick woman used to be all right. She and her husband was summer folks over in town. They used to picnic over here on the outside. It was Joe Dyer—he's always talkin' to summer folks—told 'em the government was goin' to build the new station and sell this one by sealed bids. I heard them talkin' about it. They was sittin' right down there on the beach, eatin' their supper. They was goin' to put in a fire-place and they was goin' to paint it bright colors, and have parties over here—summer folk notions. Their bid won—who'd want it?—a buried house you couldn't move.

TONY: I see no bright colors.

BRADFORD: Don't you? How astonishin'! You must be color blind. And I guess *we're* the first party. *(laughs)* I was in Bill Joseph's grocery store, one day last November, when in she comes—Mrs. Patrick, from New York. "I've come to take the old life-saving station," she says. "I'm going to sleep over there tonight!" Huh! Bill is used to queer ways—he deals with summer folks, but that got *him*. November—an empty house, a buried house, you might say, off here on the outside shore—way across the sand far from man or beast. He got it out of her, not by what she said, but by the way she looked at what he said, that her husband had died, and she was runnin' off to hide herself, I guess. A person'd feel sorry for her if she weren't so stand-offish, and so doggon *mean*. But mean folks have got minds of their own. She slept here that night. Bill had men hauling things till after dark—bed, stove, coal. And then she wanted somebody to work for her. "Somebody," says she, "that doesn't say an unnecessary word!" Well, then Bill come in to the back of the store, I said, "Looks to me as if Allie Mayo was the party she's lookin' for." Allie Mayo has got a prejudice against words. Or maybe she likes 'em so well she's savin' of 'em. She's not spoke an unnecessary word for twenty years. She's got her reasons. Women whose men go to sea ain't always talkative.

(The CAPTAIN *comes out. He closes the door behind him and stands there beside it. He looks tired and disappointed. Both look at him. Pause.)*

CAPTAIN: Wonder who he was.

BRADFORD: Young. Guess he's not been much at sea.

CAPTAIN: I hate to leave even the dead in this house. But we can get right back for him. *(a look around)* The old place used to be more friendly. *(moves to outer door, hesitates, hating to leave like this)* Well, Joe, we brought a good many of them back here:

BRADFORD: Dannie Sears is tendin' bar in Boston now.

(The three men go; as they are going around the drift of sand ALLIE MAYO *comes in carrying a pot of coffee; sees them leaving, puts down the coffee pot, looks at the door the* CAPTAIN *has closed, moves toward it, as if drawn.* MRS. PATRICK *follows her in.)*

MRS. PATRICK: They've gone?

*(*MRS. MAYO *nods, facing the closed door.)*

MRS. PATRICK: And they're leaving—him? *(again the other woman nods)* Then he's—? *(*MRS. MAYO *just stands there)* They have no right—just because it used to be their place—! I want my house to myself!

(Snatches her coat and scarf from a hook and starts through the big door toward the dunes.)

ALLIE MAYO: Wait.

(When she has said it she sinks into that corner seat—as if overwhelmed by what she has done. The other woman is held.)

ALLIE MAYO: *(to herself)* If I could say that, I can say more. *(looking at the woman she has arrested, but speaking more to herself)* That boy in there— his face—uncovered something—(her open hand on her chest. But she waits, as if she cannot go on; when she speaks it is in a labored way—slow, monotonous, as if snowed in by silent years)* For twenty years, I did what you are doing. And I can tell you—it's not the way. *(her voice has fallen to a whisper; she stops, looking ahead at something remote and veiled)* We had been married—two years. *(a start, as of sudden pain. Says it again, as if to make herself say it)* Married—two years. He had a chance to go north on a whaler. Times hard. He had to go. A year and a half—it was to be. A year and a half. Two years we'd been married.

(She sits silent, moving a little back and forth.)

The day he went away. *(not spoken, but breathed from pain)* The days after he was gone.

I heard at first. Last letter said farther north—not another chance to write till on the way home. *(a wait)*

Six months later. Another, I did not hear. *(long wait)* Nobody ever heard. *(after it seems she is held there, and will not go on)* I used to talk as much as any girl in Provincetown. Jim used to tease me about my talking. But they's come in to talk to me. They'd say—"You may hear *yet*." They'd talk about what must have happened. And one day a woman who'd been my friend all my life said—"Suppose he was to walk *in*!" I got up and drove her from my kitchen—and from that time till this I've not said a word I didn't have to say. *(she has become almost wild in telling this. That passes. In a whisper)* The ice that caught Jim—caught me. *(a moment as if held in ice. Comes from it. To* MRS. PATRICK *simply)* It's not the way. *(a sudden change)* You're not the only woman in the world whose husband is dead!

MRS. PATRICK: *(with a cry of hurt)* Dead? My husband's not *dead*.

ALLIE MAYO: He's not? *(slowly understands)* Oh.

(The woman in the door is crying. Suddenly picks up her coat which has fallen to the floor and steps outside.)

ALLIE MAYO: *(almost failing to do it)* Wait.

MRS. PATRICK: Wait? Don't you think you've said enough? They told me you didn't say an unnecessary word!

ALLIE MAYO: I don't.

MRS. PATRICK: And you can see, I should think, that you've bungled into things you know nothing about!

(As she speaks, and crying under her breath, she pushes the sand by the door down on the half buried grass—though not as if knowing what she is doing.)

ALLIE MAYO: *(slowly)* When you keep still for twenty years you know—

things you didn't know you knew. I know why you're doing that. *(she looks up at her startled)* Don't bury the only thing that will grow. Let it grow.

(The woman outside still crying under her breath turns abruptly and starts toward the line where the dunes and the woods meet.)

ALLIE MAYO: I know where you're going! *(*MRS. PATRICK *turns but not as if she wants to)* What you'll try to do. Over there. *(pointing to the line of woods)* Bury it. The life in you. Bury it—watching the sand bury the woods. But I'll tell you something! *They* fight too. The woods! They fight for life the way that Captain fought for life in there!

(Pointing to the closed door.)

MRS. PATRICK: *(with a strange exultation)* And lose the way he lost in there!

ALLIE MAYO: *(sure, somber)* They don't lose.

MRS. PATRICK: Don't lose? *(triumphant)* I have walked on the tops of buried trees!

ALLIE MAYO: *(slow, somber, yet large)* And vines will grow over the sand that covers the trees, and hold it. And other trees will grow over the buried trees.

MRS. PATRICK: I've watched the sand slip down on the vines that reach out farthest.

ALLIE MAYO: Another vine will reach that spot. *(under her breath, tenderly)* Strange little things that reach out the farthest!

MRS. PATRICK: And will be buried the soonest!

ALLIE MAYO: And hold the sand for the things behind them. They save a wood that guards a town.

MRS. PATRICK: I care nothing about a wood to guard a town. This is the outside—these dunes where only beach grass grows, this outer shore where men can't live. The Outside. You who were born here and who die here have named it that.

ALLIE MAYO: Yes, we named it that, and we had reason. He died here *(reaches her hand toward the closed door)* and many a one before him. But many another reached the harbor! *(slowly raises her arm, bends it to make the form of the Cape. Touches the outside of her bent arm)* The Outside. But an arm that bends to make a harbor—where men are safe.

MRS. PATRICK: I'm outside the harbor—on the dunes, land not life.

ALLIE MAYO: Dunes meet woods and woods hold dunes from a town that's shore to a harbor.

MRS. PATRICK: This is the Outside. Sand *(picking some of it up in her hand*

Caught in the Ecotone

and letting it fall on the beach grass) Sand that *covers*—hills of sand that move and cover.

ALLIE MAYO: Woods. Woods to hold the moving hills from Provincetown. Provincetown—where they turn when boats can't live at sea. Did you ever see the sails come round here when the sky is dark? A line of them—swift to the harbor—where their children live. Go back! *(pointing)* Back to your edge of the woods that's the *edge of the dunes.*

MRS. PATRICK: The edge of life. Where life trails off to dwarfed things not worth a name.

(Suddenly sits in the doorway.)

ALLIE MAYO: Not worth a name. And—meeting the Outside!

(Big sense of the wonder of life.)

MRS. PATRICK: *(lifting the sand and letting it drift through her hand.)* They're what the sand will let them be. They take strange shapes like the shapes of blown sand.

ALLIE MAYO: Meeting the Outside. *(moving nearer; speaking more personally)* I know why you came here. To this house that had been given up; on this shore where only savers of life try to live. I know what holds you to these dunes, and draws you over there. But other things are true besides the things you want to see.

MRS. PATRICK: How do you know what they are? Where have you been for twenty years?

ALLIE MAYO: Outside. Twenty years. That's why I know how brave they are. *(indicating the edge of the woods. Suddenly different)* You'll not find peace there again! Go back and watch them *fight!*

MRS. PATRICK: *(swiftly rising)* You're a cruel woman—a hard, insolent woman! I knew what I was doing! What do you know about it? About me? I didn't *go* to the Outside. I was left there. I'm only—trying to get along. Everything that can hurt me I want buried—buried deep. Spring is here. This morning I *knew* it. Spring—coming through the storm—to take me—take me to hurt me. That's what I couldn't bear—*(she looks at the closed door)* things that made me know I feel. You haven't felt for so long you don't know what it means! But I tell you, Spring is here! And now you'd take *that* from me— *(looking now toward the edge of the woods)* the thing that made me know they would be buried in my heart—those things I can't *live* and know I feel. You're more cruel than the sea! "But other things are true besides the things you want to see!" Outside. Springs will come when I will not know that it is spring. *(as if resentful of not more deeply believing what she says)* What would there be for me but the Outside? What was there for you? What did you ever find after you lost the thing you wanted?

ALLIE MAYO: I found—what I find now I know. The edge of life—to hold life behind me—

(A slight gesture toward MRS. PATRICK)

MRS. PATRICK: *(stepping back)* You call what you are life? *(laughs)* Bleak as those ugly things that grow in the sand!

ALLIE MAYO: *(under her breath, as one who speaks tenderly of beauty)* Ugly!

MRS. PATRICK: *(passionately)* I have *known* life. I have known *life.* You're like this Cape. A line of land way out to sea—land not life.

ALLIE MAYO: A harbor far at sea. *(raises her arm, curves it in as if around something she loves)* Land that encloses and gives shelter from storm.

MRS. PATRICK: *(facing the sea, as if affirming what will hold all else out)* Outside sea. Outer shore. Dunes—land not life.

ALLIE MAYO: Outside sea—outer shore, dark with wood that once was ships—dunes, strange land not life—woods, town and harbor. The line! Stunted straggly line that meets the Outside face to face—and fights for what itself can never be. Lonely line. Brave growing.

MRS. PATRICK: It loses.

ALLIE MAYO: It wins.

MRS. PATRICK: The farthest life is buried.

ALLIE MAYO: And life grows over buried life! *(lifted into that; then, as one who states a simple truth with feeling)* It will. And Springs will come when you will want to know it is Spring.

(The CAPTAIN and BRADFORD appear behind the drift of sand. They have a stretcher. To get away from them MRS. PATRICK steps farther into the room; ALLIE MAYO shrinks into her corner. The men come in, open the closed door and go in the room where they left the dead man. A moment later they are seen outside the big open door, bearing the man away. MRS. PATRICK watches them from sight.)

MRS. PATRICK: *(bitter, exultant)* Savers of life! *(to ALLIE MAYO)* You savers of life! "Meeting the Outside!" Meeting—*(but she cannot say it mockingly again; in saying it, something of what it means has broken through, rises. Herself lost, feeling her way into the wonder of life)* Meeting the Outside!

(It grows in her as CURTAIN lowers slowly.)

Tess Gallagher

The Woman Who Raised Goats

Dear ones, in those days it was otherwise.
I was suited more to an obedience
of windows. If anyone had asked,
I would have said: "Windows are my prologue."

My father worked on the docks
in a cold little harbor, unhappily
dedicated to what was needed
by the next and further
harbors. My brothers
succeeded him in this, but when I,
in that town's forsaken luster, offered myself,
the old men in the hiring hall creeled
back in their chairs, fanning themselves
with their cards, with their gloves.
"Saucy," they said. She's saucy!"

Denial, O my Senators,
takes a random shape. The matter
drove me to wearing
a fedora. Soon, the gowns, the amiable
forgeries: a powdery sailor, the blue silk
pillow given by a great aunt, my name
embroidered on it like a ship, the stitched
horse too, with its red plume and its bird eyes
glowing, glowing. There was the education
of my "sensibilities."

All this is nothing to you.
You have eaten my only dress, and the town
drifts every day now
toward the harbor. But always,

above the town, above
the harbor, there is the town,
the harbor, the caves and hollows
when the cargo of lights
is gone.

Gloria Anzaldúa

El otro México

> El otro México que acá hemos construido
> el espacio es lo que ha sido
> terriroio nacional.
> Esté el esfuerzo de todos nuestros hermanos
> y latinoamericanos que han sabido
> progressar.
> —Los Tigres del Norte

> The *Aztecas del norte* . . . compose the largest single tribe or nation
> of Anishinabeg (Indians) found in the United States today . . . . Some
> call themselves Chicanos and see themselves as people whose true
> homeland is Aztlán [the U.S. Southwest].
> —Jack D. Forbes

Wind tugging at my sleeve
feet sinking into the sand
I stand at the edge where the earth touches ocean
where the two overlap
a gentle coming together
at other times and places a violent clash.

Across the border in Mexico
  stark silhouette of houses gutted by waves,
    cliffs crumbling into the sea,

Caught in the Ecotone

silver waves marbled with spume
gashing a hole under the border fence.

Miro el mar atacar
la cerca en Border Field Park
con sus buchones de agua,
an Easter Sunday resurrection
of the brown blood in my veins.

Oigo el llorido del mar, el respiro del aire,
my heart surges to the beat of the sea.
In the gray haze of the sun
the gulls' shrill cry of hunger,
the tangy smell of the sea seeping into me.

I walk   through the hole in the fence
to the other side.
Under my fingers I feel the gritty wire
rusted by 139 years
of salty breath of the sea.

Beneath the iron sky
Mexican children kick their soccer balls across,
run after it, entering the U.S.

I press my hand to the steel curtain—
chainlink fence crowned with rolled barbed wire—
rippling from the sea where Tijuana touches San Diego
unrolling over mountains
and plains
and deserts,
this "Tortilla Curtain" turning into *el río Grande*
flowing down to the flatlands
of the Magic Valley of South Texas
its mouth emptying into the Gulf.

1,950 mile-long open wound
dividing a *pueblo*, a culture,
running down the length of my body,
staking fence rods in my flesh,
splits me   splits me
me raja   me raja

Gloria Anzaldúa   49

This is my home
this thin edge of
barbwire.

But the skin of the earth is seamless.
The sea cannot be fenced,
el mar does not stop at borders.
To show the white man what she thought of his
arrogance,
Yemaya blew that wire fence down.

This land was Mexican once,
was Indian always
and is.
And   will be again.

Yo soy un puente tendido
del mundo gabacho al del mojado,
lo pasado me estirá pa' 'trás
y lo presente pa' 'delante.
Que la Virgen de Guadalupe me cuide
Ay ay ay, soy mexicana de este lado.

Annie Dillard

. . . .

Fall, 1855, the settlement called Whatcom

The sailor put down the helm and Ada Fishburn felt the boat round up towards the forest. She stood in the bow, a supple young woman wearing a brown shawl and a deep-brimmed sunbonnet that circled her face. She carried her infant son, Glee, in her arms.

Without a sound the schooner slipped alongside a sort of dock that met the water from the beach. This dock represented the settlement on Bellingham Bay. Ada Fishburn had been sailing in Puget Sound and along this unbroken

Caught in the Ecotone

forest every day for almost a week. The same forest grew on the islands they passed, too: the trunks rose straight. She had seen enough of this wall of forest to know that even when the sun and all the sky shone full upon it, and the blinding sea glinted up at it, it was always dark.

From behind her on deck Ada heard her older son, Clare, singing a song. Clare was five—a right big boy for five, long in the leg bones like his father—and life suited him very well, and he found his enjoyment. She glanced back and saw her husband, Rooney, moving their four barrels, their five crates, their four kegs, and the rolled feather-bed to the rail. Young Clare climbed up on everything barefoot, as fast as Rooney set it down on the deck. Rooney tied the two cows and gave the ropes to Clare to hold, and the boy sang to them, half-dead as they were. Neither man nor boy glanced up to see where he was getting off, which was a mercy, one of few, for she herself scarcely minded where she was since she lost her boy Charley on the overland road, but she hated to see Rooney downhearted, when he staked his blessing on being on this place, and look at it.

Ada and Rooney hauled their possessions off the dock. The baby, Glee, stayed asleep, moving its lips, and missed the whole thing. The schooner sailed on north and left them there.

It was the rough edge of the world, where trees came smack down to the stones. The shore looked to Ada as if the corner of the continent had got torn off right here, sometime near yesterday, and the dark trees kept on growing like nothing happened. The ocean just filled in the tear and settled down. This was Puget Sound, and some straits that Rooney talked about, and there was not a thing on it or anywhere near it that she could see but some black ducks and humpy green islands. Salt water wet Ada's shoes if she stood still. Away out south over the water she made out a sharp line of snow-covered mountains. From the boat she had seen a few of such mountains poking up out of nowhere, including a big solitary white mountain that they had sailed towards all morning, that the forest now hid; it looked like its sloping base must start up just back there behind the first couple rows of trees. God might have created such a plunging shore as this before He thought of making people, and then when He thought of making people, He mercifully softened up the land in the palms of his hands wherever He expected them to live, which did not include here.

Rooney inspected the tilting dock. He folded his thin body double and studied the pilings and planks from underneath as if the dock were the wonder of the world. When he stood up again, Ada tried to read his expression, but she never could, for his bushy red beard seemed to grow straight down out of his hat, and only the tip of his nose showed. She watched him tear off some green grass blades at the forest edge and feed them to the spotted cows. Then he disappeared partway up a steep trail near the dock, returned, and set off up the beach.

Ada stayed in the silence with their pile of possessions. Her feather-bed was on top, on the barrels, to keep it dry. She poked one of its corners back in the roll so it would not pick up sand from the barrels. Deep inside the bonnet, her bow-shaped mouth was grave. Her dark brows almost met above her nose; her eyes were round and black. She made herself look around; her head moved slowly. The beach was a narrow strip of pebbles, stones, and white old logs laid end to end in neat rows like a necklace where the beach met the forest. Young Clare got right to breaking sticks off beach logs and throwing them in the water. Then he ran along the logs, and every time he stopped, Ada saw his bony head looking all around. It was October. The layer of cloud was high and distant, and the beach logs and the quiet water looked silver.

Ada said to herself, "For we are strangers before thee, and sojourners, as were all our fathers: our days on earth are as a shadow, and there is none abiding." The clouds overhead were still. There were no waves. A fish broke the water's sheen. It was not quite raining, but everything was wet.

A while later she saw a few frail smokes and some cabins under the trees back of the dock; she missed seeing the cabins at first because they were down among the roots of the trees, and she had been searching too high, thinking the trees were smaller. In all those days of sailing past the trees, she had nothing to size them by. Rooney came back beside her and said nothing. While Ada stared at the glassy water and the dark islands near and far, here came an Indian man.

The Indian man, in a plug hat, was paddling a dugout canoe in smooth water alongshore. He had another canoe trailing behind him, and no one in it. He was a smooth-bodied, almost naked man, whose face had a delicate, modest expression. The plug hat sat oddly high on his head. He held a paddle low in one hand, and he pushed its top lightly with the other hand; his round, bulging shoulders moved. The silver water closed smoothly behind his path. Little Clare must have caught sight of him, for he came flying down from the logs to the shore.

The man beached the log canoe. Rooney took the few long-legged steps to the water. Clare marched directly into the water to try to help, and the man looked down at the boy and his wet britches with a trace of smile. He brought the other canoe alongshore and, wading, lifted the tan grass mats that decked

Caught in the Ecotone

its red interior. What was in this second canoe was feathers. It was white goose feathers, just loose under the mats. Ada looked out at Rooney; his mouth behind his red beard showed nothing, but she could see that he glanced at her from under his hatbrim.

The man came forward and said his name was Chowitzit. They knew he must be a Lummi Indian, for the schooner man said the local people were Lummis, and "right friendly." He had said, in fact, that the settlement at Whatcom "would have starved to death a dozen times" without the Lummis. Now the Lummi man and Rooney shook hands. He had a wide face and a small nose; he wore an earring made of something pale and hard. He indicated, speaking English in a tender voice and making gestures, that he was selling the feathers. Ada saw that around one of his wrists was a tattooed bracelet of black dots. He said that the price of the whole canoeload of feathers was "two cups of molasses." If they needed less than the whole canoeload, they could just take what they needed. He barely moved his lips when he spoke. His voice lilted.

They had just debarked from a schooner full of molasses; they had two kegs of molasses right there on the beach: everybody in their wagon train had molasses. They had molasses when they had no water. Molasses was plenty cheap for them, that is, but on the other hand, they needed no feathers. Rooney told the fellow no, and thanked him. He added that they could use fresh fish or meat or vegetables if he could get them. He could. Rooney thanked him again, and his high voice cracked. It was all coming home to Rooney here, Ada thought, where one powerful effort was ending, and another was beginning.

They tied the cows and left their outfit on the beach. Chowitzit led them up the hillside on a short trail through the woods by a creek. From behind Rooney, Ada watched Chowitzit's sure feet on the steep trail. In the past six months she had engaged in a great many acts of commerce with a great many native men of many tribes, and had accustomed herself to the sight of grown men's buttocks. Clare ran on ahead, ran back, and said, "Here's a house," which she could plainly see, a log house across the creek from what she knew was Felix Rush's sawmill.

The log house was low in the forest, and there were stumps and slash smoking all around the dirt. The door was open. Chowitzit walked straight inside, and the Fishburns hung back on the bare ground. Ada glimpsed a blue apron, a white woman's face. She heard the woman greet the bare-legged Chowitzit with glad sounds, and they started talking. Then the woman came out, all smiling and showing her long gums, and caught hold of Ada, hauled her inside, and began to weep. She put her arms around her, and Ada gave in to weeping too. The baby woke up and commenced to bawl. Rooney went out to have a look at the mill.

Chowitzit had taken off his hat in the house, and Ada saw that the top of his head was flattened into a wedge, so his forehead sloped back. He and the woman, who was Mrs. Lura Rush, made a stir over puny Glee equally, as if neither had ever encountered such a thing as a baby.

Growing Up Coastal

When I reach the top of the dunes with Kali, I see my favorite view, the Atlantic Ocean. This morning, I see day-after-a-storm waves, gray and a bit reckless. I know this shoreline intimately; yet every time I come upon it, the scene is slightly different. Watching today's rough and active ocean, I try to recall the many variations of this scene. My earliest memories of this beach date back to 1959. My parents began camping at the shore when I was just three years old. They would pack their aging Oldsmobile with an army tent, army cots, scratchy wool army blankets, and for me and my sister the pillows from our beds. On a Friday night we would leave the suburbs behind and drive to Hither Hills campgrounds. Saturday mornings I would wake up the moment the sun broke through the loosely tied tent flaps. My mother, father, and sister, still sleeping in their creaking wooden-legged cots, were never early beach risers, but I prided myself on being the first one to the edge of the water each morning. The feel of sand on my feet, the smell of salty ocean air, and the movement and sounds of the waves were (and are) as natural to me as breathing.

Growing up coastal teaches one how to tell time by the tides and seasons. Many of the writers in this section reflect their sense of internal growth as they learn more about their coastal home environments. Celia Thaxter grows up on the Isles of Shoals as a lighthouse keeper's daughter. Although she marries at sixteen and moves away from the islands, her coastal environment indelibly shapes her perceptions of the world. Thaxter is unable to leave the islands permanently, and year after year she returns for the summers. Her book *Among the Isles of Shoals* documents elements of her life, a life she found idyllic.

Growing up tidal is not necessarily growing up with the perfect balance of the pull of the moon and sun on different parts of the rotating earth. As Mary Karr remembers in her memoir *The Liars' Club*, sometimes a child's experiences on the shore are exceptionally frightening. The shore, after all, can be a wild environment filled with storms and wreckage. In the memoir, as Mary and her sister, Lecia, play on a Gulf of Mexico beach ravaged by Hurricane Carla, far from the not-so-watchful eyes of their parents, Lecia is attacked by a man-of-war. Mary both thrills at the prospect of such excitement and fears the consequence that Lecia might die. While one moment Mary has been taunting Lecia and happily playing on the shore, she finds her next moment filled with Lecia's screams for help. The beach is, as Mary learns, a deceptive place filled with hidden dangers and life lessons.

Some of the other writers in this section show how young women, sometimes through interior or exterior struggles, come of age. Kerry Neville Bakken creates a much-too-young female character who mistakes male sexual attention for real caring and has her first sexual experience at the beach. The young girl protagonist of Sarah Orne Jewett's story "A White Heron" ultimately sees through the guise of the handsome young hunter-ornithologist and instead protects the life of the rare shorebird he seeks.

The women who write about the coast from the perspective of an insider offer some of the clearest insights into the way the forces of nature press against the forces of culture to shape one's identity. They see not only the romanticized coast but the fish bones, barnacles, gutweed, eel grass, and whelk egg cases as well as the human trash strewn on the beach. Their works contain a lifetime of observation.

As I continue east along the shore with Kali, who is now far ahead of me and chasing the waves, I trek along the very edge of the shore, allowing the water to wash up on my feet and soak my ankles. The forward press and roll of my feet in the sand leaves temporary footsteps, the same sorts of mysterious footprints I wondered about when I was a child.

Celia Thaxter

From *Among the Isles of Shoals*

In a series of papers published not many years ago, Herman Melville made the world acquainted with the "Encantadas," or Enchanted Islands, which he describes as lying directly under the equator, off the coast of South America, and of which he says: "It is to be doubted whether any spot of earth can, in desolateness, furnish a parallel to this group." But their dark volcanic crags and melancholy beaches can hardly seem more desolate than do the low bleached rocks of the Isles of Shoals to eyes that behold them for the first time. Very sad they look, stern, bleak, and unpromising, yet are they enchanted islands in a better sense of the word than are the great Gallipagos of which Mr. Melville discourses so delightfully.

There is a strange charm about them, an indescribable influence in their atmosphere, hardly to be explained, but universally acknowledged. People forget the hurry and worry and fret of life after living there awhile, and, to an imaginative mind, all things become dreamy as they were to the lotus-eaters, to whom

> "The gushing of the wave
> Far, far away did seem to mourn and rave
> On alien shores."

The eternal sound of the sea on every side has a tendency to wear away the edge of human thought and perception; sharp outlines become blurred and softened like a sketch in charcoal; nothing appeals to the mind with the same distinctness as on the mainland, amid the rush and stir of people and things, and the excitements of social life. This was strikingly illustrated during the late war, which, while it wrung the heart of the whole country, and stirred the blood of every man, woman, and child on the continent, left the handful of human beings upon these lonely rocks almost untouched. The echoes of woe and terror were so faint and far they seemed to lose their significance among the many-voiced waters they crossed, and reached at last the indifferent ears they sought with no more force than a spent wave.

Celia Thaxter

Nine miles of the Atlantic Ocean intervene between these islands and the nearest point of the coast of New Hampshire; but from this nearest point the coast-line recedes gradually, in dim and dimmer distance, to Cape Ann, in Massachusetts, twenty-one miles away at the southwest, and to Cape Ned-dock, in Maine, sixteen miles distant in the northeast (in clear weather another cape is faintly distinguishable beyond this), and about one third of the great horizon is filled by this beautiful, undulating line of land, which, under the touch of atmospheric change, is almost as plastic as the clouds, and wears a new aspect with every turn of wind and weather.

Sailing out from Portsmouth Harbor with a fair wind from the northwest, the Isles of Shoals lie straight before you, nine miles away,—ill-defined and cloudy shapes, faintly discernible in the distance. A word about the origin of this name, "Isles of Shoals." They are supposed to have been so called, not because the ragged reefs run out beneath the water in all directions, ready to wreck and destroy, but because of the "shoaling," or "schooling," of fish about them, which in the mackerel and herring seasons, is remarkable. As you approach they separate, and show each its own peculiar characteristics, and you perceive that there are six islands if the tide is low; but if it is high, there are eight, and would be nine, but that a breakwater connects two of them. Appledore, called for many years Hog Island, from its rude resemblance to a hog's back rising from the water, when seen from out at sea, is the largest and most regular in shape. From afar, it looks smoothly rounded, like a gradually sloping elevation, the greatest height of which is only seventy-five feet above high-water mark. A little valley in which are situated the buildings belonging to the house of entertainment, which is the only habitation, divides its four hundred acres into two unequal portions. Next, almost within a stone's throw, is Haley's Island, or "Smutty-nose," so christened by passing sailors, with a grim sense of humor, from a long black point of rock stretching out to the southeast, upon which many a ship has laid her bones. This island is low and flat, and contains a greater depth of soil than the others. At low tide, Cedar and Malaga are both connected with it,—the latter permanently by a break-water,—the whole comprising about one hundred acres. Star Island contains one hundred and fifty acres, and lies a quarter of a mile southwest of Smutty-nose. Toward its northern end are clustered the houses of the little village of Gosport, with a tiny church crowning the highest rock. Not quite a mile southwest from Star, White Island lifts a lighthouse for warning. This is the most picturesque of the group, and forms, with Seaveys's Island, at low water, a double island, with an area of some twenty acres. Most westerly lies Londoner's, an irregular rock with a bit of beach, upon which all the shells about the cluster seem to be thrown. Two miles northeast from Appledore, Duck Island thrusts out its lurking ledges on all sides beneath the water, one of them running half a mile to the northwest. This is the most dangerous of the islands, and, being the most remote, is the only one visited to any great degree by the shy sea-fowl that are nearly banished by civilization. Yet even now, at low tide, those long black ledges are often whitened by the dazzling plumage of gulls whose exquisite and stainless purity rivals the new-fallen snow. The ledges run toward the west and north; but at the east and south the shore is bolder, and Shag and Mingo Rocks, where, during or after storms, the sea breaks with magnificent effect, lie isolated by a narrow channel from the main granite fragment. A very round rock west of Londoner's, perversely called "Square," and Anderson's Rock, off the southeast end of Smutty-nose, complete the catalogue.

Smutty-nose and Appledore are almost united by a reef, bare at low tide, though a large vessel can pass between them even then. Off the landing at White Island the Devil's Rock rolls an incessant breaker, and makes an attempt to reach the shore perilous in any but the serenest weather. Between Londoner's and Star is another, hardly bare at low tide; a perpetual danger, for it lies directly in the path of most of the sailing vessels, and many a schooner has been "brought up all standing" by this unexpected obstacle. Another rock, about four miles east of Appledore, rejoices in the significant title of the "Old Harry." Old Harry is deeply sunk beneath the surface, and never betrays himself except in great storms, when an awful white spray rises afar off, and the Shoalers know how tremendous are the breakers that send it skyward.

The names of the towns, Appledore, Gosport, and along the coast, Portsmouth, Newcastle, Rye, Ipswich, Portland, Bangor, Newbury, Amesbury, Salisbury, and many more, are all borrowed from towns on, or not far from, the coasts of England and Wales, as may be seen from the maps of those countries. Salisbury Beach fronts our islands. Amesbury lies farther inland, but the gentle outline of Po Hill, in that town, is the last eminence of any importance on the southern end of the coast line.

The dividing line between Maine and New Hampshire passes through the group, giving Appledore, Smutty-nose, and Duck Islands to Maine, and the rest to New Hampshire; but their allegiance to either is a matter of small importance, the few inhabitants troubling themselves but little about what State they belong to. Till within a few years no taxes were required of them, and they enjoyed immunity from this and various other earthly ills as completely as the gulls and loons that shared their dwelling-place.

Swept by every wind that blows, and beaten by the bitter brine for unknown ages, well may the Isles of Shoals be barren, bleak, and bare. At first sight nothing can be more rough and inhospitable than they appear. The incessant influences of wind and sun, rain, snow, frost, and spray, have so bleached the tops of the rocks, that they look hoary as if with age, though in the summer-time a gracious greenness of vegetation breaks here and there the stern outlines, and softens somewhat their rugged aspect. Yet so forbidding are their shores, it seems scarcely worth while to land upon them,—mere heaps of tumbling granite in the wide and lonely sea,—when all the smiling, "sapphire-spangled marriage-ring of the land" lies ready to woo the voyager back again, and welcome his returning prow with pleasant sights and sounds and scents that the wild wastes of water never know. But to the human creature who has eyes that will see and ears that will hear, nature appeals with such a novel charm, that the luxurious beauty of the land is half forgotten before one is aware. Its sweet gardens, full of color and perfume, its rich woods and softly swelling hills, its placid waters, and fields and flowery meadows, are no longer dear and desirable; for the wonderful sound of the sea dulls the memory of all past impressions, and seems to fulfil and satisfy all present needs. Landing for the first time, the stranger is struck only by the sadness of the place,—the vast loneliness; for there are not even trees to whisper with familiar voices,—nothing but sky and sea and rocks. But the very wildness and desolation reveal a strange beauty to him. Let him wait till evening comes,

"With sunset purple soothing all the waste."

and he will find himself slowly succumbing to the subtile charm of that sea atmosphere. He sleeps with all the waves of the Atlantic murmuring in his ears, and wakes to the freshness of a summer morning; and it seems as if morning were made for the first time. For the world is like a new-blown rose, and in the heart of it he stands, with only the caressing music of the water to break the utter silence, unless, perhaps, a song-sparrow pours out its blissful warble like an embodied joy. The sea is rosy, and the sky; the line of land is radiant; the scattered sails glow with the delicious color that touches so tenderly the bare, bleak rocks. These are lovelier than sky or sea or distant sails, or graceful gulls' wings reddened with the dawn; nothing takes color so beautifully as the bleached granite; the shadows are delicate, and the fine, hard outlines are glorified and softened beneath the fresh first blush of sunrise. All things are speckless and spotless; there is no dust, no noise, nothing but peace in the sweet air and on the quiet sea. The day goes on; the rose changes to mellow gold, the gold to clear, white daylight, and the sea is sparkling again. A breeze ripples the surface, and wherever it touches the color deepens. A seine-boat passes, with the tawny net heaped in the stern, and the scarlet shirts of the rowers brilliant against the blue. Pleasantly their voices come across the water, breaking the stillness. The fishing-boats steal to and fro, silent, with glittering sails; the gulls wheel lazily; the far-off coasters glide rapidly along the horizon; the mirage steals down the coast-line, and seems to remove it leagues away. And what if it were to slip down the slope of the world and disappear entirely? You think, in a half-dream, you would not care. Many troubles, cares, perplexities, vexations, lurk behind that far, faint line for you. Why should you be bothered any more?

"Let us alone. Time driveth onward fast,
And in a little while our lips are dumb."

And so the waves, with their lulling murmur, do their work, and you are soothed into repose and transient forgetfulness.

I well remember my first sight of White Island, where we took up our abode on leaving the mainland. I was scarcely five years old; but from the upper windows of our dwelling in Portsmouth, I had been shown the clustered masts of ships lying at the wharves along the Piscataqua River, faintly outlined against the sky, and, baby as I was, even then I was drawn, with a vague longing, seaward. How delightful was that long, first sail to the Isles of Shoals! How pleasant the unaccustomed sound of the incessant ripple against the boat-side, the sight of the wide water and limitless sky, the warmth of the broad sunshine that made us blink like young sandpipers as we sat in triumph, perched among the household goods with which the little craft was laden! It was at sunset in autumn that we were set ashore on that loneliest, lovely rock, where the lighthouse looked down on us like some tall, black-capped giant, and filled me with awe and wonder. At its base a few goats were grouped on the rock, standing out dark against the red sky as I looked up at them. The stars were beginning to twinkle; the wind blew cold, charged with the sea's sweetness; the sound of many waters half bewildered me. Someone began to light the lamps in the tower. Rich red and golden, they swung round in mid-air; everything was strange and fascinating and new. We entered the quaint little old stone cottage that was for six years our home. How curious it seemed, with its low, whitewashed ceiling and deep window-seats, showing the great thickness of the walls made to withstand the breakers, with whose force we soon grew acquainted! A blissful home the little house became to the children who entered it that quiet evening and slept for the first time lulled by the murmur of the encircling sea. I do not think a happier triad ever existed than we were, living in that profound isolation. It takes so little to make a healthy child happy; and we never wearied of our few resources. True, the winters seemed as long as a whole year to our little minds, but they were pleasant, nevertheless. Into the deep window-seats we climbed, and with pennies (for which we had no other use) made round holes in the thick frost, breathing on them till they were warm, and peeped out at the bright, fierce, windy weather, watching the vessels scudding over the intensely dark blue sea, all "feather-white" where the short waves broke hissing in the cold, and the sea-fowl soaring aloft or tossing on the water; or, in calmer days, we saw how the stealthy Star-Islander paddled among the ledges, or lay for hours stretched on the wet seaweed, with his gun, watching for wild-fowl. Sometimes the round head of a seal moved about among the kelp-covered rocks. A few are seen every winter, and are occasionally shot; but that are shyer and more alert even than the birds.

We were forced to lay in stores of all sorts in the autumn, as if we were fitting out a ship for an Arctic expedition. The lower story of the lighthouse was hung with mutton and beef, and the store-room packed with provisions.

In the long, covered walk that bridged the gorge between the lighthouse and the house, we played in stormy days; and every evening it was a fresh excitement to watch the lighting of the lamps, and think how far the lighthouse sent its rays, and how many hearts it gladdened with assurance of safety. As I grew older I was allowed to kindle the lamps sometimes myself. That was indeed a pleasure. So little a creature as I might do that much for the great world! But by the fireside our best pleasure lay,—with plants and singing birds and books and playthings and loving care and kindness the cold and stormy season wore itself at last away, and died into the summer calm. We hardly saw a human face beside our own all winter; but with the spring came manifold life to our lonely dwelling,—human life among other forms. Our neighbors from Star rowed across; the pilot-boat from Portsmouth steered over, and brought us letters, newspapers, magazines, and told us the news of months. The faint echoes from the far-off world hardly touched us little ones. We listened to the talk of our elders. "Winfield Scott and Santa Anna!" "The war in Mexico!" "The famine in Ireland!" It all meant nothing to us. We heard the reading aloud of details of the famine, and saw tears in the eyes of the reader, and were vaguely sorry; but the fate of Red Riding-Hood was much more near and dreadful to us. We waited for the spring with an eager longing; the advent of the growing grass, the birds and flowers and insect life, the soft skies and softer winds, the everlasting beauty of the thousand tender tints that clothed the world,—these things brought us unspeakable bliss. To the heart of Nature one must need be drawn in such a life; and very soon I learned how richly she repays in deep refreshment the reverent love of her worshipper. With the first warm days we built our little mountains of wet gravel on the beach, and danced after the sandpipers at the edge of the foam, shouted to the gossiping kittiwakes that fluttered above, or watched the pranks of the burgomaster gull, or cried to the crying loons. The gannet's long, white wings stretched overhead, perhaps, or the dusky shag made a sudden shadow in mid-air, or we startled on some lonely ledge the great blue heron that flew off, trailing legs and wings, stork-like, against the clouds. Or, in the sunshine on the bare rocks, we cut from the broad, brown leaves of the slippery, varnished kelps, grotesque shapes of man and bird and beast that withered in the wind and blew away; or we fashioned boats from bits of driftwood, manned them with a weird crew of kelpies, and set them adrift on the great deep, to float we cared not whither.

Sarah Orne Jewett

A White Heron

1

The woods were already filled with shadows one June evening, just before eight o'clock, though a bright sunset still glimmered faintly among the trunks of the trees. A little girl was driving home her cow, a plodding, dilatory, provoking creature in her behavior, but a valued companion for all that. They were going away from the western light, and striking deep into the dark woods, but their feet were familiar with the path, and it was no matter whether their eyes could see it or not.

There was hardly a night the summer through when the old cow could be found waiting at the pasture bars; on the contrary, it was her greatest pleasure to hide herself away among the high huckleberry bushes, and though she wore a loud bell she had made the discovery that if one stood perfectly still it would not ring. So Sylvia had to hunt for her until she found her, and call Co'! Co'! with never an answering Moo, until her childish patience was quite spent. If the creature had not given good milk and plenty of it, the case would have seemed very different to her owners. Besides, Sylvia had all the time there was, and very little use to make of it. Sometimes in pleasant weather it was a consolation to look upon the cow's pranks as an intelligent attempt to play hide and seek, and as the child had no playmates she lent herself to this amusement with a good deal of zest. Though this chase had been so long that the wary animal herself had given an unusual signal of her whereabouts, Sylvia had only laughed when she came upon Mistress Moolly at the swamp-side, and urged her affectionately homeward with a twig of birch leaves. The old cow was not inclined to wander farther, she even turned in the right direction for once as they left the pasture, and stepped along the road at a good pace. She was quite ready to be milked now, and seldom stopped to browse. Sylvia wondered what her grandmother would say because they were so late. It was a great while since she had left home at half past five o'clock, but everybody knew the difficulty of making this errand a short one. Mrs. Tilley had chased the hornéd torment too many summer evenings herself to blame any one else for lingering, and was only thankful as she waited that she had Sylvia, nowadays, to give such valuable assistance. The good woman suspected that Sylvia loitered occasionally on her own account; there never was such a child for straying about out-of-doors since the world was made! Everybody said that it was a good change for a little maid who had tried to grow for eight years in a crowded manufacturing town, but, as for Sylvia herself, it seemed as if she never had been alive at all before she came to live at the farm. She thought often with wistful compassion of a wretched dry geranium that belonged to a town neighbor.

"'Afraid of folks,'" old Mrs. Tilley said to herself, with a smile, after she had made the unlikely choice of Sylvia from her daughter's houseful of children, and was returning to the farm. "'Afraid of folks,' they said! I guess she won't be troubled no great with 'em up to the old place!" When they reached the door of the lonely house and stopped to unlock it, and the cat came to purr loudly, and rub against them, a deserted pussy, indeed, but fat with young robins, Sylvia whispered that this was a beautiful place to live in, and she never should wish to go home.

The companions followed the shady woodroad, the cow taking slow steps, and the child very fast ones. The cows stopped long at the brook to drink, as if the pasture were not half a swamp, and Sylvia stood still and waited, letting her bare feet cool themselves in the shoal water, while the great twilight moths struck softly against her. She waded on through the brook as the cow moved away, and listened to the thrushes with a heart that beat fast with pleasure. There was a stirring in the great boughs overhead. They were full of little birds and beasts that seemed to be wide-awake, and going about their world, or else saying good-night to each other in sleepy twitters. Sylvia herself felt sleepy as she walked along. However, it was not much farther to the house, and the air was soft and sweet. She was not often in the woods so late as this, and it made her feel as if she were a part of the gray shadows and the moving leaves. She was just thinking how long it seemed since she first came to the farm a year ago, and wondering if everything went on in the noisy town just the same as when she was there; the thought of the great red-faced boy who used to chase and frighten her made her hurry along the path to escape from the shadow of the trees.

Suddenly this little woods-girl is horror-stricken to hear a clear whistle not very far away. Not a bird's whistle, which would have a sort of friendliness, but a boy's whistle, determined, and somewhat aggressive. Sylvia left the cow to whatever sad fate might await her, and stepped discreetly aside into the bushes, but she was just too late. The enemy had discovered her, and called out in a very cheerful and persuasive tone, "Halloa, little girl, how far is it to the road?" and trembling Sylvia answered almost inaudibly, "A good ways."

She did not dare to look boldly at the tall young man, who carried a gun over his shoulder, but she came out of her bush and again followed the cow, while he walked alongside.

"I have been hunting for some birds," the stranger said kindly, "and I have lost my way, and need a friend very much. Don't be afraid," he added gallantly. "Speak up and tell me what your name is, and whether you think I can spend the night at your house, and go out gunning early in the morning."

Sylvia was more alarmed than before. Would not her grandmother consider her much to blame? But who could have foreseen such an accident as this? It did not appear to be her fault, and she hung her head as if the stem of it were broken, but managed to answer "Sylvy," with much effort when her companion again asked her name.

Mrs. Tilley was standing in the doorway when the trio came into view. The cow gave a loud moo by way of explanation.

"Yes, you'd better speak up for yourself, you old trial! Where'd she tuck herself away this time, Sylvy?" Sylvia kept an awed silence; she knew by instinct that her grandmother did not comprehend the gravity of the situation.

She must be mistaking the stranger for one of the farmer-lads of the region.

The young man stood his gun beside the door, and dropped a heavy game-bag beside it; then he bade Mrs. Tilley good-evening, and repeated his way-farer's story, and asked if he could have a night's lodging.

"Put me anywhere you like," he said. "I must be off early in the morning, before day; but I am very hungry, indeed. You can give me some milk at any rate, that's plain."

"Dear sakes, yes," responded the hostess, whose long slumbering hospitality seemed to be easily awakened. "You might fare better if you went out on the main road a mile or so, but you're welcome to what we've got. I'll milk right off, and you make yourself at home. You can sleep on husks or feathers," she proffered graciously. "I raised them all myself. There's good pasturing for geese just below here towards the ma'sh. Now step round and set a plate for the gentleman, Sylvy!" And Sylvia promptly stepped. She was glad to have something to do, and she was hungry herself.

It was a surprise to find so clean and comfortable a little dwelling in this New England wilderness. The young man had known the horrors of its most primitive housekeeping, and the dreary squalor of that level of society which does not rebel at the companionship of hens. This was the best thrift of an old-fashioned farmstead, though on such a small scale that it seemed like a hermitage. He listened eagerly to the old woman's quaint talk, he watched Sylvia's pale face and shining gray eyes with ever growing enthusiasm, and insisted that this was the best supper he had eaten for a month; then, afterward, the new-made friends sat down in the doorway together while the moon came up.

Soon it would be berry-time, and Sylvia was a great help at picking. The cow was a good milker, though a plaguy thing to keep track of, the hostess gossiped frankly, adding presently that she had buried four children, so that Sylvia's mother, and a son (who might be dead) in California were all the children she had left. "Dan, my boy, was a great hand to go gunning," she explained sadly. "I never wanted for pa'tridges or gray squer'ls while he was to home. He's been a great wand'rer, I expect, and he's no hand to write letters. There, I don't blame him, I'd ha' seen the world myself if it had been so I could."

"Sylvia takes after him," the grandmother continued affectionately, after a minute's pause. "There ain't a foot o' ground she don't know her way over, and the wild creatur's counts her one o' themselves. Squer'ls she'll tame to come an' feed right out o' her hands, and all sorts o' birds. Last winter she got the jay-birds to bangeing here, and I believe she'd 'a' scanted herself of her own meals to have plenty to throw out amongst 'em, if I hadn't kep' watch. Anything but crows, I tell her, I'm willin' to help support,—though Dan he went an' tamed one o' them that did seem to have reason same as folks. It was round here a good spell after he went away. Dan an' his father they didn't hitch,—but he never held up his head ag'in after Dan had dared him an' gone off."

The guest did not notice this hint of family sorrows in his eager interest in something else.

"So Sylvy knows all about birds, does she?" he exclaimed, as he looked round at the little girl who sat, very demure but increasingly sleepy, in the moonlight. "I am making a collection of birds myself. I have been at it ever since I was a boy." (Mrs. Tilley smiled.) "There are two or three very rare ones I have been hunting for these five years. I mean to get them on my own ground if they can be found."

"Do you cage 'em up?" asked Mrs. Tilley doubtfully, in response to this enthusiastic announcement.

"Oh, no, they're stuffed and preserved, dozens and dozens of them," said the ornithologist, "and I have shot or snared every one myself. I caught a glimpse of a white heron three miles from here on Saturday, and I have followed it in this direction. They have never been found in this district at all. The little white heron, it is," and he turned again to look at Sylvia with the hope of discovering that the rare bird was one of her acquaintances.

But Sylvia was watching a hop-toad in the narrow footpath.

"You would know the heron if you saw it," the stranger continued eagerly. "A queer tall white bird with soft feathers and long thin legs. And it would have a nest perhaps in the top of a high tree, made of sticks, something like a hawk's nest."

Sylvia's heart gave a wild beat; she knew that strange white bird, and had once stolen softly near where it stood in some bright green swamp grass, way over at the other side of the woods. There was an open place where the sunshine always seemed strangely yellow and hot, where tall, nodding rushes grew, and her grandmother had warned her that she might sink in the soft black mud underneath and never be heard of more. Not far beyond were the salt marshes and beyond those was the sea, the sea which Sylvia wondered and dreamed about, but never had looked upon, though its great voice could often be heard above the noise of the woods on stormy nights.

"I can't think of anything I should like so much as to find that heron's nest," the handsome stranger was saying. "I would give ten dollars to anybody who could show it to me," he added desperately, "and I mean to spend my whole vacation hunting for it if need be. Perhaps it was only migrating, or had been chased out of its own region by some bird of prey."

Mrs. Tilley gave amazed attention to all this, but Sylvia still watched the toad, not divining, as she might have done at some calmer time, that the creature wished to get to its hole under the doorstep, and was much hindered by the unusual spectators at that hour of the evening. No amount of thought, that night, could decide how many wished-for treasures the ten dollars, so lightly spoken of, would buy.

The next day the young sportsman hovered about the woods, and Sylvia kept him company, having lost her first fear of the friendly lad, who proved to be most kind and sympathetic. He told her many things about the birds and what they knew and where they lived and what they did with themselves. And he gave her a jack-knife, which she thought as great a treasure as if she were a desert-islander. All day long he did not once make her troubled or afraid except when he brought down some unsuspecting singing creature from its bough. Sylvia would have liked him vastly better without his gun; she could not understand why he killed the very birds he seemed to like so much. But as the day waned, Sylvia still watched the young man with loving admiration. She had never seen anybody so charming and delightful; the woman's heart, asleep in the child, was vaguely thrilled by a dream of love. Some premonition of that great power stirred and swayed these young foresters who traversed the solemn woodlands with soft-footed silent care. They stopped to listen to a bird's song; they pressed forward again eagerly, parting the branches,—speaking to each other rarely and in whispers; the young man going first and Sylvia following, fascinated, a few steps behind, with her gray eyes dark with excitement.

She grieved because the longed-for white heron was elusive, but she did not lead the guest, she only followed, and there was no such thing as speaking first. The sound of her own unquestioned voice would have terrified her,—it was hard enough to answer yes or no when there was need of that. At last evening began to fall, and they drove the cow home together, and Sylvia smiled with pleasure when they came to the place where she heard the whistle and was afraid only the night before.

2

Half a mile from home, at the farther edge of the woods, where the land was highest, a great pine-tree stood, the last of its generation. Whether it was left for a boundary mark, or for what reason, no one could say; the woodchoppers who had felled its mates were dead and gone long ago, and a whole forest of sturdy trees, pines and oaks and maples, had grown again. But the stately head of this old pine towered above them all and made a landmark for sea and shore miles and miles away. Sylvia knew it well. She had always believed that whoever climbed to the top of it could see the ocean; and the little girl had often laid her hand on the great rough trunk and looked up wistfully at those dark boughs that the wind always stirred, no matter how hot and still the air might be below. Now she thought of the tree with a new excitement, for why, if one climbed it at break of day, could not one see all the world, and easily discover whence the white heron flew, and mark the place, and find the hidden nest?

What a spirit of adventure, what wild ambition! What fancied triumph and delight and glory for the later morning when she could make known the secret! It was almost too real and too great for the childish heart to bear.

All night the door of the little house stood open, and the whippoorwills came and sang upon the very step. The young sportsman and his old hostess were sound asleep, but Sylvia's great design kept her broad awake and watching. She forgot to think of sleep. The short summer night seemed as long as the winter darkness, and at last when the whippoorwills ceased, and she was afraid the morning would after all come too soon, she stole out of the house and followed the pasture path through the woods, hastening toward the open ground beyond, listening with a sense of comfort and companionship to the drowsy twitter of a half-awakened bird, whose perch she had jarred in passing. Alas, if the great wave of human interest which flooded for the first time this dull little life should sweep away the satisfactions of an existence heart to heart with nature and the dumb life of the forest!

There was the huge tree asleep yet in the paling moonlight, and small and hopeful Sylvia began with utmost bravery to mount to the top of it, with tingling, eager blood coursing the channels of her whole frame, with her bare feet and fingers, that pinched and held like bird's claws to the monstrous ladder reaching up, up, almost to the sky itself. First she must mount the white oak tree that grew alongside, where she was almost lost among the dark branches and the green leaves heavy and wet with dew; a bird fluttered off its nest, and a red squirrel ran to and fro and scolded pettishly at the harmless housebreaker. Sylvia felt her way easily. She had often climbed there, and knew that higher still one of the oak's upper branches chafed against the pine trunk, just where its lower boughs were set close together. There, when she made the dangerous pass from one tree to the other, the great enterprise would really begin.

She crept out along the swaying oak limb at last, and took the daring step across into the old pine-tree. The way was harder than she thought; she must reach far and hold fast, the sharp dry twigs caught and held her and scratched her like angry talons, the pitch made her thin little fingers clumsy and stiff as she went round and round the tree's great stem, higher and higher upward. The sparrows and robins in the woods below were beginning to wake and twitter to the dawn, yet it seemed much lighter there aloft in the pine-tree, and the child knew that she must hurry if her project were to be of any use.

The tree seemed to lengthen itself out as she went up, and to reach farther and farther upward. It was like a great main-mast to the voyaging earth; it must truly have been amazed that morning through all its ponderous frame as it felt this determined spark of human spirit creeping and climbing from higher branch to branch. Who knows how steadily the least twigs held themselves to advantage this light, weak creature on her way! The old pine must have loved his new dependent. More than all the hawks, and bats, and moths, and even the sweet-voiced thrushes, was the brave, beating heart of the solitary gray-eyed child. And the tree stood still and held away the winds that June morning while the dawn grew bright in the east.

Sylvia's face was like a pale star, if one had seen it from the ground, when the last thorny bough was past, and she stood trembling and tired but wholly triumphant, high in the tree-top. Yes, there was the sea with the dawning sun making a golden dazzle over it, and toward that glorious east flew two hawks with slow-moving pinions. How low they looked in the air from that height when before one had only seen them far up, and dark against the blue sky. Their gray feathers were as soft as moths; they seemed only a little way from the tree, and Sylvia felt as if she too could go flying away among the clouds. Westward, the woodlands and farms reached miles and miles into the distance; here and there were church steeples, and white villages; truly it was a vast and awesome world.

The birds sang louder and louder. At last the sun came up bewilderingly bright. Sylvia could see the white sails of ships out at sea, and the clouds that were purple and rose-colored and yellow at first began to fade away. Where was the white heron's nest in the sea of green branches, and was this wonderful sight and pageant of the world the only reward for having climbed to such a giddy height? Now look down again, Sylvia, where the green marsh is set among the shining birches and dark hemlocks; there where you saw the white heron once you will see him again; look, look! white spot of him like a single floating feather comes up from the dead hemlock and grows larger, and rises, and comes close at last, and goes by the landmark pine with steady sweep of wing and outstretched slender neck and crested head. And wait! wait! do not

move a foot or a finger, little girl, do not send an arrow of light and consciousness from your two eager eyes, for the heron has perched on a pine bough not
far beyond yours, and cries back to his mate on the nest, and plumes his feathers for the new day!

The child gives a long sigh a minute later when a company of shouting catbirds comes also to the tree, and vexed by their fluttering and lawlessness the
solemn heron goes away. She knows his secret now, the wild, light, slender
bird that floats and wavers, and goes back like an arrow presently to his home
in the green world beneath. Then Sylvia, well satisfied, makes her perilous
way down again, not daring to look far below the branch she stands on, ready
to cry sometimes because her fingers ache and her lamed feet slip. Wondering
over and over again what the stranger would say to her, and what he would
think when she told him how to find his way straight to the heron's nest.

"Sylvy, Sylvy!" called the busy old grandmother again and again, but nobody
answered, and the small husk bed was empty, and Sylvia had disappeared.

The guest waked from a dream, and remembering his day's pleasure hurried to dress himself that it might sooner begin. He was sure from the way the
shy little girl looked once or twice yesterday that she had at least seen the
white heron, and now she must really be persuaded to tell. Here she comes
now, paler than ever, and her worn old frock is torn and tattered, and smeared
with pine pitch. The grandmother and the sportsman stand in the door together and question her, and the splendid moment has come to speak of the
dead hemlock-tree by the green marsh.

But Sylvia does not speak after all, though the old grandmother fretfully
rebukes her, and the young man's kind appealing eyes are looking straight in
her own. He can make them rich with money; he has promised it, and they are
poor now. He is so well worth making happy, and he waits to hear the story
she can tell.

No, she must keep silence! What is it that suddenly forbids her and makes
her dumb? Has she been nine years growing, and now, when the great world
for the first time puts out a hand to her, must she thrust it aside for a bird's
sake? The murmur of the pine's green branches is in her ears, she remembers
how the white heron came flying through the golden air and how they
watched the sea and the morning together, and Sylvia cannot speak; she cannot tell the heron's secret and give its life away.

Dear loyalty, that suffered a sharp pang as the guest went away disappointed
later in the day, that could have served and followed him and loved him as a

dog loves! Many a night Sylvia heard the echo of his whistle haunting the pasture path as she came home with the loitering cow. She forgot even her sorrow at the sharp report of his gun and the piteous sight of thrushes and sparrows dropping silent to the ground, their songs hushed and their pretty feathers stained and wet with blood. Were the birds better friends than their hunter might have been,—who can tell? Whatever treasures were lost to her, woodlands and summer-time, remember! Bring your gifts and graces and tell your secrets to this lonely country child!

Edna St. Vincent Millay

Memory of Cape Cod

The wind in the ash-tree sounds like surf on the shore at Truro.
I will shut my eyes . . . hush, be still with your silly bleating,
    sheep on Shillingstone Hill . . .

They said: Come along! They said: Leave your pebbles on the sand and come
    along, it's long after sunset!
The mosquitoes will be thick in the pine-woods along by Long Nook, the wind's
    died down!
They said: Leave your pebbles on the sand, and your shells, too, and come along,
    we'll find you another beach like the beach at Truro

Let me listen to the wind in the ash . . . it sounds like surf on the
    shore.

Impression: Fog off the Coast of Dorset

As day was born, as night was dying,
The seagulls woke me with their crying;
And from the reef the mooing horn
Spoke to the waker: Day is born
And night is dying, but still the fog
On dimly looming deck and spar
Is dewy, and on the vessel's log,
And cold the first-mate's fingers are,
And wet the pen wherewith they write
"Off Portland. Fog. No land in sight."
—As night was dying, and glad to die,
And day, with dull and gloomy eye,
Lifting the sun, a smoky lamp,
Peered into fog, that swaddled sky
And wave alike: a shifty damp
Unwieldy province, loosely ruled,
Turned over to a prince unschooled,
That he must govern with sure hand
Straightway, not knowing sea from land.

Mary Karr

· ·

Chapter 5, *The Liars' Club*

My daddy watched Hurricane Carla come up the Intercoastal Canal from the Gulf. He claimed to be high in a sort of crow's nest at the time, behind a thick glass wall that let him look out over half the county. The crow's nest was on a giant tower facing the refinery, beyond which lay the oil-storage tanks, and finally the canal, a glorified ditch that Houston oilmen had spent a fortune having dug so they could boat their oil from offshore rigs right to the refineries. Daddy later said the tower swayed back and forth in the gale. He and Ben Bederman swore they had to hold on to the countertops while the rolling chairs slid around. Through the observation window, they watched a gray wall of water twenty feet high move up the canal toward town. I can almost see my daddy cock his head and squint like it was some animal he was tracking in the distance. He even took a minute to point with his ropy arm when he was telling the story, like the tidal wave was coming right at us that minute. "It was like a whole building made out of water," he said. I later had cause to wonder how his view was so clear in the midst of the storm. But hearing him tell it, you would never doubt he'd somehow actually cowboyed his way through it all.

Remarkably enough, the hurricane didn't go in at Leechfield, this despite the fact that a tidal wave had been dead set on a course that would have squashed every remaining citizen flat as a roach. The odds on a direct hit had been high. But the storm took a weird turn, the kind of dodge people later likened to a fast quarterback barely scooting around some bullnecked lineman. The move was a forty-to-one fluke. Just before Carla came ashore at Leechfield, the storm stopped almost dead in place; then it made a sixty-degree turn. Only the edges swept over East Texas, the rest flying full force into Cameron, Louisiana, which hadn't battened down at all.

Cameron's preparations wouldn't have mattered much, though, since a good hunk of the Gulf of Mexico essentially lifted itself up and then toppled over right on the low-lying town. People shinnied up trees, trying to get away from the rising water. Civil Defense did what they could at the last minute, and some families managed to outrun the flood in their cars when the radio announced where the storm was heading in. But a lot of people didn't happen to have their radios turned on. Casualties were high. The TV ran footage of guys in hip waders sloshing through their own living rooms, feeling around underwater for pieces of furniture that hadn't washed away.

The storm also flooded the bayous and brought all manner of critters from both salt and fresh water right into buildings and houses. When the water went down, one guy I read about in the paper found an eight-foot nurse shark flopping on his kitchen tiles. Whole bunches of people opened dresser drawers to find cottonmouths nesting next to their balled-up socks. There were also nutria-rat bites, kids mostly, toddlers who got cornered in their own yards. The rats were as big as raccoons and had front teeth shaped like chisels with bright orange enamel on them, which made the attacks particularly scary to think about. Neighbors came back to town bringing stories about cousins or friends of friends who'd been bitten, then gone through the agonizing rabies shots in the belly. I was a vulture for this kind of story.

Grandma died during all of this, of course. It turned out that she hadn't been fully dead at Auntie's, just in a coma. I've been told that she actually came out of that coma and spent a few days bedridden back at our house in Leechfield before she died. I don't remember it that way. Apparently I just blanked out her last visit along with a lot of other things. She died, and I wasn't sorry.

The afternoon it happened, Frank Doleman came to the door of my second-grade class with Lecia in tow. Mrs. Hess told me to get my lunch box and galoshes. Out in the hall, Lecia was snubbing into a brown paper towel that covered half her face so I couldn't see if she was ginning out real tears or just making snotty sounds in her head. Uncle Frank kneeled down eye-level to tell me that Grandma had "passed away." I remember this phrase seemed an unnaturally polite way of putting it, like something you'd hear on *Bonanza*. All the local terms for dying started more or less coursing through my head right then. *She bought the farm, bit the big one, cashed in her chips,* and my favorite: *she opened herself up a worm farm.* (I had the smug pleasure once of using this term up north and having a puzzled young banker-to-be then ask me if these worm farmers in Texas sold worms for fishing, or what.)

I sat in the back of Uncle Frank's white convertible going home with Lecia blubbering nonstop in the front bucket seat and him putting his hammy hand on her shoulder every now and then, telling her it was okay, to just cry it out. What was running through my head, though, was that song the Munchkins sing when Dorothy's house lands on the witch with the stripy socks: "Ding dong, the witch is dead." I knew better than to hum it out loud, of course, particularly with Lecia making such a good show, but that's what I thought.

Daddy was squatting on the porch in his blue overalls and hard hat, smoking, when we pulled up. He'd obviously been called right out of the field. He was dirty and smelled like crude oil when he hugged Lecia and me, one under each arm. Our principal didn't pause, though, before shaking his hand, didn't even dig out his hankie to wipe the oil off his palm after he shook. He was partial to white starched shirts, but knew when to set that aside.

While Uncle Frank backed out, Daddy and Lecia and I stood together a minute at the head of the driveway waving bye-bye. I remember leaning across the front of his blue work shirt to tell Lecia that was some good crying she did, to which she lowered the paper towel so I could finally see her face. It was like a coarse brown curtain dropping to show a mask entirely different than the grinning one I'd expected. Her eyes and nose were red and her mouth was twisted up and slobberly. All of a sudden, I knew she wasn't faking it, the grief I mean. It cut something out of me to see her hurt. And it put some psychic yardage between us that I was so far from sad and she was so deep in it.

It must have pissed Lecia off too, somehow, that gap between her misery and my relief. Later that evening, Daddy was frying up a chicken, and she chased me down over something mean I'd said about Grandma. She was fast even then (in junior high, she would run anchor on the four-forty relay), so I didn't make it a half turn around the yard before she caught me by the back collar and yanked me down from behind. The collar choked off my windpipe, and the fall knocked the breath out of me. Before I knew what hit me, she had me down on my back in the spiky St. Augustine grass.

She sat on my chest with her full weight. Her knees dug into the ball sockets of both my shoulders. She said take it back. I sucked up enough wind to say I wouldn't. I tried bucking my pelvis up to throw her off. Then I tried flinging my legs up to wrap around her shoulders, but she had me nailed. Still I wouldn't take it back. All I had to fight back with was my stubbornness (which I'd built up by being a smart mouth and getting my ass whipped a lot). I never actually won a stand-up fight, with Lecia or anybody. Hence my tendency to sneak up blindside somebody weeks after the fact. But I could sure as hell provoke one and then drag it out by not giving in. I took a warped sort of pride in this, though I can see now it's a pitiful thing to be proud of—being able to take an ass-stomping.

I don't know how long she had me pinned. Her knees dug twin bruises in my shoulders. I found them when putting on my pajamas that night, the size and shape of big serving spoons. She kept me there a while. The sky was going pink. I could hear Daddy's spatula on the skillet scraping chicken drippings for cream gravy. Finally, she got tired of my not giving in and decided to spit in my eye. She hawked up a huge boogery gollop from way back in her throat, pausing every now and then to tell me she was fixing to huck it at me. It had bulk and geometry. It was hanging in a giant tear right over my face, swinging side to side like a pendulum, when Daddy came slamming out the screen to haul her off me.

That night in bed I could hear her crying into her pillow, but when I put my hand on her shoulder, she just shrugged me off.

Mother was on her way to bury Grandma during all this. Thank God, because Lecia and me fighting always made Mother sit down crying. She had always longed so fiercely for a sister that she couldn't understand why we whaled on each other.

Anyway, while Lecia was trying to spit in my eye, Mother was driving across the Texas desert in Grandma's old Impala, heading from the hospital in Houston to Lubbock and the funeral. She says that she wore her black Chanel suit with Grandma's beige-and-ivory cameo, which her great-grandmother had brought from Ireland. She also wore pearl earrings, and a white pillbox hat of the type Jackie Kennedy had on when her husband was shot. (It is a sad commentary on the women of my family that we can recite whole wardrobe assemblages from the most minor event in detail, but often forget almost everything else. In fact, the more important the occasion—funeral, wedding, divorce court—the more detailed the wardrobe memory and the dimmer the hope of dredging up anything that happened.) She took the trip solo because she didn't want to upset us. Or so she told us on the phone. "There's no need for y'all riding all the way out there just to get upset" was how she put it. That sudden surge of maternal feeling seems odd to me now. I mean, we'd already seen all manner of nastiness and butchery, including Grandma's lopped-off leg at M. D. Anderson Hospital. Plus we'd watched Grandma achieve whole new levels of Nervous as the cancer ate out her brain. It just didn't make sense.

For years Lecia had me convinced that Mother left us behind because she was hauling Grandma's body in the backseat of the Impala. Lecia fed me this lie pretty soon after we got off the phone with mother that night, and I swallowed it like a bigmouthed bass. I needed an excuse for being left behind, I guess. The truth—that we were murder on her nerves, which were already shot—must have been too much for me. In bed one morning I asked Lecia why didn't Mother just put Grandma in the trunk. Lecia propped up on her elbow and said that wasn't very nice for your dead mother. Following that same line of logic, I figured out for myself that she wouldn't let anybody truss the old lady on top of the car like a deer, just so we'd all get to ride out too. So for years, I pictured Mother driving the five hundred miles across Texas with Grandma's corpse stretched out on the backseat. (I guess it wasn't till I read William Faulkner's *As I Lay Dying*, where the kids are dragging their dead mother across Mississippi, and the stink gets so bad and the flies and maggots get at her, that I began to figure that some ambulance had probably carted the body back. Mother had small tolerance for odors.)

The trip must have been grisly. The newly dead do, after all, rent a lot of skull space from us. So I still imagine Mother alone in that car with some ghost of her dead mother sitting beside. Mother was driving at night as Grandma would have, for the cool and lack of traffic night provided. It's a fourteen-hour drive, and the sky can get awful black in that time, like a big black bowl somebody set over you. One pair of headlights can put you in a trance with the white road dashes coming up in them at exact intervals. And as John Milton says, "The mind is its own place, and in itself / Can make a heav'n of hell, a hell of heav'n. I myself am Hell."

I sometimes want to beam myself back to the old Impala so Mother won't have to make that drive alone. I always picture myself being incredibly useful—pouring coffee from the thermos or finding something of a soothing and classical nature on the radio—never whining or asking to pee as I surely would have. Maybe I would roll down all the windows just to shoo the mean ghost of my grandmother out.

Mother had left us at home because she was hurt. For her, being hurt meant drawing into herself. (Old joke: What's the loneliest place in Louisiana? Bayou Self.) And that's where I have to leave her, alone on the dark highway with the cacti rearing up and falling back down as she passes.

Grandma's death gave me my first serious case of insomnia. When I lay in bed next to Lecia's solid, sleeping form, that picture of Grandma's pale arm with the ants would rear up behind my closed eyes. With it came a low humming in my head—a sound like a crazy cello player sawing the same note over and over, or like a zillion bees coming up out of the ground. In fact, that humming was the sound our car tires had made on the Orange Bridge when Mother either did or didn't try to crash through the guardrail and fly us screaming down to the river. If I kept my eyes open, the humming stopped. If they fell closed, even for a second, that humming would swamp over every good thought I'd ever had. Nights, I lay awake with my eyes burning. What I was protecting myself against on these vigils was, in fact, my own skull, which must be the textbook definition of early-onset Nervous if ever there was one.

That small psychic crisis kicked off a metaphysical one. Why was everybody so fired up about nature all the time, and God? These kids sitting around me with their heads crooked earnestly over their giant drawing papers seemed to have forgotten that the ocean had decided for no good reason to dislodge itself on top of hundreds of people across the river in Louisiana. Our bodies could have been the ones people saw on TV newsreels after school. Families on these film clips went from one child-sized body bag to another— the bags having been lined up in rows across some movie-theater parking lot. The sheriff would unzip the bag's top a little bit, and the daddy would peer in, then shake his head no. Then he'd step back while the sheriff rezipped before going on to the next bag. This happened over and over till the sheriff finally unzipped the face the family was looking for—little Junior or baby Jackie, blue-skinned and bloated, tongue black and sticking out.

Growing Up Coastal

The cameras didn't show those faces, of course. But Daddy had seen plenty guys dead in war. I remember he rubbed the sleeve of his faded chambray shirt and said that a human face could go just as blue as that. He also said it wasn't the coldness of a dead man's skin that gave you the willies, but how the skin went hard all over, so touching him was like touching wood or concrete.

During this talk, we were sitting in bed eating dinner, a habit we'd gone right back to after Grandma died. Only we'd added the drone of TV news. Its blue-white light was our family hearth. "I shit you not," Daddy said as he tore off a hunk of biscuit. "You touch a dead man sometime." He took a swallow of buttermilk. "Hard as that table. Got no more to do with being alive than that table does."

That description didn't scare me so much as the news footage of some daddy folding in on himself once he'd recognized a kid's face. The mothers cried too, of course, and bitterly. But they seemed better equipped for it. They held each other while they cried, or fell to their knees, or screamed up at the sky. But you could tell by the moans and bellows those grown men let out that their grief had absolutely nowhere to go. I watched from the middle of my parents' bed, a steaming plate of beans and biscuits balanced on my patch of covers, while one grown man after another buckled in the middle like everything inside him was going soft all at once, and I knew that the dead child's face would stay on each daddy's eyeballs forever. I stopped trusting the world partly from seeing how those meaty-faced men bellowed under the shadowy bills of their tractor caps or cowboy hats.

The rest of the second grade seemed immune to all this misery. Or they took our escape from the storm as a testament to our moral superiority. It was a sign from God that prayers had been answered, something to be pious about.

I asked Carol Sharp at recess didn't she think that the people over in Cameron had said any prayers before the storm came in. And she said that maybe God thought Leechfield Baptists somehow better Christians than folks over in Louisiana. They were probably Catholic anyway, she said. We were riding in the middle of the merry-go-round during this discussion. It was standard playground stuff, industrial steel painted fire-engine red. You had to brace yourself on these metal sawhorses to keep from flying off once the kids shoving it around got it up to speed. Once we were whirling pretty good, I tried to pry Carol's fingers loose from her sawhorse, but she hollered to Shirley Carter to help. They both tickled me deep in my armpits till my own fingers came loose, and I went flying, the whole playground going blurry under me as I flew. I skittered across the asphalt and ground to a stop on bloody knees, my plaid skirt hiked around my waist so my underpants showed. I was screaming to Carol Sharp that her Jesus was a mewling dipshit (a phrase I'd picked up from one of mother's less-than-Christian tirades) when Mrs. Hess picked me up by the waist and carried me wrangling and cussing back to her room.

I was given as box of crayons and plopped at a desk that faced a bulletin board of crayon drawings. Mrs. Hess instructed me to make something pretty by the end of recess. The pictures tacked over me pissed me off worse—a spotted butterfly settling in the middle of a daisy, a sailboat bobbing on neatly sloping blue waves, a smiling yellow sun.

I wore my black crayon down to the nub during that recess period, making a sky full of funnel clouds. Over and over I sharpened the point on the back of the box, then quickly made it dull again doing the narrowing spirals. It was a big piece of paper and shiny with black crayon before I was through. On a green hill in the background, I drew grave mounds in brown and topped them off with white crosses, each penciled with "R.I.P."

That truth—that death came in a big blind swipe—was gradually taking form in my head, picking up force and gaining motion like its own kind of storm. It was drawing me away from the other kids in a way I didn't even notice. They still saw the world as some playground smiled over by God. I couldn't, and their innocence rankled me to the point of fury. When Baptist girls standing next to me on the choir risers got all misty-eyed singing about the purple mountains' majesty, I would often elbow or jostle them out of nothing but spite. If they turned my way in outrage, I'd make a wide-eyed apology. I couldn't help myself. Sundays, when Carol Sharp came home from Bible school—her black hair pinched and shining in twin plastic barrettes, her petticoat sticking her pink skirt out sideways—and announced, while I was digging for worms in the flower box, how God had made me from the dirt, I said I wasn't dirt, and I wasn't God's Barbie doll either. And why would God set Death loose among us like some wind-up robot destroyer if he loved us so much. Carol was ready for this. "There are some mysteries in life the Lord doesn't want us to understand," which serene declaration caused me to turn our garden hose on her full force. Something in me had died when Grandma had, and while I didn't miss her one iota, I keenly felt the loss of my own trust in the world's order.

Leechfield itself would make you think that way—the landscape, I mean. You needed to watch out for the natural world down there, to defend yourself against it. One fall morning I was crossing a meadow to a sugarcane field with a friend's family when the bird dogs that had been running alongside the men

Growing Up Coastal

with rifles turned and went into a hard point right at one little girl's feet. Somebody's daddy told us all to freeze still, which we did. He took aim with his Winchester where this four-year-old was standing in her red Keds, scared enough to wet her pants. When he fired, a rattlesnake flew thirty feet in the still air. It landed with a plop in the weeds, where dogs fell on it. You might well start toting a rifle or shotgun around after that, for reasons that had nothing to do with other human beings. It's nature itself, revered in other climates, that's Leechfield's best advertisement for firearms. The woods held every species of poisonous snake, spider, and rabid biting creature available in that latitude.

Even at the beach, there were signs warning you had to stay out of the eel-grass because of the alligators. The Gulf itself was warm as dishwater, and brown. There were stingrays and sea snakes under its surface. Shark attacks were not unheard-of, though nobody had been completely toted off by one in decades. The undertow could drag your ass to Cuba before you even knew you'd been sucked down.

And it was on this wretched strip of shore at McFadden Beach that we took a family day trip once Mother came back.

We'd no idea she was coming home that day. She had just walked in the back door one morning without so much as a howdy. Daddy said, Hello, Joe, can I get you some coffee? She just waggled her head in a loose way, like one of those dogs you see on a dashboard with a long spring for a neck. Lecia and I must have flung ourselves on her right off, because I remember Daddy telling us not to bird-dog her the minute she hit the door.

She sat down on a kitchen stool, and we plopped down on the linoleum at her feet. She was in her stocking feet, which was no surprise since she always said that driving would ruin a good pair of heels like nothing else. Anyway, there were little runs in the stockings, narrow black ladders starting up over her toes. I got to fiddling with one of these right off. I pulled it a little bit so the run got longer and skittered up her shin. Then I pulled a little more to make it creep up over her knee where it got wide. I said did that tickle, and she just patted my hand in an idle way. She still hadn't said word one. She was massaging her temples with her eyes closed.

Lecia started rubbing Mother's feet, which were as twisted up as any dancer's, knotty and calloused from decades of high heels. (Lecia became an adult devotee of such heels. Once at a party in Boston, a loafer-wearing debutante suggested jokingly to her that if God had wanted women to wear heels, he wouldn't have designed our feet as He did. Lecia replied that if God hadn't intended us to wear heels, She wouldn't have made our legs look so great in them.) Lecia's rubbing put me in mind of somebody from the Bible. Then Daddy came over and started digging his thumbs deep into Mother's shoulder muscles. This made her head flop back. She must have felt like Gulliver being swarmed on by the little people. And, looking up from the floor, I thought she was way taller than I'd remembered. (Silence can make somebody bigger, I've come to believe. Grief can, too. A big sad silence emanating from someone can cause you to invest that person with all manner of gravitas.) There were pouches under her eyes that hadn't been there before, and streaks dried in her rouge from where she'd been crying on the drive home. But her lipstick was fresh and shiny and the color of a dark plum. She'd touched it up in the car, and that's the last thought I had before my memory fuzzed over.

The next day we went to the beach to cheer Mother up—a good plan, in theory. The only reports of Lubbock we'd been able to drag out of her were that the funeral had been sparsely attended, the trip out and back long. She'd spent the whole week alone or in the company of her mother's witchy sisters.

But really our family didn't excel at outings of any kind. Put us in close quarters—inside the un-air-conditioned Ford, say, in our bathing suits, with our legs sweat-stuck to the vinyl—and things got ugly. Toward the end of this particular drive, Lecia and I leaned like vampires over the backseat repeating "Mama-Daddy-Mama-Daddy" in unison, in a fast auctioneer's prattle, until Daddy's huge arm came swinging at us about neck level. We ducked down, and the car went surging over a sand dune. Then we slid down to McFadden beach and the Gulf.

It was dusk. We always went then to miss the crowd, although the state of the shore would have kept most sane people away at any hour. There'd been some kind of hurricane back-tide or oil spill, so you could smell whole schools of dead fish stinking on the beach as soon as you got out of the car. You parked right on the sand, facing the waves. Daddy started unloading stuff out of the trunk.

Lecia and I raced down to the water, assuming Mother would be behind us. Having been reared in the desert, Mother could spend the better part of daylight sitting near the tide cross-legged, dribbling wet sand through her fingers to build up the squiggly turrets of a castle. She couldn't swim worth a damn but adored floating in an inner tube. She could lie back and doze for hours while the swells bobbed her up and down. But that day, she didn't even get her ankles wet. We got down to the water in our suits and stared leaping over the shorebreak right off. Finally we spotted her back by the eelgrass dunes, walking away from the car. The sun was low on my right. I had to shade my eyes to make her out. She moved into a patch of pale sun and then out again. She turned into a shadow.

Then that shadow was climbing the weathered steps of a beer joint called the Breeze Inn. It was a little screened-in shack, really, high on spindly stilts. More than one storm had blown it over, but they kept propping it back up. Inside was a bar for the shrimpers and for the fellows needing a bump of something to help them get through their family picnics. There was also a pinball machine, usually played by sunburnt kids looking pissed off and waiting for their daddies to finish the last swallow and come back to swimming or cooking hot dogs. I studied Mother while she walked up the steps of the Breeze Inn in her black bathing suit. She wore an old white shirt of Daddy's for a coverup. Like a lot of women with great legs, she had a way of tiptoeing along an invisible line, especially on stairs. It made her butt kind of prissy, and I remember that bothered me somehow, too. She was carrying a sketch pad the size of a small card table, like she was planning to draw the fishermen, but I knew with a cold certainty while I stood ankle-deep in that lukewarm water that she was climbing up there to get drunk.

Maybe that pissed me off, because all of a sudden, I wheeled around to Lecia and whooshed as much of the Gulf at her as I could move with two cupped hands. She tried to cover her face so her bangs wouldn't get wet, but she was pretty well soaked. She was giving me the finger for having done this when Daddy stepped out from behind the trunk of the car.

But instead of just letting her hand relax, so he wouldn't see her shooting the bird, she hid the whole hand behind her head, still frozen in the fuck-you position. She stood there like that for way longer than it might have taken her to relax her hand.

I can still see Daddy coming down the beach toward us. He had his black swim trunks on, and black basketball Keds. He'd put on a red Lone Star baseball cap and was slipping into his blue work shirt while he came toward us. He had the easy glide of men who labor for an hourly wage, a walk that wastes no effort and refuses to rush. His barrel chest and legs were pale. There was a wide blood-colored scar up one shin where one of Lee Gleason's quarter horses had thrown Daddy, then dragged him around the corral till six inches of white shinbone was visible on that leg. On the same leg, just above the knee, there was a knot of iron-blue shrapnel bulging under the skin left over from the war. Still, he didn't limp one bit coming toward us. He had an amused squint on his face. Maybe he even knew that Lecia was hiding that fuck-you finger in back of her neck, and that tickled him.

He stood on the packed sand and called to us. "Y'all come on out from there. I want you to look at something." We followed him up the beach.

We passed what looked like the whole roof off a good-sized shed. There were also stinking loads of dead fish, a whole school of mullet all facing one direction and blank-eyed, looking like they'd leapt up all at once and the wave that had carried them had just evaporated before they came down. Daddy also took a minute to flip over a baby stingray with his shoe so we could see its face. It had wide-spaced eyes and a little slit of a mouth like something you's cut out of pie dough.

About hollering distance from our car, we could see a dozen men spread out over the beach in a seining party. Basically, it's a poor man's fishing, seining, a good way to scoop fish out of the water without neither bait nor boat nor patience. All you need is eight to ten partners and a long net about four or five feet high. First, the seiners wade out to sea together in a pack. If you were watching and couldn't make out that somebody was carrying the rolled-up net, you might think it was a mass suicide or some weird form of baptism, because people tend to wade out in their clothes. They wear canvas shoes so their feet don't get cut, and blue jeans or light khakis so nothing can sting their legs. You catch the best stuff by heading a good ways out, past the little sandbars that keep the shorebreak choppy. Daddy always said you have to go as far offshore as you can without getting dragged off by the Gulf Stream heading for the Florida Keys. The water's liable to get neck-deep on somebody short, and guys seining hold their beer cans up out of the waves while they walk out. (These cans get chucked into the surf when empty, of course, with no *mea culpa* to the environment.) Once the men figure the water's verging on deep enough, they fan out from each other, unrolling the net while they do it, passing it hand to hand, till it's pretty straight. All told, it might be thirty or forty yards long. Then everybody just walks back to the beach real slow, each fellow hanging on to his hunk of net, which strains out whatever swims in its path. By the time they get back to the beach, the net's loaded with creatures and takes some work to get laid out flat on the sand. Then you walk along the net picking out whatever's fit to eat.

They must have been done with the seining for a while on that particular evening because by the time we got up level with them, I spotted a washtub of seawater cooking over a big fire back by their trucks. You could smell the crab-boil spices—onion and garlic and probably whole ropes of Mexican peppers. Down by the water, two of the guys carrying white bait buckets were stooping to untangle soft-shell crabs and shrimp. One of these, a crewcut guy in camouflage pants, straightened up from the beach holding a little shark two or three feet long in his hands. He told somebody named Bucky to run and get the Polaroid. This set somebody (Bucky presumably) loping back to the car. Then the shark-holding guy (who was wearing pink rubber gloves of the type grandmas use to wash dishes) asked Daddy if his girls wanted to see the hammerhead, and Daddy said sure.

I'd never seen a shark up close before, and what struck me was how chinless it was, its mouth drawn low down where its neck should have been. This gave it a deep, snaggle-toothed frown and kept it from looking very smart. Plus its whole body was one big muscle. It couldn't have weighed more than fifteen or twenty pounds, but the guy was having to fight to hold it, yelling over to Bucky to hurry. The shark, meanwhile, was thrashing from side to side in the air. Finally, Daddy helped the man pin the thing on the sand with his foot so Lecia and I could feel how rough its skin was. I rubbed it the wrong way (exactly, Daddy pointed out to me, as he had told me not to do) and it chafed the skin off my fingers like sandpaper. In the black-and-white picture from Bucky's Polaroid camera, Lecia is looking solemnly at the shark, which is blurred into a kind of swinging bludgeon in the fellow's gloved hands, and Daddy is grinning a little bit too hard, and I am studying my bloody fingers like they're some code I'm about to crack. What was on my mind was Mother vanishing up those steps to drink, taking herself Away. There's no picture of that worry, of course. I can only guess it from the crease in my forehead.

Farther down the beach, we hit a kelp bed full of dead men-of-war, which was what Daddy had wanted us to see. There were more of these tangled up in the brown ribbons of kelp than I'd ever seen in one place before. The storm had blown them in, and Daddy wanted us to look out for them. If you've never seen a man-of-war, it's something right out of science fiction. The head's a translucent globe about the size of a softball and full of air, so it floats on top of the water, clear in places, but full of sunset-type colors in others— royal blue and red-violet, the colors bleeding into each other. A bunch of men-of-war bobbing on a wave looks at a slant like water flowers—lily or lotus, even. The colors are that strong. You can poke the head with a finger and feel it give like a bubble-gum bubble. But the tentacles dangling down under the surface hold serious poison. They're fuchsia and grow yards long. They sway around where you can't see them just looking for a leg to wrap onto, or so Daddy told us that afternoon. We knew jellyfish better. They had short hard tentacles that stayed in one place. We'd both been stung by jellyfish, and it was about like a honeybee sting. Plus you could just pick one up by the head and pitch it away if it brushed against you. Daddy said that a man-of-war could wrap around you like an octopus, suck itself tight to your leg so no amount of pulling could unwrap it. He said if we saw one of those bubbles on a wave, to clear out of the water, even if it looked like it was ten yards away. The tentacles could reach that far. They had little suckers that ran down each tentacle and could sting you through each one of those, a thousand times all at once, worse than a nest of hornets. The creature could kill a grown man if he had a weak heart or something. Daddy wasn't one for idle warnings, so we backed away from the kelp pretty quick.

Maybe by the time he had vanished up the steps of the Breeze Inn to keep Mother company Lecia had forgotten to be scared. We were horsing around in the water. If we had a cent's worth of caution in us that day, we spent it trying to stay lined up with the car, since even a light undertow could pull you sideways a mile down the beach before you knew it. Lecia was a ways out by this time, hip deep at least. I remember she dove into a brown wave just before it crested so the white soles of her feet disappeared in it. *Like the tailfin of a mermaid,* I remember thinking. After the wave broke, she bobbed up on the backside of it, behind the white water, her blond hair all slicked back like a seal's.

Maybe I hung on the sand because I remembered Daddy's warning. I do recall kicking around the shorebreak and wondering very specifically what Mother was drinking and how much. I yelled to Lecia did the Breeze Inn just serve beer. This was a big question, since Mother didn't even drink beer, not on her worst hungover morning. Lecia ignored me and twisted around to dive into the next swell. (The terrible thing about children—I'd like to mention here—is that they're so childish.) When Lecia surfaced again, I yelled again. This time I waved my hands to show how dire I was feeling about my question. I couldn't remember if the Breeze Inn sold mixers, in which case I wondered did Mother have her purse with her. A purse might hold a fifth of vodka. I could picture the giant sketch pad but no purse. Was that right? I hopped up and down and pointed back to the bar. Lecia drew her face down into a grimace that mocked my expression. She flapped her arms like a chicken. She turned and dove again. It was then that I started scanning around for something to chuck at her, nothing too hurtful really, a pebble or a light hunk of driftwood.

I spied a huge cabbage-head jellyfish on the sand. It was a dull white color. It looked like a free-floating brain knocked out of somebody's skull. I found a pole to pick it up, stabbing up under the hard white tentacles till it was pretty deep on the stick with its inner goop squooshing out. This was the perfect weapon to chase Lecia with, jellyfish being somehow like roaches in their ability to make her squeal. I stood in the shorebreak and brandished it like a head

Growing Up Coastal

on a pole, holding it angled away from myself so none of the poison would get on me. She'd backed up into a big piece of chop. The white top of the wave slapped over her head and got her hair in her face. She must have had hair spray in it, because it stayed glued together in a kind of slab, and she started rubbing her eyes with a fury. She was still rubbing with one hand when she started squealing.

At first I thought she was screaming to mock me. It was such a high-pitched squeal, like a little shoat hog might make. Then she danced up and down in the water, pumping her knees too high. I kept wielding the jellyfish on the pole at her. If anything, I was happy because I was really scaring her with it. I waded out a little closer to her. I wanted her to stop making fun of me so I could find out what kind of liquor license they had at the Breeze Inn. But of course she kept squealing. The slab of hair over her eyes shielded her face. But when she began swatting and slapping at her leg below the water, I backed up pretty quick. Maybe a braver child would have rushed to help her. I was not a braver child, though. I backed up slow, afraid if I took my eyes off her she might vanish below the surface in the jaws of some sea creature. After a while, I dropped the pole and ran as fast as I could to the bar.

It was a hard run in deep sand from the waterline to the steps of the Breeze Inn. My feet sank and couldn't get traction, like the run in a bad dream.

Mother and Daddy ran back with me all the way down to the beach, but once they got there, they seemed way too calm. I mean, neither of them lit a cigarette or anything, but it took a long time before either of them really did much.

The guy in the camouflage pants had dragged Lecia out of the water while I was fetching my parents. He was kneeling beside her with his pink grandma gloves on when we came up. Lecia sat on the sand with her legs straight out in front of her like some drugstore doll. She had stopped squealing. In fact, she had a glassy look, as if the leg with the man-of-war fastened to it belonged to some other girl. She wasn't even crying, though every now and then she sucked in air through her teeth like she hurt. The camouflaged guy with the pink gloves was trying to peel the tentacles off her, but it was clumsy work. Mother was looking at Daddy and saying what should they do. She said this over and over, and Daddy didn't appear to be listening.

I sat down hard on the sand next to Lecia. I was getting that tight, buckled-down feeling in my stomach like I'd had during the hurricane. I wrapped my arms around my knees, bowed my head, and prayed to a god I didn't trust a prayer that probably went like this: *Please let Lecia not die. Make Daddy think of something fast. Don't let them chop off her leg either.* . . . But all of a sudden, there was that humming noise again, running underneath the prayer like an electrical current in my head. I opened my eyes fast so it went away.

Daddy finally scouted around for a sharp shell and cut the head of the man-of-war and then popped it like an old balloon. But he saw quick that that didn't do any good. The tentacles stayed wrapped around Lecia's leg, which had started to swell up. Up near her hip joint the tentacles came together where the bubblehead had been. They fanned out down her leg all the way to the ankle. Where the guy with gloves had picked off a length, I could see tiny circle marks left behind where it had suctioned onto the flesh. The flesh was pulpy where these had been attached. There were perfectly circular blisters rising up. This wasn't supposed to happen with Daddy around, I thought. I recalled a story of Daddy's in which he'd stood drunk on this very beach with Jimmy Bent, the most badass Cajun in four counties. Jimmy had been drunk too, on Tennessee whiskey. It was a seining party. Girls in capri pants had been sitting along an old log they used for a bench. The girls were eating shellfish from the kettle of crab boil when Jimmy started shooting at Daddy's feet with a Colt .45, saying, "It takes a strong man to dance in the sand." And Daddy saying back, "I'm a strong man, Jimmy," dancing till one of their seining buddies got up behind Mr. Bent and cracked him on the skull with a stick. That story came back to me as proof of my daddy's omnipotence. People weren't supposed to get hurt with him around.

The next instant I can see, they've somehow gotten all the tentacles off, and there are bright red welts around Lecia's leg in a swirly pattern, like she's been switch-whipped with willow branches. Mother has dug a trench in the sand for the leg, and she is packing wet sand on it, trying to get the swelling down the way you would with a poultice or mustard plaster. The leg doesn't look much like a leg anymore. The skin is too tight and inflamed. It looks to me like the gray blood sausage Cajuns make called boudain. There are more people standing around—all the men from the seining party and a family, and the light is fading fast behind all their heads. The sky has gone gray, and the colors from everybody's clothes seem muted, like somebody has sprinkled us all with lime. Somebody gives Lecia a slug of Coca-Cola, and she spits it right back out. She's going pale all over, to match the leg.

In the next slide, dark finally comes. Daddy is talking off to the side with some lawman about what hospital to take Lecia to—High Island or Port Arthur: which is closer, which better. Somebody's had the idea of turning everybody's car headlights on us, so lights shoot at us from all kinds of crazy angles. I am kneeling right next to Lecia, holding her hand, but I don't want to look at her face. The last time I checked it out, it was the color of the moon that's starting up. Mother is washing that face with a little damp Wash'n Dri cloth she got out of a foil packet in her purse, and I can smell the antiseptic from that under the sea smell and the musty smell of vodka they've given Lecia mixed up with Coke to help with the pain. Instead of looking at Lecia, I am paying big attention to the Gulf, which has moved farther away, breaking in long, electric-white lines in the dark.

Mother starts talking. She says the light in the breaking waves is caused by phosphorus. She is telling Lecia this like Lecia's listening. Mother's voice is very whispery and makes me want to go to sleep. There are, in salt water, she says, microscopic sea animals that get excited by the turmoil of water and so give off light when waves break. One night the three of us took off all our clothes—a phosphorus night like this—and went skinny-dipping. Daddy picked our clothes off the sand and laughed at us from his truck. "You crazy, woman," he yelled to Mother, but there was joy in it. Then the waves ate his voice, and I dove in and watched my whole body light up.

Probably I was falling asleep on somebody's lap, because that's what I see us doing. Mother and I are flying underwater like lightgreen phantoms. It reminds me of the Matise painting that she'd razored out of one of her art books and taped up over the bathtub. In it the women dance nude in a circle. And we are like those huge women, fluid and pale, Mother and I. Ahead of us in the green water, I can see Lecia's pale white feet like the neon tailfin of a mermaid slipping away just out of reach.

I was sure in my sleep that Lecia was fixing to die, which is why, I guess, I slept so deeply. I had wished her dead a thousand times, even prayed for it, no less fiercely than I'd prayed for Grandma to die. Now God, who had done me the kindness of killing Grandma, was taking payment for that kindness by killing Lecia too, poisoning her in the leg with a man-of-war, all because I had chased her with a jellyfish, all because she had mocked me when I was scared. I was a child—three feet tall, flat broke, unemployed, barely literate, yet already accountable somehow for two deaths.

I don't remember the hospital at all. Lecia and Mother rode there in the highway patrol car, I guess, with Daddy and me following behind. I slept next to Daddy while he drove home. The car slipped off the shoulder at one point, so I jerked awake and saw all that blackness rushing by the window with the stars getting long and streaking away behind me. Then he said to lay down, that Lecia was in the backseat. He told me the old lie that everything was fine and just to lay down. And that's what I did.

The next morning I counted more than a hundred water blisters on Lecia's leg where the man-of-war had wrapped around it. She'd been ordered to stay in bed but seemed perfectly happy to lie there with her puffy leg propped on a pillow. I was so grateful she hadn't died that all day I played servant to her empress. I brought her chicken pie for lunch on Mother's bone china and spent my own money buying her peppermint swirls at the drugstore. I broke out the *Encyclopedia Britannica* and read aloud to her about squids the length of battleships and massive shark attacks on shipwrecked sailors during World War II.

By the next day, she was charging neighborhood kids a nickel to see her blisters, a dime to touch one, and a quarter to pop one with a straight pin we'd dunked in alcohol. Sometime during those transactions, she got mad at me and eventually got out of bed to stuff me once more into the dirty clothes hamper that pulled out from the bathroom wall. I heaved my body against the hamper to open it a slot, but the heavy lid fell back closed and mashed my fingers before I could get out. I wished her dead again, Lecia. I sat in the dark among the sandy towels and damp bathing suits for nearly an hour before she finally let me out. It seems Daddy had gone back to work, and Mother had gone to bed for the foreseeable future. There was no one else around.

Kate Braverman

Small Craft Warnings

It was the winter my grandmother Danielle discovered candles and scents. It was her season of fragrances and textures, she often said that. If I had been younger, I might have thought she had become a witch, that's how intensely she breathed the creamy flames into her body, how her whole torso contrived to sculpt itself around the squat glass vases that held the fragrant wax in a kind of embrace.

But my grandmother Danielle was not a witch. She was merely corrupt and sociopathic. That's how my mother described her. It was January. I know that, absolutely, because my mother had taken me to her mother's house on my birthday and then left me there. I wasn't precisely abandoned. I knew my

Growing Up Coastal

mother would return for me, that I wasn't in immediate danger. This time, my mother had gone to Paris.

She did this periodically, sold what we had managed to accumulate, took me to my grandmother Danielle's, and left me there while she went to Amsterdam, Rome, Vienna, London, and now France. She claimed it was research for her dissertation. She had grants and fellowships to attest to the importance of her scholarship. My grandmother and I both agreed, with perfect nonverbal communication, that my mother's European jaunts had nothing to do with furthering human understanding of sculpture or architecture, design or graphics or any of the other evolutions my mother's studies had taken across the decade.

"She can't find her own angle," Danielle told me, smoking a cigarette in the sun-room. Her voice was smooth with certainty and contempt. "She can't invent her own spin. That's why she spends her life staring at other people's faces and walls."

I didn't know what to say. There were evolutions everywhere. There were progressions, and the stakes inexorably rose. Now there was the complication of my grandmother's increasingly unsavory personal affairs. My mother had to arrange her European sojourns to coincide with periods when we were on speaking terms with Danielle. My grandmother was only in our lives sporadically, when she was between men. When my mother realized that Danielle was alone, she seized the moment, deposited me in the house on the hill, and stayed in Europe until her fellowship expired.

The entire process usually took five or six months. Then it was over. My mother returned as if she had only been gone for a weekend, and we resumed our life as it had been. I was used to sleeping on sofas and constantly changing schools. I thought it was simply another irritating and nonsensical part of childhood, like vaccinations and orthodontia, like the violin for a year, the piano for three years, and teachers who were blatantly unfair, who always favored the blonds who had doctors for fathers.

I was used to sudden departures and arrivals that disappointed, how nothing matched the description, not the apartment complex or the neighborhood, not the school or the park or the beach. Someone wrote glossy paragraphs in italics about deep-tufted grassy lawns, but that had nothing to do with my life.

"You'll learn plenty from your grandmother," my mother said, in a hurry. Suddenly, my grandmother had been revised, cleansed of sin and taint. There were always generous dispensations when my mother had a plane to catch. "Danielle's better than seventh grade. Trust me."

"What about school?" I asked. I wasn't even sure I cared if I went back to school again or not. The water fountain by the cafeteria was, in whatever school I went to, perpetually broken, the pretty girls with names like Lisa and Julie got better grades and school had already failed me.

I was leaning against a wall. Our suitcases were packed. My mother's were tagged for TWA Airlines. We both had sleeping bags. I hadn't washed my hair in two weeks. It occurred to me that I had nothing left to lose.

"School? School?" My mother repeated, lighting a French cigarette, staring at the rising gray calligraphy of the smoke and considering the strange syllable as if she had never encountered it before.

"Don't I have to go to school?" I repeated. I knew I was right. This was mandatory.

"Christ. You're so American," my mother decided, annoyed. "All over the world, kids have adventures. They hitchhike through Africa. They walk to India. Only Americans worry about school. They believe there's some correlation between civilization and education," she postulated, exhaling smoke.

"Is there?" I demanded.

"Of course not, you idiot," my mother yelled. "Look at this country." Then we drove to my grandmother's house.

My grandmother had a real house in the hills above Santa Monica. My mother and I always lived in apartments—in an interminable hell of graduate-school limbo—was my mother's description. "Dante couldn't have imagined this," my mother once said. She was talking about Van Nuys.

I was momentarily stunned when first seeing Danielle's house again, how substantial it was on the top of the hill, after the exactly one hundred and seven blue flagstone steps you had to climb to the front door. The door was behind a gray iron lattice. You had to be buzzed through the bars, which were twined with bougainvillea and wisteria. It was like a form of blue initiation.

"Do you know what style this house is?" my mother asked.

I considered colonial, traditional, and contemporary, Cape Cod, California bungalow, English country, the classic Spanish of the late '20's. I looked at my mother's face, searching for clues. She was wearing her anonymous airport persona, no makeup, a scarf in her hair, blue jeans and layers that made her appear unattractively large. The look that said I'm not interesting on any level, don't mug or rape or bomb me. I was still sorting through possible architectural styles when my mother said, "It's called Marrying Well Repeatedly." She laughed.

Danielle's house was made from the sorts of materials my mother and I never had, wooden floors in fine vertical strips, enclosed orange tile patios that always felt cold under my feet, built-in cabinets and built-in book shelves in a dark wood that glistened as if it had just been polished. The house seemed not built or constructed but rather composed. Danielle had real canvas paintings on her walls, and whole sides of rooms were glass and looked down at the canyon and, farther, the city.

At night, I thought I was experiencing vertigo, watching the lights of Los Angeles that seemed to want to rise to meet the lights of the helicopters and planes that were landing. The light was everywhere alive, like an entity, and it seemed volitional, capable of choosing its own function, whether it wished to be a blue airport guide light or one lone green beacon floating on a buoy in the Santa Monica Harbor. Or a lemon-yellow porch light, a traffic light with three predicable phases or something more dazzling, like a display-case window strung with multiple bulbs flaunting their possibilities like a litter of gold and amber things I imagined sounded like bells. The city could be a kind of music if one was attentive and knew how to listen.

Then my mother was buzzing us through the iron lattice. I knew I was already learning to listen in an entirely new way. There were aviaries of color strung on invisible wires. There were transformations in sequences of sunlight and moonlight and smoke. There were chimes and chords inside stones and ways to open them, gut them, make them reveal their secrets of wind and rain. Then my grandmother opened the door.

I remember this particular visit as being not a night sojourn but rather an afternoon one. I think of my grandmother in her study with the door closed and half a dozen vanilla candles burning. She made rooms into rituals. She had housewarmer candles in heavy squat glass vases, and she would lean over them as they burned, breathing the vanilla smell deep into her body. I thought of exotic cargoes in the holds of ships, mangoes and Chinese vegetables in colors like glazed violet and cerulean. That's how she was taking the odor into her lungs, like she was a vessel containing it. I recognized bodies were for storage and transport.

"I never understood opulence," my grandmother said. It was during my first week back in her house. "I never understood taste or smell. I never had the ABC's."

She is elegant and sad, grave, her face like pewter. She is at her desk, her bare feet pressed into a flower-print Moroccan rug. A man who loved her or loved her money gave her that rug, and she would rub her feet into it. I wanted to peel off pieces of her skin and, like flower petals, keep them pressed between pages of books I would never lose.

In my memory of this visit, it is always winter in her study, the smallest room in the house. It is completely permeated with her fragrances. She is holding a glass-encased candle in her two hands, breathing the flamey vapor in, eyes closed. I think she could eat it, like a sacred food, a wafer, a bit of unleavened bread. I watch as she bends her face so close to the fire, her bangs are sometimes singed. I smell burned hair then, mixed in with the vanilla. It is like a sour red wire in the midst of what I imagine melted orchids smell like, something bewitched and lacquered. I thought magic was something that could be identified, cut out and laminated, like a photograph in a wallet.

"Vanilla shares the same properties as orchids," Danielle told me. "The Empress of China ate orchids. She smoked opium. The combination drove her mad."

My grandmother's voice was hoarse, rough edged, like she had opened her mouth to too much wind. It was a throat things had blown into, autumn leaves the red of maples in abrupt transit, leaves russet and auburn. And rocks, and the residues of olive and almond trees with their sweet and subtle scents.

"Do you hear her voice? That's what forty years of pot smoking will do for you," my mother had once said. "That woman must eat nails."

I thought there were mysterious essences, ways of being transmuted that came through the skin. I must have thought sex was like that, some conjunction of rain-forest night-blooming flower that entered you and changed you forever. I lacked systematic processes of discrimination then. I lurched between beacons of intuition, rage and sorrow. I knew what the stones know in their pretense of sleep. I knew city lights longed to be freed from their flagrant neon signs, from their overly representational prisons. They dreamed of being released, allowed to loiter instead in stained-glass cathedrals. They wanted to pour their bodies into the faces and capes of saints. I believed in immaculate conception and spontaneous combustion. I believed in aliens from outer space and vampires, prophecy and the resurrection of the dead. I had déjà vu many times each day. I was thirteen.

My grandmother was in her study, reading sporadically, underlining passages in yellow Magic Marker. She was saving sections of poems and novels for me to read later, even though she knew I probably wouldn't. I wasn't even going to junior high school anymore. But that was the least of it. Danielle said everything she loved would be out of fashion by the time I was an undergraduate. Pablo Neruda. Octavio Paz. T. S. Eliot. Sylvia Plath.

"I know," I told her with mock sympathy. "There won't even be books when I grow up. The whole world will be on-line."

My grandmother shrugged. "Oh that," she said, dismissing the future she had so recently lamented with a flick of her wrist. "That's irrelevant. I finally understand all gestures are egocentric. This has nothing to do with you," she said holding the yellow pen in the vanilla-thickened air, as if she was leading an invisible yellow orchestra. I imagined she was conducting something composed entirely of brass, some real instruments, others that were creatures, alive, like rare insects with intricate wings that could be taught when to buzz and when to be mute.

I thought my grandmother could read minds. I thought she had mastered telepathy. There were burning candles all over the house and I thought she would die from fire or smoke inhalation before she died from heart disease. Heart disease sounded vague and open to interpretation, phases, and gradations. It lacked definite borders. It seemed like something creeping so slowly, one could forget about it entirely. It would never march far enough to catch my grandmother at the top of one hundred and seven perfect stone stairs a man who had loved her had built for her. It had taken him an entire summer, dawn to dusk. My grandmother with her permanently blond hair, with her size-six figure, with her tennis games and her convertible sports car. She was too fast for this disease. After all, my grandmother was the keeper of the scented flame.

I believed Danielle was somehow camouflaged by her fragrances and how they folded invisible leaves and fronds around her shoulders, her suddenly too thin neck. I thought nothing could find her beneath that woody vanilla, that startled, burned, sweet whiteness that wasn't magnolias or moonlight, not roses with tiny baby mouths, but something intrinsic to skin itself. That's what gave the vanilla its poignancy. It was the way it interacted with my grandmother's flesh, mysteriously, like a night forest where anything is possible.

I sensed there were confusions in her skin. There were always too many possibilities. Her body continually betrayed her, in one way or another. First there had been the men too young for her, long-haired men who took drugs and didn't have jobs. The men Danielle collected that forced my mother to repeatedly shun her. There were long periods when my grandmother was viewed as contaminated. We could not visit. She was living with a bass player from a second-rate San Francisco band.

"Not even San Francisco. They're from a garage in Vallejo. An opening act in its one best moment," my mother had assured me.

That was Danielle's most recent lapse, a liaison with a man thirty years younger than she. I had glimpsed them on the street once, purely by accident. He was blond like my grandmother and slight, thinner than she was. I had at first thought he was a woman. Then my mother said I could not visit, could not spend the night in the house on the hill where I had my own bedroom painted in my favorite shade of purple, August Lilac. This man was the worst yet, my mother informed me. The ultimate blond bimbo, she called him, and because he was now officially living in the house on the hill, I was not even allowed to telephone.

It took two years for the blond man to pass from my grandmother's house and life, and there were details my mother didn't even want to discuss. Something about the paintings and the car, something about tailored suits and the silver, something that had nothing to do with burglary. Now there was the matter of how my grandmother's body was again betraying her, this time with the heart disease.

It was the first year I was officially a teenager and I was hungry for symbols. I thought I possessed an innate capacity for metaphor. My grandmother crossed borders with her skin and now her heart was rotting. My grandmother gave herself to bad men, men who were merely opening acts, salaried players, for Christ sake, my mother had said, and now, as a result, she was going to die.

My beliefs about death were ambiguous, barbaric, phobic. I closed my eyes and entered a realm of phantasmagoria. Sometimes I did not even need to close my eyes for this to occur. I believed rooms were haunted. I thought there were creatures caught between two worlds, some warp in the space/time continuum that existed just behind my left shoulder. I entertained the notion that death was the consequence of bad thoughts and immoral actions. I was convinced that there were machines for reading thoughts and decoding images and if one strayed, graphically, sexually, a kind of plaque formed in your arteries. After enough such nights, you would need open-heart surgery, a bypass and a transplant and even that probably wouldn't work.

If Danielle needed it, I would give her my heart. I wanted to write a will, bequeathing my organs to her if I was shot or killed in a car crash. Then I realized my grandmother was too beautiful for death. Her skin was very white, it reminded me of her porcelain teacups, which she always drank from, the bone-thin cups with their gold rims and tiny violet flowers like a faint blue pulse on their sides. It was like they were breathing.

We often had tea together in the late afternoons. "Use objects," Danielle said, "or they're just boring pretensions." She was pouring tea from a pot that was three hundred years old. It had belonged to a warlord's fourteen-year-old concubine. My grandmother had carried it back from China herself.

I could watch her drink tea indefinitely, for afternoons or years. She had long blondish hair with a hint of red and freckles across her face and arms. Her eyes were huge and completely blue, so blue they looked painted. They were a blue I rarely saw in human beings. They reminded me of chemicals and bodies of water in certain seasons, fall perhaps, when the wind blows from the north. Danielle wore tight black lace leggings under miniskirts and very high heels, no matter where she was going. She looked nothing like me. I was much darker, olive skinned, and I was heavy, my bones were big, my head and feet and hands were larger than hers.

"You're sturdy," Danielle reassured me, smoking a cigarette I knew contained marijuana. I could smell it. "You'll live through the winter. What's wrong with that?"

It was the real, not metaphorical winter that I was thirteen and I wasn't going to school. Danielle never brought up the subject. After all, only Americans were compulsive about attending classes. The rest of the world spent their time having adventures, creating sculptures and paintings and enjoying good medical care. They went to palaces to live with warlords. As if reading my thoughts, Danielle said, "Lets' do something exciting. I want to learn to sail."

She made two quick phone calls, and it was done. Everything seemed to be happening so fast. The space between ideas and their slow enactment was diminishing, and I was glad. We drove the red convertible Jaguar to the marina, and a man named Gordo appeared with a sailboat and a smile.

It was a California February rocked clean by storms, by fires and floods in the hills, by an earthquake, by elements that had scrubbed and anointed it. It was the clean-to-a-subatomic level that only California knows in the pause between disasters, in its intervals of pure color. These are the stalled moments when you know Los Angeles is chartreuse and lime. These are the subdued tropics where the green molts along the alleys and boulevards between the red of the poinsettias and the tanning of the sycamores. It is in February in Los Angeles that you know redemption is cyclic and eternal, indigenous like the palms and the desert winds and the crumbling cliffs above the Pacific.

Gordo motored us out of the marina. First, he put up the mainsail and then, as we left the artificial channel and entered the gray-blue bay, he raised the headsail. There were reasons for what he was doing; he was explaining the order of procedures to Danielle, the special knots the ropes required, how they must be rolled away, but I wasn't listening. The sails were called sheets, and Danielle said, "That's one thing I've always been good with."

"I can sure see that," Gordo answered with a laugh. He looked at my grandmother, but he couldn't see her withered heart, how the vessels were collapsing. Her cargo would be trapped. It would be lost at sea, mingling itself with doubloons and heirloom linen, with pianos and trinkets, with silver music boxes and love letters and all the things that never reach home. Danielle wasn't going to return to her port of origin, either.

We were sailing the harbor, which I decided was a kind of gray-hazel, capable of blue or green. It was a substance for a sorcerer. There were unknown variables. I could see the Santa Monica Mountains rising behind what looked like toy buildings. The mountains were the color of festering jade. It was suddenly very cold. Afternoon was like a slap, and I thought, yes, of course, it is in the air that we are redeemed.

I was standing next to Danielle. She leaned over to me suddenly and whispered in my ear, "What if one life isn't enough? What if three dimensions aren't right?" She was staring at the deceptive shifting bay, at the fluid mirror. "What if I can't find the coordinates home?'

"But you can," I said, without hesitation. It wasn't an act of kindness. It wasn't deliberate or contrived. It was like breathing in and out. I loved her.

After that, we drove to the dock almost every day. I had begun to see the city with a new clarity. The boulevards were festooned and desiccated with ornamental plum trees and leaves that looked like leather pouches. I thought I could live off the land if I had to. There were hybrid hibiscus near the fence by the dock. They were the size of a clenched fist or a stabbed heart. No one asked me about school.

Our teacher, Gordo, would be waiting with his down vest over a denim shirt, with his smell of cigarettes and cold bay. My grandmother would not remove her high heels until we were already on the sail boat. She seemed small in her tennis shoes, close to the ground and her coffin. We usually had the same boat, the *Gabrielle Rose*. The name was painted in pink cursive letters. But the stern didn't indicate where it was from. Los Angles had somehow taken over the world. It went without saying.

Then we were motoring out to the bay. We were attaching the halyard to our mainsail. We were cleating our ropes. We were unfurling the headsail with our winch. We were working our sheets, setting our course, aiming north to Malibu or south past the airport. We were on a broad reach, a close haul. We were tacking to starboard, we were jibing to port. The ocean was a hall of blue mirrors with a kinetic language. There were stairs down, currents and reasons.

The air was so utterly without interruption that it wasn't air as it is ordinarily known but rather an avenue for deciphering. There was no residue, no litter of foul pastels. Everything was abnormally etched the way white rock is. I could see the details on the individual houses and condominiums near the shore. I could identify their balconies, their sun decks, their garden roofs with banks of assertive red geraniums.

I would duck as the mainsail swung and my grandmother yelled, cheerfully, "Hard a-lee," into the agitated wind. I thought she was saying "heartily," and somehow talking about her heart, how it was dissolving in her chest cavity, how it was beating erratically, how it was somehow fading like stamps on an old passport. Where we enter and where we depart, all of it fading.

I thought of tattoos, how they too were blue and how they faded. I considered the question of whether or not you could actually see a tattoo fade. This would only be possible if you were able to watch time pass. It would be a matter of adjusting the machinery. Watching time pass was a sort of paradox. I spent my afternoons on the hazel Santa Monica Bay, constructing conceptual contradictions about time and space.

The last afternoon we went sailing was on a red-flag day at the beginning of March. We passed the red flag by the Coast Guard station and I said, "Shouldn't we turn back?"

I had been with my grandmother for nearly three months. My mother hadn't sent a single postcard. My grandmother was meeting with her lawyer and drafting her will. I knew a red flag meant small craft warnings.

Gordo looked at Danielle and shrugged. "Just the tail end of a real small storm," he said. "I wouldn't lose sleep over it."

Danielle studied the triangular flag shaking in the wind. "I've always liked red," she said. "It's festive, like blood and brandy. Let's keep going."

We entered the bay, and the wind was suddenly tame. It was the wind that returned after serious punishment, subdued and normal. We were on the cusp between seasons. I wanted my grandmother to live until spring. It occurred to me that there is no imprecision on the cusp between seasons. The zones surrounding seasons have their own identities, their own assurances, languages and passwords. This day the edges were elegant under a grainy pewter half-light that reminded me of a new razor. The place between actual seasons is filled with tiny roses in transition. There are murders and amputations in the garden. There are choirs on the sandy floors beneath oceans.

That evening, my mother would be waiting back at the house on the hill. She would take me away with her. I would stand at a window of a new apartment, looking for the gutted stars in their coral burrows. I would see the moon, in multiple identities, hanging like clothes drying on a balcony or a flank on a meat hook. I would start school the next morning with a headache and a bad attitude.

I would come to know dusk and abhor it, the stainless steel gray in which I saw something like fine spiders encroaching toward the stars. The stars were far above the stucco, abstract in their fatal distance, anchored in their sullen silver. It was better than lying down and the affliction of dreams. Later still, I would spend what remained of my adolescence trying to reconstruct my last frayed season with my grandmother.

I remember once, driving home in the red Jaguar after one of our first sailing lessons, we passed a homeless woman lying on her side on a strip of green in the middle of a boulevard. "That's courage," Danielle said.

"That's mental illness," I replied.

"You're so conventional," Danielle laughed. There was nothing mean in her tone. "Can't you imagine choosing vagrancy? No address or chest x-rays? No florist or priest? Only a vast clarity at the juncture? Do you understand?"

"No," I said.

"I wish I had her conviction," Danielle told me. We were driving east along Wilshire Boulevard, and I knew she was talking about the homeless woman. "Some women divest themselves of sabbath. Sin becomes a kind of flame, a blue friend warm in your hand. Some women divest themselves of answers. Cause and effect, balancing the checkbook, rotating the linen. Jesus. I wish I'd gotten a tattoo."

"Of what?" I tried to imagine her porcelain skin with a green rose on the shoulder. Or a heart, perhaps, with a black guitar in the center.

"A blue crescent moon on my thigh. Done in jail ink. Something I couldn't be put in the family plot with." My grandmother smiled.

What I remember with the most clarity is that red flag March day when we sailed Santa Monica Bay for the last time. I had stayed up all the previous night, alone in the sun-room with its three-sided windows, knowing I wouldn't be living there long. Danielle needed a cane now. She refused to use it, walked with it slowly from room to room, holding it, like a misshapen star lily. Her expression seemed astonished, that she would have this wooden implement, that any of this would be happening to her.

I saw a shooting star that March night. I thought the stars were burning down like red flowers, poinsettias or hibiscus. I knew I would spend the rest of my life standing alone at one window or another, considering the heavens. I would be solitude, distilled and refined. I would be alone beneath the coral reefs of constellations. I knew they were merely somber russet shells, uninhabited bodies of water abandoned as they slept. I thought this is why we often wake and feel wounded. There have been splinters of star as we slept and some of these red disks lodged in our flesh.

At my grandmother's house, I could tell time by the bells from St. Anthony's Cathedral. Danielle came and stood beside me at precisely five. She was wearing a red silk bathrobe she had gotten on a trip to Thailand. There were red dragons and red chrysanthemums embossed on the red silk. You had to see the design with your fingers. They were meant to be traced by someone who loved you. Danielle had taken a young man with her on that cruise. I hadn't been allowed to see her for eight months. I knew. I counted and remembered. I had a calendar. I didn't hitchhike through Africa or marry soldiers, but I kept track of things. Now her hair looked too thin. Her eyes were streaked with red. She was smoking a cloisonné pipe.

"What is that?" I asked.

"Opium," my grandmother said. "It's very hard to get. Do you want some?"

I said no. But after a moment, in which I heard the five bells die like five distant bullets, the residue of a drive-by shooting hitting someone else's infant, I inquired, voice soft, "Can I sit on your lap?"

"I thought you'd never ask," Danielle said. She sat on a sofa in the living room. I perched myself on her thighs. The bells from St. Anthony's had not quite faded, had contrived somehow to remain in the air. The bells were a sort of net, a kind of tattoo in the darkness, an embroidery that lingered. Everything was the color of stained silver.

"Ah, the somber hour of church bells plying their trade through the night. Time for remorse and abstinence. If you have the time," my grandmother said. Then she put her arms around me, pressed me hard against her wrapped-in-red-silk chest, and wept, loud and broken. I touched the dragons with my cheek. Then she howled.

In the morning, we sailed on the red-flagged, small craft warning harbor. "Hard a-lee!" Danielle cried, again and again.

I thought she was talking about her heart, how there were waves in it, channels, eddies, sandbars, places where you must post triangular warning signs. We are all like that, with our hearts littered form the residues of dredging and storms. It is always a season of small craft warnings. You sail into it, face first, as if you were canvas. You consider only the essence of red, the core, with its festive implications.

We sailed all day, through the day, sifting its hours and increments into navigational knots. We cleated it. We reinvented time and travel. The harbor filled with spilled cargoes form sunken galleons. There were silver Peruvian flutes and fine linens. There were white jungle orchids and bolts of white lace for bridal dresses with patterns you could only recognize with your hands. There were fields of white poppies and strands of drowned pearls, and everything smelled of vanilla.

Danielle was yelling something into the wind as the mainsail swung, her voice hoarse and charged from a variety of self-inflicted sabotage. Certainly she was talking about her heart and how it belonged to the sea and the wind and the fluid elements, tattooed and unfading, the deceptive hazels and silvers in which we do not randomly drift. And of all that occurred to me then and later, this is the one truth of which I remain absolutely convinced.

Kerry Neville Bakken

Vigil

Normally, before the divorce, my mother would have been going to the beach with us, dressed in her black bathing suit with the built-in tummy sucker, floppy straw hat with the chewed brim, and flip-flops which protected her feet from discarded syringes. Normally she would have proclaimed this to be a perfect beach day—slight breeze, a few clouds to take the edge off the sun, a new Danielle Steele book to read. But she was no longer normal. She was on her way to colon therapy. Once a month, Dr. Grabo, her holistic healer, cleaned her colon of the dietary toxins and his assistant massaged her temples with aromatic oils. My mother assured us it was a comfortable cleansing; not the run-of-the-mill enema.

My mother rummaged under the seat, pulling out used tissues, yoga fliers, fuzzy Lifesavers, flattened raisins, and a tube of SPF 30 which she pressed into Kara's hand. "Just use it for once," she begged, "otherwise you'll look like Grandma Joe." This was my mother's threat every summer—Grandma Joe's skin looked like it had been cross-stitched with wrinkles.

Kara had been working on the ideal tan since the first sunny days of March. She sat in the backyard surrounded by tinfoil reflectors, face turned up to the sun, shivering in her bikini, as the last of the snow melted. By July, she had reached maximum color—deep even bronze.

"Or you'll get skin cancer," my mother continued. "Lesions, on the side of your nose. Great, big, cavernous lesions."

Kara's nose was smooth and freckle-free, her vanity unfazed by the dire predictions. "They're be a cream or pill by then," she said, handing the tube back to my mother.

Since the divorce, my mother had become convinced that our newfound happiness and security was threatened by a toxic world, and Kara, convinced that the future promised an all-purpose Super Retin-A that would cure every ill—wrinkles, skin cancer, pimples, and PMS.

My mother passed the sunblock to me. "Here Gina, you still have baby skin." Kara laughed, I stuck my tongue out. My mother apologized for the unintended insult. "All I meant is that there's still hope for you."

I was thirteen, and it was a fact that I no longer had baby skin—had indeed been the first of my friends to go to the dermatologist to get blackheads worked out, whiteheads popped open, and my very own prescription cream. Allison and Jeannie were jealous of my jump-start on clear skin. Sometimes I brought the tube to school to share it with them, and they talked wistfully of the day when their mothers would spring for a professional consultation.

My mother reset the radio back to her AM talk show and sighed, "Can the two of you try to get along for the afternoon? Kara, remember I'm trusting you to watch out for Gina. And don't swim if there's an undertow." And then she kissed us off, leaving the two of us together.

We walked to the edge of the boardwalk and Kara stopped, loosened her hair from the scrunchie, rolled the waist of her cutoffs past her hipbones, pulled off her T-shirt, adjusted the straps of her bikini and said, "Just don't sit near me, okay?"

"Why? Are you meeting Sean?" Kara kept her diary in the closet with my father's things—the things left behind—Star Wars video collection, one scuffed wingtip shoe, dirty sock stuffed inside, suit forgotten at the drycleaners, four rolls of undeveloped film from the last family vacation on Cape Cod, his box of business cards—"Vincent DiFerrari, Assistant Regional Manager, Westec Residential Alarm Systems"—and a shoebox full of shotglasses pocketed from bars across Long Island's South Shore. It was the only place in the house my mother consciously avoided. We referred to it as *that* closet—the chafing dish was in *that* closet, could I get it? The big golf umbrella was in *that* closet, top shelf, could Kara reach it? *That* closet became Kara's own private confessional. In her diary, hidden behind a box of old slides, Kara wrote that she had almost gone all the way with Sean. They were at a keg party and snuck off into a bedroom, and she let him feel her up and down but he wasn't mature enough to be the one.

Kara swung her beachbag over her shoulder and stepped out into the sand. "Fifteen feet, Gina. That's as close as you come."

My mother read *Psychology Today*, snipping articles and tacking them to the refrigerator with post-it notes on top. Kara—Read This!! Gina—This One's For You!! She left articles about depression next to my cereal bowl in the morning, about body image under Kara's Fat Free yogurt container, about mother-daughter dynamics taped to the bathroom mirror. Citing her experts, she explained that Kara was asserting her boundaries since she was sixteen going on seventeen, since we shared a room, since I was the younger sister, since she was becoming an *individuated* woman, whatever that meant. Basically, following the experts' advice, she devised a system. Kara and I each had the bedroom to ourselves for one uninterrupted hour each day. I usually didn't use my hour, but I knew how Kara used hers—I could hear her chanting, "I love my breasts and they love me. Soon they'll grow to a 36c." She suffered from a small boob complex; my mother's side, the Kelleher's, referred to their boobs as mosquito bites. Kara had actually reached the low end of a B-cup, an accomplishment worth noting at family dinners. Aunt Susie, Aunt Patty, and Grandma Joe said that it must have been the Italian blood from our father's side, and then they sized up my chest and said maybe it was just a fluke.

Besides creative visualization, Kara also practiced kissing on the wall. An entire wall was covered with closed-mouth smooches, pursed-puckers, and open-O's in plums and reds and pinks—the range of Revlon colors. My mother said that when this stage passed we'd just paint over the wall in a color of my choice. I knew if our father still lived with us the wall would have remained the original Rosepetal Pink.

But after the divorce, my mother had grown understanding of Kara's emotional turbulence. For two months, Kara stopped talking, cut school, ran away to friends' houses. She finally opened her mouth about two weeks before Christmas and asked to be taken to the Gap to pick out her presents. My mother returned the clothes she'd picked out at Macy's, afraid that her choices had been foolish—wrong sizes, wrong colors, wrong styles, not what Kara would want. Silence became Kara's means to a new wardrobe, new CD's, later curfews, locked bedrooms. But at night I heard her crying, face stuffed into

Growing Up Coastal

the pillow, and when I crept into bed with her, she sometimes said she was okay, and rubbed my back, and we fell asleep next to each other; but sometimes she told me to leave her alone and stay out of her life.

Field 3, Jones Beach was known to all Long Islanders as the singles bar of beaches. Muscle guys strutted around in skimpy briefs, their things swaying in the breeze like some sort of external tonsil; shoulders shined and buffed with baby oil; they wore Gold's Gym tank tops and called girls "babe." Groups of girls stretched across king-sized sheets, stomachs pulled tight, backs arched, knees bent, poised like Rockettes ready to do a kickline; they passed around the *Cosmo Quiz*—"Are You A Heartbreaker or a Heartacher?"—and misted each other's bodies with Hawaiian Tropic Darque Tanning Oil. And as long as people weren't drowning or puking in the water, lifeguards ignored the alcohol.

Field 4 was the family beach—noses smeared white with zinc oxide, fluorescent flowered beach umbrellas lined the shore, skirted bathing suits covered saddlebags and cellulite, bald spots were concealed from the sun under an assortment of caps, visors, toupees; garbage cans were filled with sand soggy diapers. There was mini-golf, bocci, volleyball, and Italian ices. I liked Field 4 because there were things to do; Kara liked Field 3 because there were people to see.

Kara picked a patch of sand near a bunch of guys building a beerwall with empty cans; it started at their heads and traveled around the outer edge of the towels. They were all wearing bathing suits of various plaids and baseball caps with names of colleges. Kara flapped her blanket in the breeze and let it settle. She shimmied out of her cutoffs, dripped baby oil down her legs, over her stomach, up her arms, and trailed lipbalm over her mouth with her fingertips. I watched the guys nudge each other and watch her. But Kara just stretched and sighed and went to sleep. I counted off fifteen feet and set up camp a little less melodramatically—bath towel, SPF 30, salami sandwich, thermos of Tang, mystery book. I didn't want to be noticed, didn't want their strange eyes wandering over my skinny, level body.

My father kept a stash of *Playboy*s in the attic, not hidden in some dark corner, but in stacks next to the Christmas Tree box. I don't know why he saved them all, all the pictures looked the same—naked women wrapped in gauze or posed in front of rain smudged windows or sprawled on animal skin rugs. They didn't look remotely like me, or how I even thought I might look. They were big, and full, and unashamed. The only part of the magazine that I could relate to was the personal data page for the centerfolds—they liked ten-nis, poetry, bagels, kindness; they disliked boxing, dishonesty, pot roast, golf. I didn't like to think of my father looking at all these naked women, all these bodies.

An hour passed quietly—I read, Kara slept, the guys drank and stayed carefully to themselves. When Kara woke, she flipped to her stomach, ran her fingers under the bikini bottoms, adjusting the elastic, unzipped her backpack, and unwrapped a can from a layer of tinfoil. She cracked the beer open, sipped, and smiled at the guys.

I knew Kara drank; she hid a bottle of vodka behind a pile of stuffed animals crammed under her bed—Paddington Bear, Cabbage Patch Kid, and Garfield were her partners in crime. Before she went out with her friends, she drank vodka from an "Italian Stallion" shotglass left over from Dad Days. She hid that in a drawer behind her hidden Victoria's Secret underwear. She knew I knew, said drinking wasn't such a big deal, that Dad just didn't know how to drink. Late at night I heard her in the bathroom throwing up, gagging, flush-ing, and brushing her teeth. My mother hadn't noticed, which was strange because she could smell a gas leak five blocks over, smell my dad's whiskey breath through a sinus infection. I could smell it on Kara; she smelled like my dad only sweeter—Mom only smelled of her patchouli.

My mother was on a "healing journey"; she'd been going to a therapy group called "Visualizing the New You—Learning to Break with the Stale Self"—you can guess where Kara's boob mantra came from. She started burn-ing patchouli instead of Garden Fresh potpourri, wore silver earrings instead of pearl knots, and nodded with understanding when I said I failed my history test. Over cups of herbal tea, she comforted, "Sister Saint Thomas doesn't know how to teach the French and Indian War with imagination."

During the divorce, Mom made piles and piles of grilled cheeses. Velveeta and Wonder Bread, her comfort food. French toast, grilled with cheese, for breakfast, grilled cheese with tomatoes for lunch, grilled cheese with bacon for dinner. She bought Velveeta by the crate and stored loaves of bread in the freezer just in case she ran out. After the first few weeks of this feeding frenzy, I suggested we go to the diner for salads, burgers, anything non-cheesy, to which she replied, "That's okay. I love grilled cheese," with the same gusto she used when announcing, "That's okay. I love the gristly pieces." She ate grilled cheese because that's all that was left for her, all that she was hungry for. For my father, she'd cooked full-palate meals: grilled steak, herb potatoes, green beans almondine, Caesar salad, and black forest cake. For herself, she could only cook bland tasteless food; she said her tastebuds had shriveled up the day my father moved out. In five months, Mom gained forty pounds, popped the buttons on skirts, gave up on zippers, and only wore pants with elastic waistbands.

The day she signed the divorce papers, she stood in front of the full-length mirror in her underwear and cried for two hours, pinching the folds of her stomach, the skin under her arms, the bottom of her butt. And then suddenly she stopped and glared back at herself. "Never again," she said to us, "will you see me like this." She rummaged through her sewing box, handed Kara a tape measure, handed me a pencil and paper, and demanded the measurements of her waist, hips, thighs, calves, neck, chest, even her ankles. "Nothing," she said, "will go unaccounted for." I watched from the bed, catching Kara's puzzled and fearful glances in the mirror as she circled my mother's body like a tailor, wrapping the tape around one thigh, then the other, calling out numbers that lost their meaning as I wrote them in little columns: chest–41, thigh–19, ankle–8, rear end–53. From that day on, Kara and I had to measure my mother weekly, adding, subtracting, pulling the tape tighter to make the numbers smaller. Little by little, she shrank, her body began to disappear, until I knew we had lost her. My mother was right, we never did see her like that again.

While on her "journey," she gave up caffeine, sugar, and fat; instead, she drank herbal teas, got her colon cleaned, had a friend named Helen, an expert in the "rebirthing" process. Helen wanted to guide me through my "rebirth"; she said it would help me "keep a whole self while going through the fragmenting experience of adolescence." I declined; from what I saw of the birth movie in religion class, it was bad enough the first time. Helen and Mom went to Weight Watchers, joined a ladies-only gym, meditated to fake birds' songs in the living room. Kara and I were left to ourselves. I was partial to luncheon meat—salami, bologna, prosciutto, anything but olive loaf. Kara picked at salads, claimed she was getting fat, that she inherited Mom's body and had to start "regulating" her food—she even counted the calories in toothpaste.

Kara threatened death if I ratted on her drinking, which I didn't believe, but wouldn't test. We shared a bedroom so it would have been easy for her to smother me with a pillow in the middle of the night or cut out my tongue with her nail scissors. I wouldn't have said anything though. My mother told Helen over the phone that she was still "grieving" over the divorce, and maybe she just needed a week away from it all—Kara, me, Massapequa, Long Island—to kick back on a Caribbean Island, swinging in a hammock, and drinking root juices out of coconut shells. Helen offered to babysit, said my mother should rediscover her needs while she was still young, "Hell, have a fling with a sailing instructor in Aruba." But Mom said she was out of vacation time, even out of personal days, and besides, didn't feel like a fling with a twenty-year old who would want to have sex with the lights on. I didn't want to upset my mother's grieving process with the news that Kara was drinking like our father. I didn't want Helen to "rebirth" me while babysitting. I didn't want to think of my mother having a fling.

There isn't much to do at the beach by yourself except to look at people between catnaps, or stare at the sand. I watched the way girls walked at the water's edge in pairs, how they passed men—swishing their feet slowly through the surf or walking heel-toe through the sand, defiant and proud, or slouching, arms crossed over stomachs. I watched couples grease each other, make-out, give wedgies, unhook straps. I watched the gulls steal bits of pretzels, bread, garbage. I found ten cigarette butts, six beer caps, two tampons, and one condom, smashed, buried, and forgotten in the sand. An old man wandered up from Field 4, skimming the sand with a metal detector. He'd stop, dig furiously with a small spade, pick something out and toss it away. My father once rented a metal detector when we were on Cape Cod. Kara and I spent hours pacing the beach with him in the late afternoon, which was, according to him, "the best time for loot." The people would be gone, and all the lost money, broken necklaces, forgotten watches would ours for the picking. He said we could keep anything we found as long as it wasn't historical, since, after all, pirates had buried treasure in those shifting sands. He told us about Spanish doubloons worth millions, about chests filled with jewels, about all we could do with the money. Kara found three dollars worth of change; I found a gold chain, twisted and tarnished, the clasp missing. My father looked at it, held it up to the fading sun, and tossed it back out to the sea. It was junk, he said, "electroplated crap." He returned the detector, said it was a waste of money and vacation time. Kara whispered to me that he was wrong, that I had found gold and he just didn't know it.

After the old man had disappeared down the beach, I watched Kara, how she played with the ends of her hair, twisting it around her fingers, how she let her bikini straps slide down her shoulders, how she wiggled her toes and swatted at imaginary sandflies. By the end of the second hour, they were all friends—the six plaid guys and Kara. They talked about school, college, and Kara lied, said she was a sophomore at Penn State, one of the names not written in hunter green across their caps. I watched her drink three beers of her own and stack them neatly by her side. By the end of the third hour, she drank two beers from their cooler. They adjusted the beerwall so her blanket fit inside. She talked mostly to a guy called Murphy, junior, University of Michigan, PolySci major, burned shoulders and back. He sat closest to her, passing beers, bumping into her side. He offered to re-oil her, and Kara smiled, leaned into her knees, offered her back. His hands moved confidently over her shoulders, under her straps, and she giggled. My sister was ticklish along her sides. She didn't kick him away like she would have kicked me. My sister called me a snoop, a busybody, a brat. My mother told me to give Kara breathing room. But there was no one else to smell breath and count meals. No one else to pay attention.

My mother worried that I was too detached from my father, that I took so completely to the divorce, was happy he was gone. She said it wasn't natural, that I was blocking, repressing, denying—that one day she'd be watching Oprah, and there I would be, center stage, head resting on Oprah's shoulder, telling all the world that the reason I killed was because of my parents' divorce. She was convinced that my easy adjustment was a honeymoon period, that in the years to come, I would have relationship problems, hate men, have boyfriends who gave me black eyes because I wasn't sullen and hostile like Kara.

I don't know why she couldn't understand that I was happy he left. Happy that she stopped eating grilled cheeses, stopped crying, stopped nursing hangovers, calming anger, closing doors. That I couldn't react like Kara; I could only watch her, stick close, play her shadow. Because who else would have known where she hid her vodka, her diary, her ticklish spots?

Murphy anchored his feet in the sand and tugged Kara up from her towel. She swayed back and forth, as if the weight of the breeze could knock her around like a styrofoam cup. Murphy draped his arm around her shoulder and they stumbled around towels, radios, legs, and coolers to the water. I followed, keeping my distance. When they were thigh deep, Murphy lunged and tackled her; Kara screeched, landing hard in shallow water. I laughed. She looked so stupid smiling up at Murphy, as if it didn't hurt at all. Murphy shrugged and paddled out deeper.

I swam after them, parallel to them, bobbed up for air, trying to catch their words, but could only hear them laughing between the waves. And then they were kissing. Kara had her legs wrapped around his back; Murphy had his fingers under her straps, tried to unhook the back of her bikini. Kara slapped at his chest and screeched again. I dove under the water and swam back to shore. I was good at keeping track of things. At school, I could always tell who had a new haircut, a new boyfriend, a new jacket; who had their period, who didn't. I liked to know where people were—I liked to be the one with the information. I gave up on keeping track of my father. He went too far—always moving around—first Phoenix, then Las Vegas, Boca Raton, then Seattle; he had to keep up with the action, the next housing boom. He said there was a fortune to be made in the alarm business out West—new residents, new city, new fears; New York was dried up, the niche already filled. I didn't think his alarm prospects could be any better than New York, and so I suspected he didn't want to be kept track of, measured against the rest of us. I remember him drinking, remember his strangeness, how his words didn't sound right, how his movements seemed wrong. My mother used to call it "Daddy's make-believe time." She said, "Make believe Daddy's a lion. Remember at the zoo how loud they were?" Or, "Make believe it's just thunder and lightning. Just electricity and rain outside." When I was older, I counted his drinks and he yelled at me, said he didn't need anyone keeping track of him.

Kara doesn't remember—or doesn't want to. All she remembers is the end. Mom smashing the empty bottles in the street. Mom packing Dad's clothes in boxes. Mom erasing the messages that asked for another chance.

Sometimes I felt that I was the only sane one left in our house; that I was the gauge that measured how far we'd wandered from each other. My mother had turned into a fuzzy smear of pastel colors and wheat germ. Kara had threatened my life. I was lonely, addicted to salami and afternoon talk shows that discussed dysfunction and co-dependence.

On their way back from the water, Murphy staggered over to the guys, rolled into the sand, and opened a beer. Kara detoured, stopped at my towel.

"Move it," I said. She was dripping water all over my book and blocking the sun.

"You're okay, right?" she plopped down and squeezed water from her hair.

"I'm fine."

She pulled her fingers through her hair, catching them in knots. "I'm covered in sand from head to toe," she said, and picked off the stray strands of hair that clung to her nails. "Aren't they cute, Gina? What about the guy I was with? Did you see us?"

"They seem older."

"That's the point. They are." She waved at them, but they were intent on a game of hackysack. Murphy tried to kick the hackysack and wiped out in the sand.

Kara pressed a finger into her belly and a white print appeared. "Look, Gina. I'm burning."

"Maybe we should call Mom."

Kara stood up. "I don't feel like leaving. And remember? Colon cleaning day."

"Then put on my 30. You should be more careful."

She traced the outline of white-skinned straps over her shoulder. "Oh well. What's done is done. Four months of work wasted. Now I'll start to peel. You'll be here right? Because I'm going with Murphy. We're going to listen to the radio in his car. You'll watch my stuff, right?"

"But it's so hot."

"Please, Gina. I'll be back soon."

I sighed and nodded. Kara tiptoed up to Murphy and whispered in his ear. He nodded. They walked back up the beach, to the boardwalk, and out into the parking lot. I watched their heads, mostly Kara's blond one—disappear down a row of cars.

I waited for them to return, squinted at every couple, every blond girl in a bikini, in a one-piece, in shorts. It didn't matter. I stood watch, as the guys drank beer, drifted off to sleep. Every now and then, one would roll over and say something about Kara and Murphy, but mostly about Kara, and they would laugh. I hated them.

I thought about finding a lifeguard, explaining that I couldn't find my sister and she had my heart medication and I think she went out to the parking lot for sunscreen, but oh God, my heart was going crazy. I thought about pressing my face to every car window until I found them. I thought about throwing my sandwich at the plaid guys, wait for the seagulls to attack, then demand her release. Instead, I stood in the hot sand, without flip-flops, letting it burn my feet, hoping that the moment I couldn't stand the pain would be the moment they came back. I tried this ten times. I tried telepathy. I tried holding my breath. I tried to stare at the sun, tried to do the un-do-able, to bring Kara back from what she was doing. I prayed.

I felt her shadow fall across my body before I saw her—it was light, then dark, and then it waited. I looked up. Kara's hair was clumped in tangles from the salt, mascara smudged beneath her eyes, bikini top uneven—a sort of mermaid gone bad look. "Are you okay?"

She shrugged and sat down. "Do I look a mess?"

A purple bruise sat on the curve of her neck, speckled red like a tetanus shot. I touched it and asked, "He hurt you?"

"A hickey. Oh my God, I've never had a hickey. It's gross and all, but kind of cool, right? Like a love tattoo."

"It looks like he bit you."

"He was a great kisser. And he's twenty. Can you believe that?"

The side of her bikini bottom was twisted around, the tag on the outside. I tried to tuck the tag in, untwist the material, but realized she'd have to take the bottoms off to straighten it out.

Kara's eyes were closed and she rocked back and forth. "Gina, I don't feel so good. Maybe I should go to the bathroom." She took a deep breath, said "Oh no," and I knew she was going to be sick. When Kara had the flu a few years ago, she'd developed the air gulp-oh, no technique, so I was prepared. She threw up all over my towel and book, splattering my legs. She stopped herself quickly and sat straight, as if nothing had happened. "They didn't see that, did they?"

"Who?" I wiped my legs, dabbed the book with a clean corner of the towel, tried not to breathe in her fumes.

"Murphy. The guys. It didn't look like I was throwing up, right? I mean, it's not like I made a scene."

"What are you talking about? You just puked your guts in the middle of a crowded beach, all over yourself, all over me, and all you care about is how you looked puking?"

Kara began to cry.

I wiped a string of spit from her mouth with my sweatshirt. She looked terrible and smelled worse. "You look fine," I lied. "Besides, they weren't looking over here." And that was the truth. They were all down at the water, throwing around a football. Murphy never looked back.

We stayed in the ladies room stall for an hour. Kara knelt in muddy water, on concrete, and threw up again and again. I held her hair back, flushed the toilet, wiped the seat. All the way through the heaving though, she kept talking about him. "He's cute, isn't he? I gave him my number," or, "Do I look any different? Any older? What'll I tell Mom when he calls?"

"Don't tell her anything," I answered, "and fix your bottoms. They're all twisted." She didn't look any different, at least not in the way she wanted. Just messy, and sad. Sister Mary Louise told us in Family Life Class that the day a girl loses her virginity out of wedlock is the saddest day of her life. I thought she was lying, trying to scare us, but maybe she knew how it turns out.

Growing Up Coastal

Kara fingered the tag. "That's funny. I didn't even notice I put them on wrong." She stepped out of them, right there, in front of me—Kara who locked the bedroom to change, who accused me of trying to sneak peeks, stepped out of her bottoms and untwisted them. But she couldn't pull them back on; her hands were shaking and she started crying again. So I knelt in the puddle, placed her feet through the holes, tugged the bottoms up, past her knees, over her thighs, to her hips. And I peeked, quickly, not knowing what to look for. Except maybe blood.

During one of her pauses, I called home, left a message for my mother to pick us up ASAP, as soon as her colon was clean enough, because Kara was sick. I wanted to tell her that I hated her and Kara, and my father and the stupid beach and guys but I didn't. I hung up and leaned against the hard metal box and closed my eyes.

I left Kara sitting on the curb, sipping a coke; her knees were scoured red, her hair pulled back up in the scrunchie. I went back to the beach to gather our things—threw the towel, book, and Kara's empty cans in the garbage. The guys were flopped on their backs, sleeping, some snoring, the beerwall now a complete circle around the edges of their towels. Murphy was on the end, baseball cap covering his face, stomach bright pink. His arm was smeared with blue ink that had washed off. I wondered if he had memorized Kara's number. If he remembered she went to Penn State. That he bit the side of her neck.

We waited by the curb for a long time. It began to rain and the beach cleared out; lightning crackled across the water and there was a mad rush for cars. Everyone whined about the traffic, about the day being ruined, about wet bathing suits in cars. Kara and I just sat there, shivering. I could tell she was searching the crowd, scanning the cars that pulled out of the lot. But she never tried to wave anyone down.

When my mother finally swung up, honking the horn and flashing head-lights, as if we could have missed her, as if we weren't the last ones left, Kara said, "Don't say anything to Mom about today, okay?" I nodded and Kara climbed into the backseat, I climbed into the front.

"I think there's some blankets in the back. I must have just caught the rain." Mom said. She didn't look at us and I wondered if she knew how late she was. I wondered where she had been.

Kara passed a blanket and I wrapped myself inside. We were quiet all the way to the parkway, listening to the garden hotline talk about mulching and pruning and Japanese beetles chewing through tomato plants. Mom stole glances at both of us while switching lanes. "Is something wrong?" she finally asked, turning down the radio. "I'm sorry I was late. But Dr. Grabo was behind schedule. A woman with colitis needed an emergency drainage. I came when I could."

"Kara doesn't feel well. She's sick," I said.

She twisted around. Kara was stretched across the seat. "Kara, honey, you feel sick?" She felt her forehead. "You feel okay. But God, look at you. You're all sunburned. I told you to be careful with the sun."

"I'm fine," Kara said "it's not that bad."

"She didn't wear the sunblock," I said.

"Your eyelids are practically purple. And your chest. You'll be covered in blisters, you know." Mom sighed. "Helen says a cold chamomile bath helps a sunburn. I'll run one for you when we get home."

"I said I'm fine. So I'm fine. Just take it easy with the brakes and my stomach will be fine."

"You feel sick to your stomach? You just may have a touch of sunstroke. Do you know you can die from sunstroke? Gina, you didn't notice her burning up?"

I shrugged. "You can't see a sunburn right away. It comes out later."

For the rest of the ride we listened to the windshield wipers thump back and forth at top speed, keeping time, counting miles. My mother hummed along to her Whitney Houston tape, a little off-key, hands clenched around the steering wheel; Kara breathed steadily in and out, sleeping I supposed; I counted off exits, waiting patiently for ours. It took an hour and a half because of the rain and lightning and accidents that piled up on the side of the parkway. When we finally turned into the driveway and rolled to a stop, I had the courage to look back at Kara. Only she wasn't sleeping, she was curled up in the seat, eyes scrunched closed. And she was crying, but trying hard not to. "Mom, would you look. I told you she was sick."

My mother saw her, maybe even smelled her, and nodded.

Kara threw up once more, and my mother held her hair back, pressed a wash-cloth to her forehead. Kara was furious, "Stop babying me, goddammit. I can take care of myself." My mother ignored her, and ran a chamomile bath. She tried to help Kara out of her wet clothes, but Kara pushed her away. My mother sighed and said, "Gina, why don't you give us some privacy. You can start dinner if you want. And close the windows so the rain doesn't ruin the

Growing Up Coastal

furniture." She hugged me to her, still smelling of patchouli but more like my mother. "She'll be fine, Gina. Just a ruined tan. Maybe she learned her lesson."

Kara stood in the middle of the bathroom, hair scraggly, body shaking, bikini straps hanging off her shoulders, arms folded tightly across her chest, and she said, so quietly I almost didn't hear, "Fuck you, Mom. You don't know anything."

My mother was silent, then shrugged. "Don't think I'm impressed, Kara. I've heard it all. But I'll forgive you for it, unlike your father. We'll chalk it up to hormones and sunburn, okay?" My mother tentatively smiled, but Kara didn't, she just glared back, with the same look my mother had in her eyes that day in front of the mirror, wild beyond anger, propelled by the determination to leave us all behind. I knew, at that moment, that I could never bring Kara back.

The lights went out at dusk. The electric company said a main power line went down and it would be a few hours, maybe morning, before it would be back on. I made salami sandwiches, dandelion root iced tea, and lit candles. We sat around the table, not saying much, watching the storm through the sliding glass doors. A big limb from the oak tree snapped off, the patio table and umbrella blew over, the metal garbage can clattered down the driveway. But inside the kitchen, we just sat, sipped, and nibbled on the sandwiches, willing ourselves to forget what had happened. Kara massaged aloe vera lotion into her skin so she wouldn't peel and look like a leper. My mother talked about the healing properties of herbs, how dandelion root helped upset stomachs, depression, headaches, and irritability—a cure for all our ills that day. I let Kara French-braid my hair, sat still for her and didn't scream when she accidentally tugged too hard. Honestly, she could have pulled all my hair out and it wouldn't have mattered because it was like it used to be. When we were emptying the dishwasher, Kara whispered, "Thanks, Gina."

I bent over, to rescue a knife fallen way in back, and said, "You were careful, weren't you?"

She tugged on the end of my braid and tried to smile. "No problemo, Gina. We can pretend like today never happened."

Later, I left Kara and Mom together in the kitchen. I sat on the stairs hoping to hear confessions or apologies, reconciliation. I wanted something, I suppose, to make it all right again, something to absolve me, to relieve me from my watch.

Observers and Naturalists Explore the Marginal World

While Kali is occupied with a starfish on the beach, I take the time to watch the bank swallows fly in and out of their dune homes. I follow their light and quick movements as carefully as I can, but the sun, the shadows, and some optical trick of my astigmatic vision make them disappear and reappear like magic. All quick energy and grace, they circle above me, dark flickering in the clear morning light.

As a young girl I always wanted the names for the things I saw at the beach, but my urban-born parents did not know which birds were which or what the bushes and grasses and trees were called. Even worse, my father would give things his own names, "That's a Sidney bird. And that one, with the lipstick, well, that's a Sadie bird." My mother would chime in with her version of naming, "We should call this a flat petal–rose bush, because, well, it's obvious that someone forgot to give these roses all the petals they deserve." Later on I would find people and books to help me attach names to the coastal flora and fauna. There were, of course, many naturalists writing about coasts, defining and interpreting coastal ecology, and some of the most prominent coastal naturalists have been women.

In 1955, the *New York Times* bestseller list included two books about the coast written by women: Anne Morrow Lindbergh's *Gift from the Sea* and Rachel Carson's *The Edge of the Sea*. Both books brought to the reader naturalists' observational visions of the shore. Carson's reputation as a marine zoologist provided readers with a scientific knowledge blended with her very personal attachment to the shore, and Anne Morrow Lindbergh wove her life philosophies with descriptions of the coast. Both of these books are excellent examples of early ecofeminist texts; they are texts in which the observers sought to express what Janis Birkeland has noted as the "interrelations among self, societies, and nature" in her essay "Ecofeminism: Linking Theory and Practice" (18). It was as though the subject itself—the coast, a place where two different ecosystems meet, land and water—provided the impetus for books that would necessarily blend new and different ways of thinking and writing about nature and humanity.

Whether the writers included in this section of the anthology have scientific training or not, they all spend much of their time observing the details of coastal life. Sometimes they use scientific terms and provide labels for their reader, and other times they use highly descriptive language and offer an open vision of the coast. Often their observations lead to uniquely female interpretations of the shore, such as Sandra McPherson's "Edge Effect," while other writers, such as Jennifer Ackerman and Mary Parker Buckles, use their training as journalists to write vivid and questioning portraits of the now acutely evident environmental problems found along our fragile coasts. Ackerman and Buckles cannot resist the urge to enter the word pictures they create, and both women rely on an interdisciplinary approach to their subject, blending literature, science, sociology, philosophy, history, environmentalism, and religion.

For these writers, the place they write about is crucial to their understanding of themselves and to the broader vision of humans and nature. By examining edge spaces, these writers raise critical questions of the relationships and conflicts between culture and nature. Like the landscape they write about, they integrate discourses and disciplines to create a metaphoric margin rich in thought and commentary.

I call Kali away from the hole she is digging in the sand, notice a "Sadie" bird—a herring gull—smile, and continue east toward town. It's still early in the morning, plenty of time to keep walking.

Rachel Carson

The Marginal World

The edge of the sea is a strange and beautiful place. All through the long history of Earth it has been an area of unrest where waves have broken heavily against the land, where the tides have pressed forward over the continents, receded, and then returned. For no two successive days is the shore line precisely the same. Not only do the tides advance and retreat in their eternal rhythms, but the level of the sea itself is never at rest. It rises or falls as glaciers melt or grow, as the floor of the deep ocean basins shifts under its increasing load of sediments, or as the earth's crust along the continental margins warps up or down in adjustment to strain and tension. Today a little more land may belong to the sea, tomorrow a little less. Always the edge of the sea remains an elusive and indefinable boundary.

The shore has a dual nature, changing with the swing of the tides, belonging now to the land, now to the sea. On the ebb tide it knows the harsh extremes of the land world, being exposed to heat and cold, to wind, to rain and drying sun. On the flood tide it is a water world, returning briefly to the relative stability of the open sea.

Only the most hardy and adaptable can survive in a region so mutable, yet the area between the tide lines is crowded with plants and animals. In this difficult world of shore, life displays its enormous toughness and vitality by occupying almost every conceivable niche. Visibly, it carpets the intertidal rocks; or half hidden, it descends into fissures and crevices, or hides under boulders, or lurks in the wet gloom of sea caves. Invisibly, where the casual observer would say there is no life, it lies deep in the sand, in burrows and tubes and passageways. It tunnels into solid rock and bores into peat and clay. It encrusts weeds or drifting spars or the hard, chitinous shell of a lobster. It exists minutely, as the film of bacteria that spreads over a rock surface or a wharf piling; as spheres of protozoa, small as pinpricks, sparkling at the surface of the sea; and as Lilliputian beings swimming through dark pools that lie between the grains of sand.

The shore is an ancient world, for as long as there has been an earth and sea there has been this place of the meeting of land and water. Yet it is a world that keeps alive the sense of continuing creation and of the relentless drive of life. Each time that I enter it, I gain some new awareness of its beauty and its deeper meanings, sensing that intricate fabric of life by which one creature is linked with another, and each with its surroundings.

In my thoughts of the shore, one place stands apart for its revelation of exquisite beauty. It is a pool hidden within a cave that one can visit only rarely and briefly when the lowest of the year's tides fall below it, and perhaps from that very fact it acquires some of its special beauty. Choosing such a tide, I hoped for a glimpse of the pool. The ebb was to fall early in the morning. I knew that if the wind held from the northwest and no interfering swell ran in from a distant storm the level of the sea should drop below the entrance to the pool. There had been sudden ominous showers in the night, with rain like handfuls of gravel flung on the roof. When I looked out into the early morning the sky was full of gray dawn light but the sun had not yet risen. Water and air were pallid. Across the bay the moon was a luminous disc in the western sky, suspended above the dim line of distant shore—the full August moon, drawing the tide to the low, low levels of the threshold of the alien sea world. As I watched, a gull flew by, above the spruces. Its breast was rosy with the light of the unrisen sun. The day was, after all, to be fair.

Later, as I stood above the tide near the entrance to the pool, the promise of that rosy light was sustained. From the base of the steep wall of rock on which I stood, a moss-covered ledge jutted seaward into deep water. In the surge at the rim of the ledge the dark fronds of oarweeds swayed, smooth and gleaming as leather. The projecting ledge was the path to the small hidden cave and its pool. Occasionally a swell, stronger than the rest, rolled smoothly over the rim and broke in foam against the cliff. But the intervals between such swells were long enough to admit me to the ledge and long enough for a glimpse of that fairy pool, so seldom and so briefly exposed.

And so I knelt on the wet carpet of sea moss and looked back into the dark cavern that held the pool in a shallow basin. The floor of the cave was only a few inches below the roof, and a mirror had been created in which all that grew on the ceiling was reflected in the still water below.

Under water that was clear as glass the pool was carpeted with green sponge. Gray patches of sea squirts glistened on the ceiling and colonies of soft coral were a pale apricot color. In the moment when I looked into the cave a little elfin starfish hung down, suspended by the merest thread, perhaps by only a single tube foot. It reached down to touch its own reflection, so perfectly delineated that there might have been, not one starfish, but two. The beauty of the reflected images and of the limpid pool itself was the poignant

Observers and Naturalists Explore the Marginal World

beauty of things that are ephemeral, existing only until the sea should return to fill the little cave.

Whenever I go down into this magical zone of the low water of the spring tides, I look for the most delicately beautiful of all the shore's inhabitants— flowers that are not plant but animal, blooming on the threshold of the deeper sea. In that fairy cave I was not disappointed. Hanging from its roof were the pendant flowers of the hydroid Tubularia, pale pink, fringed and delicate as the wind flower. Here were creatures so exquisitely fashioned that they seemed unreal, their beauty too fragile to exist in a world of crushing force. Yet every detail was functionally useful, every stalk and hydranth and petal-like tentacle fashioned for dealing with the realities of existence. I knew that they were merely waiting, in that moment of the tide's ebbing, for the return of the sea. In the rush of water, in the surge of surf and the pressure of the incoming tide, the delicate flower heads would stir with life. They would sway on their slender stalks, and their long tentacles would sweep the returning water, finding in it all that they needed for life.

And so in that enchanted place on the threshold of the sea the realities that possessed my mind were far from those of the land world I had left an hour before. In a different way the same sense of remoteness and of a world apart came to me in a twilight hour on a great beach on the coast of Georgia. I had come down after sunset and walked far out over the sands that lay wet and gleaming, to the very edge of the retreating sea. Looking back across that immense flat, crossed by winding, water-filled gullies and here and there holding shallow pools left by the tide, I was filled with awareness that this intertidal area, although abandoned briefly and rhythmically by the sea, is always reclaimed by the rising tide. There at the edge of low water the beach with its reminders of the land seemed far away. The only sounds were those of the wind and the sea and the birds. There was one sound of wind moving over water, and another of water sliding over the sand and tumbling down the faces of its own wave forms. The flats were astir with birds, and the voice of the willet rang insistently. One of them stood at the edge of the water and gave its loud, urgent cry; an answer came from far up the beach and the two birds flew to join each other.

The flats took on a mysterious quality as dusk approached and the last evening light was reflected from the scattered pools and creeks. Then birds became only dark shadows, with no color discernible. Sanderlings scurried across the beach like little ghosts, and here and there the darker forms of the willets stood out. Often I could come very close to them before they would start up in alarm—the sanderlings running, the willets flying up, crying. Black skimmers flew along the ocean's edge silhouetted against the dull, metallic gleam, or they went flitting above the sand like large, dimly seen moths. Sometimes they "skimmed" the winding creeks of tidal water, where little spreading surface ripples marked the presence of small fish.

The shore at night is a different world, in which the very darkness that hides the distractions of daylight brings into sharper focus the elemental realities. Once, exploring the night beach, I surprised a small ghost crab in the searching beam of my torch. He was lying in a pit he had dug just above the surf, as though watching the sea and waiting. The blackness of the night possessed water, air, and beach. It was the darkness of an older world, before Man. There was no sound but the all-enveloping, primeval sounds of wind blowing over water and sand, and of waves crashing on the beach. There was no other visible life—just one small crab near the sea. I have seen hundreds of ghost crabs in other settings, but suddenly I was filled with the odd sensation that for the first time I knew the creature in its own world—that I understood, as never before, the essence of its being. In that moment time was suspended; the world to which I belonged did not exist and I might have been an onlooker from outer space. The little crab alone with the sea became a symbol that stood for life itself—for the delicate, destructible, yet incredibly vital force that somehow holds its place amid the harsh realities of the inorganic world.

The sense of creation comes with memories of a southern coast, where the sea and the mangroves, working together, are building a wilderness of thousands of small islands off the southwestern coast of Florida, separated from each other by a tortuous pattern of bays, lagoons, and narrow waterways. I remember a winter day when the sky was blue and drenched with sunlight; though there was no wind one was conscious of flowing air like cold clear crystal. I had landed on the surf-washed tip of one of those islands, and then worked my way around to the sheltered bay side. There I found the tide far out, exposing the broad mud flat of a cove bordered by the mangroves with their twisted branches, their glossy leaves, and their long prop roots reaching down, grasping and holding the mud, building the land out of a little more, then again a little more.

The mud flats were strewn with the shells of that small, exquisitely colored mollusk, the rose tellin, looking like scattered petals of pink roses. There must have been a colony nearby, living buried just under the surface of the mud. At first the only creature visible was a small heron in gray and rusty plumage— a reddish egret that waded across the flat with the stealthy, hesitant movements of its kind. But other land creatures had been there, for a line of fresh tracks wound in and out among the mangrove roots, marking the path of a racoon feeding on the oysters that gripped the supporting roots with projections from their shells. Soon I found the tracks of a shore bird, probably a sanderling, and followed them a little; then they turned toward the water and were lost, for the tide had erased them and made them as though they had never been.

Looking out over the cove I felt a strong sense of the interchangeability of land and sea in this marginal world of the shore, and of the links between the life of the two. There was also an awareness of the past and of the continuing flow of time, obliterating much that had gone before, as the sea had that morning washed away the tracks of the bird.

The sequence and meaning of the drift of time were quietly summarized in the existence of hundreds of small snails—the mangrove periwinkles—browsing on the branches and roots of the trees. Once their ancestors had been sea dwellers, bound to the salt waters by every tie of their life processes. Little by little over the thousands and millions of years the ties had been broken, the snails had adjusted themselves to life out of the water, and now today they were living many feet above the tide to which they only occasionally returned. And perhaps, who could say how many ages hence, there would be in their descendants not even this gesture of remembrance for the sea.

The spiral shells of other snails—these quite minute—left winding tracks on the mud as they moved about in search of food. They were horn shells, and when I saw them I had a nostalgic moment when I wished I might see what Audubon saw, a century and more ago. For such little horn shells were the food of the flamingo, once so numerous on this coast, and when I half closed my eyes I could almost imagine a flock of these magnificent flame birds feeding in that cove, filling it with their color. It was a mere yesterday in the life of the earth that they were there; in nature, time and space are relative matters, perhaps most truly perceived subjectively in occasional flashes of insight, sparked by such a magical hour and place.

There is a common thread that links these scenes and memories—the spectacle of life in all its varied manifestations as it has appeared, evolved, and sometimes died out. Underlying the beauty of the spectacle there is meaning and significance. It is the elusiveness of that meaning that haunts us, that sends us again and again into the natural world where the key to the riddle is hidden. It sends us back to the edge of the sea, where the drama of life played its first scene on earth and perhaps even its prelude; where the forces of evolution are at work today, as they have been since the appearance of what we know as life; and where the spectacle of living creatures faced by the cosmic realities of their world is crystal clear.

Anne Morrow Lindbergh

Channelled Whelk

The shell in my hand is deserted. It once housed a whelk, a snail-like creature, and then temporarily, after the death of the first occupant, a little hermit crab, who has run away, leaving his tracks behind him like a delicate vine on the sand. He ran away, and left me his shell. It was once a protection to him. I turn the shell in my hand, gazing into the wide open door from which he made his exit. Had it become an encumbrance? Why did he run away? Did he hope to find a better home, a better mode of living? I too have run away, I realize, I have shed the shell of my life, for these few weeks of vacation.

But his shell—it is simple; it is bare, it is beautiful. Small, only the size of my thumb, its architecture is perfect, down to the finest detail. Its shape, swelling like a pear in the center, winds in a gentle spiral to the pointed apex. Its color, dull gold, is whitened by a wash of salt from the sea. Each whorl, each faint knob, each criss-cross vein in its egg-shell texture, is as clearly defined as on the day of creation. My eye follows with delight the outer circumference of that diminutive winding staircase up which this tenant used to travel.

My shell is not like this, I think. How untidy it has become! Blurred with moss, knobby with barnacles, its shape is hardly recognizable any more. Surely, it had a shape once. It has shape still in my mind. What is the shape of my life?

The shape of my life today starts with a family. I have a husband, five children and a home just beyond the suburbs of New York. I have also a craft, writing, and therefore work I want to pursue. The shape of my life is, of course, determined by many other things; my background and childhood, my mind and its education, my conscience and its pressures, my heart and its desires. I want to give and take from my children and husband, to share with friends and community, to carry out my obligations to man and the world, as a woman, as an artist, as a citizen.

But I want first of all—in fact, as an end to these other desires—to be at peace with myself. I want a singleness of eye, a purity of intention, a central core to my life that will enable me to carry out these obligations and activities

Observers and Naturalists Explore the Marginal World

as well as I can. I want, in fact—to borrow from the language of the saints—to live "in grace" as much of the time as possible. I am not using this term in a strictly theological sense. By grace I mean an inner harmony, essentially spiritual, which can be translated into outward harmony. I am seeking perhaps what Socrates asked for in the prayer from the *Phaedrus* when he said, "May the outward and inward man be at one." I would like to achieve a state of inner spiritual grace from which I could function and give as I was meant to in the eye of God.

Vague as this definition may be, I believe most people are aware of periods in their lives when they seem to be "in grace" and other periods when they feel "out of grace," even though they may use different words to describe these states. In the first happy condition, one seems to carry all one's tasks before one lightly, as if borne along on a great tide; and in the opposite state one can hardly tie a shoe-string. It is true that a large part of life consists in learning a technique of tying the shoe-string, whether one is in grace or not. But there are techniques of living too; there are even techniques in the search for grace. And techniques can be cultivated. I have learned by some experience, by many examples, and by the writings of countless others before me, also occupied in the search, that certain environments, certain modes of life, certain rules of conduct are more conducive to inner and outer harmony than others. There are, in fact, certain roads that one may follow. Simplification of life is one of them.

I mean to lead a simple life, to choose a simple shell I can carry easily—like a hermit crab. But I do not. I find that my frame of life does not foster simplicity. My husband and five children must make their way in the world. The life I have chosen as wife and mother entrains a whole caravan of complications. It involves a house in the suburbs and either household drudgery or household help which wavers between scarcity and non-existence for most of us. It involves food and shelter; meals, planning, marketing, bills, and making ends meet in a thousand ways. It involves not only the butcher, the baker, the candlestickmaker but countless other experts to keep my modern house with its modern "simplifications" (electricity, plumbing, refrigerator, gas-stove, oil-burner, dish-washer, radios, car, and numerous other labor-saving devices) functioning properly. It involves health; doctors, dentists, appointments, medicine, cod-liver oil, vitamins, trips to the drugstore. It involves education, spiritual, intellectual, physical; schools, school conferences, car-pools, extra trips for basket-ball or orchestra practice; tutoring; camps, camp equipment and transportation. It involves clothes, shopping, laundry, cleaning, mending, letting skirts down and sewing buttons on, or finding someone else to do it. It involves friends, my husband's, my children's, my own, and endless arrangements to get together; letters, invitations, telephone calls and transportation hither and yon.

For life today in America is based on the premise of ever-widening circles of contact and communication. It involves not only family demands, but community demands, national demands, international demands on the good citizen, through social and cultural pressures, through newspapers, magazines, radio programs, political drives, charitable appeals, and so on. My mind reels with it. What a circus act we women perform every day of our lives. It puts the trapeze artist to shame. Look at us. We run a tight rope daily, balancing a pile of books on the head. Baby-carriage, parasol, kitchen chair, still under control. Steady now!

This is not the life of simplicity but the life of multiplicity that the wise men warn us of. It leads not to unification but to fragmentation. It does not bring grace; it destroys the soul. And this is not only true of my life, I am forced to conclude; it is the life of millions of women in America. I stress America, because today, the American woman more than any other has the privilege of choosing such a life. Woman in large parts of the civilized world has been forced back by war, by poverty, by collapse, by the sheer struggle to survive, into a smaller circle of immediate time and space, immediate family life, immediate problems of existence. The American woman is still relatively free to choose the wider life. How long she will hold this enviable and precarious position no one knows. But her particular situation has a significance far above its apparent economic, national or even sex limitations.

For the problem of the multiplicity of life not only confronts the American woman, but also the American man. And it is not merely the concern of the American as such, but of our whole modern civilization, since life in America today is held up as the ideal of a large part of the rest of the world. And finally, it is not limited to our present civilization, though we are faced with it now in an exaggerated form. It has always been one of the pitfalls of mankind. Plotinus was preaching the dangers of multiplicity of the world back in the third century. Yet, the problem is particularly and essentially woman's. Distraction is, always has been, and probably always will be, inherent in woman's life.

For to be a woman is to have interests and duties, raying out in all directions from the central mother-core, like spokes from the hub of a wheel. The pattern of our lives is essentially circular. We must be open to all points of the compass; husband, children, friends, home community; stretched out, exposed, sensitive like a spider's web to each breeze that blows, to each call that comes. How difficult for us, then, to achieve a balance in the midst of these contradictory tensions, and yet how necessary for the proper functioning of our lives. How much we need, and how arduous of attainment is that steadiness preached in all rules for holy living. How desirable and how distant is the ideal of the contemplative, artist, or saint—the inner inviolable core, the single eye.

With a new awareness, both painful and humorous, I begin to understand why saints were rarely married women. I am convinced it has nothing inherently to do, as I once supposed, with chastity or children. It has to do primarily with distractions. The bearing, rearing, feeding and educating of children; the running of a house with its thousand details; human relationships with their myriad pulls—woman's normal occupations in general run counter to creative life, or contemplative life, or saintly life. The problem is not merely one of *Woman and Career, Woman and the Home, Woman and Independence.* It is more basically: how to remain whole in the midst of the distractions of life; how to remain balanced, no matter what centrifugal forces tend to pull one off center; how to remain strong no matter what shocks come in at the periphery and tend to crack the hub of the wheel.

What is the answer? There is no easy answer, no complete answer. I have only clues, shells from the sea. The bare beauty of the channelled whelk tells me that one answer, and perhaps a first step, is in simplification of life, in cutting out some of the distractions. But how? Total retirement is not possible. I cannot shed my responsibilities. I cannot permanently inhabit a desert island. I cannot be a nun in the midst of family life. I would not want to be. The solution for me, surely, is neither in total renunciation of the world, nor in total acceptance of it. I must find a balance somewhere, or an alternating rhythm between these two extremes; a swinging of the pendulum between solitude and communion, between retreat and return. In my periods of retreat, perhaps I can learn something to carry back into my worldly life. I can at least practice for these two weeks the simplification of outward life, as a beginning. I can follow this superficial clue, and see where it leads. Here, in beach living, I can try.

One learns first of all in beach living the art of shedding; how little one can get along with, not how much. Physical shedding to begin with, which then mysteriously spreads into other fields. Clothes, first. Of course, one needs less in the sun. But one needs less anyway, one finds suddenly. One does not need a closet-full, only a small suitcase-full. And what a relief it is! Less taking up and down of hems, less mending, and—best of all—less worry about what to wear. One finds one is shedding not only clothes—but vanity.

Next, shelter. One does not need the airtight shelter one has in winter in the North. Here I live in a bare sea-shell of a cottage. No heat, no telephone, no plumbing to speak of, no hot water, a two-burner oil stove, no gadgets to go wrong. No rugs. There were some, but I rolled them up the first day; it is easier to sweep the sand off a bare floor. But I find I don't bustle about with unnecessary sweeping and cleaning here. I am no longer aware of the dust. I have shed my Puritan conscience about absolute tidiness and cleanliness. Is it possible that, too, is a material burden? No curtains. I do not need them for privacy; the pines around my house are enough protection. I want the windows open all the time, and I don't want to worry about rain. I begin to shed my Martha-like anxiety about many things. Washable slipcovers, faded and old—I hardly see them; I don't worry about the impression they make on other people. I am shedding pride. As little furniture as possible; I shall not need much. I shall ask into my shell only those friends with whom I can be completely honest. I find I am shedding hypocrisy in human relationships. What a rest that will be! The most exhausting thing in life, I have discovered, is being insincere. That is why so much of social life is exhausting; one is wearing a mask. I have shed my mask.

I find I live quite happily without those things I think necessary in winter in the North. And as I write these words, I remember, with some shock at the disparity in our lives, a similar statement made by a friend of mine in France who spent three years in a German prison camp. Of course, he said, qualifying his remark, they did not get enough to eat, they were sometimes atrociously treated, they had little physical freedom. And yet, prison life taught him how little one can get along with, and what extraordinary spiritual freedom and peace such simplification can bring. I remember again, ironically, that today more of us in America than anywhere else in the world have the luxury of choice between simplicity and complication of life. And for the most part, we, who could choose simplicity, choose complication. War, prison, survival periods, enforce a form of simplicity on man. The monk and the nun choose it of their own free will. But if one accidently finds it, as I have for a few days, one finds also the serenity it brings.

Is it not rather ugly, one may ask? One collects material possessions not only for security, comfort or vanity, but for beauty as well. Is your sea-shell house not ugly and bare? No, it is beautiful, my house. It is bare, of course, but the wind, the sun, the smell of the pines blow through its bareness. The unfinished beams in the roof are veiled by cobwebs. They are lovely, I think, gazing up at them with new eyes; they soften the hard lines of the rafters as grey hairs soften the lines on a middle-aged face. I no longer pull out grey hairs or sweep down cobwebs. As for the walls, it is true they looked forbidding at first. I felt cramped and enclosed by their blank faces. I wanted to knock holes in them, to give them another dimension with pictures or windows. So I dragged home from the beach grey arms of driftwood, worn satin-smooth by wind and sand. I gathered trailing green vines with floppy red-tipped leaves. I picked up the whitened skeletons of conch shells, their curious hollowed-out shapes faintly reminiscent of abstract sculpture. With these tacked to walls and propped up in corners, I am satisfied. I have a periscope out to the world. I have a window, a view, a point of flight from my sedentary base.

I am content. I sit down at my desk, a bare kitchen table with a blotter, a bottle of ink, a sand dollar to weight down one corner, a clam shell for a pen tray, the broken tip of a conch, pink-tinged, to finger, and a row of shells to set my thought spinning.

I love my sea-shell of a house. I wish I could live in it always. I wish I could transport it home. But I cannot. It will not hold a husband, five children and the necessities and trappings of daily life. I can only carry back my little chan-nelled whelk. It will sit on my desk in Connecticut, to remind me of the ideal of a simplified life, to encourage me in the game I played on the beach. To ask how little, not how much, I can get along with. To say—is it necessary?— when I am tempted to add one more accumulation to my life, when I am pulled toward one more centrifugal activity.

Simplification of outward life is not enough. It is merely the outside. But I am starting with the outside. I am looking at the outside of a shell, the outside of my life—the shell. The complete answer is not to be found on the outside, in an outward mode of living. This is only a technique, a road to grace. The final answer, I know, is always inside. But the outside can give a clue, can help one to find the inside answer. One is free, like the hermit crab, to change one's shell.

Channelled whelk, I put you down again, but you have set my mind on a journey, up an inwardly winding spiral staircase of thought.

Amy Clampitt

The Outer Bar

When through some lacuna, chink, or interstice
in the unlicensed free-for-all that goes
on without a halt out there all day, all night,
all through the winter,

one morning at low tide you walk dry-shod across
a shadowy isthmus to the outer bar,
you find yourself, once over, sinking at every step
into a luscious mess—

a vegetation of unbarbered, virgin, foot-thick
velvet, the air you breathe an aromatic
thicket, odors in confusion starting up
at every step like partridges

or schools of fishes, an element you swim through
as to an unplanned, headily illicit
interview. The light out there, gashed
by the surf's scimitar,

is blinding, a rebuke—Go Back! Go back!—
behind the silhouetted shipwreck (Whose?
When did it happen? Back in the village
nobody can tell you),

the bell buoy hunkering knee-deep in foam,
a blood-red-painted harbinger. How strange
a rim, back where you came from,
of familiar portents

reviewed from this *isola bella*, paradise
inside a prison rockpile—the unravished
protégé of guardians so lawless, refuge
moated up in such a shambles!

Observers and Naturalists Explore the Marginal World

Your mind keeps turning back to look at them—
chain-gang archangels that in their prismatic
frenzy fall, gall and gash the daylight
out there, all through the winter.

Denise Levertov

Singled Out

Expanse of gray, of silver.
Only this one rockstrewn
shallow bay singled out
to be luminous jade.
                    Its breakers
sing hard, sing loud, the sound
heard on the hilltop. Perhaps
the red-tailed hawk, swaying its flight
so much higher, hears it as well.

Warning

Island or dark
hollow of advancing wave?
Beyond
surf and spray a somber
horizontal. As if the sea
raised up
a sudden bulwark.
A menacing land, if land—
frowning escarpment, ephemeral
yet enduring, uncharted,
rumored. If wave,

a thundered prophetic word
in ocean's tongue, a bar of blackest
iron brandished aloft
in two fists of a water-god,
a warning not meant kindly.

Mary Oliver

. . . .

At the Shore

This morning
      wind that light-limbed dancer was all
            over the sky while
                  ocean slapped up against
                        the shore's black-beaked rocks
row after row of waves
      humped and fringed and exactly
different from each other and
      above them one white gull
            whirled slant and fast then
                  dipped its wings turned
                        in a soft and descending decision its
leafy feet touched
      pale water just beyond
breakage of waves it settled
      shook itself opened
            its spoony beak cranked
                  like a pump. Listen!
                        Here is the white and silky trumpet of nothing.
Here is the beautiful Nothing, body of happy,
      meaningless fire, wildfire, shaking the heart.

Observers and Naturalists Explore the Marginal World

Gretel Ehrlich

Santa Rosa

Green, no one here remembers when it started. Maybe three days ago, after seven months of brown. "It comes on like blindness," one of the cowboys says. "One day the green puts your eyes out, and you didn't even see it coming." I'm standing on the mountainous top of Santa Rosa island off the Santa Barbara coast. Out across the channel waters—white-capped, big-swelled, and shark-glutted—I can see, on the California mainland, the ridge where my house is perched. From there, the view down a canyon perfectly frames Santa Rosa. It is as if this marine shard were the missing half of the land where I live, the other side of my green mind. Santa Rosa island is shaped like a four-pointed star plucked in the middle and dropped. The east and west arms reach for the shore of the next islands in the chain. They were once linked together in a sixty-mile-long island: now the passages between them are cross-currented, choppy, wild, and dangerous, churning gyres rotating counterclockwise, mixing warm water into the cold and bathing the islands in clear seas. At 53,000 acres, Santa Rosa is the second largest of the eight Channel Islands and has been run as a cattle ranch for almost a hundred years by the Vail and Vickers families. Plunging down a rough dirt track in the Vails' battered pickup truck, we go east toward Bechers Bay, the steep land splaying out into broad coastal grasslands. Two foxes, endemic to the island, pounce on a field mouse, oblivious to our passing, reminding me that the four northern islands—Anacapa, Santa Cruz, Santa Rosa, and San Miguel—are sometimes called the Galapagos of the Northern Hemisphere.

We pass a stand of Torrey pines. Tall and thin-limbed, they are pruned by the raging winds that have driven some people on this island crazy. We cross a creek, and the land grows broader. Salt grass tightens its hold on sandy coastal bluffs as a hard northwesterly wind surges our way. Below us the bay is held by a wide curve of sand where snowy plovers nest, and to the southeast a stream widens into a freshwater estuary where egrets and herons prance and stalk, performing their near-motionless ballets. As we descend to the lee side of the island, a feeling of calm engulfs me.

Islands remind us of our intrinsic solitude, yet they usually stand in relationship to a greater body of land and so also teach us about relatedness, just as the islands in a Japanese garden must rest in harmony with the garden.

In our travels we are lured to islands, as if crossing their watery boundaries will endow us with a more vivid sense of ourselves set apart from the maddening fray. But once there, the plangent wholeness of the place blossoms forth: grasses, flowers, birds, trees, streams, animals all distinguished by having gotten there and survived, having been bound together by the frame of limited space.

We follow a long narrow barranca called the Wreck because the British ship *Crown of England* went aground here in 1894. Swales of green flatten out near shore as waves break with sharp reports, as if to say: "Home at last. I have come such a long way."

Near a set of sorting corrals for cattle, a meandering stream is still mostly dry, and a single tree's tortured trunk twists upward from bedrock.

"There never was much in the way of vegetation in this canyon," foreman Bill Wallace tells me, "and after last year's floods, even that was swept away."

We cross the creek and follow the coast west to a beach where cattle take their morning rest on the sand. At low tide, eelgrass is swept up on the brown rock, and jade green waves break like windowpanes on the bare bones of the island.

Beyond, a black ridge bends down to the sea, and from around its snout a plug of fog spews continually, never coming onto land.

Another day, the green has intensified. "Who needs a damned watch around here?" one of the men says. "The grass grows an inch every minute."

The southwest coast of the island is paradisiacal. Accordioned by a winter storm in Hawaii, I am on my favorite part of the island, China Camp, once an abalone camp of Chinese fishermen. A set of corrals and a small two-room cabin on the coastal plain overlook the ocean.

"Used to camp here when we were gathering," Russ Vail says. "I've traveled around some, and I guess this is one of the most beautiful spots in the world," he adds quietly, then looks west toward San Miguel. "The other one is next door."

As we come down off the mountain, hundreds, maybe even thousands, of western meadowlarks fly up, land, and throw their heads back in ecstatic song. This whole island is musical, a meadowlark orchestra.

Now the thick roll of fog that pulled past black rock yesterday twists overhead, and I feel as if I were riding a sea turtle, a great green back floating in mist. Waves that are lapis and foam break through the fog at the fringes of this tiny universe, and a seal observes me from the trough between sets of waves.

In Arlington Canyon we come across the site of Phil Orr's camp. An archeologist with the Santa Barbara Museum of Natural History, Orr did research on early man here on Santa Rosa for twenty years, from 1947 to 1967.

"He was a little crazy," Al Vail says, bemused. "Lived in a cave, fed the damned foxes, and spent years looking around for bones."

Orr theorized that hunter-gatherers lived on these islands as long ago as 35,000 years, though current thinking dates humans here to less than a third of that. Before those people, there were dwarf mammoths, giant mice, sea otters, and flightless geese. Even though the geology of the West is relatively new, the island seems old, having weathered continuous habitation by animals and humans for more years than we know.

Down by the shore Arlington Creek empties out into another estuary loaded with ducks. Huge beams from a wrecked boat are strewn in grass, and an elephant seal, his face and neck scarred from a lifetime of fighting, is slumped across a hummock of kelp, dead.

Fog billows over us and San Miguel disappears. An island may represent apartness and isolation, but that too is only an aspect of its stepping-stone unity with the whole. How do you know you are apart if you do not know there is something other—other islands, a mainland?

When Juan Cabrillo sailed into the Santa Barbara Channel in 1542, the Chumash people greeted him in their plank canoes, called *tomols.* They called what we know as Santa Rosa by the name Wi'ma—driftwood.

Each island had its own dialect, and the island tribes remained distinct from the Chumash who lived in villages along the mainland from Malibu to San Simeon.

They thought of the channel as a stream to step over. "I make a big step," one Chumash islander song goes. "I am always going over to the other side. I always jump to the other side, as if jumping over a stream of water. I make a big step."

With these words, sung in Santa Rosa island dialect, the Fox Dance began, the participants moving in a circle from fire to fire taking up offerings of *islay,* wild cherries. At the end, when the fox dancer whirled around and around under his weighted headdress, another song was sung in Cruzeño—the language of Santa Cruz island: "March! There comes the swell of the sea, the wood tick is drowning."

There were many dances—the Swordfish, Barracuda, Arrow, and Skunk, and the haunting chant of the Seaweed Dance: "I walk moving my brilliance and feathers. I will always endure in the future. . . ."

But they did not endure. They were gone—moved to the mainland—by 1817.

"There are many ghosts on this island," Nita Vail, Al's daughter, tells me.

On Bechers Bay is the main ranch house, the oldest standing house in Santa Barbara County, built in 1865. It is plain and rickety.

When I slept there, the winds seized and shook it, and two elegant Torrey pines outside the door swayed with the house's shaking.

Behind the house two red barns are still standing, but the original bunkhouse is gone. An old cook named Henry fell asleep with a cigarette in bed, burning it down, with himself and his dog in it. For years afterward the Vails said they could hear Henry walking around, clanking pots and pans in the middle of the night.

All afternoon we stroll luxuriant Lobos Canyon, one of the deepest and most unusual barrancas of them all. Year-round springs feed watercress, reeds, and sedge grasses. A snipe flies up as I splash through the stream, and an orange-crowned warbler sings in a small tree. As we tunnel down, the canyon walls grow taller; they are sheaves of sandstone, carefully etched with fine lines as if music had been written on them, the notes erased by the wind. Here and there shallow caves have been smoothed out by the island's hard winds, and in one amphitheater, a long tooth of rock hangs down from the roof of a cave, as if from the roof of some orange giant's mouth.

Downstream. More green: reeds, grasses, ferns, Toyon—California holly—and willows grow tall, and even the colonies of lichen on boulders stand up as if starched. A forty-foot-high wall is feathered into delicate filaments that look like the underside of a mushroom, sun-splashed and edible.

"I would like to die here," Nita says, "except I love this canyon so much, I'd want to stay alive to savor it."

As would I.

Observers and Naturalists Explore the Marginal World

Cynthia Huntington

The Edge

The beach goes on forever, a membrane between two worlds. I walk that disappearing line, along the edge of it, where the water slams up on shore and its movement reverberates through my entire body. A billion grains of sand shift underfoot and cold water crashes at my feet, once every seven seconds. This is no-man's-land, where nothing grows, a place of contention and disorder, of broken forms, and litter that stinks in the sun. Here the great beat of the ocean falls back, finding its limit; the waves curl as they hit and burst into particles, tossing molecules of water and salt into the air. The shore thrums softly with each blow, and, sloping downward, dives under water. And in all this beat and surge the victims are casually cast up, things of one world that can't live in the other.

Bodies float up and begin to rot in the rich air. A new moon pulled the tide high up the beach last night, leaving long, scalloped ridges of wrack and flotsam to mark its retreat. Shells with their insides gone soft and black, wet crumbling snail meat, and unhatched fish eggs all bloated and stinking in their sac membranes, lie strewn across the sand. A kind of sponge called dead man's fingers swells and dries pale in the sun, a six-fingered amputee, porous and reeking. The upper beach is studded with debris: nests of driftwood, cans, and dense, salt-rotten boards, bottles ground to a dull sheen by the waves' thrashing, tangled string and garish shreds of fishnet dyed orange and red, acid yellow, and the dire green of deepest sea caverns. I kicked up a light bulb wrapped in black electrical tape and sticking half out of the sand, a glass mummy loosening its bandages. These things belonged once to the land and were lost. They return strangely changed, with the smell of that other world all over them. A snarled fishing line, trailing a plume of kelp and a plastic detergent bottle, slams back and forth in the shallows; up ahead in the sand, something small and ghostly is burrowing out of sight.

It's a bright, cold morning down here among the wrecks. I'm walking at a slant, left foot low, right foot high, one side to the water and one leaning upland, heading east and south towards Truro. The high beach is flatter, but the sand up there is soft; here at the waves' edge is firmer footing. Up ahead in the east, the sun spreads an oily sheen across the water. The sky is pale, with a foam of sea clouds stirred into it, as if someone had poured white paint into blue without mixing them thoroughly. Along the horizon, a thin white line appears, tracing the border of sea and sky, a gap between the worlds where another light shines through.

Past the opening where Snail Road cuts through the foredune, an intersection marked by two posts in the sand and some jeep tracks that end abruptly at the tide line, I press forward into an empty landscape. Three gulls ride high above the waves, their wings barely moving as they float on an offshore breeze. The shoreline stretches away in an arc, following the curve of the earth, and drops down into the sky. Down here only the barest co-ordinates mark a position—there are no landmarks, everything flat and bright. My hand above my eyes, I scan the front of the sand bar, hoping for a glimpse of whales, but it's still too early. The finbacks will be here in June.

In late May the back shore is almost empty of life. The spring migrations raced through in April: geese and arctic terns headed to the northern tundras and cold inland lakes of Canada and Greenland. In town their hurried night flights woke us; cries of passage echoed in our dreams. Deeper inland, warblers streamed through the woods, flitting in and out among the spiky branches of pine and beach plum. Blackburnians, magnolias, blackpolls, and Tennessees, they rested, fed, and moved on, followed in turn by our summer residents, the kingbirds, catbirds, phoebes, and swallows, who are gathering now in woods and marshes along the highway. Most of our ocean birds have disappeared—even the herring gulls, who seem otherwise never to forsake our company, have begun scattering to nesting colonies along Monomoy and Long Point. Today a few immature gulls, too young to breed, strut importantly down the beach, meeting up with a company of smaller, pretty laughing gulls, just in from the Carolinas.

Some birdhouses poking up over the hill were the first sign I was nearing Thalassa: gradually the peak of its roof rose into view above the crest, then came a small dip in the grasses where the footpath winds down the hill, not noticeable really, unless you know how to look for it. The passage of people over sand is ghostly, fleeting. Where Frenchie's shack faces the beach, thrusting its little screened porch out ahead of it, the dunes open slightly to allow a glimpse of its shingled front. Yeats ago a sand dune moved in and covered this shack, burying it up to its windows, and rather than dig it out whoever owned it then simply built on top of it, making this the only shack in local record with a basement.

Past Frenchie's, still shuttered and dark inside, and past Thalassa, with its pointy roof rising over the foredune, around the bend and beyond the cliff where the beach gets narrow and almost disappears at high tide, some terns were flying, making high, nervous cries above the whitecaps. These were least terns, little sea swallows with black caps, forked tails, and temperaments as quick and tense as bees. They seem to dislike the land, and only come on shore reluctantly to nest, where they exhibit all the paranoia of exile. They began arriving last week from South America, and are getting ready to mate and scratch out their nests on the sand. One would approach the shore and veer off, as if losing nerve, then turn and take it out on his neighbor, wheeling and crying out in an accusing tone. By midsummer their nervousness will flower into a hysteria that will send them diving at the heads of intruders, but today they only followed me complaining, making a quivering company along shore. And when they had had enough of me, they flowed away into the sky.

After the terns I saw no one, just a disconsolate crow jabbing at a reeking pile of eel-grass, and a half-dead skate I nearly stepped on at the water's edge, a flat, gelatinous carpet heaved up cold on the wet sand. I stopped and poked it with my foot, and it rose up with a shudder, revealing its white underside, its gaping v-mouth gulping the fatal air. From deep covered sockets on top of its head its eyes stared and rolled as the thing with a prodigious effort flipped on the sand, lashed its horny tail and fell back. That must have been the last gasp because the next wave lifted it and it rode back and forth in the waves, its wings flopping uselessly.

My shadow trails me as I walk south. There are no shacks out this far and little sign of life. The beach gets narrow, then wide again; grass grows down to the tide line, then the shore is cut back in a steep scarp sloping upward for a hundred yards. Along the rim where the waves have torn at the edge of the grasses, black, salt-soaked roots hang exposed in midair. A plover skids past with a plaintive cry. Where am I? I could be anywhere. The scene is all flatness and falling away—the empty strip of beach running down the side of the globe, the blue dome of sky curving down to meet it. Past Pilgrim Heights, maybe, certainly not so far as Head of the Meadow. I can't be sure. What at a distance seems to be a wreck unburying itself turns out, as I approach, to be a tree limb bucked about in the waves. A whale's carcass rises out of the sand, but as I come closer it becomes a bleached log, salt white, with stubs of broken limbs.

I stop and open my water bottle. The tide has turned, and small waves wash up over the hard berm. Teasing the edge, they sizzle, fizz, and run back down to the water. Behind my, I notice my footprints running at an angle up the beach, swelling and darkening as water rises in them from below. Without my paying attention, the incoming tide has pressed me higher inland as I walked. This visible evidence of change is unexpectedly startling. "Time and motion, time and motion . . . of course," I think, to reassure myself.

Here is the point of creation, a beat that has been going on since time began. The present: breaking, moving, clashing, never to be repeated; the world teetering on a point of balance. The waves make old music, tearing at the shore, singing, "you must change, change," as they press forward on the land, a movement widening, center to circumference, opening until it breaks. Offshore a small boat drifts east with the current; there's a dragger about a mile down, in close pulling for scallops. Overhead, a pale broad sky floats off into space, not even seeming to touch the horizon.

The sun is high now; I need to think about heading back. If I turn around the scene will all be new, this sheet of sand before me, the endless border of sea and land, and offshore a green curl of wave breaking over the sandbar. You can't bend time backward; even the way home is another going forward, and the waves never repeat, or rest. One curve leads to another, endlessly disappearing. I walk, balanced on an invisible line that only exists in motion. And wherever I step, waves are tearing the ground away beneath my feet.

The sky is cold; its air is thin. I walk in the sky, bathed in sky, holding onto this narrow shore where the sea approaches and retreats before me. A line of sand grains forms at the shoreline and presses inland, a single line, then another. I give a moment to looking both ways, but I walk the edge, my head turned toward the path, the line without width or depth. The beach goes on forever and I walk that disappearing line, into time that opens to the pressure of my passing and closes behind me, complete.

Observers and Naturalists Explore the Marginal World

Jennifer Ackerman

Prologue, *Notes from the Shore*

I live in a small town by the sea. It sits just inside Cape Henlopen at the bottom lip of the Delaware Bay. Summer mornings, salt air sifts through the screen on my open window. Companies of gulls settle on my rooftop or sail around the church steeple across the way. On gray days, the foghorn out in the harbor bleats like a cow deprived of its calf.

One is always aware of the sea in Lewes, can feel its broad, enduring presence just over the fat humps of sand dunes. It affects people as surely as it breeds rhythms into the fiddler crab. When the wind is from the east, the saltwater leans in strong, and the sun rises pink under a moist haze. Stamps mate shamelessly. Bread molds in a day. In big storms, the ocean seems to empty its belly, and even a solid house like mine feels ephemeral. The hackberry trees weep floods of tears; my drainspout gives up altogether, spewing a wide waterfall that feeds a pool at the foot of the stairs. In the small tidal marsh at the center of town, chill water rises to the tips of the cordgrass so that only specks of green show, like a lawn in a pointillist painting. When the tide shrinks, the mudbanks exhale that sharp, salty smell.

Some days, a thick sea mist creeps backward over the dunes and infiltrates the town with the ghost of deep water; then the place feels as if it were adrift, unanchored to anything.

This coast is a rhythmic landscape cut from marshes and sand described by an early Dutchman as "beautifully level." Age by age the ocean has risen; age by age it falls again, sweeping back and forth across the coastal plain. The ground around Lewes supports flowering plants that fare well in thin sandy soil: beach heather, bayberry, groundsel, beach pea. Because the ocean tempers the swing of seasons, it is a twin province of north and south, home to species that ordinarily do not mix. Bald cypress, muscadine grape, loblolly pine, and sweetleaf push up from their southern habitats; wild cherry, beach plum, sassafras, and laurel creep down from the north. Such northern species as eider ducks meet true southerners like the brown pelican and black vulture.

Spring and fall, flocks of migrating birds flow north and south overhead. In

May, shorebirds descend from the night skies to feed on our margins. Swallows mass under the August sun, stippling the dunes and beading the phone wires. When the temperature falls, the air reverberates with the calls of snow geese, which gather by the thousand in the stubby cornfields like raucous crowds on a public beach. In winter, flotillas of scoters and scaups play the edges of the sea.

The Siconese Indians called this spot Sickoneysinck, or "place where there is a gentle sound from the movement of things." Early Dutch colonists called it Zwaanedael for the wild swans. Today Lewes is a town of twenty-five hundred, though the population swells in summer. It has been spared the development that mars so much of this coast thanks in part to the clouds of mosquitoes that once bred in the marshes and ponds, and to the presence of two strong-smelling fish-fertilizer plants on its bay shore, which perfumed the streets, especially when the wind was from the east.

Our main thoroughfare, Savannah Road, got its name from the flat farmland over which it traveled. Some of this land remains, and roadside stands piled high with sweet white corn and cantaloupes still populate the county highways in summer. But with the death of the fish factories in the late sixties, Lewes has grown into nearby Wolfe Neck, Gills Neck, and Holland Glade, slapping down over forest and farmland subdivisions with names that memorialize what has been razed.

At the only stoplight in town, Savannah intersects Pilottown Road, which runs along the Lewes canal. This is the old neighborhood of the river pilots, men charged with navigating large vessels through the swift, narrow channel of the Delaware to ports upstream. When the wind is right, you can hear their boats go out, the throbbing engines louder than most other boats. The pilots are still considered the elite and their houses are among the biggest and best in town, with tall attic windows once used to scan the horizon for incoming ships. Maps of the Delaware Bay are peppered with reminders of the old terror of the cold gray deeps: Ship John Shoal, Joe Flogger Shoal, Old Bare Shoal, Deadman Shoal, The Shears. The bay is a drowned river valley of modest size, about seventy-five miles north to south from its head at Chester, Pennsylvania, to its broad mouth at Cape Henlopen and Cape May. Unlike the Chesapeake Bay, its shoreline is not shredded by necks and coves but smooth and regular, like a beet. It receives a vigorous infusion of freshwater from the Delaware, the Schuylkill, and a dozen or so smaller rivers—the Neversink, Smyrna, Mispillion, Murderkill, Broadkill—which mixes at the mouth with saltwater from the sea. The floor of the bay is strewn with ships that have foundered over the past three centuries, casualties of the shoals that radiate fingerlike north and west from its mouth and sometimes rise nearly to the surface. Before the advent of the river pilots, it is said, the curbs of the town's sidewalks were built from the masts of wrecked vessels.

Most of the houses in Lewes are small, modest frame houses from the 1700s or large Victorian affairs built during the railroad boom of the late nineteenth century. The older ones have long sloping roofs, dormer windows, and cypress shingles hand-cut from virgin trees felled in the swamps near Laurel, Delaware, now weathered to a soft gray. They have that native sense of geometry and proportion, compatible in mood and color with the beach, the marsh, the sea. The Victorian places, on the other hand, stand out like big showpieces, fussy with scrollwork and ornately carved porches. The house I live in is one of these. My father and stepmother bought it twenty years ago, when it was an oversized, shabby elephant of a place, grayish white like dried salt. They fell in love with it largely because of the dozens of giant double-hung windows that admit sunlight from all sides. Over the years they fixed it up and slowly furnished it with odd pieces hand-picked from local estate sales. Then they generously offered up its three apartments to a tribe of relatives: brother, daughter, mother, two elderly aunts—the one quiet and polite, the other, voluble and brusque but with a big, generous spirit that still haunts the place, along with the stray cats she adopted. And finally, my husband and me, who came here three years ago with the plan to start a family of our own here.

When I arrived, I set as my goal to look closely at the daily nature around me and by so doing, come to know the place a little. There is not a great deal on this coast that recalls the landscape of my childhood. My roots lie in the interior, in rolling deciduous woodland. Few of us have the privilege of living as adults in the place we lived in as children. Even fewer of us die where we were born. I have moved eight times in the last nine years. How many landscapes can fit inside the human heart?

At first I felt disoriented here, as if I had been spun round blindfolded and set down reeling, wondering from which quarter the winds usually blew and whether this shroudy brown fog was typical of my share of coast. I missed the hiss of wind in high trees and the sweet vegetable smell of humus and decaying leaves. I saw only the barren mud flats, the sly sameness of the marsh. I saw only surfaces.

A native landscape enters a child's mind through a meld of sensations: the smell of seaweed or hay, the sound of cicadas, the cold grit of stone. It is all heart and magic, confusion rather than order, but the feeling it evokes is wholly satisfying and lasting. Gaining this kind of deep familiarity with a landscape other than your native one is like learning to speak a foreign language. You can't hope for quick or easy fluency. You work from the outside in, by accumulating a vocabulary of observed details. You learn where things happen in the rhythmic revolutions of the days and the year, which shrubs harbor families of grackles, which stands of beach plum send out sprays of August bloom, where the hognose snake waits for its toad and the toad, for its fly. Slowly the strange becomes familiar; the familiar becomes precious.

In my time here, I've learned that the slick dark mud flat is fidgety with hidden creatures, that life here is equally in the rapid pulse of perceptible change and in the slow pull of long time, that with a small nest egg of facts about a place comes a sea of questions. I've learned that the way in to a new landscape is to pull at a single thread. Nearly always it will lead to the heart of the tangle.

Osprey, *Notes from the Shore*

The temperature this morning is 82 degrees. The relative humidity is 85 percent. The wind is all by the sea; here in the bay it is quiet and warm. I've come to the cape in the hopes of seeing a pair of osprey, newly mated and nesting on a wooden platform by the bay. But the birds are nowhere in sight. Instead I spot a photographer in a three-piece suit, and his subjects, a groom in tails and a bride in a starchy white, high-necked gown. It is a pretty scene: Behind the pair, dunes stretch to the sea, patchy mats of beach heather exploding with the yellow bloom of May. But the bride seems annoyed. Her satin pumps fight the avalanching dunes, heels probing the sand like the bill of a willet. She reaches out to the groom to steady herself, removes a shoe, and empties a long stream of grit. She looks young, barely twenty. Beads of sweat soak the lace rimming her veil. The flies are up; the warm air carries the stench of creatures rotting on the flats.

Yesterday I was lucky enough to catch the ospreys copulating. Through my scope I could see the female in intimate detail perched on the edge of the platform, her glistening yellow eyes, the dusky shafts of her breastband, the soft green-gray of her feet. Her mate circled above, white belly shining in the sun. He whistled piercing notes, then dropped suddenly, dipping below the platform and swooping up to hover directly above her. He settled on her back gently, barely touching her with clenched talons, flapping his wings for balance. She tipped forward slightly, raising her tail high to the side to receive him. I watched, a little ashamed of my magnified view. They coupled in silence for twenty or thirty seconds. Then the female, with a light flutter of wings, shrugged off her mate, who slowly banked upward and slipped sidewise across the sky.

The osprey leapt into my heart from my first days here. For one thing, the big bird is easy to identify. So many shorebirds are what ornithologists call "LBJs," little brown jobs. These I tried to pin down in my notes with some vague hope of identifying them later. But the osprey's size, its white belly and dark carpal patches, its wings kinked at the wrist, gave it away. So did its slow whistled call, a penetrating *kyew, kyew,* which drifts down from overhead. I occasionally mistook a high-flying osprey for a gull, but eventually learned to read its pattern of flight: shallow wingbeats interspersed with long glides. Its movement was more purposeful and deliberate than a gull's, less flighty. The osprey's huge nests, most of them in open, public places, and its showy method of hunting—a dazzling power dive ending in a burst of spray—mad it a conspicuous neighbor, familiar and expected.

When I was seven or eight I went bird-watching with my father from time to time. I remember rising before dawn reluctantly and heading out, stiff, sleepy, my shoes damp with dew. In a family of five girls, time alone with my dad was a rare pleasure, not to be missed. The two of us would feel our way along the towpath between the C & O Canal and the Potomac River, cool breeze on the backs of our necks, companionable in late starlight. We moved quietly, all eyes for the small woodland birds we hoped to spy from a distance. It would begin with one bird, maybe two, chipping away at the dark. Then the clear whistled note of a cardinal would rise and the trilling of a wood thrush, and the songs would pass from one bird to another, their swelling sounds lifting me up by my ears. As the stars faded and branches emerged against the sky, sudden small shapes would appear and disappear, fluttering and darting about, flashing between the leaves: sparrows, finches, warblers, which I could just barely make out in the darkness. I didn't try to identify them. At that hour the world was theirs. On the ride home in the car, I would sift through my father's well-thumbed volume of Roger Tory Peterson's *Field Guide to North American Birds*, neatly indexed with plastic tabs marking the division of families: *Paridae* (titmice), *Sittidae* (nuthatches), *Troglodytidae* (wrens), and *Parulidae* (wood warblers). I was a pushover for the neat little manual, a fine tool for thinking about diversity and order in the world.

What birds I saw on those excursions were mostly woodland species. When it came to shorebirds I was utterly lost. Some species were easy to pin down. The ruddy turnstone, for instance—a squat, aggressive little bird with a harlequin mask—or the black-bellied plover, with its long, elegant black bib. But the sandpipers were a different story. Peterson calls the littlest ones "peeps," the white-rumped, the semipalmated, the least. There are rules, of course—the least is the smallest, its diminutive size earning it the species name *minutilla;* the semipalmated has a shorter, stouter bill—but judging either bill or body size at a distance seemed hopeless. Then there was the matter of plumage, which changes from season to season like foliage and which differs from male to female, from juvenile to immature to adult. Same bird, different disguises. No sooner had I nailed down the various appearances of one migratory species than another had taken its place. It's no wonder Aristotle came up with the theory of transmutation: Birds change species with the seasons, he said. Redstarts, common in Greece throughout the summer, became robins in winter; summer garden warblers changed into winter black caps. He claimed to have seen the birds midway in their metamorphoses. Anyone who has tried to identify fall birds in their shabby molting plumage can understand the mistake.

I eventually found a tutor in Bill Frech, a kind, owlish man, now eighty, who has been a devoted observer of winged things since he was twelve. Bill is up and away every morning at dawn to make his rounds in a VW with a scope mounted on the window. Though he claims not to have any special knowledge of winds or weather, he knows where the birds will be on any particular day, where heavy rains form pools of standing water that draw glossy ibises and egrets, which hayfields have been cut over recently, making good habitat for golden plovers, which buoys offer refuge to storm petrels in heavy wind. He sees what he sees, he says, and a good part of his pleasure is in the chanciness of the enterprise. One morning might yield nothing more interesting than a common goldeneye or an upland plover, while the next turns up a stray swallow-tailed kite hovering over the Lewes water tower; an Australian silver gull, or two thousand gannets riding out a storm behind Hen and Chickens Shoal.

Bill sees the world of light and motion not in a continuum, he says, but in frozen frames, a series of discernible stopwatch tableaux, which helps him spot his quarry. He scours the edges of the land, the broad sweep of sky and sea, one section at a time, and nearly always turns up a bird. I have tried to learn to do this, to look for spots of stillness on the tossing sea, for movement among the stubble of a cut field, but I often miss the mark and must have my eye directed. Bill carries no field guides. He depends less on fieldmarks to identify a bird than on its jizz, a term that comes from the fighter pilot's acronym GIS for General Impression and Shape. He has taught me to recognize a semipalmated plover or to distinguish a yellowlegs from a willet without quite knowing how I do so, just as one recognizes a friend from a distance not by individual characteristics, but by shape and gait. Most sandpipers walk and probe, while the plover runs and pecks, runs and pecks. Spotted sandpipers teeter. The Maliseet Indians of Maine understood this. They called the bird *nan a-mik-tcus,* or "rocks its rump." The sanderling flies steadily along; the plover's flight is wilder, full of tilting twists and turns. Most warblers dart through trees, but myrtle warblers drift. Knowing the jizz of a bird is especially useful when it comes to identifying high-flying species: Canada geese flap constantly; cormorants glide, long black necks in eternal pursuit of tiny tufted heads; gannets dip like goldfinches; pelicans alternate flaps with a short sail. As Bill filled my head with these rules of thumb, the species slowly separated and gained names.

I have the good fortune to live within a three-mile radius of five active osprey nests. One sits atop a platform on the double cross-arms of an old utility pole in the marsh at the center of town, hard by a railroad and King's Highway. The highway carries the crush of traffic disgorged from the Cape May–Lewes ferry, a steady stream of tourists hell-bent for a seaward peep. Another nest occupies a channel marker, a fancy site complete with a flashing red light powered by a solar panel and two bright orange warning signs. The rest sit on duckblinds and man-made platforms. The ospreys seem unbothered by all the human activity surrounding these sites. They are adaptable, versatile sorts, with a predilection for human ruins. An unkempt chimney, a vacant house, or a pile of fence rails gone back to nature draws them in. On an island in the Chesapeake Bay that was once a bombing range, ospreys nest on the busted-up car bodies used as targets. One pair set up housekeeping on the surface of an unexploded thousand-pound bomb.

Every year, within a day or two of St. Patrick's Day, as schooling fish move into the sun-warmed waters of the bay, the ospreys arrive on the south wind for the breeding season. They fly high and circle overhead, greeting each mudbank, each twist of creek with a high, clear whistle. Invariably a notice appears in the local paper: "The fish-hawk, Delaware's harbinger of spring, has finally arrived."

The spectacle of courtship follows soon after. The young male selects a nesting site and then begins an aerial display, a slow, undulating flight high in the sky. Once an understanding is struck between a male of good property and his discriminating partner, nest building begins. The pair is up and down, in and out all day, scouring the neighborhood for appropriate materials. Ospreys are pack rats and indefatigable renovators. Though they nest in the same site from year to year, the nests themselves are often destroyed between seasons and so need considerable repairs. The birds don't seem particularly interested in permanence or stability. John Muir purportedly rode out a hurricane sitting on an eagle's nest. Ornithologist Alan Poole said he wouldn't trust his weight to an osprey nest on a blue windless day. At the nest near King's Highway, I've watched males bring in cornstalks, cow dung, crab shells, a fertilizer bag, a toy shovel, a slice of floor mat, and the doilylike remnants of fish net. Even this eclectic nest doesn't hold a candle to one John Steinbeck found in his Long Island garden, which contained three shirts, a bath towel, an arrow, and a rake.

The male plays hod carrier to the female's bricklayer. She has definite ideas about how things should be arranged and fulfills her task with zeal. The loose mass grows up and out until it looms like a giant mushroom cap against the horizon. Nest finished, the female turns broody, sitting deep in the nest cup so that only her head shows. The male brings her fish and often spells her while she perches nearby and consumes her meal head first, with a kind of horrible delicacy.

When I'm at a loss to explain some bit of bird biology or behavior I've observed, I turn to Arthur Cleveland Bent's mighty twenty-volume series on the *Life Histories of North American Birds* (Bill Frech started acquiring copies of the books in the 1920s, when the U.S. Government Printing Office sent them out free. He got all but the last three volumes, which he had to buy from the publisher.) The organization of these volumes is tidy and pleasing. The section on ospreys, for instance, lists the bird's full Latin name, *Pandion haliaëtus carolinensis*. Then the common name, from the Latin *ossifraga*, or sea eagle. Then come sections filled with copious details on courtship, nesting, plumage, voice, enemies, and eggs, all enhanced by the observations of a large company of tipsters. Here's Mr. Clinton G. Abbott's catalogue of osprey calls:

> The commonest note is a shrill whistle, with a rising inflection: *Whew, whew, whew, whew, whew, whew, whew.* This is the sound usually heard during migration; and when the bird is only slightly aroused. When she becomes thoroughly alarmed it will be: *Chick, chick, chick, cheek, cheek, ch-cheek, ch-cheek, cheereek, chezeek, chezeek,* gradually increasing to a frenzy of excitement at the last. Another cry sounds like: *Tseep, tseep, tseep-whick, whick, whick-ick-ick-ck-ck,* dying away in a mere hiccough.

It is no easy task to record a bird sound on paper, and you have to admire the efforts of Abbott. One crotchety contributor expresses disappointment in this range: "All these notes . . . seem inadequate to express the emotions of so large a bird."

For the latest field studies on ospreys, I turn to Alan Poole's book, *Ospreys: A Natural and Unnatural History.* Here are hundreds of businesslike facts: the number of minutes of hunting necessary to meet the daily food requirements of an osprey family (195), the percentage of eggs lost from an average clutch in New York (68%) and in Corsica (21%), the total population of breeding pairs in Britain (45) and along the Chesapeake Bay (1,500).

According to both Bent and Poole, ospreys are traditional, one could even say conservative, birds. A female selects her mate not by his fancy flight, melodious song, or flamboyant feathers, but by his choice of homes. The birds favor the top limbs of large, mature, isolated trees. In a typical old-growth forest, fewer than one in a thousand trees suit. On this coast, where mature forests are mostly gone, the birds resort to distinctly unnatural sites: telephone poles, channel markers, fishing piers, and duck blinds. They favor overwater sites, which offer good protection from raccoons and other four-legged predators, but are of no use against winged carnivores such as the great horned owl. I've seen these formidable hunters perched on the Lewes water tower, heard them caterwauling in the dark, and found their pellets in the pine forest, packed solid with bones, feathers and fur.

Ospreys are thought to mate for life. However, a recent story in *The New York Times* tells me that there is almost no such thing as true monogamy in the animal kingdom. It reports that scientists are uncovering evidence of philandering in species after species, withering the notion of lovingly coupled birds. With sophisticated spying techniques, they are spotting members of supposedly faithful pairs—purple martins, barn swallows, black-capped chickadees—flitting off for extramarital affairs. With DNA fingerprinting, they've compiled dossiers on the adulterers. One of the few known examples of true monogamy, they say, is a rodent living in the weeds and grasses of the midwestern prairies, a homely little vole called *Microtus ochrogaster*, which is utterly committed to its mate.

Still, it is fairly well established that adultery is rare among ospreys, and there are stories of fervent conjugal devotion. Bent reports the story of a bird whose mate was killed when a bolt of lightning struck her nest. The male refused to abandon the site, perching in a nearby tree all summer, a bird-shaped picture of bereavement. He returned the following year and stood vigil for another season.

A typical osprey clutch consists of three eggs, which Bent describes as "the handsomest of all the hawks' eggs . . . roughly the size of a hen's egg." Bent collected eggs most of his life, saved the orbs as trophies, laying their speckles in a cabinet fragrant with that peculiar pungent egg odor. "I shall never forget my envious enthusiasm," he writes, "when a rival boy collector showed me the first fish hawk's eggs I had ever seen." He goes on to describe the range of their appearance in loving detail: "The shell is fairly smooth and finely granulated. The ground color . . . may be white, creamy white, pinkish white, pale pinkish cinnamon, fawn color, light pinkish cinnamon, or vinaceous-cinnamon. They are usually heavily blotched and spotted with dark rich browns or bright reddish browns, bone brown, liver brown, bay, chestnut, burnt sienna, or various shades of brownish drab."

It was after reading this description that I bought a scope to watch more closely the activities of the ospreys nesting near King's Highway. I couldn't see the eggs themselves: They sat too low in the nest. But sometime late in the second week of June, they hatched. The newborn chicks were unfinished things, fuzzy flesh poking up from the bottom of the nest, as naked and helpless as a human baby, and no less perishably tender. Unlike such precocial birds as plovers and sandpipers, which go forth into the world straight from the egg, young ospreys take some coddling. Despite a steady stream of fish delivered by its parents, one chick died ten days later. The survivor, a fat squab with golden pinfeathers and thick black eye stripes, turned mobile at about four weeks, pestering its mother for fish and backing up now and again to squirt feces over the nest's edge. By midsummer, fatted on shad and flounder, puffed up on menhaden, it was flapping its scrawny wings, testing flight.

One warm, still day later that summer, I watched a young osprey fishing in the bay. The water was alive with hundreds of silver fish that split the calm, sun-smoothed surface. The bird flew high from the southwest, slowly spiraled down to seventy or eighty feet, and began to stalk the shallows. The bright eye opened, the head lowered, the wings folded, then the feet thrust forward and the bird dropped like a feathered bomb, striking the water with a burst of spray.

Millions of generations of natural selection have made these birds good at what they do. Though ospreys have been known to take snakes, turtles, voles, and even baby alligators, 99 percent of their diet is fish, and they play every piscine angle. They spot fish from hundreds of feet above the water, even bottom fish with superb camouflage, like flounder. They penetrate the sun's glare or a dark, rippled water surface and adjust their strike to compensate for light refraction. With an eye membrane called a pecten, they change focus instantly to keep the fish in perfect view as they plunge. They hit the water at speeds of twenty to forty miles per hour. Their dense, compact plumage protects against the force of impact; a flap of tissue on top of the beak closes over the nostrils to shut out the splash. The bird's strong, sinewy legs are superbly adapted for catching and holding slippery prey. Sharp talons, curved and of equal length, can snap shut in a fiftieth of a second. One toe swings back so that the osprey can clutch its prey with two claws on either side. Short spines on the base of the bird's toes and footpads ensure a firm grip.

With several deep wingbeats, this young bird rose slowly, shook its wings, and shifted the wildly flapping quiver of silver in its broad talons so that it rode headfirst, like a rudder. I watched until nothing could be seen of it but the dark V-sign of wings against the sky.

Aldo Leopold once wrote about the physics of beauty in the sand hills of Wisconsin. "Everybody knows . . . that the autumn landscape in the north woods is the land, plus a red maple, plus a ruffled grouse. In terms of conventional physics, the grouse represents only a millionth of either the mass or the energy of an acre. Yet subtract the grouse and the whole thing is dead. . . . A philosopher has called this imponderable essence the *numenon* of material things." For me, the osprey supplies the same kind of motive power to this place.

In the 1950s and '60s, this coast nearly lost its numenon to DDT, what Rachel Carson called the "elixir of death." March brought few homecomers, June grew no aerie. The toxic brew did more damage to the osprey than had been done by decades of egg collecting, hunting, and habitat destruction.

During World War II, the U.S. Army had used DDT to combat body lice among its troops, successfully breaking the chain of typhus infection. After the war, farmers and government workers began using the pesticide as a weapon against mosquitoes and agricultural pests. Its hazards were recognized from the beginning. Two researchers from the U.S. Fish and Wildlife Service published a paper in 1946 warning of the dangers of DDT. They had found that spraying in New Jersey endangered blue crabs. In Pennsylvania, it was brook trout; in Maryland, birds, frogs, toads, snakes, and fish. Still, for almost three decades, most of the East Coast's shoreline and marshes were blanketed with DDT in an effort to eradicate the common salt-marsh mosquito. Long-lasting and easily dispersed, the pesticide spread over the earth in much the same pattern as radioactive fallout, carried aloft by wind and deposited on the ground in rainfall. By the 1960s, it permeated wildlife all around the globe, even lodging in tissues of Adélie penguins in Antarctica.

The highest concentrations of DDT residues were found in carnivorous birds at the top of the food chain: bald eagles, peregrine falcons, ospreys. The pesticide found its way into plankton and phytoplankton (microscopic plants and algae such as diatoms and dinoflagellates), which were eaten by shellfish, insects, and other creatures, which were eaten by fingerlings, which were in turn eaten by larger fish, which were caught by osprey. The concentration of the pesticide increased as much as ten times with each level in the chain. (Fish also accumulate toxins by absorbing pollutants directly through their gills.) What started out as a minute amount of DDT in water or plants ended up as a big dose in fish and an even bigger dose in the fatty tissues of birds of prey.

Ospreys can rid themselves of small amounts of some toxins: mercury, for instance. They excrete it from the blood into growing feathers, which are eventually molted—a technique that works only during the molting season. But mercury occurs in nature; DDT is man-made. Birds have had no time to evolve a way to rid their bodies of the poison. As the toxin accumulates in fatty tissues, it blocks the efficient metabolism of calcium and so makes the shell of an osprey's egg brittle, cracked by a touch of fingers. When a female settles down to incubate, she crushes her clutch beneath her.

Around the turn of the century, the ornithologist Alexander Wilson remarked that he saw osprey "thick about Rehoboth Bay," some twenty nests within a half-mile range. A concentrated colony flourished then at Cape Henlopen, with twenty-three nesting pairs, probably drawn by the dense schools of menhaden that crowded the waters of the lower bay. By 1972, when DDT was finally banned in the United States, populations of ospreys here and elsewhere along the northeast coast had plummeted to a small fraction of their former numbers. When Bill Frech came to Lewes in 1977, there were forty-six nesting pairs of osprey in all of Delaware. That year, observers across the bay at Cape May counted just over a thousand migrating osprey during the whole autumn season. Since the 1970s, the birds have somehow recovered their numbers. In October of 1989, nearly a thousand birds were spotted passing through Cape May on a single day. At last count, Delaware had seventy-five nests.

Most ospreys along this coast make impressive annual migrations in orbit with the seasons, traveling south to the tropics in fall and north again in spring to breed. Young birds travel both ways alone. The migration route they follow is not learned, but acquired in the egg, carried in them by the accident of ancestry. A young osprey fledged in Lewes goes south to Peru or Venezuela to winter in the hot mists and vast swamps of the Amazon, and returns after a year or two to breed on the very same stretch of temperate shore where it fledged.

I know the gift of being able to find home is not allotted merely to these birds. Moose return annually to the same summer range. Bears transported more than fifty miles from their territory come back to it within days. Something in the cold brains of sea turtles guides them to their natal beaches after prodigious migrations of thousands of miles. Even limpets seem to know their way home, crawling back to a favorite scar or dimple on a rock at low tide, even if the face of the rock they cross had been hammered or chiseled into oblivion. Terns, swallows, gulls, and song sparrows, as well as shore birds— piping plovers, ruddy turnstones, and sanderlings—all return to the same nesting ground in what is called *ortsreue,* or "place faithfulness." A strong attachment to birthplace makes good biological sense, of course. In a familiar landscape, animals have an easier time finding nesting sites and prey and avoiding predators. Biologist Ernst Mayr once remarked that birds have wings not so much for the purpose of getting away to a place but for the purpose of getting home.

Still, it seems astonishing that a young osprey, only a few months old, can take off over land and water and travel south three thousand miles; then, years later, head sure and direct, without guidance, back to the precise point of its infancy. Scientists believe that members of a pair stay together because they share a deep affinity for the same stretch of marsh or shore. Apparently ospreys carry an image of home in their heads that is sharp and well defined. How does a young bird register this place? What are its landmarks of sight and smell? Is it, as Lamarck said, that the environment creates the organ? Does our particular wash of blue and white bore those bright golden eyes and code the neurons that stream into those kinked wings? Do our mottled currents and patterns of marsh grass brand a bird, saying, Come toward this shore? There may be other sensual messages sent by the earth, undetected by us, but which a bird is innately prepared to receive. Although scientists suspect that some consciousness of the exact magnetic topology and field strength of a nesting area has something to do with it, no one really knows. "It's a black box sort of thing," one ornithologist told me. Somehow this stretch of shore works a kind of magic against all others to pull its progeny from the sky.

When I was twelve, the school I went to sat on a hillside near a mature deciduous wood. At lunchtime, I often retreated to a small clearing some distance from the school to eat my sandwich and reflect on the morning's events. One day I sat on a log, peeling bark from a stick, and pondering the news that had struck our family a few weeks before: my father was leaving my mother. It was a warm, breezy day. Sunlight moving in and out of the clouds shattered the leafy surfaces with flecks of gold. I hadn't noticed trouble between my parents, engrossed as I was in my own awkward passing into adolescence. No shouting, no slamming doors. Suddenly this. The sunglasses my mother had been wearing for days couldn't conceal from me her wet face, her bafflement and sense of betrayal. I was at that age when I yearned above all else to be invisible, the way a Fowler's toad is invisible against the sand of the pine forest floor. The rift between my parents made me stand out and pick sides. It set me adrift, hunting for stable sanctuary in what had come to seem a shifting, unreliable world.

These woods were comforting and familiar. I knew their mossy hummocks and decaying stumps as well as any place I'd ever known. But this day I saw something new. Glancing up from the stick in my hand, I noticed a vibrating white dot about the size of a firefly in the trunk of an oak tree some distance from where I sat. It was more an absence than a presence, a tiny pulsating hole. I stared and stared. The hole slowly grew into a crescent, then a large ragged horseshoe, a sizeable bite that should have split the tree in two. But the top half of the trunk just hung there like a stalactite. Still the hole grew, spreading in pulses until it swallowed nearby bushes and trees in white-hot light. It was as if my woods were being punched out or sucked up in a shiny boiling void. I couldn't shift my gaze from the growing hole, and a sense of horror stole over me. I got up and stumbled blindly out of the woods. By this time my hands were numb, dead weight at the ends of my arms, like dangling lumps of dough. Nausea roiled my insides; then a dot of hot pain shot through my temple and set the right side of my head throbbing.

This was my first experience with the aura of a classical migraine headache. The visual disturbance, the scintillating, zigzaggy chasm, is called a scotoma, meaning darkness or shadow. I rarely have such attacks anymore. I've learned to fend them off by lying down in darkness and focusing on that first tiny flash of white light, concentrating it until it shrinks into a pinpoint and pops out of existence. But I still think of that first aura not merely as a chaotic burst of firing among the thin wires of my brain but as a sudden, complete extinction of place.

Oddly enough, that pleat in my perception held a vision of the future. Several years later, when I returned to visit those woods, I found them gone. In their place was a thick cluster of row houses that clung like barnacles to the edge of the hill, and I was struck anew by a sense of disorientation and loss.

This sensation is not peculiar to humans. The loss of familiar surroundings, the destruction of refuge, is no doubt felt by animals, perhaps even more keenly than by our kind. I once saw something like this happen to a pair of osprey that for more than a decade had nested on a dilapidated pier behind the old fish factories. The pier was used in the 1950s and '60s to offload the giant nets of menhaden. When the factories closed, the pier fell into disuse; all that was left was a set of rotting pilings with a few cross timbers, disconnected from the land. One fall, developers bulldozed the fish factories to build condominiums and tore up the old pier. When the osprey returned that March, I watched them circle the empty water for hours in bewilderment. They hung around for days, perching on a nearby utility pole and watching the site, apparently recollecting a structure now made of air.

Stories are told of species that retain an image in their heads of places that have long disappeared. Monarchs migrating over Lake Superior fly south, then east, then south again, as if reading the echoes of a long-vanished glacier. Year after year, pilot whales on their autumn migrations strand themselves on the beaches of Cape Cod, as if unwilling to accept the presence of a twelve-thousand-year-old geological upstart that has parked itself in the middle of a migratory path they have followed for millions of years. American toads return to breed in ponds that have long since been paved over, drawn by some insubstantial vapor, some aura of home.

Studies of human preferences for landscapes have found that our tribe tends to favor savannalike land—flat, grass-covered landscape studded with trees, where we had our origins and earliest home. Also promontories overlooking water. Some scientists even speculate that somewhere along the way we veered off the common primate course of evolution not just by winging down from trees, but by going toward the sea. The seashore, with its abundance of edibles—fish, mollusks, turtle and bird eggs, digestible plants—and of shells, vines, kelp, and driftwood for tools, was the home of emergent humanity.

I like this idea that our earliest home landscapes are buried deep, embedded in our minds like an anchor at great depth, that we know in some dark, birdly way where we want to go.

Beauty may, indeed, lie in the genes of the beholder. Ospreys have been around for something like fifteen million years, long before we ever set foot on seashores. In our burgeoning minds, shore has never been separate from bird, so perhaps at some level, the two are joined in an inexplicable sweetness of union. Perhaps the osprey exists on a mental map of an earlier world passed down from our ancestors, and the bird in its landscape enters us like the parental. Perhaps it is also the other way around: Perhaps *he* contains *us* as part of his element, having seen us through the ages, through our infancy and the whole tumult of civilized man.

I wonder, too, if the residues of old ancestral landscapes don't rise up in our minds by the same deep grooves that make the scent of hay or sunlit ferns call up an episode from childhood, so that we act on buried instinct—like a dog at the hearth who turns slowly around and around on himself, tamping down a circle of imaginary grass—so that for the sake of marking her union in a meaningful way, a young bride puts up with salt stench and sand in her shoe.

Mary Parker Buckles

. . . .

The Shore

Many paths lead to water from where I live. Some are journeys of the eye through glass and screen. In winter my sight travels from the large coastal oak out to islands framed by its boughs and, far beyond, to splinters of sun that underline Long Island's north shore. This allows morning to begin while a sliver of moon still lodges in the oak's crossed limbs.

Some paths are recollections. After a season of record snowfall my back exulted as it pressed into the warmth of Sound-side bedrock. A few snows had been heavy enough to outfit this stone in white spats above the dark water of high tide. As the tide receded, a sharp line remained to define where earth began.

The best path is literal and direct. It runs from the bottom of my front steps to the top of the rocky slope overlooking the Sound. The first ten strides lead me through evergreens that serve as a windbreak for the house and garden. A dozen more and I'm across a lane and out onto turf browned by repeated freezings and the unending thoughtlessness of geese. The rest of the trip requires forty-six steps and is often breezy.

Simply to stand here and look out is to be entertained. Diving ducks court shamelessly on these sheltered waters from late autumn through early spring. There are buffleheads and oldsquaws and two species of scaups and red-breasted mergansers with their head crests like worn-out toothbrushes. These waterfowl are small, the sprightly buffleheads weighing only three-quarters of a pound.

Observers and Naturalists Explore the Marginal World

The birds vanish under water to feed. This distinguishes them from mallards and other surface-feeding ducks, called dabblers. It also makes guesswork of tracking a particular individual, since flock members often surface fifty feet from where they plummet. When thirty or forty ducks forage at once, the water gathers them and shoots them back to the top with alacrity, and whole stretches of liquid dance with the motion.

Before the cold lifts and the diving ducks head north, I'm likely to see the mergansers mate just a few feet offshore. A hen will swim low in the water with a wild look in her eye. A drake who's been flirting by dipping his angled, outstretched neck will try to seduce her, climbing on backward sometimes. I'll chuckle, knowing little of wet chivalry's trials. He will correct his mistake and find success. For an instant the locked pair may swim with the drake clutching the back of the hen's crest in his red beak, the hen not quite drowning. The it will be over. The two ducks may never approach each other again, their species' habit being to put on flashy nuptial plumage and choose new partners every spring.

When the flocks are far from shore, I sometimes watch their dives and reappearances over the backs of browsing geese and pheasants. Then the ducks' fleetness forms a living fringe that extends the margins of the land. Occasionally the telescope picks up a raft of forty or fifty scaups out near the islands, which are several hundred yards away. When they're not feeding, these birds bob along the shelf of the Sound, their white abdomens bookended by dark breasts and rumps.

As the diving ducks become increasingly restless prior to their departure for nesting, great and snowy egrets and the black- and yellow-crowned nightherons arrive to stand motionless along the water's edge. They gather their bodies into S's and hunches and other uncomfortable-looking postures that they appear to hold for weeks at a time. By late in the month the sheltered waters of the Sound seem drained of quickness, as if skateboarders had somehow become supplanted by aloof royals.

The herons do not starve. Their energy is simply different from the ducks': it's spent in rhythms of boom and bust. After a long period of immobility, a neck lunges violently toward a fish in the shallows—the Sandman with a seizure.

Casts of characters replace one another here predictably over the course of seasons. Yet there are moments when the world seems unrehearsed. On April 17, the mewings of cedar waxwings caused me to look up into the crown of a cedar rooted a quarter of the way down the rocky shore. Thirty of the birds were beginning to feed there, fluttering while they tried to balance on the berry-rich branches. As they fell silent with feasting, the movement of their many wings gave the tree itself a sense of lightness, as if it, too, vibrated in the pale air.

I watched the acrobats for several minutes. In groups of three and four they began to fly from the needled greenery onto stones beneath it, where runoff from the previous evening's rain formed tiny rivulets and pools. Though waxwings are terrestrial birds, these individuals slaked their thirst just above the tide line before they flew back up to their tree. They dropped and returned, dropped and returned, with a regularity that bridged water and land like a tangible line.

Soon the entire flock moved to the deciduous tree next door. Its limbs were still winter-bare, and I could see the waxwings clearly. Their dramatic black masks hinted of bandits as the birds sat fluffed up against the cold. They peeled out, kissed the cedar in passing, and evaporated en masse.

A freshening wind off the water sometimes sends me inland a few yards, along a ragged lane that separates an old apple orchard from a grove of pines. I've seen as many as seven deer at a time explode quietly from these conifers, their tails erect and flashing white. Before I can breathe, they've leaped across the road and melted into the hardwoods and hemlocks that surround the gnarled fruit trees.

The end of this lane leads down to water protected from the wind. The route is an improvised affair—part road, part raccoon trail, part just the memory of picking my way along massive boulders and bedrock that give out onto sand. Slow going, it promises, to the extent that anything can, a close approach to creatures I don't otherwise see. In warm weather, if the tide is out beyond the derelict wall that forms a lagoon here, I have a chance of finding panicked flounders swimming among the clouds of seaweed. And sluggish, foot-long worms—blue ones, with apricot "legs" that move in waves. It is not possible— ever—to see the great blue heron at close range. As a pointed stone rises to bite me in the leg, the bird utters three nasal croaks and lifts off for more solitary shores.

Often when a big flyer leaves me to myself like this, I think about what a consummate spot I've come to. At odd moments in my previous, inland life I pondered what I would value most on land bordering water. Would broad stretches of sugary sand like the sand of the tropics be appealing? Would evergreens, marching along rock shores as in Maine? Or would I prize a wave-echoing sanctuary, a place to garden like the heaven Celia Thaxter chronicled in *An Island Garden*? Those flower colors, which artist Childe Hassam captured in the New Hampshire light! Those spire-like shapes, and vines that

Observers and Naturalists Explore the Marginal World

shade a lookout to sea! Amazingly, miraculously it seems at times, I found it all—trees, stone, sand, a seaside garden—the variety of being concentrated in this one glorious setting near a cove.

At the cove's head, within close proximity of the water, mountain laurel rises ten feet tall. The plants grow close together; in places their twisted trunks limit how far I can penetrate. Behind the laurel hells, which is what the dense patches are called, open forest floor is covered in matted leaves and in remnants of the plant called, quite wonderfully, wild sarsaparilla. Young sassafrasses stretch toward the light of clearings.

A small sand beach lies across the road from the laurels. Cradling it are thirty-foot-high curved banks of rock and soil. Trees extend down the banks to about fifteen feet above the tide line. The lower stone is devoid of major vegetation except in the few spots that hold marsh grasses. The overall configuration is that of a giant U, with the beach tucked into the closed curve between two headlands.

Alternating coves and headlands are typical along the north shore of the Sound. Michael Bell, author of *The Face of Connecticut*, compares the arrangement to a meter of poetry. "Like Shakespearean couplets," he writes, "place names along the Coast are paired, a 'convex' name followed by a 'concave' name: Hammonasset Point, Clinton Harbor; Bluff Point, Mumford Cove; Indian Neck, Branford Harbor. And on and on down the line."

This beach and cove, like many others along the Sound, attract beer cans and other throwaways that remind me I don't live near wilderness. Juice bottles, and braided ropes, and pink ribbons that wished someone three yards of "Happy Birthday Happy Birthday Happy Birthday," and aquamarine sea glass, and one-quart plastic containers printed with the words "Ursa Super Plus SAE 40 Heavy Duty Engine Oil" above the red-and-white Texaco star are all here.

After storms huge windrows of oyster shells lie tossed together on the sand with jingle shells and clamshells and blue-mussel valves, slipper shells, the occasional perfect conch. The whole lot often ends up bound into bolsters by seaweed. Giant waves fling the heaviest shells, oysters mostly, well above the coastal stone and onto the dark soil and leaf litter. In the calm that follows they look like bits of tissue strewn across the landscape.

An enormous white oak rooted on the bank overhangs this beach. I collect a handful of its acorns when I find them. They remind me of the thoroughly adolescent notes I used to leave curled inside acorns from my parents' yard. I wrote my brief announcements ("Meet me on the bridge, James Dean!" "Read this and die!") on strips of paper the size of those found in Chinese fortune cookies. After I rolled the strips into circles around my fingertips, I sealed the ends with saliva, removed each acorn's cap, and scooped out the pulp. When the hollow became large enough to hold a single scroll, I stuffed one inside and put the cap back on.

I thought of the ark as a tidy package of anticipation, since its existence was a secret known only to myself. I placed it and several others like it inside a dresser drawer in the house. I hoped someone would lift the linens and find the treasures. No one did. Nevertheless, I still think of acorns as vehicles for communication between unseen parties and myself. They are my own digital chip. There's a message in that drawer, still.

Here along the Sound the oak itself is the message. A predominantly oak forest hopscotched across much of southern New England during the 10,000 years that preceded the European immigration. (Historian William Cronon describes the precolonial woods as a "mosaic of tree stands with widely varying compositions.") The southern New England Indians burned and cleared many acres of woodlands. But their communities relocated seasonally, which gave altered tracts time to restore themselves.

British and other European settlers who began arriving here in the early seventeenth century hacked the forest down in the process of clearing the land for fuel and housing and a more permanent style of agriculture. The largest, straightest trees—white pines, initially—were singled out for the masts of sailing ships. By some estimates three-fourths of the southern New England woodlands were gone by 1840.

In 1864 George Perkins Marsh's ground-breaking book *Man and Nature* called attention to the devastating environmental effects of deforestation. Within the next two decades, partly in response and partly out of fear about the economic consequences of deforestation, many Northeastern farmers abandoned stony land that they or their forebears had cleared, fenced, and impoverished; and they didn't stop moving until they reached Connecticut's Western Reserve in Ohio or other areas in the fertile Midwest. Ironically, the migration gave the Northeastern forest a chance, once again, to begin healing on its own.

Now, little more than a century later, the oak forest has make a remarkable comeback. Stone walls originally built along the edges of fields currently lace up returning woods. Oaks and their co-dominants hickory and tulip poplar extend today from southern New England all the way into Tennessee.

As the trees have returned, wild turkey, black bear, and other native pre-Revolutionary forest creatures have re-established themselves as well. (The connection between oaks and deer ticks transmitting Lyme disease has only recently become clear: the numbers of infected insects are now known to increase dramatically in response to extra-large crops of acorns produced every three to four years. The huge crops initiate a population explosion in acorn-loving white-footed mice, from whom the ticks are infected with the disease-causing organism.)

Though the success of these woodlands is sweet, the Northeast's second-growth forests are never free of threats to their future. Development, acid rain, and clear-cutting are just a few. Nonetheless, the very fact of the woodlands' presence in this populous region of the country is nothing short of astounding. As Bill McKibben points out in his book *Hope, Human and Wild*, this is one of the unheralded triumphs of the past one hundred years of conservation history.

Intertidal Zone

As if frightened of waves, the thin-footed least sandpiper keeps from getting its feet wet. Or tries to. Its rounded profile moves on legs that are the written sign for kisses: XXXXX. My pen cannot draw the marks as fast as the legs can cross.

The bird surprises me by seeming unafraid. We share the spring rain. In its view I am a giant stillness, perhaps a tree, given my standing height and open green umbrella. I was planted before it flew onto the sloping sand ten feet away from me.

We are both here because we need something: the bundles of living and dead tidal fragments that have washed over the low seawall and onto the beach behind two side pockets of salt marsh. Drying now, the bundles form several sets of erratic peaks and dips, like suspect EKGs placed one above the other. Seen as a panorama, they repeat the crescent shape of the shoreward push of water and suggest an amphitheater's curved seats. For me the tidal arcs are undeciphered scripts that may contain some clue to this marginal place. For the peep, they hold food. The bird chases along and picks among the tidbits with its bill.

The tide is rising. Broad fingers of water gently lift the scallops of debris nearest the Sound, move them up the incline a fraction of an inch, and withdraw. They leave behind undulating, fibrous ridges. Above them, a previous tide left contoured clusters of shells and of marine algae that now look broiled by the sun to a rich maroon. Segmented, hollow stalks of a plant reminiscent of bamboo make up the shallow arc farthest from the water.

I glance down. The peep cannot ride a surge to shore, but falters in the same wave that drowns my shoes. These repeating crescents necklace the intertidal zone.

The oars fight the swift water. I cannot control the slant of their blades beyond the gunwale or the speed with which salty liquid pours off the blade ends after each hard stroke. The drops blend back into the Housatonic River beside the marsh called Nells Island. I cannot tell where the river stops and starts.

Neither can I fathom the tall cordgrass plants that live along this vague boundary. A single stem appears to thrive in every element but fire, and often in three at once.

I guide the dinghy into a thumb of quieter water. All around me, the strong current stretches the completely submerged plants into pale-green flames, transforming the stems into underwater lightning that zigzags and flickers. It bends and tugs lower portions of amphibious clumps as if they were handfuls of long hair. The exposed parts of those clumps are a farmer's field of leaves. I reach out and touch the pointed tips above August's rising tide.

Still farther in, entire stands of the grass breathe air. Water covers only the roots. Some stems culminate in steeples of tiny blond flowers that rise higher than my head. The plants return tapered reflections, dark on the silver-backed brine.

I cannot yet explain why some plants swim in place while other like them wade. I only know this pliancy contains the marsh.

The red swimming trunks of a man and the aquamarine bottle tilted to a woman's lips provide the only real color in my view of a distant island. It is the week prior to Memorial Day, not quite the Season. Yet the temperature is 80 degrees. In my telescope the couple walk barefoot, through heat waves, on the sand and the dun stones.

I scan the island's breadth. Near the water irregularly cantilevered ledges of brown overhang the dark sand, which toward the upland lightens to biscuit. The ledges' top surfaces want to be green. But they are not. From this distance they still seem a nondescript hue, a retarded stepchild of the sweet-smelling and already twice-mown grass beneath my feet.

The tide is falling. For a moment the shadow of a cloud cloaks the island in winter light, and even the subtle hues flatten. The surrounding water goes to slate. As the sun begins to saunter around a point, a wide band of blue-mussel-shell blue shows its cool tint. This island cummerbund is new, probably the legacy of last winter's pushy ice. Growing through it, or appearing to, is a line of green leaves. I judge them to be a foot tall. Behind the interwoven midden, single stems of last year's reed grass bend their tan plumes in the wind.

To the west an American oystercatcher in three-quarter profile—one, not the more usual pair—stands motionless as the sun returns the shock of hot orange to its beak. The island transcends this wait in time and light.

Sandra McPherson

Edge Effect

Arcadia Beach, Oregon

Even under a petroglyphic coastal overcast,
the sand flushes with a heat almost innocent,
unhurt as it burns, and thus it is so often
the purest place for us as children.

Now, when we imprint its edge, we know it will wash.
While we may squint, its glint is broken lenses.
Rubbing sand in my palm, I feel
vision in that hand. I see

to reach outside the wet breathing ribcage
of the horizon. At my blind side,
basalt: shearable, towerable, and able to abide
long hours and average eons. The cliff

houses its resident eyes in caves,
in nests, down crevices, in hives. Ships,
if sensitive, may feel watched. And underfoot,
beneath goat-stepping wet opals of old toenails,

whole orbits of washed-in sea gooseberries
kindle a gaze up every few feet, glassies
convexing the vista, oculists' models of the eye's
hermaphroditic twin, paired in one single flesh

as we, with two eyes in one head, are mated for sight.
Merely to move forward, I tear draglines
of gull prints, their scuff's slight stickiness
to land before they fly. Beneath gulls' high ride,

every second villager's the best imagist
he or she can be for sea stacks' rough allure
offshore. It's all the brush-fingered seem to see.
Their garden or kitchen studios hatch water-slender

watercolors, stout sumi-e outlines, stolen styles—
expropriated eyes—of great but landlocked artists
of any continent but this. They line the palisades,
hold mirrors to the sea, even gladly to fog.

The whole subduction zone
calls painter for a briefing every day—
and every day the wet description dries.
But here, far up the littoral, I feel another congregation;

I sense they are inspecting everything going by.
Backbone, backbone, backbone
of stones: Stack three, you have a god: a minor one
improves on none. It's a beach outing

for a gang of almighties. Each has a base, a trunk, a head,
a jutting chin. Or driftwood eyebrows.
They are more than pillars, rock on rock.
One probes with seaweed field glasses, alert with poise

not of the spy but of the curious, of the
minerally secure: What's to be seen, its body
language says, in this shred of humanity coursing
north? I feel weather-cut edges of one watcher

multiply, its brain stones' ordained postures aiming
at the sea through any shore-searcher in the way.
I feel stone necks risen to attention, each vertebra
an observation deck. Against the cliff a pantheon.

No shadows on their cheeks, they are not grim.
Gray, the are not whimsy. They stand up stark.

Observers and Naturalists Explore the Marginal World

What does "stark" mean anyway? Didn't Anne G. say
my father-in-law George's weightroom

"looked so stark"? Those dumbbells no longer made,
their deadweight laid out in increments
of hardship, increasing as hardship will, the barbells
propped like desolate businessmen at the final gate

of an airport concourse, present only to pick up
another drear and cunning company joe
whose name they hold penned on a pitiful placard. . . .
Stark. Can it mean pure? utter? simple? strong?

Sometimes I've seen eighty-year-old George standing
on his head, upside-down power, a restacking
of stones, right there on his gunboat-stern
cement basement floor, rebuilding, rearranging the cairn,

his body well-trained to be ancient, an Old World
stonemason. Why should bone be the most
solid-seeming part of a god around a mind?
Isn't a skull just a showcase for eyes? The fact that feet

in air come down, rocks tumble in time,
deduce to abdomen, thorax, small insect head,
almost back to diagram, that one
frost crystal brings the stone church to the ground,

excuses or defends erecting this toppler
while one can. Gods *are* hard. But longer life-tested sand
is soft. I hear one rock fall, the highest stone, on point,
fall backwards, and here we turn, we must turn, back,

as we would if we had any children with us,
not ready to take them beyond the falling of the gods
and yet permitting them to hear
the softness of their landings,

where wounds will bathe, bedded in sand,
one edge rushing over to enfold the other.

Love and Desire
in the Littoral Zone

As Kali and I reach the edge of town, we see the familiar sight of teenagers who have slept all night on the beach. There are four pairs of feet and only one arm poking out from a tumble of blankets. Kali is ever sensitive as she walks around the teenagers, but she cannot resist investigating the remains of their bonfire and disturbs their sleep when she accidentally collapses a small tower of cans they have erected around the fire pit. The night beach calls to potential lovers of all ages: they walk barefoot along the edge of the water, look at the stars, relax, talk, and sometimes snuggle into the sand. When I was a teenager, my interest shifted, for a while, from the birds, the waves, and the book I inevitably carried around to the activity in town and on the beach. It was as though one day I suddenly realized there were other people on the beach. I noticed, for the first time, something that had been going on all along—the rituals of beach mating behavior, of suntanning, of the ways boys and girls peeked at each other from their beach blankets, and of the desire that opens up along the shore.

The beach has long been a seductive place as well as a place for seduction. Before the proliferation of modern beach resorts with singles weekends and happy hours, poets, writers, philosophers, artists, and of course those who visited or lived by the coast understood the allure of the shore. Lena Lencek and Gideon Bosker note in their book *The Beach: The History of Paradise on Earth* that "the intense physical experience of the seashore—the scouring of the sand, the stroking of the wind, the slapping of the water—were interpreted by Romantics as impersonal analogues to erotic contact" (106). The shore often presented visitors with a sense of the forbidden as they moved away from solid ground and edged closer and closer to the wildness of the ocean. Too, beach attire presented men and women with new challenges to established moral views on how much of the body could or should be revealed. The bikini, introduced in 1946, was absolutely shocking and liberating, and it was inevitable. Love, romance, desire, and sex are all part and parcel of what takes place in the littoral zone.

In this section, the writers express various levels of desire; some show us a sexual fantasy, as does Emily Dickinson in her well-known poem, "Wild Nights—Wild Nights!" In *The Story of Avis,* Elizabeth Stuart Phelps paints, for her main character, an intimate awakening that takes place during a wild winter storm. Avis Dobell stands on a reef during the height of a storm when the male protagonist, Philip Ostrander, comes to her rescue. By the end of the experience, filled with all the fabled heroism of Saint George and the Dragon, Avis now sees Mr. Ostrander as a Scandinavian god. The storm awakens her desires and Phelps suggests her passionate nature in connection to the barely survivable storm.

Many of these writers express a sexual freedom, an escape from propriety that can be found at the coast as they experience the combination of the wildness of the ocean in conjunction with the safety of the land. These authors tell us how important it is for many of their characters to leave behind their domestic or other realities in order to experience a new or more open kind of intimacy in their lives.

Now that Kali has disturbed the tangle of people under the sandy damp blankets, I think we should move on and leave the young lovers to experience the remainder of their morning in peace. The next stretch of beach is more difficult to navigate, requiring a climb on some slippery rocks, but it is also a more dramatic stretch of coastline. I check to make sure Kali remains full of energy, give her some fresh water, and then we continue east.

Emily Dickinson

Wild Nights—Wild Nights!

Wild Nights—Wild nights!
Were I with thee
Wild Nights should be
Our luxury!

Futile—the Winds—
To a Heart in port—
Done with the Compass—
Done with the Chart!

Rowing in Eden—
Ah, the sea!
Might I but moor—Tonight—
In Thee!

I started Early—took my Dog

I started Early—took my Dog—
And visited the Sea
The Mermaids in the Basement
Came out to look at me—

And Frigates—in the Upper Floor
Extended Hempen Hands—
Presuming Me to be a Mouse
Aground—upon the Sands—

But no Man moved Me—till the Tide
Went past my simple Shoe—
And past my Apron—and my Belt
And past my Bodice—too—

And made as He would eat me up—
As wholly as a Dew
Upon a Dandelion's Sleeve—
And then—I started—too—

And He—He followed—close behind—
I felt His Silver Heel
Upon my Ankle—Then my Shoes
Would overflow with Pearl—

Until We met the Solid Town—
No One He seemed to know—
And bowing—with a Mighty look—
At me—The sea withdrew—

Elizabeth Stuart Phelps

. . . .

From *The Story of Avis*

> My saul, ye maun blythe-bid
> the Lord, ettlin' his carriage
> the cluds; on wings o' the
> win' making' speed:
> Errand-runner he make o' the
> blasts, and loons o' his ain,
> *the bleeze o'lowe.*
> —Scotch Psalms

If Philip Ostrander expected Miss Dobell to join his German class, he was doomed to what it is not exactly correct to call a disappointment. Probably he did expect it. The other young ladies had all joined. Young ladies were apt to join any classes which he chanced to open without undue reluctance. He had been in the frequent way of this sort of thing, in the natural course of that griping struggle with ways and means which had brought the keen-eyed,

Love and Desire in the Littoral Zone

poverty-ridden boy from an uncultivated New-Hampshire home to one of the most brilliant positions which New England had then to offer.

For it was now considered, as Avis heard from her father when she had been at home a little while, quite assured that Mr. Ostrander would ultimately take the geological chair through the probation of the assistant professorship. True he was not a Harmouth graduate, this the professor regretted keenly; but his shining talents burned the more conspicuously for this disadvantage. And that he had refused a position in his Alma Mater to compass those two years in Germany, by which a promising young man expected, with some confidence, fifteen or twenty years ago, to become immediately "distinguished," had naturally recommended him to the Harmouth perceptive Faculty.

Coy was right when she said that Mr. Ostrander was thought in Harmouth to be remarkably versatile.

At all events, a versatility which can be converted into a dollar an hour is not to be despised by a Harmouth tutor; and Ostrander held the rudder of his yet unanchored craft with a very easy hand.

In this matter of the German lessons—which, requiring but the slightest type of attention, left him space for a good deal of revery,—he was conscious of watching narrowly to see what Miss Dobell would do. During the afternoons which he spent in the sunny parlors of the Harmouth ladies, with the prettiest girls in the city chirping gutturals at his feet, or in the evenings which he devoted to Barbara Allen's fine renderings of Schumann, he made no attempt to deny that the young artist occupied certain large untraveled spaces upon the map of his fancy. It is more than possible, that if Avis had drifted into the German class; if there had been established between them that time-honored relation of master and pupil, which, always fraught with the sweetest possible perils to man and woman, is more stimulating to the imagination of the pupil than of the master; if Avis, too, had sat and chirped at his feet, then—well, *what* then?

Possibly Ostrander assumed that then the delicate poem opened one day at vespers in the Madeleine would hardly have been found worth the reading, and the radiant, undiscovered country would have scarcely compelled the explorer over the threshold.

Possibly, too, both nature and experience would have taken his brief, had he been tried for this assumption. Ostrander, at this period of his life, protected himself against the ambuscades of his own temperament with that forethought which an unmarried man of thirty is clearly expected to have acquired. But he experienced a singular sense of relief and expectancy, when several weeks had passed, and Miss Dobell did *not* join the German class.

That sibyl of the Madeleine perhaps possessed the fine old classic instinct which every year he thought grew rare and rarer among women. She must, it seemed, be absolutely sought.

Some pressing Faculty business took him, before the vacillating April days were quite over, to Professor Dobell's house. He called at dusk, and aunt Chloe invited him to tea. He hesitatingly refused; but when she said,—

"Then come next Friday, Mr. Ostrander: it is a long time since we have had the pleasure, and I notice my brother is always in good spirits when you have been to see us," he accepted the invitation at once. He did not in the least attempt to wrestle with his motive in this innocent bit of scene-shifting, but allowed himself to be led blindfold by it. His wish to see that girl again had become imperative. Ostrander had the deepest respect for whatever he found really imperious in himself.

With Friday, the New-England April weather had assumed one of the caprices which we tolerate so tenderly in any born coquette; and snow fell heavily. The day before had been as gentle as a baby's dream. Avis worked in the studio in the garden without a fire; and one of the college-boys brought Ostrander a tuft of saxifrage from the pale-green promise of the meadows. That morning the wind lay in the east sleepily enough; but by noon the air was blurred with the large, irregular spring flakes, as if Nature had taken a wayward fancy to fold herself in a Japanese screen. In the afternoon, when Ostrander had strolled out of town, and down the shore to see the surf, the drifts were already piling high. He tramped through them lightly enough, in the rubber-boots which are the chief end of man in New England, and with his soft silk cap drawn over his eyes, and his powerful figure bent a little with the first languid action of a wrestler upon it, yielded himself to the intoxication of the winter shore.

Few greater passions pass more readily into the permanence and fidelity of love than the passion for the sea. Ostrander had an elemental kinship with it in himself, which every year of his life had intensified. He sometimes wished that he was quite sure he cared as much for any human creature as he did for Harmouth Harbor. He struck off down the drifted beach toward the Light. The wind was in his face. Through the opaque air he could see rudely defined, like the values of a vast, unfinished sketch, the waves leap and slip and fall upon the glazed cliffs, and across the narrow reef from which the light-house shot sheer against the sky. He pushed on down, perhaps a mile, to find a shelter; and there, with the tide at his feet and the spray in his face, flung himself upon the freezing rocks, possessed with a kind of fierce but abundant joy.

Love and Desire in the Littoral Zone

The Light stood just across the bay where the Harbor widened to the sea; it might have been a dozen rods or so from where Ostrander sat. The reef, traversable at low tide, ran from it to a gorge within the cliff. The well-defined metallic tints common to the New-England coast—the greens and reds and umbers, the colors of rust, of bronze, of ruins—covered the reef. The gorge was a vein of deep purple lava, which to Ostrander's educated eye told the story of a terrible organic divorce.

The wave that tore its heart out at his feet was throbbing green; but, beyond that, the inrolling tide, the chalky outline of the Light, the harbor-mouth, the narrowing horizon, the low sky, all the world, lay gray beneath the footsteps of the dizzy snow. The wind was rising from the sullenness of a blow to the anger of a gale; and the crash of the breakers which he could see had a shrill, petulant sound set to the boom of those unseen across the bay.

Was it the lawlessness of all this, or the law of it, that thrilled Ostrander? Was it the passion, or the purpose, which commanded him? Was the eternal drama of unrest an outlet, or an inlet, to his nature; an excitant, or a sedative? It were hard to say. The young man asked himself the question, but found a shrug of his fine shoulders the most intelligent answer at his command.

Or perhaps we must admit that there was as much rheumatism as philosophy in that shrug. It certainly was growing very cold, and darkening fast.

Ostrander had been somewhat sheltered by the cliff at whose feet he sat; so much so, that he was quite unaware of the extent to which the wind had risen. A man does not sit very long upon an ice-covered rock; but a few moments will suffice to let loose the prisoned temper of an April gale. When he turned to get back to the beach, he found the wind racing through the lava-gorge at the rate of perhaps eighty miles an hour, and the snow seething under his feet before the first oncoming of the heavy, breeze-swept tide.

He stopped to pull up his coat-collar, as he would now have the storm at his back; as he did so, the fog-bell began to toll from the Light, and he turned instinctively at the sound.

At that moment he saw a figure between himself and the light-house, moving slowly shorewards along the reef. It was the figure of a woman—it was the figure of a lady, slight and delicately dressed. It was not so dark but that he could see that she moved with great difficulty. The reef was jagged as a saw, and glared with the thin, blue, cruel ice. It ran at an angle to the northward, and took the whole sweep of the easterly gale.

Ostrander, as he watched her, felt the blood tingle about his heart. He believed that there was but one lady in Harmouth who would have taken a walk to the light-house on such a day. Did Miss Dobell know that not one woman in one hundred could get across that reef in a blow like this? The light-keeper must have been mad to let her start.

It seemed that the light-keeper himself was coming to that late and useful conclusion. Dimly through the snow Ostrander saw the flash of the lantern with which he had accompanied her to the reef's edge. There was still much sickly light in the air, and the lantern shone pale and ghastly. The man gesticulated violently, and seemed to be shouting unheard words. Ostrander remembered suddenly how shallow the rocks grew in sloping to the little island. The rising tide had probably cut between the keeper and the lady, and by this time distinctly severed them.

Ostrander hesitated no longer, but ran swiftly out upon the reef.

She was making her way valiantly enough, perhaps without any more than a vague and not unpleasant consciousness of possible peril. The gale took the heavy drapery of her skirts and long waterproof cloak in a cruel fashion, winding them about and about her limbs. She looked very tall in the waning light, and there was a certain grandeur in her motions. She stood out against the ice-covered rock like a creature sprung from it, sculptured, primeval, born of the storm.

As Ostrander ran along the reef, he saw her stop or stagger, hesitate, then stoop slowly, and take to her hands and knees. She rose again in a moment, and stood cowering a little, afraid or unable to stretch her full height to the force of the gale, which seemed to Ostrander something satanic, now that he was in the teeth of it upon that reef. Could a blind, insensate force of Nature, so many feet of atmospheric pressure to the square inch, obedient to a powerful, and, on the whole, kindly-disposed Creator, set the whole weight of its brute organism to work with this devilish intelligence, to beat a delicate woman, blow by blow, to death? There seemed something so profoundly revolting to Ostrander's manhood in this idea, just then, that it did not occur to him, that he was not the only man in the world who had ever experienced his first genuine defiance of fate in some stress of peril sprung upon a woman whom he would have given— What would Ostrander have given to save her?

It seemed to him at that moment that he would have given his young life; for as he crept along the reef—now swiftly, that he might reach her, and then slowly, that he might not startle her—she threw up her arms, and fell.

He came leaping from rock to rock, and would possibly have plunged into the water; but through the dusk he heard her voice.

She said, "I have not fallen into the water. Can you get over to that great purple rock?"

She spoke so quietly, that he was completely re-assured about her until he crawled over under the prodding gale, and, dashing the snow out of his eyes, looked down. She had slipped from the edge of the reef, and hung at full-length along the slope of a huge bowlder. The slope was perhaps twenty feet long, and very gradual: it was covered with ice. The spray froze in his face as he looked over. The water was breaking across her feet. She clung with both hands to the polished edge of the bowlder: there was blood upon the ice where she had clutched and beaten it away. But perhaps the fact which came most distinctly to Ostrander's consciousness was, that the tips of her fingers were absolutely without color.

The first thing which he did was to tear off his fur gloves, and, leaning over the reef, stretch both his warm hands upon hers. The water sucked between the reef and the bowlder in a narrow, inky stream.

"You are right," she said: "they *were* getting frost-bitten. There. Now I can hold myself easily enough as long as I must. Mr. Ostrander, do you find it very slippery upon the reef?"

"Not in the least," said Ostrander grimly, grinding his heel into the ice.

"Can you brace yourself sufficiently to put one foot against the bowlder?"

"I should hope so."

"Only one foot, please, and only one hand. Do not try to get upon the bowlder, and do not step between the bowlder and the reef. Do you under-stand?"

"Miss Dobell, give me one hand now—slowly. Raise your fingers, one at a time, and put them into mine."

"Do you understand that you are not to come upon the bowlder?"

"If you do not give me your hand immediately, I cannot possibly answer for what I shall do."

"Promise me, that, if I slip, you will let go."

"I promise nothing. Give me your hand!"

"Promise that you will not let me drag you after me."

"I promise any thing. For God's sake, give me, this instant, the fingers of your right hand!"

She gave them to him with that, obediently enough. She lifted them one by one from the ice; one by one he slipped his own under them, slid the palm of his hand slowly under the palm of hers; so cautiously, but with the full prehensile force of her own supple touch to help him, reached and grasped her wrist. Avis had firmer fingers than most women; but they were supple as withes.

"Now, the other!"

They managed it with the other more nervously, for the water was now dashing freely in their faces.

"Now I am quite firm upon the reef. I shall draw you easily up. Do you trust me perfectly that I know what I am about?"

"Perfectly. Do you remember, that, in case of an accident, only *one* must slip."

"I remember."

"Very well."

"Are you ready?"

"Quite ready."

It seemed to Avis but a moment's work; and they sat crouched and panting side by side upon the broad surface of the reef. She could not possibly have said how she came there. Her most definite thought was a perfectly new conception of the power of the human hand. Ostrander's controlled, intelligent grasp challenged the blind mood of the gale: it was iron and velvet, it was fury and pity; as if the soul of the storm had assumed the sense of a man.

As soon as might be, for the tide was rising fast, they made their way across the reef, and sat down for a moment's breath upon the shore. Neither had yet spoken. Ostrander had not, indeed, released the grip which he had of Miss Dobell's hand. Avis was the first to break the silence which had fallen upon them. She said,—

"I am afraid I have killed the bird."

"I beg your pardon?" said Ostrander, staring.

"I went over to the Light to see about the birds that are brought by the storm," said Avis, exactly as if nothing had happened. "The keeper gave me a little blue-jay that he picked up under the light-house. He thought it might live; and I wrapped it in my cloak-pocket. Ah, see! No: it is alive."

"Give it to me," said Ostrander, adopting the young lady's tone very quietly. "You are too much chilled to keep it. And now are you able to get on a little? The tide is becoming really troublesome; and the walk is longer than I wish it were."

He took the bird, and, unfastening his coat, wrapped it in his breast. Avis, looking up through the dusk, thought how tenderly the little act was done.

"The poor thing flutters against my heart," said Ostrander in his exquisitely-modulated tones. He had one of those voices into which all the tenderness of the nature ows readily, like the meadows which are the first to receive the freshet of the river. And then Ostrander was really sorry for the bird.

Avis made no reply. She took his arm in silence, and in silence they passed through the lava-gorge, and out upon the drifted beach. There she stopped and looked back. The fog-bell was tolling steadily, and under the gray sheen of the snow the grayer mist stole in.

"I have always wondered exactly what made this gorge," she said, quite as if she and Ostrander had only come out on a little geological expedition. "What was torn out of the heart of the rock?"

"Nothing was torn out," said Ostrander. "The two sides of that gorge are thrust apart by flood or fire. They were originally of one flesh. It was a perfect primeval marriage. The heart of the rock was simply broken."

Avis stood for a moment in the purple shadow of the cleft, into which the water was now bounding high. A certain awe fell upon them both as Ostrander spoke. Instinctively they glanced from rent side to rent side of the divorced cliff, and then into one another's faces. Stirred by the strain of peril and the thrill of safety, Avis's excited imagination took vivid hold of the story of the rock. It seemed to her as if they stood there in the wake of an awful organic tragedy, differing from human tragedy only in being symbolic of it; as if through the deep, dumb suffering of Nature, the deeper because the dumber, all little human pains went seething shallowly, as the tide came seething through the gorge. In some form or other, the motherhood of earth had forecast all types of anguish under which her children groaned; had also thrilled, perhaps, beneath all forms of joy. Suppose the bridal gladness or the widowed pathos of a rock. Suppose the sentient nature of a thing adapted to its reticence. What story, then, in sea or shore, in forest, hills, and sky, in wind and fire, in all things whose mighty lips were sealed! Suppose she herself, gone mute as the mutest of them, cognizant of their secret, joined to their brotherhood, were dashing on the tide across the lava-gorge.

As they turned away, she leaned rather heavily upon his arm, and tremulously said,—

"I suppose, Mr. Ostrander, if it had not been for you"—

"Ah, no, no!" interrupted Ostrander quickly. "The light-keeper would have got out the boats. I have only saved you a pretty cold bath. Pray let us not talk of that.—But indeed," he added, abruptly changing his tone, "I begin to understand why the people in the novels always *are* saving each other's lives. It is just another instance of the absolute naturalness of much that we are all used to call unnatural in fiction."

"And why?" asked Avis, without the least apparent awkwardness.

"Because nothing acquaints two people like the unconventionalities of danger. It seems to me—pray pardon me—as if I had known you for a long time."

Avis made no reply; and they struck out upon the drifting shore. They seemed to have been taken up now, and driven by the gale behind them, as if they had been scooped into the hollow of a mighty hand.

"And nothing isolates," continued Ostrander, "like the interchange of emotions which any such experience involves. See now," added the young man, looking about the desolate shore, "how lonely we seem. It would be easy to think that there was no other life than ours in all this world."

He turned as he spoke, and would have stood face to the wind; but the mighty hand which had gathered them swept them imperiously on, as if it conceived them to have been bent upon some terrible errand of its own.

Perhaps Ostrander, too, had received quite his share of the excitement that April afternoon. He was in some sense rather a guarded man in his habit of speech among women, sufficiently cautious not to involve himself in those little ambiguous sallies of the lip to which young ladies attach an importance which a man reserve for affairs. He caught himself in thinking that he did not know another woman in the world to whom he could have made that speech without a savage and humiliating fear of misinterpretation.

With a little of the madness of any rarely-tasted license, he plunged on,—

"How like you it was, in the midst of all that, to tell me to get upon the *purple* rock!"

"How do you know it was like me?" laughed Avis, as they struggled through the snow.

"I think I have always known what would be like you," said the young man in a lower voice, "since I saw you in the Madeleine."

There is a certain shade of expression peculiar to a man's face, which every woman knows, but few understand. It falls as far short of the flash of over-mastering feeling on the one hand as it does of self-possession on the other. Its wearer is at once constrained to admire, and predetermined not to love; and precisely in so far as he is unconscious even to that predetermination does this delicate play of the features take on the appearance of the strongest emotion.

It was not so dark but that Avis, looking up through the storm, saw that sensitive expression dart across Ostrander's face. Then the lines about his mouth subsided, his eye cleared, he lifted his head, and it was gone. She need not be a vain woman, only an inexperienced one, who read in such a facial change a tenderness which it by no means bespeaks. Avis, being neither the one nor the other, suffered nothing more than a slight feeling of surprise.

"I suppose," he added, after a few minutes' profound attention to the problem: given darkness, a lady, and a snow-drift four feet high, how to flounder through the latter with that grace which it will be a pleasure to reflect upon to-morrow,—"I suppose *you* now went home, and thought what a rude American you had seen. I was glad when I saw you come into the Chaucer Club. I have always felt that I owed you an apology for that stare."

He said this with the manner of one who is conscious of having said an uncommon thing, and hastens to wrench out of it a common-place significance.

"Not in the least," said Avis with composure. "I owe the making of a very satisfactory little sketch to you. I put you into sepia, on a neutral gray. Couture took a great fancy to that sepia."

"If I have been in any sense the cloak across which your royal feet have stepped upon the muddy road to glory, or the royal road to glory, or—my metaphor is gone mad, and I give it up," said Ostrander, with the carelessness which conceals rather than expresses meaning. "At all events, I am glad you made the sketch. We are getting along bravely. Are you very cold?"

"Not much. Only my hand which I bruised. Thank you! No, I should be very unhappy to take your glove. How is my bird, Mr. Ostrander?"

"I forgot the bird!"

He sought for it very gently with his free hand, and said,—

"It lives. It is quite warm. But it does not stir."

"Why," said Avis as they drew in sight of her father's house—"why should we disturb my father by telling him about that slip upon the rock?"

"Why, indeed? You are very wise and right. We will not talk of it."

"I have been away from him so many years," said Avis in the almost timid way she had when her gentlest feeling was aroused, "that, now I am come back, I find I like to spare him all possible pain, even a little one like this. And *now,* Mr. Ostrander, how is my bird?"

The light fell full upon his face when they stopped without the door. The snow lay lightly on his beard and bright hair. He looked like a young Scandinavian god.

He slipped his hand very tenderly under his shaggy coat as he stood there looking down at her.

"I hope all is well with the poor thing," said he. But the bird upon his heart lay dead.

Sea Longing

A thousand miles beyond this sun-steeped wall
   Somewhere the waves creep cool along the sand,
   The ebbing tide forsakes the listless land
With the old murmur, long and musical;
The windy waves mount up and curve and fall,
   And round the rocks the foam blows up like snow,—
   Tho' I am inland far, I hear and know,
For I was born the sea's eternal thrall.
I would that I were there and over me
   The cold insistence of the tide would roll,
   Quenching this burning thing men call the soul,—
Then with the ebbing I should drift and be
   Less than the smallest shell along the shoal,
Less than the sea-gulls calling to the sea.

Woman on Sand

my eye the coastline disappears on
gray horizon he moves a vision a child searches
for seashells amid litter beer cans cig butts
broken glass my heart the pieces bleed
cool water/dead cum

the loving is the needing

he shows me the sculpture
the naked woman of sand a silicone siren
entrenched in the music of her pain
abandoned to inquisitive eyes
her lover gone on to greater adventures

the loving is the healing

yes. i could smother the child/pillow to face
the fears and trusts. what must be done
end suffering/torture/starvation
love does the right thing in his eyes
mercy. free him. anguish. free him
move on. urban pastures, slum sky

the loving is the wanting

we travel. i am aware of his question
it beats against my heart, tries to get in
someday. maybe. i will answer. when time
for now there is the long hard drive
speeding up slowing down taking curves

the loving is

cruising. our arms. clutching
each other. tongues deep into mouth and throat
become one/the other. embrace/the beach the wave.
i can't swim it covers me. i drown

the next day they find me on the shore
he's gone on to other adventures

the loving. the killing

The Mapmaker's Daughter

the geography of love is terra infirma

it is a paper boat
navigated by mates
with stars in their eyes

cartographers of the fiery unknown

it is the woman's sure hand
at the helm of twilight, the salt
compass of her desire

the map of longing is at the edge
of two distant bodies

it is the rain that launches thirst
it is the palm leaf floating on waters
far from shore

the secret passage into the interior
is in my intemperate estuary

the sweet and languorous flowering
is in the caliber of your hands

the circular motion of our journeying
is the radius of sky and sea, deep
territories we name
after ourselves

Mary Hood

· ·

First Things First

It was early September when the whales came back, bringing sorrow with them. The Captain was away, far out in the Stream, a day beyond the horizon. Deep-sea charter. As he left, he had given Faye a list (the way he generally did) of little deeds to accomplish: to ask, to pay, to tell, to look for, to clean, to find, to write, to cancel, to call—that sort of list, a wife's list—and also to buy stamps and get to the bank. Definitely to get to the bank. He had underlined it.

So Faye had asked, and paid, and told, and found; she had written and called and canceled and cleaned; she had bought the stamps. Now there was only the banking left to be done and it was Saturday and the bank closed at noon precisely. Since there was plenty of time, and the weather was good, she walked.

That big house the Captain had built Faye out on the bluff stood about a mile from the village. A fine low modern house with a lot of glass, but dark, even at noon still dark and cool because of the sheltering oaks. The housekeeper bicycled away down the shell road to her own family comforts at night. When the Captain was late, or away overnight, Faye's mother worried.

"Come home," Mrs. Parry would tell her every time. She said it that September morning too. They'd talk on the phone all hours, not long distance. Her mother had that to be thankful for. But there was that gulf between them, more daunting than open water, which Faye's marriage to what Mrs. Parry thought of as a "foreigner" had only widened.

"He was born here, same as I was," Faye uselessly pointed out.

"His mama don't talk to me," Mrs. Parry said. "She's got my number."

"She doesn't speak English!" Faye said.

"That's what I said," Mrs. Parry said. "He's foreign."

Faye had to laugh.

Mrs. Parry had been a naturalized war bride, convent-educated, with a French father and a Vietnamese mother. Her English was good enough for running a business, though she still counted and kept books in Vietnamese, prayed in Latin, and sang in French.

"Road runs both ways, Mama," Faye always reminded her. "You come here."

Her mother was welcome and knew it. But she had the shop to run—couldn't just lock the door and go flittering, as she called it. Still, if she had taken the notion to find Faye and spend the day with her, she could have been over to the bluff in a blink, by boat or car, both—thanks to the Captain—at her disposal. Leagues farther by land, of course, because of having to go around to North End and cross the gut on the drawbridge—sometimes raised, stopping the whole world for a bargeload of pine stumps or a dallying yacht or a string of luckless shrimpers—but even so, the causeway, the land, was her choice when she chose. Faye was like her in that, in preferring the land route. They both loved the water, and Faye even had a handful of diving medals, but that was in a pool, not open water. They weren't good sailors. Brave enough, but seasickly.

Through the pay telescope in the municipal park, Faye's mother kept a weather eye on things across the marsh inlet. She'd walk down there after work most evenings, with far from the random change in her pocket, to swivel the scope around like a pro, fixing the focus on the Captain's roof and sunset-shining windows straight across the sound. Madonna blue shutters, heavenly blue, Faye called it, matching it in the morning glories she planted on the back terrace.

"Everything the Captain has is touched with blue," Faye had told her mother early on, as an icebreaker, a casual remark to get the conversation on track. Her mother liked the color blue. "The name of his boat is the *Blue Lady*," Faye added.

"In Spanish?" her mother accused, leaning way into the dryer drum to haul out another armload for fluff and fold.

"No," Faye said.

They worked on the load together, efficient from long practice, eyes as blank and hands as quick as a bank teller's. They didn't talk, but this wasn't a quarrel. The machines were very loud back there, and Faye liked to wear her little pocket radio and earphones to drown it out. If her mother needed to say something, she'd reach across and touch Faye's arm—they worked that close—and Faye would drop the headset on her neck and listen. They had hand signals too, for when words weren't needed, and a light as well as a buzzer for the drive-through window.

Some sudden niceness, a deference to Faye's maidenhood, prompted Mrs. Parry to reach out, and sort the men's underwear from the heap and fold it herself, as though Faye might Get Ideas. Faye was grown, graduated, bound to marry someday, yet when Mrs. Parry studied her and thought, Soon, she

Love and Desire in the Littoral Zone

shook her head no, and would go on shaking it. She was muttering to herself when she went to wait on the customer at the drive-through window, and she was still muttering when she came back.

"How do you know his boat's name is in Spanish?" Faye asked, about fifteen minutes later, not hostile, not defensive, but with that same friendly everyday open-faced look that had led her through high school to honors on the debate team.

"Lucky guess," Mrs. Parry said.

"Nope," Faye said. "It's in English same as our shop sign."

"How do you know?"

Faye smiled. "I asked."

"*Blue Lady*," her mother said. "All blue? Blue and white? Some folk paint that blue on sills and doors to ward off the evil eye."

"*Some*," Faye said. You mean voodoo . . . That's not why, so far as I know," Faye said, after thinking it over. "He likes blue!" There was still a lot to guess about, but it proved true that the Captain was as proper a Catholic as a proud man—with no faith in luck or island mojo—could be. There Faye differed. She couldn't take things easy—as a matter of dealt cards, fated events, and *que será*. Susceptible to anguish over possibilities, prey to alarms for love, she believed in intercession, did what she could to prevent harm's befalling.

When they were newly married, she used to go down to their little dock and hold up the gas lantern to guide his launch safe home, even in bad weather, especially in bad weather, as though the light in her hands had drawing power amplified by love. It never once—that mote of faith and home fire—winked out in the wind, though the storm flags on the Coast Guard pole might be snapping flat square open: small craft warnings. Only a few nights that bad; the Captain was too keen a soul at his work, held his craft and crew too dear to risk them in critical winds.

Sometimes Faye's mother would struggle down to the park and aim the viewfinder of the pay scope across the whitecaps, trying to see Faye's lovelight. Abroad in weather like that, because driven by devotion, same as Faye. Simple enough to figure. If Faye didn't answer her phone, her mother knew what to dread, where to head, bundled against the elements. Faye's was the greater peril. The park at least had handrails and streetlights, and if you fell, you landed on earth.

"A mother's love is one kind of suffering," according to Father Ockham, Mrs. Parry's priest, "with the stages built in. Like the Stations of the Cross." Love like Faye's had precedents too, but no path. Like wildfire. Inviting backfire to keep it in bounds. "Oh, she can be a queen, no arguing with her," Mrs. Parry admitted. "Which is to say," Father Ockham agreed, "she's nineteen."

The Captain had a telescope of his own, but Faye couldn't see her mother's roof from there, because of the jog in the street and the trees, not because she had never bothered to look back. She wasn't ashamed of Parry's A-1 Dry Cleaning and Laundry, or of growing up over the shop. She even joked that it was the steam that kept her wavy hair—heavy, heavy, never cut in her whole life, caught in a barrette so it swung almost to her waist in back—from being as straight as her mother's. She would have gone on working there after marriage if the Captain had let her.

From the day Faye had been able to print both letters and numbers, she had helped in the shop. Her parents had set up a milk crate for her to stand on and she served as their counter girl, quick at numbers, and good at remembering faces and orders. She could make reliable change from first grade on, and could answer the phone sensibly when her father was out making deliveries and her mother was still learning to speak English. Faye was their only child.

The Sisters at Saint Joseph skipped her forward across second grade and fourth, and she repeated the year in between, when her father died; Faye was only eight. For a long time they had looked up, she and her mother both, when the shop door opened and the little bells rang, expecting him to come back. The usual staggering and drift of sudden loss. Bankruptcy loomed, then receded.

Mrs. Parry—who had never learned to drive, and preferred to go by foot or on bicycle—hired a driver for the delivery van, but relied on Faye more and more. The business slowly righted, like their life. When Faye turned sixteen and graduated from her learner's permit, she took over the deliveries before and after school. That saved on payroll.

Mrs. Parry didn't just hand Faye the keys to the van and say, "Go!" Because she was small and plain, and because Faye was not, Mrs. Parry signed them both up for self-defense lessons—evenings—and together they learned precaution. As for the van, Faye had to promise seatbelt always, hitchhikers never, doors locked all around, no entering homes of strangers, and this: "Assume it's you or them. If they're going to kill you, make them do it first, don't let them drag you off somewhere and strew your bones in sawgrass so deep we won't find you till marsh hen season." Faye always laughed and promised. And kept the gas tank full, good rubber on the wheels. Practical paranoia. It wasn't retreads or blems that blew, front and rear curbside, and left her stranded out there on the dead end at Cedar Point with only one spare tire and nothing to do but knock at a stranger's door.

Love and Desire in the Littoral Zone

That time of day, no one was home. All the men off fishing or at the docks wishing they were. Wives labored in their hairnets and rubber boots at the crab plant, or were pulling linens and turning out rooms at the motels on the strip, or keeping books at the icehouse, checking groceries at the plaza, flipping burgers or waffles, whatever. Gainfully employed, every one of them. Grandfolks too. No old-timers sitting on their porches. All go-getters, not a thriftless soul around, just dogs, a cat on a window ledge, chickens in a backyard, a few gulls and grackles skulking around the garbage cans.

Faye was out of luck. She went house to house, knocking, calling. A quiet street, a shortcut, Faye had hoped, around heavy traffic on the boulevard heading to the toll bridge. A dead end, she now saw. A block from the river, the houses lichen-colored and some boarded up, sagging, next to newer little cottages of cinderblock and jumbo brick, so small they appeared to have burst at the seams and let life spill out into the grassless yards, toy-strewn, bright flowers in gaudy containers and beds outlined in shells. From the trees, like graybeard moss, the nets hung to be mended.

Finally Faye saw an open door, daylight spearing straight through an old two-story house front to back, through patched screen doors. She knocked and knocked. Calling hello, leaning against the screen, her eyes shielded by her hands, calling "Someone? Anyone!"

At last, footsteps. Slow, heavy. A nightmare of a noise, unsteady, coming on. What had Faye interrupted? She almost fled. If she had!"

He loomed, rumpled, wordless. "Big man," she told her mother later. Before she finished describing, Mrs. Parry said, certain, "Tom Rios." Not a bad guess; not a bad man. His brother was the one with the devil-in-a-white-shirt reputation, not Tom.

Faye didn't know any of them, or anything about them. Different parish. Besides, her mother never let her loiter around Lupo's, by the docks. Brought her up on Main Street, not the bay. Walked with her to parochial school, teaching her eyes down, no glancing in windows, no swaying or dawdling past those balmy doorways of the warehouses breathing out their exotic airs from bales and bundles and piles of hides and herbs, the sweet stores of vanilla deertongue, clover, coffee and tea and tobacco, spices, lumber, crates of plunder stenciled from all over the world. What child wouldn't stare and dream? But Mrs. Parry nipped her along, like a stock dog after a stray lamb in wolf territory.

Bayfront. Lupo's the capital of that rough ward. Where Cuban captains and crews took their time over Cafe Bustelo—"Terrible coffee," Faye's mother complained, judging not by the taste but by the stains, having had the contract for those linens, weekly pickup and drop-off, couldn't *get* those stains out, had to agree about that from the first order—and read the newspapers and argued and bragged. When Lupo's rebuilt after the fire, they put in dinettes and booths, all Formica, and went to Styrofoam cups and plastic spoons. Paper napkins in little dispensers on the tables. "Flimsy, no class," Mrs. Parry decided. No more checkered cloths, no curtains at all, kitchen towels done by the linen service that did for the motels on the interstate. Progress. That was a major customer Mrs. Parry had lost, in the rocky years before Faye got her driver's license, so she had never gone in there, never knew who Tom Rios was till she walked up to his house and said, "I've had an accident. Truck dropped cinder blocks in the road and didn't even stop. I couldn't miss them all."

He didn't say anything.

Faye explained, "I blew my horn but he just gave me—gave me a gesture, and then drove on."

Nothing. He just stood there. She turned from the door and glanced back up and down the deserted street, pushed her bangs off her forehead, the bracelets on her wrist chinging slightly. She ran her finger over the eye-level patched place on the screen and read him the bottom line. "I need a wrecker, see?"

When he still just stood there, she wondered if he was drunk, or didn't speak English, or both. She tried out her B-plus high school Español. "May I use your telephone, please?" Not let me, or I must, but may I, and please.

He seemed to be thinking it over. Maybe he was Greek? Could be Greek. Fierce eyes, dark—circled like a panda's. She added, in all the Greek she knew besides Merry Christmas, "Good Morning." And again, in English, "please." He turned and walked away, deep into the dark heart of the house. Left her standing there.

"Mister!" she called to his back.

"It's not locked," he answered tonelessly, in English as good as her Spanish. He vanished into the dim front room. She heard a chair sigh as he sank into it. The phone was on the wall in the hall. After looking around through the screen one more time, and breathing a prayer, she opened the door and went toward it.

The bird in its covered cage stared at her listlessly when she peeked. Days of droppings were piled under its perch; the water was cloudy, the seed cup empty of all but husks. The bird was puffed, eyes almost shut, one foot retracted into disheveled feathers. Faye dropped the cover back.

Outraged, she called out. "What's the matter here?"

The man answered, "Dial six, then your number, not long distance."

So Faye dialed.

They put her on hold.

All the time she waited, she could see the outline of Tom Rios sitting there in the dark, his uncombed head. Everything in the house needed care, food, light, action. A stack of unopened mail lay on the table beside a couple of wilting dish gardens with florist cars attached: "In Sympathy."

Someone had died here. Faye didn't want to know who or why. The flurry and rites were over, and this was what remained. She just wanted the wrecker to come and let her go on her way; she didn't want to be involved, wished she had never walked into this, longed to be gone, to forget it all. And was ashamed for wishing it. For penance, she promised she would open that birdcage door and put her hand in and pour seeds and change the water dish, though she had never touched a bird before, and the possibility that it might flutter, or fly at her and try to escape, or, worse, settle on her hand, grip around her finger with its scaly little claws, made her spine ache, and her mind faint. But if she would do that much, it would prove she wasn't afraid of the grief and death in this strange house, that she wasn't just turning and running away. She could do that much, anyway, before she left that man alone, as the rest of the world had done.

Through the back door she saw the browning pots of funeral mums and a tub of sun-scalded poinciana, foil and ribbons still fresh. The pinecone weights on the cuckoo clock on the wall behind her had reached the floor, and time had stopped at two-fifteen. Day or night didn't matter, that was plain enough.

No "what next" to the whole house . . . She puffed the chaff out of the feed cup and poured in a handful of seeds and a bit of stale muffin she picked up off the counter. The water sparkled when she put it back in the cage, fresh. All the time she held her breath, not only against the odor, but also against the possibility the bird might act wild. All it did was humbly begin eating with a tiny cracking and tonguing of the seeds. Relieved, she latched the door, leaving the cover half off the cage to let the sunlight in.

When she went into the dark parlor where Tom Rios sat, to offer to pay for the phone call, he was just sitting on the wallowed sheet on the sofa, as though he'd been sleeping there for weeks, or trying.

"Forget it," he said. To every offer—no thanks; about the blinds, let them stay down; no thanks about the coffee she could make in a moment; no thanks to toast or cereal or juice.

She swooped down on the dish gardens and took them to the sink and drenched them, set them on a sunny sill. That was the end of her good deeds, her nerved-up meddling. "I'll wait outside," she told him, almost whispering.

Held her bracelets so they wouldn't chatter or bangle, just that bright little female noise seemed irreverent. She regretted her perfume, and her happiness. What sort of trouble were two flat tires and a snapped tie-rod, weighed against death?

Faye tiptoed to the edge of the porch and sat on the top step, her sandaled feet in the stinging-hot April sun. She decided it must be the man's wife that had died, because if a woman who loved a man were not dead, she would be here, right that moment, to help him get through this awfulness.

The porch offered a good vantage; she could see the road, hear the phone if the wrecker company had to call back. She was so intent on listening for that, she didn't at first notice the bird whistling. It was so important to her to believe that it was the caged bird, she didn't want to make sure, but she had to know, what good was believing a lie? She leaned against the dark screen door and stared; the bird sat in the sun-struck corner of the cage, preening and mumbling. Straight through the house were the parched flowers in the backyard.

Maybe she should go around back, see if there was a hose lying there, so she could water the poinciana. Somehow this didn't qualify as one of what her mother called Faye's Save the World Merit Badge projects. She had just got to her feet when Vic Rios drove up, the brother.

If he noticed Faye's van kneeling against the curb down the block, he never worried about it. The bad tires were not visible, the cracked headlight and grazed fender not extraordinary in that neighborhood.

When Faye saw he was coming to that very house, she moved to one side of the steps, and started down, explaining, "Leaving," off balance, flustered, as though she had been caught trespassing. As though Vic Rios—that devil-in-a-white-shirt—were the Law, arresting in brass and navy blue. Open collar, no tie, very, very tan. He came up the lower steps two at a time. Watching him, Faye fell.

"Whoa," he said. Reaching to help her up.

"I'm all right." Furious with embarrassment, angry, as always, at pain when it was her own. She never could bear sympathy, preferred to go off by herself to shed any tears. Did but most certainly did not want his hands on her. Brushed herself, and him, off.

He shrugged and went on across the porch and into the house without knocking. So he belonged, she knew that much about him, and that was all. He hadn't spoken another word, just "Whoa."

The wrecker came right away. The driver didn't know the people in the neighborhood, no. So Faye left, not knowing Vic Rios's name, or how they'd meet again, or if. She didn't let it obsess her; she had plenty to do, and more to think about. She didn't cruise around, seeking. Never had been goody-goody faithful at mass but took the slow way past the idlers in doorways—the sort that's a tart at heart.

She wanted what one often wants, but yearned no more than natural or seemly. Wanted it to happen, but never, till she met Rios, had she been sure. Cristo had gotten close to making her feel lonely, but none of those cocky, low-riding, beer-buzzed, night-prowling others in their crazy cars!—or the clam-baking, beach-dancing, golden-boy yearbook-heros—no, not even Cristo, the National League's numero-uno draft pick bucking home from college in that army-surplus jeep—not a one prevailed. They took her spare time, not her whole heart.

So why him, the Captain, at first sight? It was that sudden. And of course they ran into each other again soon; fate doesn't need a map. It might not have been right but it was real. And they made plans, from the beginning. Mrs. Parry only insulted Faye once asking if she was sure.

Who made the wedding dress? Mrs. Parry. "Anything you can dream up," she promised. Graduated to bifocals sewing seed pearls onto cream. Three weights of peau de soie, clouds of lace, silk tulle veiling soft as mist; even the mitts were hand-fashioned. Hundred and fifty dollars a yard wholesale wouldn't begin it. Both mother and daughter shopped for fabrics with their fingertips, knew fabric quality by touch as much as by eye, in any light. They were unsparing. "Once in a lifetime," they agreed.

The shears through that night-chilled silk! "Like cutting smoke in a dream," Mrs. Parry marveled. The right ideas came to her, her hands moved with a mind of their own. Years of alterations, custom tailoring for others, had practiced her for this perfection. They worked mornings in the loft, shutters wide open for the land and sea breezes. Month of May, daylight savings, nine A.M. It was hot already.

"Like swimming naked," Faye muttered, "by starlight." She had her eyes closed and was drawing a cool scrap over her bare arm, up across her throat, testing it with her lips.

"Alone?" What mother wouldn't ask?

Faye's eyes blinked open.

"Alone!" She frowned, considering it.

Her mother stitched faster, thinking, *Sure as God, it's time.*

Through two rehearsals the Captain's mind wandered far from the harbor, but on the actual day, when Faye hove into the chapel fully rigged, his attention dropped anchor. He stared like a statue. Faye's mother counted that a compliment and took at least partial credit. It is not easy to teach lace to cleave and flex decently on warm curves and hollows. The newspaper photographs, good as they were, didn't do justice.

The portraits succeeded better, so well in fact, the photographer was using an unauthorized copy of one of the hand-colored one in his studio window, for an example of his finest work, he was that pleased; but the Captain put a stop to it as soon as someone mentioned it to him, in praise, a few weeks after the honeymoon: roared over to the studio from bayfront, during fishing hours, leaving his clients waiting at the dock, while he cleared it up once and for all.

"My wife's not bait," he explained simply. He was raging, but quiet. Very convincing. Customers in the shop fell back toward the door, in case it came to assassination of more than character. "I won't have her trolled as chum for suckers." He left the man's easel overturned in a cloud of tossed bills. It wasn't piracy, for he paid, then strolled calmly out with the picture under his arm. Faye's portrait wound up on Mrs. Parry's wall, a profile shot, backlit. Wearing her grandmother's earrings. That was her something old. Faye was glancing over her shoulder, side-to-back view, the button pearls and handmade loops highlighting her straight spine. Here and there Faye's mother could see little places she would've got perfect with one more fitting; it was all she could do not to touch up the dress anyway, afterwards, when Faye laid it off forever, to be cleaned and boxed for storage and posterity.

Faye wore a linen suit—blue to please the Captain—for going away. They hid their rented car, locked till the last moment, in a nearby garage, so no tin cans, no shaving soap, no balloons, no streamers. No posing. Toss the bouquet, duck and flee, his hand urgent and claiming. They were in such a hurry. That was the picture the FBI chose; they didn't keep it, but it came back marred.

Love and Desire in the Littoral Zone

Sandra McPherson

Ocean Water Absorbs Red, Orange, and Yellow Light

in a flash
and allows only the green and blue
        to penetrate the depths.
As we love deeply those we love,
        they are our blue and green.

        And what if
the sex so easily replaced by next
        and next times is the last,
lapsing into the Dalai Lama's
        "method of coping with lust":

        Sometimes in
my dreams there are women. When such
        dreams happen, immediately
I remember, "I am monk."
        A tidal zone is like sex—

        wet rocks
a flesh, the flexing of anemones
        hung like cat balls, shoulder carryalls,
or hummingbird nests from outcrops,
        seaweed bodies long together,

        hanks, skeins,
warps, lariats, the paraphernalia of dead
        ocean cheerleaders. The *appearance*
of a beautiful face, a body,
        however beautiful, decomposes

to a skeleton.
The *fffsss* of wave-water lowers
    into round gravel,
floods silver areolas of turban snails,
    and dry flashes into wet—

    When we penetrate
to human flesh and bones, NO
    beauty, is there?
A couple in a sexual experience is happy
    for that moment. Then very soon

    trouble begins.
The holy man's viewpoint is before
    one's born body chemicals
gladden the flesh and find for it
    long moments within the seconds,

    gasps
that replace clock-ticks. And he
    should dream of profounder women,
or men, to make irrelevant
    the slowing or quickening

    of the skeleton,
however it drags in eternity.
    "Deposit/withdrawal/deposit/withdrawal,"
the lover says of waves. You have
    to love each other's

    elements,
healthful calcium, the stone earbones
    as delicate to seduction
as to fine mineral rain embedding
    a fossil. And, like the field guide

    for driftwood,
the feeling guide to human bones
    can help identify why strong
light through countless self-
    absorbed literal

    Love and Desire in the Littoral Zone

(and even literary)
rosy-natured human nipples keeps on
    descending to these cores,
the bluegreen chassis inside
    the down-sworling body,

      the red
and yellow femurs surfaced together
    in the opened crypt
or tossed at last on shore
    among carnelians and agates drying,

      arousing
color when wet, even the inexpressive
    skull seen to be homely
as an ecstasy of gaping mouth
    returned to the wild

as the outermost open mind.

Marshall Gulch Beach, Sonoma coast

Andrea Barrett

· · · · · · · · · · · · · · · · · · · ·

The Littoral Zone

When they met, fifteen years ago, Jonathan had a job teaching botany at a small college near Albany, and Ruby was teaching invertebrate zoology at a college in the Berkshires. Both of them, along with an ornithologist, an ichthyologist, and an oceanographer, had agreed to spend three weeks of their summer break at a marine biology research station on an island off the New Hampshire coast. They had spouses, children, mortgages, bills; they went, they later told each other, because the pay was too good to refuse. Two-thirds of the way through the course, they agreed that the pay was not enough.

How they reached that first agreement is a story they've repeated to each other again and again and told, separately, to their closest friends. Ruby thinks they had this conversation on the second Friday of the course, after Frank Kenary's slide show on the abyssal fish and before Carol Dagliesh's lecture on the courting behavior of herring gulls. Jonathan maintains that they had it earlier—that Wednesday, maybe, when they were still recovering from Gunnar Erickson's trawling expedition. The days before they became so aware of each other have blurred in their minds, but they agree that their first real conversation took place on the afternoon devoted to the littoral zone.

The tide was all the way out. The students were clumped on the rocky, pitted apron between the water and the ledges, peering into the tidal pools and listing the species they found. Gunnar was in the equipment room, repairing one of the sampling claws. Frank was setting up dissections in the tiny lab; Carol had gone back to the mainland on the supply boat, hoping to replace the camera one of the students had dropped. And so the two of them, Jonathan and Ruby, were left alone for a little while.

They both remember the granite ledge where they sat, and the raucous quarrels of the nesting gulls. They agree that Ruby was scratching furiously at her calves and that Jonathan said, "Take it easy, okay? You'll draw blood."

Her calves were slim and tan, Jonathan remembers. Covered with blotches and scrapes.

I folded my fingers, Ruby remembers. Then I blushed. My throat felt sunburned.

Ruby said, "I know, it's so embarrassing. But all this salt on my poison ivy—God, what I wouldn't give for a bath! They never told me there wouldn't be any *water* here...."

Jonathan gestured at the ocean surrounding them and then they started laughing. *Hysteria,* they have told each other since. They were so tired by then, twelve days into the course, and so dirty and overworked and strained by pretending to the students that these things didn't matter, that neither of them could understand that they were also lonely. Their shared laughter felt like pure relief.

"No water?" Jonathan said. "I haven't been dry since we got here. My clothes are damp, my sneakers are damp, my hair never dries...."

His hair was beautiful, Ruby remembers. Thick, a little too long. Part blond and part brown.

"I know," she said. "But you know what I mean. I didn't realize they'd have to bring our drinking water over on a boat."

"Or that they'd expect us to wash in the ocean," Jonathan said. Her forearms were dusted with salt, he remembers. The down along them sparkled in the sun.

"And those cots," Ruby said. "Does yours have a sag in it like a hammock?"

"Like a slingshot," Jonathan said.

For a half an hour they sat on their ledge and compared their bubbling patches of poison ivy and the barnacle wounds that scored their hands and feet. Nothing healed out here, they told each other. Everything got infected. When one of the students called, "Look what I found!" Jonathan rose and held his hand out to Ruby. She took it easily and hauled herself up and they walked down to the water together. Jonathan's hand was thick and blunt-fingered, with nails bitten down so far that the skin around them was raw. Odd, Ruby remembers thinking. Those bitten stumps attached to such a good-looking man.

They have always agreed that the worst moment, for each of them, was when they stepped from the boat to the dock on the final day of the course and saw their families waiting in the parking lot. Jonathan's wife had their four-year-old daughter balanced on her shoulders. Their two older children were leaning perilously over the guardrails and shrieking at the sight of him. Jessie had turned nine in Jonathan's absence, and Jonathan can't think of her eager face without remembering the starfish he brought as his sole, guilty gift.

Ruby's husband had parked their car just a few yards from Jonathan's family. Her sons were wearing baseball caps, and what Ruby remembers is the way the yellow linings lit their faces. For a minute she saw the children squealing near her sons as faceless, inconsequential; Jonathan later told her that her children had been similarly blurred for him. Then Jonathan said, "That's my family, there," and Ruby said, "That's mine, right next to yours," and all their faces leapt into focus for both of them.

Nothing that was to come—not the days in court, nor the days they moved, nor the losses of jobs and homes—would ever seem so awful to them as that moment when they first saw their families standing there, unaware and hopeful. Deceitfully, treacherously, Ruby and Jonathan separated and walked to the people awaiting them. They didn't introduce each other to their spouses. They didn't look at each other—although, they later admitted, they cast covert looks at each other's families. They thought they were invisible, that no one could see what had happened between them. They thought their families would not remember how they had stepped off the boat and stood, for an instant, together.

On that boat, sitting dumb and miserable in the litter of nets and equipment, they had each pretended to be resigned to going home. Each foresaw (or so they later told each other) the hysterical phone calls and the frenzied, secret meetings. Neither foresaw how much the sight of each other's family would hurt. "Sweetie," Jonathan remembers Ruby's husband saying. "You've lost so much weight." Ruby remembers staring over her husband's shoulder and watching Jessie butt her head like a dog under Jonathan's hand.

For the first twelve days on the island, Jonathan and Ruby were so busy that they hardly noticed each other. For the next few days, after their conversation on the ledge, they sat near each other during faculty lectures and student presentations. These were held in the library, a ramshackle building separated from the bunkhouse and the dining hall by a stretch of wild roses and poison ivy.

Jonathan had talked about algae in there, holding up samples of *Fucus* and *Hildenbrandtia*. Ruby had talked about the littoral zone, that space between high and low watermarks where organisms struggle to adapt to the daily rhythm of immersion and exposure. They had drawn on the blackboard in colored chalk while the students, itchy and hot and tired, scratched their arms and legs and feigned attention.

Neither of them, they admitted much later, had focused fully on the other's lecture. "It was *before*," Ruby has said ruefully. "I didn't know that I was going to want to have listened." And Jonathan has laughed and confessed that he was studying the shells and skulls on the walls while Ruby was drawing on the board.

The library was exceedingly hot, they agreed, and the chairs remarkably uncomfortable; the only good spot was the sofa in front of the fireplace. That was the spot they commandeered on the evening after their first conversation, when dinner led to a walk and then the walk led them into the library a few minutes before the scheduled lecture.

Erika Moorhead, Ruby remembers. Talking about the tensile strength of byssus threads.

Walter Schank, Jonathan remembers. Something to do with hydrozoans.

They both remember feeling comfortable for the first time since their arrival. And for the next few days—three by Ruby's accounting; four by Jonathan's—one of them came early for every lecture and saved a seat on the sofa for the other.

They giggled at Frank Kenary's slides, which he'd arranged like a creepy fashion show: abyssal fish sporting varied blobs of luminescent flesh. When Gunnar talked for two hours about subduction zones and the calcium carbonate cycle, they amused themselves exchanging doodles. They can't remember, now, whether Gunnar's endless lecture came before Carol Dagliesh's filmstrip on the herring gulls, or which of the students tipped over the dissecting scope and sent the dish of copepods to their deaths. But both of them remember those days and nights as being almost purely happy. They swam in that odd, indefinite zone where they were more than friends, not yet lovers, still able to deny to themselves that they were headed where they were headed.

Ruby made the first phone call, a week after they left the island. At eleven o'clock on a Sunday night, she told her husband she'd left something in her office that she needed to prepare the next day's class. She drove to campus, unlocked her door, picked up the phone and called Jonathan at his house. One of his children—Jessie, she thinks—answered the phone. Ruby remembers how, even through the turmoil of her emotions, she'd been shocked at the idea of a child staying up so late.

There was a horrible moment while Jessie went to find her father; another when Jonathan, hearing Ruby's voice, said, "Wait, hang on, I'll just be a minute," and then negotiated Jessie into bed. Ruby waited, dreading his anger, knowing she'd been wrong to call him at home. But Jonathan, when he finally returned, said, "Ruby. You got my letter."

"What letter?" she asked. He wrote to tell me good-bye, she remembers thinking.

"My *letter*," he said. "I wrote you, I have to see you. I can't stand this."

Ruby released the breath she hadn't known she was holding.

"You didn't get it?" he said. "You just called?" It wasn't only me, he remembers thinking. She feels it too.

"I had to hear your voice," she said.

Ruby called, but Jonathan wrote. And so when Jonathan's youngest daughter, Cora, later fell in love and confided in Ruby, and then asked her, "Was it like this with you two? Who started it—you or Dad?" All Ruby could say was, "It happened to both of us."

Sometimes, when Ruby and Jonathan sit on the patio looking out at the hills above Palmyra, they will turn and see their children watching them through the kitchen window. Before the children went off to college, the house bulged with them on weekends and holidays and seemed empty in between; Jonathan's wife had custody of Jessie and Gordon and Cora, and Ruby's husband took her sons, Mickey and Ryan, when he remarried. Now that the children are old enough to come and go as they please, the house is silent almost all the time.

Jessie is twenty-four, and Gordon is twenty-two; Mickey is twenty-one, and Cora and Ryan are both nineteen. When they visit Jonathan and Ruby they spend an unhealthy amount of time talking about their past. In their conversations they seem to split their lives into three epochs: the years when what they think of as their real families were whole; the years right after Jonathan and Ruby met, when their parents were coming and going, fighting and making up, separating and divorcing; and the years since Jonathan and Ruby's marriage, when they were forced into a reconstituted family. Which epoch they decide to explore depends on who's visiting and who's getting along with whom.

"But we were happy," Mickey may say to Ruby, if he and Ryan are visiting and Jonathan's children are absent. "We were, we were fine."

"It wasn't like you and Mom ever fought," Cora may say to Jonathan, if Ruby's sons aren't around. "You could have worked it out if you'd tried."

When they are all together, they tend to avoid the first two epochs and to talk about their first strained weekends and holidays together. They've learned to tolerate each other, despite their forced introductions; Cora and Ryan, whose birthdays are less than three months apart, seem especially close. Ruby and Jonathan know that much of what draws their youngest children together is shared speculation about what happened on that island.

They look old to their children, they know. Both of them are nearing fifty. Jonathan has grown quite heavy and has lost much of his hair; Ruby's fine-boned figure has gone gaunt and stringy. They know their children can't imagine them young and strong and wrung by passion. The children can't think—can't stand to think—about what happened on the island, but they can't stop themselves from asking questions.

"Did you have other girlfriends?" Cora asks Jonathan. "Were you so unhappy with Mom?"

"Did you know him before?" Ryan asks Ruby. "Did you go there to be with him?"

"We met there," Jonathan and Ruby say. "We had never seen each other before. We fell in love." That is all they will say, they never give details, they say "yes" or "no" to the easy questions and evade the hard ones. They worry that even the little they offer may be too much.

Jonathan and Ruby tell each other the stories of their talk by the tidal pool, their walks and meals, the sagging sofa, the moment in the parking lot, and the evening Ruby made her call. They tell these to console themselves when their children chide them or when, alone in the house, they sit quietly near each other and struggle to conceal their disappointments.

Love and Desire in the Littoral Zone

Of course they have expected some of these. Mickey and Gordon have both had trouble in school, and Jessie has grown much too close to her mother; neither Jonathan nor Ruby has found jobs as good as the ones they lost, and their new home in Palmyra still doesn't feel quite like home. But all they have lost in order to be together would seem bearable had they continued to feel the way they felt on the island.

They're sensible people, and very well-mannered; they remind themselves that they were young then and are middle-aged now, and that their fierce attraction would naturally ebb with time. Neither likes to think about how much the thrill of their early days together came from the obstacles they had to overcome. Some days, when Ruby pulls into the driveway still thinking about her last class and catches sight of Jonathan out in the garden, she can't believe the heavyset figure pruning shrubs so meticulously is the man for whom she fought such battles. Jonathan, who often wakes very early, sometimes stares at Ruby's sleeping face and thinks how much more gracefully his ex-wife is aging.

They never reproach each other. When the tension builds in the house and the silence becomes overwhelming, one or the other will say, "Do you remember . . .?" and then launch into one of the myths on which they have founded their lives. But there is one story they never tell each other, because they can't bear to talk about what they have lost. This is the one about the evening that has shaped their life together.

Jonathan's hand on Ruby's back, Ruby's hand on Jonathan's thigh, a shirt unbuttoned, a belt undone. They never mention this moment, or the moments that followed it, because that would mean discussing who seduced whom, and any resolution of that would mean assigning blame. Guilt they can handle; they've been living with guilt for fifteen years. But blame? It would be more than either of them could bear, to know the exact moment when one of them precipitated all that has happened to them. The most either of them has ever said is, "How could we have known?"

But the night in the library is what they both think about, when they lie silently next to each other and listen to the wind. It must be summer for them to think about it; the children must be with their other parents and the rain must be falling on the cedar shingles overhead. A candle must be burning on the mantel above the bed and the maple branches outside their window must be tossing against each other. Then they think of the story they know so well and never say out loud.

There was a huge storm three nights before they left the island, the tail end of a hurricane passing farther out to sea. The cedar trees creaked and swayed in the wind beyond the library windows. The students had staggered off to bed, after the visitor from Woods Hole had finished his lecture on the explorations of the *Alvin* in the Cayman Trough, and Frank and Gunnar and Carol had shrouded themselves in their rain gear and left as well, sheltering the visitor between them. Ruby sat at one end of the long table, preparing bottles of fixative for their expedition the following morning, and Jonathan lay on the sofa writing notes. The boat was leaving just after dawn and they knew they ought to go to bed.

The wind picked up outside, sweeping the branches against the walls. The windows rattled. Jonathan shivered and said, "Do you suppose we could get a fire going in that old fireplace?"

"I bet we could," said Ruby, which gave both of them the pretext they needed to crouch side by side on the cracked tiles, brushing elbows as they opened the flue and crumpled paper and laid kindling in the form of a grid. The logs Jonathan found near the lobster traps were dry and the fire caught quickly.

Who found the green candle in the drawer below the microscope? Who lit the candle and turned off the lights? And who found the remains of the jug of wine that Frank had brought in honor of the visitor? They sat there side by side, poking at the burning logs and pretending they weren't doing what they were doing. The wind pushed through the window they'd opened a crack, and the tan window shade lifted and then fell back against the frame. The noise was soothing at first; later it seemed irritating.

Jonathan, whose fingernails were bitten to the quick, admired the long nail on Ruby's right little finger and then said, half-seriously, how much he'd love to bite a nail like that. When Ruby held her hand to his mouth he took the nail between his teeth and nibbled through the white tip, which days in the water had softened. Ruby slipped her other hand inside his shirt and ran it up his back. Jonathan ran his mouth up her arm and down her neck.

They started in front of the fire and worked their way across the floor, breaking a glass, knocking the table askew. Ruby rubbed her back raw against the rug and Jonathan scraped his knees, and twice they paused and laughed at their wild excesses. They moved across the floor from east to west and later from west to east, and between those two journeys, during the time when they heaped their clothes and the sofa cushions into a nest in front of the fire, they talked.

This was not the kind of conversation they'd had during walks and meals since that first time on the rocks: who they were, where they'd come from, how they'd made it here. This was the talk where they instinctively edited out the daily pleasures of their life on the mainland and spliced together the hard times, the dark times, until they'd constructed versions of themselves that could make sense of what they'd just done.

For months after this, as they lay in stolen, secret rooms between houses and divorces and jobs and lives, Jonathan would tell Ruby that he swallowed her nail. The nail dissolved in his stomach, he'd say. It passed into his villi and out to his blood and then flowed to bone and muscle and nerve, where the molecules that had once been part of her became part of him. Ruby, who always seemed to know more acutely than Jonathan that they'd have to leave whatever room this was in an hour or a day would argue with him.

"Nails are keratin," she'd tell him. "Like hooves and hair. Like wool. We can't digest wool."

"Moths can," Jonathan would tell her. "Moths eat sweaters."

"Moths have a special enzyme in their saliva," Ruby would say. This was true, she knew it for a fact. She'd been so taken by Jonathan's tale that she'd gone to the library to check out the details and discovered he was wrong.

But Jonathan didn't care what the biochemists said. He held her against his chest and said, "I have an enzyme for you."

That night, after the fire burned out, they slept for a couple of hours. Ruby woke first and watched Jonathan sleep for a while. He slept like a child, with his knees bent toward his chest and his hands clasped between his thighs. Ruby picked up the tipped-over chair and swept the fragments of broken glass onto a sheet of paper. Then she woke Jonathan and they tiptoed back to the rooms where they were supposed to be.

Choosing the Coast

Our walk takes us up past Shadmoor Bluffs along an area of beach known as Dead Man's Cove. Just recently, the bluffs have been saved from developers and turned into a state park. Even though the state has put up a large sign and created a dirt road allowing entrance into the park, Shadmoor remains a more rugged stretch of beach, and I rarely see people walking along the cove. Initially, I was afraid that tourists would see the sign and flock to the cove, but the terrain is self-sorting, and only those with determination trek here. As I contemplate how difficult it is to walk this short stretch of beach, how I have chosen to walk the shoreline rather than walk up along the road, I am also reminded that many women coastal authors have written stories about women who have chosen to live and work in coastal areas.

Women's literature has long expressed the notion that choice is not as simple as deciding between two options and then pursuing the path or object of that choice. Life priorities often ask women to set aside their personal choices so that they might raise their children or go where their husbands have jobs. Women's roles became less restrictive in the latter half of the twentieth century and their options more easily available. In the literature of the coast, readers can see women who have chosen the coastal life for a variety of reasons and needs.

The poets Edna St. Vincent Millay, May Swenson, and Amy Clampitt sought out the shore for contemplation. As they looked out through their windows or walked along the shore collecting beach glass or driftwood, they were taken with the large and subtle changes by the shore. E. Annie Proulx, in chapters from *The Shipping News*, presents her reader with the character of an aunt, who—after many years of living away from her childhood coastal home—convinces her nephew and his children to return to the shore with her. She remains stubborn in her desire to live her final years on the coast despite the decay of her old house and its isolation from the rest of the world. As the other writers included in this section notice, their characters are compelled to live close to the shore; it is satisfying, simple, and they work hard to describe in words the ways coastal life varies from life inland.

Kali and I step carefully along Dead Man's Cove, but we make good progress on our way to Montauk's favorite surfer spot, Ditch Plains. I note, with satisfaction, that today, like the works included this section, I have made a choice and despite the difficult stretches, I trek along, daydream a bit, and think about life on the coast.

Edna St. Vincent Millay

Inland

People that build their houses inland,
 People that buy a plot of ground
Shaped like a house, and build a house there,
 Far from the sea-board, far from the sound

Of water sucking the hollow ledges,
 Tons of water striking the shore,—
What do they long for, as I long for
 One salt smell of the sea once more?

People the waves have not awakened,
 Spanking the boats at the harbor's head,
What do they long for, as I long for,—
 Starting up in my inland bed,

Beating the narrow walls, and finding
 Neither a window nor a door,
Screaming to God for death by drowning,—
 One salt taste of the sea once more?

On the Edge

I was thinking, while I was working on my income tax,
here in the open angle of a V—
that the blue on the map that's water—my house
tucked into the fold of a hill, on the edge
of a ragged beak of the sea
that widens and narrows according to the tide:
"This little house will be swallowed some year.
Not yet. But threatened."

Chips are houses, twigs are trees
on the woodland ledges along the lip,
the blue throat open, thirsty. Where my chip-roof sits,
sandland loosens, boulders shift downslope,
bare roots of old trunks stumble.
The undermining and undulating lurch
is all one way, the shore dragged south
to spill into another mouth.

I was thinking while I was working: "The April sun
is warm." Suddenly, all the twigs on the privet
budded green, the cardinal flamed and called,
the maple rained its flowerets down
and spread leaf-grown. July's plush roses bloomed,
were blown. A hundred gladioli sunsets in a row
raced to die, and dyed the cove,
while the sea crawled the sand, gnawed on the cliff.

And leisurely, cracks in the flagstones happened,
leaks in the roof. The gateposts crumbled,
mortar in the stone wall loosened,
boards in the porch let the nailheads through.

Choosing the Coast

I was thinking, while April's crocus
poked out of earth on the cesspool top:
"Blueblack winter of water coming—icewhite, rockhard
tide will be pounding the side of the gaping V. . . .

"But the smell of the windfresh, salty morning,
flash of the sunwhipped beak of the sea!
Better get last year's layers of old leaves up,
before this year's green bursts out, turns brown,
comes blowing down," I was thinking
while I was working on my income tax.

A Subject of the Waves

Today, while a steamshovel rooted in the cove,
leveling a parking lot for the new nightclub,
and a plane drilled between clean clouds in the October sky,
and the flags on the yachts tied in the basin flipped in the wind,
I watched my footsteps mark the sand by the tideline.
Some hollow horseshoe crab shells scuttled there,
given motion by the waves. I threw a plank back to the waves
that they'd thrown up, a sun-dried, sea-swollen stave
from a broken dinghy, one end square, one pointed, painted green.
Watching its float, my attention snagged and could not get off
the hook of its experience. I had launched a subject
of the waves I could not leave until completed.

Easily it skipped, putting out, prow-end topping every smack
and swell. It kept its surface dry, and looked to float
beyond the jetty head, and so be loose,
exchange the stasis of the beach
for unconceived fluidities and agitations.
It set sail by the luck of its construction.
Lighter than the forceful waves, it surmounted their shove.
Heavier, steadier than the hollows they scooped behind them,
it used their crested threats for coasting free.
Unsplashed by even a drop of spray, it was casual master
of the inconsistent element it rode.

But there was a bias to the moving sea.
The growth and motion of each wave looked arbitrary,
but the total spread (of which each crease was part,
the outward hem lying flat by the wall of sky
at the dim blue other end of the bay's bed)
was being flung, it seemed, by some distant will.
Though devious and shifty in detail, the whole expanse
reiterated constancy and purpose.
So, just as the arrowy end of the plank, on a peak of a wave,
made a confident leap that would clear the final shoal,
a little sideways breaker nudged it enough
to turn it broadside. Then a swifter slap from a stronger comber
brought it back, erasing yards of its piecemeal progress
with one push. Yet the plank turned point to the tide,
and tried again—though not as buoyant, for it had got soaked.
Arrogance undamaged, it conveyed itself again
over obstacle waves, a courageous ski,
not noticing, since turned from shore, that the swells it conquered
slid in at a slant; that while it met them head on,
it was borne closer to shore, and shunted down the coast.

Now a bulge, a series of them, as a pulse quickened in the tide,
without resistance lifted up the plank, flipped it over twice,
and dumped it in the shallows. It scraped on sand.
And so it was put back. Not at the place of first effort;
a greater disgrace than that: at before the birth
of balance, pride, intention, enterprise.
It changed its goal, and I changed my ambition. Not the open
sea—escape into rough and wild, into unpredictability—
but rescue, return and rest. Release from influence
became my hope for the green painted, broken slat,
once part of a boat.

Its trials to come ashore the cold will of the waves thwarted
more capriciously than its assays into adventure made before.
Each chance it took to dig, with its bent spike,
a grip in the salvage of pebbles and weed and shell
was teasingly, tirelessly outwitted
by dragouts and dousings, slammings and tuggings
of the punishing sea. Until, of its own impulse, the sea

decided to let be,
and lifted and laid, lifted and laid
the plank inert on the sand. At tide turn,
such the unalterable compulsion of the sea,
it had to turn its back and rumple its bed
toward the other edge, the farther side of the spread.

I watched my footsteps mark the sand by the tideline.
The steamshovel rooting in the cove had leveled
a parking lot for the new nightclub.
The launch from the yacht basin whooshed around the end
of the pier, toward a sailboat with dropped anchor there,
whose claxon and flipping flag signaled for pickup.
The men with their mallets had finished sinking posts
by the gangplank entrance to the old ferry,
its hold ballasted with cement, painted green and black,
furnished with paneled bar and dining deck.
I watched them hang a varnished sign between the posts,
and letter the name: *The Ark.*
Tomorrow I must come
out again into the sun,
and mark the sand, and find my plank,
for its destiny's not done.

Beach Glass

While you walk the water's edge,
turning over concepts
I can't envision, the honking buoy
serves notice that at any time
the wind may change,
the reef-bell clatters
its treble monotone, deaf as Cassandra
to any note but warning. The ocean,

cumbered by no business more urgent
than keeping open old accounts
that never balanced,
goes on shuffling its millenniums
of quartz, granite, and basalt.

It behaves
toward the permutations of novelty—
driftwood and shipwreck, last night's
beer cans, spilt oil, the coughed-up
residue of plastic—with random
impartiality, playing catch or tag
or touch-last like a terrier,
turning the same thing over and over,
over and over. For the ocean, nothing
is beneath consideration.

The houses
of so many mussels and periwinkles
have been abandoned here, it's hopeless
to know which to salvage. Instead
I keep a lookout for beach glass—
amber of Budweiser, chrysoprase
of Almadén and Gallo, lapis
by way of (no getting around it,
I'm afraid) Phillips'
Milk of Magnesia, with now and then a rare
translucent turquoise or blurred amethyst
of no known origin.

The process
goes on forever: they came from sand,
they go back to gravel,
along with the treasuries
of Murano, the buttressed
astonishments of Chartres,
which even now are readying
for being turned over and over as gravely
and gradually as an intellect
engaged in hazardous
redefinition of structures
no one has yet looked at.

Gloria Naylor

From *Mama Day*

Somewhere behind the clouds the sun sets and the quarter moon rises. And folks are doing the things that normally come with the evening: the suppers are cooked and eaten, the babies put to bed, but this night it's with the static from radios and the blue glow of the televisions. Hurricane watch. They evacuating beyond the bridge, the Red Cross is putting up shelters, the National Guard is called into Savannah to stop the looting that might come after. Picture after picture of boarded-up stores, deserted marinas, and interviews with mayors, out-talking each other about who's bound to have the worst disaster area and how much emergency aid they been promised from Washington.

Things is always been done different in Willow Springs. First off, it ain't never crossed nobody's mind to leave. Them sitting close to the water just get back a little more, though nobody's been fool enough to build right up to the edge. Ain't been a bad hurricane in most living memories but that's the last memory to count. It's a place always been hit by storms, leaving a lick and a promise, so houses just don't get built near the water like fields don't get planted. A promise is as good as your word here, and you can learn to live like every rain is gonna be the big one. Second off, there ain't no mayor, governor, or the like. If anything gets blown down, it's understood everybody will get together to put it back up. In 1920, Miranda says, they had to redo parts of the bridge. Sure couldn't depend upon South Carolina or Georgia, since they don't collect our taxes. It's like we don't exist for them, and near about midnight when that Hurricane Watch becomes a Wait, they stop existing for us. Them televisions and radios get turned off so folks can sit in the quiet, a respectful silence, for the coming of the force.

Abigail is reading her Bible in the light from the burning fire that Miranda feeds with pieces of kindling. It gives her hands something to do with the waiting; she's tired of sitting, tired of pacing near the shuttered windows. Miranda can't get rid of the heaviness way down in her center, holding there for a reason she can't put her finger on. It ain't Cocoa in one room, and George in another, after that miserable supper with him picking at his food and her real listless, refusing to eat at all. Both suffering from heart trouble and both of 'em stubborn to beat the band. But that's to be left alone; the same passion that flared up to start all this mess can be depended upon to burn it away. And it ain't them winds building up outside; she done felt that pressure for days now and it's got a texture all its own. Naw, this was other trouble. And she'd just have to wait it out. Too much going on around her to call up what it might be.

The old walnut clock ticks on behind the soft murmuring of Abigail's voice, while far off and low the real winds come in. It starts on the shores of Africa, a simple breeze among the palms and cassavas, before it's carried off, tied up with thousands like it, on a strong wave heading due west. A world of water, heaving and rolling, weeks of water, and all them breezes die but one. *I cried unto God with my voice, even unto God with my voice.* Restless and disturbed, no land in front of it, no land in back, it draws up the ocean vapor and rains fall like tears. Constant rains. But it lives on to meet the curve of the equator, where it swallows up the heat waiting in the blackness of them nights. A roar goes up and it starts to spin: moving counterclockwise against the march of time, it rips through the sugar canes in Jamaica, stripping juices from their heart, shedding red buds from royal poincianas as it spins up in the heat. Over the broken sugar cane fields—hot rains fall. But it's spinning wider, spinning higher, groaning as it bounces off the curve of the earth to head due north. *Thou holdest mine eyes waking; I am so troubled that I cannot speak. I have considered the days of old, the years of ancient times.* A center grows within the fury of the spinning winds. A still eye. Warm. Calm. It dries a line of clothes in Alabama. It rocks a cradle in Georgia. *I call to remembrance my song in the night. I commune with mine own heart*—A buried calm with the awesome power of its face turned to Willow Springs. It hits the southeast corner of the bluff, raising a fist of water to smash into them high rocks. It screams through Chevy's Pass. *And my spirit made diligent search*—the oak tree holds. *I will meditate also of all thy work, and talk of thy doings*—the tombstone of Bascombe Wade trembles but holds. The rest is destruction.

Miranda hears it in her soul. The tall pines in the south woods go. The cypress in the east woods go. The magnolias and jasmines in the west woods go. A low moan as it spares the other place. But then a deep heaving, a pounding of wind and rains against wood. A giving. A slow and tortured giving before a summons to The Sound to rise up and swallow the shattered fragments of the bridge. *The waters saw thee, O God, the waters saw thee; they were afraid. The depths also were troubled. The clouds poured out water. The skies sent out a sound. Thine arrows also went abroad. The voice of thy thunder was in the heaven. The lightnings lightened the world. The earth trembled and shook.*

Choosing the Coast

Miranda goes over to her sister, and gently she closes Abigail's Bible. Their gnarled hands rest for a moment on the worn leather binding. Abigail puts the Bible away and sits beside Miranda to listen to the heaving, screaming winds.

Willow Springs is a barrier island, and unlike beyond the bridge, it ain't a matter of calling them winds by a first name, like you'd do a pet dog or cat, so what they're capable of won't be so frightening—a prank or something that nature, having nothing better to do, just decided to play: one time a female, one time a male. But Abigail and Miranda is sitting side by side, listening to the very first cries from the heaving and moaning outside that darkened and shuttered house. Feeling the very earth split open as the waters come gushing down—all to the end of birthing a void. Naw, them winds will come, rest, and leave screaming—*Thy way is in the sea, and thy path in the great waters, and thy footsteps are not known*—while prayers go up in Willow Springs to be spared from what could only be the workings of Woman. And She has no name.

E. Annie Proulx

Cast Away

Cast Away, to be forced from a ship by a disaster.
—*The Mariner's Dictionary*

Quoyle's face the color of a bad pearl. He was wedged in a seat on a ferry pitching toward Newfoundland, his windbreaker stuffed under his cheek, the elbow wet where he had gnawed it.

The smell of sea damp and paint, boiled coffee. Nor any escape from static snarled in the public address speakers, gunfire in the movie lounge. Passengers singing "That's one more dollar for me," swaying over whiskey.

Bunny and Sunshine stood on the seats opposite Quoyle, staring through glass at the games room. Crimson Mylar walls, a ceiling that reflected heads and shoulders like disembodied putti on antique valentines. The children yearned toward the water-bubble music.

Next to Quoyle a wad of the aunt's knitting. The needles jabbed his thigh but he did not care. He was brimming with nausea. Though the ferry heaved toward Newfoundland, his chance to start anew.

❈   ❈   ❈

The aunt had made a good case. What was left for him in Mockingburg? Unemployed, wife gone, parents deceased. And there was Petal's Accidental Death and Dismemberment Insurance Plan money. Thirty thousand to the spouse and ten thousand to each eligible child. He hadn't thought of insurance, but it crossed the aunt's mind at once. The children slept, Quoyle and the aunt sat at the kitchen table. The aunt in her big purple dress, having a drop of whiskey in a teacup. Quoyle with a cup of Ovaltine. To help him sleep, the aunt said. Blue sleeping pills. He was embarrassed but swallowed them. Fingernails bitten to the quick.

"It makes sense," she said, "for you to start a new life in a fresh place. For the children's sake as well as your own. It would help you all get over what's happened. You know it takes a year, a full turn of the calendar, to get over losing somebody. That's a true saying. And it helps if you're in a different place. And what place would be more natural than where your family came from? Maybe you could ask around, your newspaper friends, tap the grapevine. There might be a job up there. Just the trip would be an experience for the girls. See another part of the world. And to tell the truth," patting his arm with her old freckled hand, "it would be a help to me to have you along. I bet we'd be a good team."

The aunt leaned on her elbow. Chin on the heel of her hand. "As you get older you find out the place where you started pulls at you stronger and stronger. I never wanted to see Newfoundland again when I was young, but the last few years it's been like an ache, just a longing to go back. Probably some atavistic drive to finish up where you started. So in a way I'm starting again, too. Going to move my little business up there. It wouldn't hurt you to ask about a job."

He thought about calling Partridge, telling him. The inertia of grief rolled through him. He couldn't do it. Not now.

Woke at midnight, swimming up from aubergine nightmare. Petal getting into a bread truck. The driver is gross, a bald head, mucus suspended from his nostrils, his hands covered with some unspeakable substance. Quoyle has the power to see both sides of the truck at once. Sees the hands reaming up under Petal's dress, the face lowering into her oaken hair, and all the time the truck careening along highways, swaying over bridges without railings. Quoyle is somehow flying along beside them, powered by anxiety. Clusters of headlights flicker closer. He struggles to reach Petal's hand, to pull her out of the bread truck, knowing what must come (wishing it for the driver who has metamorphosed into his father) but cannot reach her, suffers agonizing paralysis though he strains. The headlights close. He shouts to tell her death is imminent, but is voiceless. Woke up pulling at the sheet.

For the rest of the night he sat in the living room with a book in his lap. His eyes went back and forth, he read, but comprehended nothing. The aunt was right. Get out of here.

※   *※*   *※*

It took half an hour to get a phone number for Partridge.

"Goddam! I was just thinking about you the other day." Partridge's voice came fresh in the wires. "Wondering what the hell ever happened to old Quoyle! When you going to come out and visit? You know I quit the papers, don't you? Yeah, I quit 'em." The thought of Mercalia on the road alone, he said, made him go to the truck driver school himself.

"We're a driving team, now. Bought a house two years ago. Planning on buying our own rig pretty soon, doing independent contracting. These trucks are sweet—double bunk, little kitchenette. Air-conditioned. We sit up there over the traffic, look down on the cars. Making three times the money I was. Don't miss newspapers at all. So what's new with you, still working for Punch?"

It only took ten or eleven minutes to tell Partridge everything, from falling in one-way love to riding nightmares, to leaning over a tableful of maps with the aunt.

"Son of a bitch, Quoyle. You been on the old roller coaster. You had the full-course dinner. Least you got your kids. Well, I'll tell you. I'm out of the newspaper game but still got some contacts. See what I come up with. Gimme the names of the nearest towns again?"

There was only one, with the curious name of Killick-Claw.

※   *※*   *※*

Partridge back on the line two days later. Pleased to be fixing Quoyle's life up again. Quoyle made him think of a huge roll of newsprint from the pulp mill. Blank and speckled with imperfections. But beyond this vagueness he glimpsed something like a reflection of light from a distant hubcap, a scintillation that meant there was, in Quoyle's life, the chance of some brilliance. Happiness? Good luck? Fame and fortune? Who knows, thought Partridge. He liked the rich taste of life so well himself he wished for an entree or two for Quoyle.

"Amazes me how the old strings still pull. Yeah, there's a paper up there. A weekly. They're looking for somebody, too. You interested, I'll give you the name I got. Want somebody to cover the shipping news. Guess it's right on the coast. Want somebody with maritime connections if possible. Quoyle, you got maritime connections?"

"My grandfather was a sealer."

"Jesus. You always come at me out of left field. Anyway, it works out, you got to handle work permits and immigration and all that. Deal with those guys. O.k. Managing editor's name is Tertius Card. Got a pencil? Give you the number."

Quoyle wrote it down.

"Well, good luck. Let me know how it goes. And listen, any time you want to come out here, stay with Marcalia and me, you just come on. This is a real good place to make money."

But the idea of the north was taking him. He needed something to brace against.

A month later they drove away in his station wagon. He took a last look in the side mirror at the rented house, saw the empty porch, the forsythia bush, the neighbor's flesh-colored slips undulating on the line.

And so Quoyle and the aunt in the front seat, the children in the back, and old Warren sometimes with the suitcases, sometimes clambering awkwardly up to sit between Bunny and Sunshine. They made her paper hats from napkins, tied the aunt's scarf around her hairy neck, fed her French fries when the aunt wasn't looking.

Fifteen hundred miles, across New York, Vermont, angling up through Maine's mauled woods. Across New Brunswick and Nova Scotia on three-lane highways, trouble in the center lane, making the aunt clench her hands. In North Sydney plates of oily fish for supper, and no one who cared, and in the raw morning, the ferry to Port-Aux-Basques. At last.

Quolye suffered in the upholstery, the aunt strode the deck, stopped now and then to lean on the rail above the shuddering water. Or stood spraddle-legged, hands knotted behind her back, facing wind. Her hair captured under a babushka, face a stone with little intelligent eyes.

Choosing the Coast

She spoke of the weather with a man in a watch cap. They talked awhile. Someone else reel footing along, said, Rough today, eh? She worried about Warren, down in the station wagon, tossing up and down. Wouldn't know what to make of it. Never been to sea. Probably thought the world was coming to an end and she all alone, in a strange car. The man in the watch cap said, "Don't worry, dog'll sleep the 'ole way across. That's 'ow dogs are."

The aunt looked out, saw the blue land ahead, her first sight of the island in almost fifty years. Could not help tears.

"Comin' 'ome, eh?" said the man in the watch cap. "Yar, that's 'ow it takes you."

This place, she thought, this rock, six thousand miles of coast blind-wrapped in fog. Sunkers under wrinkled water, boats threading tickles between ice-scabbed cliffs. Tundra and barrens, a land of stunted spruce men cut and drew away.

How many had come here, leaning on the rail as she leaned now. Staring at the rock in the sea. Vikings, the Basques, the French, English, Spanish, Portuguese. Drawn by the cod, from the days when massed fish slowed ships on the drift for the passage to the Spice Isles, expecting cities of gold. The lookout dreamed of roasted auk or sweet berries in cups of plaited grass, but saw crumpling waves, lights flickering along the ship rails. The only cities were of ice, bergs with cores of beryl, blue gems within white gems, that some said gave off an odor of almonds. She had caught the bitter scent as a child.

Shore parties returned to ship blood-crusted with insect bites. Wet, wet the interior of the island, they said, bog and marsh, rivers and chains of ponds alive with metal-throated birds. The ships scraped on around the points. And the lookout saw shapes of caribou folding into fog.

Later, some knew it as a place that bred malefic spirits. Spring starvation showed skully heads, knobbed joints beneath flesh. What desperate work to stay alive, to scrob and claw through hard times. The alchemist sea changed fishermen into wet bones, sent boats to drift among the cod, cast them on the landwash. She remembered the stories in old mouths: the father who shot his oldest children and himself that the rest might live on flour scrapings; sealers crouched on a floe awash from their weight until one leaped into the sea; storm journeys to fetch medicines—always the wrong thing and too late for the convulsing hangashore.

She had not been in these waters since she was a young girl, but it rushed back, the sea's hypnotic boil, the smell of blood, weather and salt, fish heads, spruce smoke and reeking armpits, the rattle of wash-ball rocks in hissing wave, turrs, the crackery taste of brewis, the bedroom under the eaves.

But now they said that hard life was done. The forces of fate weakened by unemployment insurance, a flaring hope in offshore oil money. All was progress and possession, all shove and push, now. They said.

Fifteen she was when they had moved from Quoyle's Point, seventeen when the family left for the States, a drop in the tides of Newfoundlanders away from the outports, islands and hidden coves, rushing like water away from isolation, illiteracy, trousers made of worn upholstery fabric, no teeth, away from contorted thoughts and rough hands, from desperation.

And her dad, Harold Hamm, dead the month before they left, killed when a knot securing a can hook failed. Off-loading barrels of nails. The corner of the sling drooped, the barrel came down. Its iron-rimmed chine struck the nape of his neck, dislocated vertebrae and crushed the spinal column. Paralyzed and fading on the dock, unable to speak; who knew what thoughts crashed against the washline of his seizing brain as the kids and wife bent over, imploring Father, Father. No one said his name, only the word *father*, as though fatherhood had been the great thing in his life. Weeping. Even Guy, who cared for no one but himself.

So strange, she thought, going back there with a bereaved nephew and Guy's ashes. She had taken the box from sobbing Quoyle, carried it up to the guest room. Lay awake thinking she might pour Guy into a plastic supermarket bag, tie the loop handles, and toss him into the dumpster.

Only a thought.

Wondered which had changed the most, place or self? It was a strong place. She shuddered. It would be better now. Leaned on the rail, looking into the dark Atlantic that snuffled at the slope of the past.

A Rolling Hitch

A Rolling Hitch will suffice to tie a broom that has no groove,
provided the surface is not too slick.
—*The Ashley Book of Knots*

On the floor behind the seat Warren groaned. Quoyle steered up the west coast of the Great Northern Peninsula along a highway rutted by transport trucks. The road ran between the loppy waves of the Strait of Belle Isle and mountains like blue melons. Across the strait sullen Labrador. Trucks ground east in caravans, stainless steel cabs beaded with mist. Quoyle almost recognized the louring sky. As though he dreamed of this place once, forgot it later.

The car rolled over fissured land. Tuckamore. Cracked cliffs in volcanic glazes. On a ledge above the sea a murre laid her single egg. Harbors still locked in ice. Tombstone houses jutting from raw granite, the coast black, glinting like lumps of silver ore.

Their house, the aunt said, crossing her fingers, was out on Quoyle's Point. The Point, anyway, still on the map. A house empty for forty-four years. She scoffed, said it could not still stand, but inwardly believed something had held, that time had not cheated her of this return. Her voice clacked. Quoyle, listening, drove with his mouth open as though to taste the subarctic air.

On the horizon icebergs like white prisons. The immense blue fabric of the sea, rumpled and creased.

"Look," said the aunt. "Fishing skiffs." Small in the distance. Waves bursting against the headlands. Exploding water.

"I remember a fellow lived in a wrecked fishing boat," the aunt said. "Old Danny Something-or-other. It was hauled up on the shore far enough out of the storm and he fixed it up. Little chimney sticking up, path with a border of stone. Lived there for years until one day when he was sitting out in front mending net and the rotten hull collapsed and killed him."

The highway shriveled to a two-lane road as they drove east, ran under cliffs, passed spruce forest fronted by signs that said NO CUTTING. Quoyle appraised the rare motels they passed with the eye of someone who expected to sleep in one of them.

❊   ❊   ❊

The aunt circled Quoyle's Point on the map. On the west side of Omaloor Bay the point thrust into the ocean like a bent thumb. The house, whether now collapsed, vandalized, burned, carried away in pieces, had been there. Once.

The bay showed on the map as a chemist's pale blue flask into which poured the ocean. Ships entered the bay through the neck of the flask. On the eastern shore the settlement of Flour Sack Cove, three miles farther down the town of Killick-Claw, and along the bottom, odds and ends of coves. The aunt rummaged in her black flapjack handbag for a brochure. Read aloud the charms of Killick-Claw, statistics of its government wharf, fish plant, freight terminal, restaurants. Population, two thousand. Potential unlimited.

"Your new job's in Flour Sack Cove, eh? That's right across from Quoyle's Point. Looks about two miles by water. And a long trip by road. Used to be a ferry run from Capsize Cove to Killick-Claw every morning and night. But I guess it's closed down now. If you had a boat and a motor you could do it yourself."

"How do we get out to Quoyle's Point?" he asked.

There was a road off the main highway, the aunt said, that showed as a dotted line on the map. Quoyle didn't like the look of the dotted line roads they passed. Gravel, mud, washboard going nowhere.

They missed the turnoff, drove until they saw gas pumps. A sign. IGS STORE. The store in a house. Dark room. Behind the counter they could see a kitchen, teakettle spitting on the stove. Bunny heard television laughter.

Waiting for someone to appear, Quoyle examined bear-paw snowshoes. Walked around, looking at the homemade shelves, open boxes of skinning knives, needles for mending net, cones of line, rubber gloves, potted meats, a pile of adventure videos. Bunny peered through the freezer door at papillose frost crowding the ice cream tubs.

A man, sedge-grass hair sticking out from a cap embroidered with the name of a French bicycle manufacturer, came from the kitchen; chewed something gristly. Trousers a sullen crookedness of wool. The aunt talked. Quoyle modeled a sealskin hat for his children, helped them choose dolls made from clothespins. Inked faces smiled from the heads.

"Can you tell us where the road to Capsize Cover is?"

Unsmiling. Swallowed before answering.

"Be'ind you aways. Like just peasin' out of the main road. On a right as you go back. Not much in there now." He looked away. His Adam's apple a hairy mound in his neck like some strange sexual organ.

Quoyle at a rack of comic books, studied a gangster firing a laser gun at a trussed woman. The gangsters always wore green suits. He paid for the dolls. The man's fingers dropped the cold dimes.

    ❧   ❧   ❧

Up and down the highway three times before they spied a ruvid strip tilting away into the sky.

"Aunt, I don't think I can drive on this. It doesn't look like it goes anywhere."

"There's tire tracks on it," she said, pointing to cleated tread marks. Quoyle turned onto the sumpy road. Churned mud. The tire marks disappeared. Must have turned around, thought Quoyle, wanting to do the same and try tomorrow. Or had dropped in a bottomless hole.

"When are we gonna get there?" said Bunny, kicking the back of the seat. "I'm tired of going somewhere. I want to be there. I want to put on my bathing suit and play on the beach."

"Me too." Both throwing themselves rhythmically against the seat.

"It's too cold. Only polar bears go swimming now. But you can throw stones in the water. On the map, Aunt, how long is this road?" Hands ached from days of clenching.

She breathed over the map awhile. "From the main road to Capsize Cove is seventeen miles."

"Seventeen miles of this!"

"And then," as if he hadn't spoken, "eleven more to Quoyle's Point. To the house. Whatever's left of it. They show this road on the map, but in the old days it wasn't there. There was a footpath. See, folks didn't drive, nobody had cars then. Go places in the boat. Nobody had a car or truck. That paved main highway we come up on is all new." Yet the signature of rock written against the horizon in a heavy hand; unchanged, unchanging.

"Hope we don't get to Capsize Cove and discover we've got an eleven-mile walk in front of us." The rasp of his nylon sleeve on the wheel.

"We might. Then we'll just turn around." Her expression was remote. The bay seemed to be coming out of her mind, a blue hallucination.

Quoyle and the road in combat. Car Disintegrates on Remote Goatpath. Dusk washed in, the car struggled up a grade. They were on the edge of cliffs. Below, Capsize Cove, the abandoned houses askew. Fading light. Ahead, the main track swallowed in distance.

Quoyle pulled onto the shoulder, wondered if anybody had ever gone over the edge, metal jouncing on rocks. The side track down to the ruined cove steep, strewn with boulders. More gully than road.

"Well, we're not going to make the Point tonight," he said. "This is as far as I think we should drive until we can get a look at the road in daylight."

"You don't want to go back to the highway, do you?" cried the aunt in her hot voice. So close to the beginning of everything.

"Yeah," said Bunny. "I want to go to a motel with TV and hamburgers and chips that you can eat in bed. And lights that go down, down, down when you turn the knob. And you can turn the television off and on with that thing without getting out of bed."

"I want fried chicken in the bed," said Sunshine.

"No," said Quoyle. We're going to stick it out right here. We've got a tent in the back and I'm going to set it up beside the car and sleep in it. That's the plan." He looked at the aunt. It had been her idea. But she bent over her purse, rummaging for something private. Her old hair flattened and crushed.

"We've got air mattresses, we've got sleeping bags. We blow up the air mattresses and fold down the backseat and spread them out, put the sleeping bags on them and there you are, two nice comfortable beds. Aunt will have one and you two girls can share the other. I don't need an air mattress. I'll put my sleeping bag on the tent floor." He seemed to be asking questions.

"But I'm so starved," moaned Bunny. "I hate you, Dad! You're dumb!" She leaned forward and hit Quoyle on the back of the head.

"HERE NOW!" The outraged aunt roared at Bunny. "Take your seat, Miss, and don't ever let me hear you speak to your father like that again or I'll blister your bottom for you." The aunt let the blood boil up around her heart.

Bunny's face contorted into a tragic mask. "Petal says Dad is dumb." She hated them all.

"Everybody is dumb about some things," said Quoyle mildly. He reached back between the seats, his red hand offered to Bunny. To console her for the aunt's shouting. The dog licked his fingers. There was the familiar feeling that things were going wrong.

❄   ❄   ❄

"Well, I'm not doing that again," said the aunt, rotating her head, tipping her chin up. "Sleeping in the car. Feel like my neck is welded. And Bunny sleeps as quiet as an eggbeater."

They walked around in the roky damp, in a silence. The car glazed with salt. Quoyle squinted at the road. It curved, angled away from shoreline and into fog. What he could see of it looked good. Better than yesterday.

The aunt slapped mosquitoes, knotted a kerchief under her chin. Quoyle longed for bitter coffee or a clear view. Whatever he hoped for never happened. He rolled the damp tent.

Bunny's eyes opened as he threw in the tent and sleeping bag, but she sank back to sleep when the car started. Seeing blue beads that fell and fell from a string although she held both ends tightly.

The interior of the station wagon smelled of human hair. An arc showed in the fog, beyond it a second arc of faint prismatic colors.

"Fogbow," said the aunt. How loud the station wagon engine sounded.

Suddenly they were on a good gravel road.

"Look at this," said Quoyle. "This is nice." It curled away. They crossed a concrete bridge over a stream the color of beer.

"For pity's sake," said the aunt. "It's a wonderful road. But for what?"

"I don't know," said Quoyle, bringing his speed up.

"Got to be some reason. Maybe people come across from Killick-Claw to Capsize Cove by ferry, and then drive out to Quoyle's Point this way? God knows why. Maybe there's a provincial park. Maybe there's a big hotel," said the aunt. "But how in the world could they make it up from Capsize Cove? That road is all washed out. And Capsize Cove is dead."

They noticed the sedgy grass in the centerline, a damp sink where a culvert had dropped, and, in the silted shoulders, hoofprints the size of cooking pots.

"Nobody's driven this fancy road in a long time."

Quoyle stood on the brakes. Warren yelped as she was thrown against the back of the seat. A moose stood broadside, looming; annoyance in its retreat.

A little after eight they swept around a last corner. The road came to an end in an asphalt parking lot beside a concrete building. The wild barrens pressed all around.

Quoyle and the aunt got out. Silence, except for the wind sharpening itself on the corner of the building, the gnawing sea. The aunt pointed at cracks in the walls, a few windows up under the eaves. They tried the doors. Metal, and locked.

"Not a clue," said the aunt, "whatever it is. Or was."

"I don't know what to make of it," said Quoyle, "but it all stops here. And the wind's starting up again."

"Oh, without a doubt this building goes with the road. "You know," said the aunt, if we can scout up something to boil water in, I've got some tea bags in my pocketbook. Let's have a break and think about this. We can use the girls' soda cans to drink out of. I can't believe I forgot to get coffee."

"I've got my camping frying pan with me, said Quoyle. "Never been used. It was in my sleeping bag. I slept on it all night."

"Let's try it," said the aunt, gathering dead spruce branches festooned with moss, blasty boughs she called them, and the moss was old man's whiskers. Remembering the names for things. Heaped the boughs in the lee of the building.

Quoyle got the water jug from the car. In fifteen minutes they were drinking out of the soda cans, scalding tea that tasted of smoke and orangeade. The aunt drew the sleeve of her sweater down to protect her hand from the hot metal. Fog shuddered against their faces. The aunt's trouser cuffs snapped in the wind. Ochre brilliance suffused the tattered fog, disclosed the bay, smothered it.

"Ah!" shouted the aunt pointing into the stirring mist. "*I saw the house.* The old windows. Double chimneys. As it always was. Over there! I'm telling you I saw it!"

Quoyle stared. Saw fog stirring.

"Right over there. The cove and then the house." The aunt strode away.

Bunny got out of the car, still in her sleeping bag, shuffling along over the asphalt. "Is this it?" she said, staring at the concrete wall. "It's awful. There's no windows. Where's my room going to be? Can I have a soda, too? Dad, there's smoke coming out of the can and coming out of your mouth, too. How do you do that, Daddy?"

❋ ❋ ❋

Half hour later they struggled together toward the house, the aunt with Sunshine on her shoulders, Quoyle with Bunny, the dog limping behind. The wind got under the fog, drove it up. Glimpses of the ruffled bay. The aunt pointing, arm like that of the shooting gallery figure with the cigar in its metal hand. In the bay they saw a scallop dragger halfway to the narrows, a wake like the hem of a slip showing behind it.

Bunny sat on Quoyle's shoulders, hands clutched under his chin as he stumped through the tuckamore. The house was the green of grass stain, tilted in fog. She endured her father's hands on her knees, the smell of his same old hair, his rumbles that she weighed a ton, that she choked him. The house rocked with his strides through a pitching ocean of dwarf birch. That color green made her sick.

"Be good now," he said, loosing her fingers. Six years separated her from him, and every day was widening water between her outward-bound boat and the shore that was her father. "Almost there, almost there," Quoyle panted, pitying horses.

He set her on the ground. She ran with Sunshine up and down the curve of rock. The house threw their voices back at them, hollow and unfamiliar.

The gaunt building stood on rock. The distinctive feature was a window flanked by two smaller ones, as an adult might stand with protective arms around children's shoulders. Fan lights over the door. Quoyle noticed half the panes were gone. Paint flaked from wood. Holes in the roof. The bay rolled and rolled.

"Miracle it's standing. That roofline is as straight as a ruler," the aunt said. Trembling.

"Let's see how it is inside," said Quoyle. For all we know the floors have fallen into the cellar."

The aunt laughed. "Not likely," she shouted joyfully. "There isn't any cellar." The house was lashed with cable to iron rings set in the rock. Streaks of rust, notched footholds in the stone like steps, crevices deep enough to hide a child. The cables bristled with broken wires.

"Top of the rock not quite level," the aunt said, her sentences flying out like ribbons on a pole. "Before my time, but they said it rocked in storms like a big rocking chair, back and forth. Made the women sick, afraid, so they lashed it down and it doesn't move an inch but the wind singing through those cables makes a noise you don't forget. Oh, I do remember it in the winter storms. Like a moaning." For the house was garlanded with wind. "That's one reason I was glad when we moved over to Capsize Cove. There was a store at Capsize and that was a big thing. But then we shifted down the coast to Catspaw, and a year later we were off to the States." Told herself to calm down.

Rusted twenty-penny nails; planks over the ground-floor windows. Quoyle hooked his fingers under the window planks and heaved. Like pulling the edge of the world.

"There's a hammer in the car," he said. "Under the seat. Maybe a pry bar. I'll go back and get them. And the food. We can make a picnic breakfast."

The aunt was remembering a hundred things. "I was born here," she said. "Born in this house." Other rites had occurred here as well.

"Me too," said Sunshine, blowing a mosquito on her hand. Bunny slapped at it. Harder than necessary.

"No you weren't. You were born in Mockingburg, New York. There's smoke over there," she said, looking across the bay. "Something's on fire."

"It's chimney smoke from the houses in Killick-Claw. They're cooking their breakfasts over there. Porridge and hotcakes. See the fishing boat out in the middle of the bay? See it going along?"

"I wanna see it." said Sunshine. "I can't see it. I can't SEE it."

"You stop that howling or you'll see your bottom warmed," said the aunt. Face red in the wind.

Quoyle remembered himself crying, "I can't see it," to a math teacher who turned away, gave no answers. The fog tore apart, light charged the sea like blue neon.

The wood, hardened by time and corroding weather, clenched the nails fast. They came out crying. He wrenched the latch but could not open the door until he worked the tire iron into the crack and forced it.

Dark except for the blinding rectangle streaming through the open door. Echo of boards dropping on rock. Light shot through glass in slices, landed on the dusty floors likes strips of yellow canvas. The children ran in and out the door, afraid to go into the gloom alone, shrieking as Quoyle, levering boards outside, gave ghostly laughs and moans, "Huu huu huu."

Then inside, the aunt climbing the funneled stairs, Quoyle testing floorboards, saying be careful, be careful. Dust charged the air and they were all sneezing. Cold, must; canted doors on loose hinges. The stair treads concave from a thousand shuffling climbs and descents. Wallpaper poured backwards off the walls. In the attic a feather bed leaking bird down, ticking mapped with stains. The children rushed from room to room. Even when fresh the rooms must have been mean and hopeless.

"That's one more dollar for me!" shrieked Bunny, whirling on gritty floor. But through the windows the cool plain of sea.

Quoyle went back out. The wind sweet in his nose as spring water in a thirsty mouth. The aunt coughing and half-crying inside.

"There's the table, the blesséd table, the old chairs, the stove is here, oh my lord, there's the broom on the wall where it always hung," and she seized the wooden handle. The rotted knot burst, straws shot out of the binding wire and the aunt held a stick. She saw the stovepipe was rusted through, the table on ruined legs, the chairs unfit.

"Needs a good scurrifunging. What mother always said."

Now she roved the rooms, turned over pictures that spit broken glass. Held up a memorial photograph of a dead women, eyes half open, wrists bound with strips of white cloth. The wasted body lay on the kitchen table, coffin against the wall.

"Aunt Eltie. She died of TB." Held up another of a fat woman grasping a hen.

"Aunt Pinkie. She was so stout she couldn't get down to the chamber pot and had to set it on the bed before she could pee."

"Square rooms, lofty ceilings. Light dribbled like water through a hundred sparkling holes in the roof, caught on splinter. This bedroom. Where she knew the pattern of cracks on the ceiling better than any other fact in her life. Couldn't bear to look. Downstairs again she touched a paint-slobbered chair, saw the foot knobs on the front legs worn to rinds. The floorboards slanted under her feet, wood bare as skin. A rock smoothed by the sea for doorstop. And three lucky stones strung on a wire to keep the house safe.

Outside, an hour later, Quoyle at his fire, the aunt taking things out of the food box; eggs, a crushed bag of bread, butter, jam. Sunshine crowded against the aunt, her hands following, seizing packets. The child unwrapped the butter, the aunt spread it with a piece of broken wood for a knife, stirred the shivering eggs in the pan. The bread heel for the old dog. Bunny at the landwash casting peckled stones. As each struck, foaming lips closed over it.

Choosing the Coast

They sat beside the fire. The smoky stingo like an offering from some stone altar, the aunt thought, watched the smolder melt into the sky. Bunny and Sunshine leaned against Quoyle. Bunny ate a slice of bread rolled up, the jelly poised at the end like the eye of a toaster oven, watched the smoke gyre.

"Dad. Why does smoke twist around?"

Quoyle tore circles of bread, put pinches of egg atop and said "Here comes a little yellow chicken to the ogre's lair," and made the morsels fly through the air and into Sunshine's mouth. And the children were up and off again, around the house, leaping over the rusted cables that held it to the rock.

"Dad," panted Bunny, clacking two stones together. "Isn't Petal going to live with us any more?"

Quoyle was stunned. He'd explained that Petal was gone, that she was asleep and could never wake up, choking back his own grief, reading aloud from a book the undertaker had supplied, *A Child's Introduction to Departure of a Loved One.*

"No, Bunny. She's gone to sleep. She's in heaven. Remember, I told you?" For he had protected them from the funeral, had never said the word. Dead.

"And she can't get up again?"

"No. She's sleeping forever and she can never get up."

"You cried, Daddy. You put your head on the refrigerator and cried."

"Yes," said Quoyle.

"But I didn't cry. I thought she would come back. She would let me wear her blue beads."

"No. She can't come back." And Quoyle had given away the blue beads, all the heaps of chains and beads, the armfuls of jewel-colored clothes, the silly velvet cap sewed over with rhinestones, the yellow tights, the fake red fox coat, even the half-empty bottles of Trésor, to the Goodwill store.

"If I was asleep I would wake up," said Bunny, walking away from him and around the house.

She was alone back there, the stunted trees pressing at the foot of the rock. A smell of resin and salt. Behind the house a ledge. A freshet plunged into a hole. The color of the house on this side, away from the sun, was again the bad green. She looked up and the walls swelled out as though they were falling. Turned again and the tuckamore moved like legs under a blanket. There was a strange dog, white, somehow misshapen, with matted fur. The eyes gleamed like wet berries. It stood, staring at her. The black mouth gaped, the teeth seemed packed with stiff hair. Then it was gone like smoke.

She shrieked, stood shrieking, and when Quoyle ran to her, she climbed up on him, bellowing to be saved. And though later he beat through the tuckamore with a stick for half an hour they saw no dog, nor sign. The aunt said in the old days when the mailman drove a team and men hauled firewood with dogs, everyone kept the brutes. Perhaps, she said doubtfully, some wild tribe had descended from those dogs. Warren snuffled without enthusiasm, refused to take a scent.

"Don't go wandering off by yourselves, now. Stay with us." The aunt made a face at Quoyle that meant—what? That the child was nervy.

She looked down the bay, scanned the shoreline, the fiords, thousand-foot cliffs over creamy water. The same birds still flew from them like signal flares, razored the air with their cries. Darkening horizon.

The old place of the Quoyles, half ruined, isolated, the walls and doors of it pumiced by stony lives of dead generations. The aunt felt a hot pang. Nothing would drive them out a second time.

Doris Betts

. . . .

Bebe Sellars: May 1968

Sunburned and stripped to shorts, Jack crossed to the bedroom wall switch. His face, hands, a V at his neck were brown from long exposure; his red torso was streaked with Bebe's cleansing cream. Bebe pulled up the sheet and closed her eyes.

As soon as the light went out, she planned to change the room to suit her. She'd wipe out the knotty pine walls first of all, think up a stone fireplace and low coals, maybe a bearskin rug, but keep the ocean's roar. She had not heard a surf like that since it beat for Irene Dunne under Dover's white cliffs.

But when Jack sat on the bed, finished undressing in the dark and then kept sitting there, she forgot. "What's the matter? Sore?"

"Don't know. Something."

In the dark, Bebe smiled. She'd heard it a thousand times. He smelled smoke when the house was not on fire. Drove as if only maniacs steered all the other cars. Expected every scratch to lead to tetanus. She reached out to pat the hot skin on his back. "A free vacation with a job offer thrown in? Looks like a piece of good luck to me."

Jack didn't trust luck. With a grunt he slid between the sandy sheets, trying to ease his sunburn gently down. Then his foot, in the signal that meant No Sex Tonight, crossed hers and hooked under the other ankle. She kissed the closest part of him, a fiery shoulder, and lazily turned her attention to the dark room. Jack liked to sleep; Bebe thought it wasteful.

Suppose, she began dreamily, this is really an old house in Cornwall with a smuggler's tunnel to the sea? She pictured it, on black and white film, a place where Ray Milland had once heard ghosts. Pressed her eyelids shut. I use the tunnel to meet a fisherman's son my family won't accept. . . . Barely did she have a plot going before Jack's foot fell loose from hers; his breath got long. Until she married Jack, Bebe had not known how far down anyone could fall, falling asleep. Nightly he dived into it, plunged, dropped to some bottom she could not remember even as a child. She threw herself onto her back without waking him and listened to the ocean grind the land. The seabreeze was so strong, the moon so high, that light as thick as milk seemed blown past the curtains, spilled over the floor. It lit up the raw pine walls and a string of coat hangers. She couldn't make Cornwall out of that.

Rolling away from his body heat made the bedsprings clash, but he never stirred. Long ago as a bride, Bebe had breathed lightly while Jack Sellars slept so deep and far away. He had been a mystery to her. Those first nights she might measure him with her flat hand laid briefly on his leg or steady chest, then touch both knobs of bone which grew below his throat. Or listen to the clock, counting. He was still mystery, although familiar, and now she made up movies while he slept. Now they were married eighteen years and when she was wakeful she could cough, flap in bed, even hum music, only to feel Jack turn as easily as a fish in water and sleep on. Sometimes he ground his teeth. Millstones.

Other times, bad times, he dreamed. The jerk of his knee would wake Bebe instantly. She could hear him some nights reciting almost wearily in the dark, "Don't do it this time. Don't do it this time." Always the same words while his body stiffened. She would start rocking him back and forth. *Wake up, Jack, all right now, it's only a dream,* hoping for once she might help him wake before the woman did it this time. Did it again. If she could change the sequence of his standard dream, who knew what else might change? And Jack would pull Bebe onto him as if she were part of the warm weight of his sleep. Sometimes, then, they made love that way. (It isn't my favorite, she thought now.) But most times he slid his prickly face against her neck and his smile lay on her skin like a wrinkle she had earned, while his muscles loosened and dropped him under sleep again.

Bebe listened now to the sea, tried to picture it and could not, almost went to the window to check. If I lived here, she wondered, could I hear the difference between high tide and low?

Will I live here? Tomorrow, Sunday, and he'd have to decide. She closed her eyes. There was some movie about a tidal wave. Burt Lancaster making love to a woman on a flat beach in the moonlight. Another filmed in green, where Jennifer Jones drowned in a storm at Land's End, just beyond the reach of Joseph Cotten's hand.

She pulled up a blanket and began to drowse to the ocean's roar, some thought half forming in her mind: How easily the sea could kill us and does not.

Bebe woke in the everlasting roar.

Once, in the hall, her mother had used a varnished conch shell for a doorstop in summertime, and Bebe had braced its noisy mouth against one ear at an age when her whole skull matched its size. Now their bedroom seemed to float deep in that seashell's core. She was forty, and had grown in instead of up.

She opened her eyes and the morning window blazed. That's how the sun looked to the conch before he died. Do conch's have eyes? Bebe rolled over in bed. Jack's eyelids quivered in his sleep. He did not really like the beach.

Feeling guilty for liking it so much, she slid her foot across the grainy sheet and clenched her toes in the hairs on his leg. At least there had been no dream. Maybe the noisy sea jammed dreams the way governments could jam enemy radios.

In a normal voice she said, "Jack?" Then louder. His breathing snagged out of rhythm once and went on.

Early—the sun rose early here. Might as well get up. She sat on the mattress edge and turned to cover him with the sheet. There were pearly water blisters on his shoulder blades. He was going to peel like a katydid. That's probably what he predicted when he first walked in the ocean's edge Saturday: *I'm going to burn and peel.*

In the mirror Bebe watched herself, naked and smiling, swing out of bed and cross the pine boards. Sea air had clouded the tall mirror. Made him look like a ghost, Jack said. Bebe liked the way it softened her face and left the wrinkles out. She turned sideways. Early in the mornings her belly was flatter

Choosing the Coast

but the scar ran across it like a streak of chalk. She patted the line with pancake makeup to match her recent tan.

She almost went to the kitchen naked before she remembered George. It was George's beach house and already she wanted him out of it. She found yesterday's shorts on the bathroom floor and shook out the sand, put on one of Jack's old shirts. George's toothbrush lay by the spigot. I hope he's hungover.

The three of them had left the kitchen in a mess. Bebe didn't care. Like brown worms, their wet cigarettes swelled in the sink. She tossed them away and wiped her fingers on Jack's shirt. The men had stayed for a last drink while she got ready for bed, and she gazed around the kitchen for clues to what had happened. Somebody had knocked over Karo syrup in a cabinet and spilled a glassy puddle—looking for ginger ale? Its shape almost matched the map they had drawn on the plastic tablecloth. Bebe leaned closer. Ballpoint ink that wouldn't ever scrub off. Have to turn the damn thing over. Correction: Who ever lives here will have to turn it over. Was anything decided while she slept—yes or no? It wasn't written on the tablecloth.

When the coffee was hot, she carried a cup onto the screen porch, braced for the sight of that endless sea, shocked when it came. Imagine having the Atlantic Ocean in your front yard every day! Even in winter she would go out in a yellow slicker and stand at its edge. Say yes, Jack. Yes.

At home in Durham, she looked from her porch at sidewalk and street through an edging of plants which hardly showed over the grass. These were slowly growing toward Jack's fine camellia hedge, rooted from cuttings under glass, which in ten years would be green and glossy with blooms the size of saucers. If a lawn mower didn't get it by mistake. That's what I'd see there, at fifty.

But here Bebe's hedge would be water, greasy gray in the early light, trimmed perfectly even against the sky. And every day it would throw up shells and seaweed, change color, move, hold up toy ships, and make that everlasting noise.

Bebe finished the coffee. I'd like still to be watching all that when I am old.

But surely Jack had already said no. Looking the gift horse in the mouth plus any other opening he could find. Getting out of the car, he had glanced at Bebe, jerking his head toward the rusty trailers propped on concrete blocks. In Bebe's mind these were already repainted and strewn with rambler roses. He said, "What do you call it?"

"Pickerel Beach," said George Bennett. "Named for the plant that grows in the marsh. You ought to like that, knowing flowers the way you do."

Jack nodded—to his knowledge of flowers, not to liking the beach. The

Doris Betts

241

whole visit had happened by accident. That's what he couldn't stand, what she and Jack had argued about even before leaving Durham. Bebe said one thing just led to another. Why should it? Jack had asked.

A few days before, they held a reunion of Jack's old army unit from World War II at Fort Bragg, and George Bennett came. Jack wouldn't go. So George had showed up in Durham with some other buddy—big surprise!—and next thing she knew they were at a beach George owned, on a free vacation, and George was asking Jack to manage the place for him.

"What a piece of good luck!" she'd said when they were alone in the bedroom, putting on swimsuits.

"I don't trust luck," said Jack, pushing a finger into his ear as if the ocean made him deaf.

Bebe laughed, pinched him when he bent to step into the knit trunks. "We wouldn't be married if it wasn't for luck."

"Yours or mine?" he asked.

Would it have killed him just to nod his head?

Later, standing knee deep in the waves, he had pointed out the trailers, the frame house where they were staying, the marsh across the road from which mosquitoes would fly out in clouds. "This beach is ugly." You'd think he was used to country clubs instead of a tract house that cost them nine thousand dollars. His idea of a vacation was to turn over the compost pile or use Bebe's old nylons to tie a grapevine to a fence.

Bebe just touched him lightly between the shoulder blades. Once she had won a set of free dishes at the bank, and Jack wasn't really glad till he checked and found only one plate was chipped. After that he bought steaks to eat off them, and a bottle of wine and table candles that smelled like hyacinths. That's how he was. Bebe didn't mind it. It seemed to her when she added weight and her throat began looking slack, he had turned back into a bridegroom. As if he felt sure of keeping her then.

So she knew he wouldn't start having a good time at the beach until he settled what the drawbacks were. He was always telling her, "Bebe, don't take things at face value. That's simpleminded."

She set her coffee cup in a chair. If I wasn't simpleminded, she thought, he'd be a bachelor yet. I met him one day; on the next he said, "Come with me," and I came. Sometimes we simpleminded people do all right.

She went out into the washed, clean air. Her lungs weren't used to it, and she had to hunch in the wind to light a cigarette. Weekdays at home, she'd be walking into the café about this time, stuffing her yellow hair into a net, making herself smile at the college boys who needed coffee before they went to

Choosing the Coast

eight o'clock class. Those boys killed Bebe, moaning how hard school was, explaining it to waitresses they never tipped whose arches fell before those boys were born. Jack ate lunch in the café with her. In the booth she could almost see his ears flare. The noises the students made, talking of books, roared for him more beautiful than the sound of conch shells. He thought they were all smart and he envied them. It hurt Bebe to watch envy on his face. She wanted to imitate Jack, wanted to whisper, "Don't take things at face value," but did not.

Bebe lay alone on the sand and the sun against her eyelids turned every blood vessel into a stream of lava. Like a network of bright rivers of the world, pouring to the sea and never filling it.

＊ ＊ ＊

While she cooked supper and talked to George Bennett, Jack crossed the highway and walked alongside the marsh matted with pickerelweed, which gave the beach its name. Bebe could see him from the kitchen window, squatting by cattail reeds at the edge of the swamp, moving on. Once a small heron, dragging legs like sticks, rose from the grasses and crossed Jack's shadow with its moving one.

"What do you think?" asked George, teetering in a chair at the kitchen table. "Will he stay?" He propped his sandy feet on another chair. George was a dentist now, and claimed it had given him varicose veins, standing all day before open mouths.

"It's up to Jack."

"You leave things up to him, do you? I like that in Southern women." She said nothing. He sweetened his drink from a bottle of Jack Daniel's. "You like it here, don't you, Bebe?"

Stirring the shrimp creole, she glanced out the window at Jack pacing the marsh's edge. I like it but Jack says I'm not hard to please. "The house needs a lot of work."

"Oh, I agree. I agree. Whatever you need. Paint it up, inlay linoleum. Air-conditioning—would you like that?"

I bet the marsh stinks up close, she thought. Jack was coming toward the house now, slapping his leg with a long reed. Bet you could make a whistle out of it, like a stalk of rye.

"The property's got a funny shape, but that comes from buying it one piece at a time," George said. He bent his half-bald head over the tablecloth sketch. "I'll drain that marsh someday if the damn government doesn't condemn the whole coast for a park. Hand me some ice, will you?"

While she loosened the cubes from the tray, he smoothed the wrinkled plastic map and talked about the future of Pickerel Beach: a housing development inland along dredged canals, and at the tip a pavilion where kids could come to dance, perhaps build a marina on the creek. His words made a slow film in Bebe's head. A merry-go-round spinning by the highway, as slowly as her spoon turned in the pan. She made Jack step on its colorful platform and drop off again. Out-of-state cars between which he might be walking toward them now. She grew Jack a beard that George Bennett would like, dressed him as captain of a deep-sea fishing boat, bringing home happy tourists with a big catch. Bebe hummed background music, putting ice in George's drink, setting out three plates for their supper. And that's me, in a back room, making hush puppies and dropping potato strips in a greasy basket, letting drunks pat me on the fanny. The legs are on loan from Betty Grable. The syndicate tries to break in at Pickerel Beach with gambling interests but . . .

"Jack needs to thinks of this as an opportunity. Why should he keep on planting bushes and mowing grass at his age? There's no future for him in Durham," George said. "Or you, Bebe."

She didn't like hearing her own arguments in George's mouth. Instantly she changed the movie and put Jack, white-smocked, inside a greenhouse surrounded by rare orchids, but the screen went blank.

Jack came up the high back steps into the kitchen and his eyes went to her first. He liked the red bathing suit, though she doubted he'd ever say so aloud.

"Smells good."

Jack was handsomer now than eighteen years ago, partly because the lines of his ruddy face made his blue eyes more astonishing than ever—even Paul Newman's eyes were second-rate. Bebe once thought if she put her own up close to them she could see halfway inside his head and watch thoughts go round, and she wanted to, since he thought more than he ever said.

They ate hungrily, George trying to promote the beach, to recall Naples in the war, to draw Jack out. Under the table Jack rubbed her leg with his. Like *that*, is it? Bebe rubbed back. George described how Fort Bragg had grown, Fayetteville's go-go bars. He asked Bebe if she'd need more cabinets in this kitchen. Didn't Jack think copper screening would be better for the porch?

"You could try running the beach for one year. Then quit if you didn't like it."

"But I couldn't get my old job back," said Jack quietly, "and I like that job."

He'd never even ask, thought Bebe. When Jack leaves a place, his life grows shut behind him and he won't go back. They were both born in the foothills of the Blue Ridge, Stone County, North Carolina, but he never went home with

Choosing the Coast

Bebe for a visit. She still had family living in Stoneville and Greenway, but all Jack's kin were gone except on the nights they visited him in the dream and made him beg, "Don't do it this time"; and then did it.

"George, you've talked everything but money," said Jack, pushing back his plate.

"Finish off with a drink and I'll get down to salary."

He's going to take the job, thought Bebe. Probably for me. She whispered, "It's up to you, honey," then said she would walk on the beach while the men talked.

Jack handed her his Audubon book off the refrigerator. "Might as well learn the bird life," he said. Always trying to improve her mind. She left the two men writing dollar marks on their napkins.

Beatrice Fetner Sellars had seen the ocean once before, age twenty, half her life ago. She had added fifteen pounds and twenty years of time, had married, miscarried, lost a father and a faulty uterus, slept with a clerk and a sailor and Jack (mostly Jack); and still the sea looked to her exactly as it had to Columbus. She could not explain this awesomeness to Jack. He was the one who read books and studied nature, made fun of her weekly movies and Hollywood magazines. She did not even want to understand these feelings she got by the ocean, merely to go on having them. That wind off the water through her hair, the sound of the tide which throbbed through her whole body—outside and inside, inescapable. She wanted to live surrounded by them both, letting the breeze and the noise invade her in some way she could not express, until the sea's rhythm and her own would be vaguely the same. She could not guess what would happen them, or even if she would recognize the moment.

She stood in the sea oats on a low dune between the house and shore. If I knew more, I could say what I mean. How the sea I can't imagine an end to reaches around and makes this same noise in Africa. How all the rain ends up here. That it all goes together.

A gull cried out and swept the ocean's edge, looking for something that had died between trips. Shading her eyes against the low sun, Bebe watched it sail lower, stiff-winged, like the wooden planes her brothers had pieced together and slung off the roof while she sat in a darkened hallway, listening to the promise inside a seashell. She opened Jack's book but could not get interested in matching some bird to its picture. The gull struck water, bounced away. She walked down the beach and birds no bigger than bantams ran away from her in the foam. Jack called them sandpipers. She flipped the book's pages. Snipe? In Stone County that was a made-up bird. Curlew. Marbled godwit—pretty name. A turnstone never left one unturned, she guessed.

Let's admit it, she thought, dropping to the packed sand. Books are not for me. She lay on her back and used Audubon for a pillow, watching the sky get darker red as the sun dropped down the sky.

As soon as Bebe got quiet, a crumb of sand fell in nearby and a crab that seemed too big for its tunnel edged out sideways. It froze, seeing her there in its path like a log. Bebe kept her eye on its sandy color, knowing if she looked away she could never find it again. The crab skittered a little closer to Audubon.

She remembered the movement. The last year Grandma Fetner lived with them—when Bebe was eight—she would creep into Bebe's bedroom and drop her curled gray hand on the bed and waggle it down the blanket. She was a little childish by then. "Comes a little spider," she would say in singsong, making her fingers travel on the wool. "Comes a little spider . . ." in a slow threat, getting faster and louder. "Comesalittlespider . . . Bite 'em in the Belly!" and her claw would leap up and drive at Bebe's middle and make her scream and try to crawl up the headboard.

The crab looked now like her hand did then. Bebe felt her skin burst into gooseflesh. She slid away. In a ball, the crab rolled down its hole.

She hadn't thought about Grandma Fetner in years. Funny how everything that ever happened is saved up in your head a hundred percent, even the shiver that flies down your skin at the proper time, even the noises of Grandma's breath and your own breath, that the blanket was dark green and the headboard felt greasy from lemon oil.

She sat up and watched the sea. If I were like Jack and got a lot out of reading books, that's what I'd want to learn about. How people remember, and why. Just as I wonder now if the crab, folded and dark in the bottom of his hole, has already forgotten what it was that scared him.

Jan DeBlieu

. . . .

Old Christmas

Every January on Hatteras Island, a week or so after most families have packed up the duties and indulgences of the holidays, the residents of Rodanthe hold a celebration known as Old Christmas. It is simultaneously a meeting of friends and a curious gathering of people with little in common but their hometown and perhaps their last names.

Old Christmas has been observed in Rodanthe on the Saturday closest to Epiphany for at least a hundred years. It is said to have had its beginnings in 1752, when England adopted the Gregorian calendar and shortened the calendar year by eleven days. According to legend, the towns of Hatteras Island were not informed of the change until decades later, and then they refused to abide by it. Whether or not the legend is true, a tradition has evolved whereby the townspeople of Rodanthe spend Christmas Day with relatives in Waves, Salvo, or southern parts of the island, then throw a party in the Rodanthe Community Center to observe the holiday a second time. The celebration is planned for local families, and although tourists are welcomed, they seldom grasp the significance of the event. Moreover, many tourists are reluctant to attend, for Old Christmas has the reputation of being a drunken brawl.

It was once customary for the men of Hatteras Island to settle their grudges against each other once a year with a fist fight after dinner on Old Christmas. The custom seldom led to anything but a few brief sparring matches, and until recent years the celebration generally was held without incident. In the 1970s, however, it became common for men looking for a brawl to arrive in Rodanthe just before dark on Old Christmas. Frequently the men were not from Hatteras Island but from mainland communities or the northern reaches of the Outer Banks, and they started picking fights as soon as they got into town. The altercations ruined the holiday for some island residents. Even though Old Christmas had been held peacefully for the past several years, a few local families refuse to attend.

On January 4, the day of the 1986 celebration, no one expected any violence. Several weeks before, family circumstances had made it necessary for me to move to Atlanta for most of the winter, but I had managed to return to Rodanthe for the weekend of Old Christmas. Late in the afternoon, I wandered down the gravel road to the community center, a small, white building that once served as the town's single-room schoolhouse. The festivities were to have started at 1 P.M. with an oyster shoot, but it was nearly 2:30 when the first guns began to fire. On the far side of a patio, sheets of plywood had been fastened to a chain-link fence and painted with orange streaks to delineate the target zones. A knot of heads bent over a stack of paper targets that someone had spread on the hood of a car. Several of the targets were untouched; the marksmen had missed them completely. One target had a hole only a quarter-inch from the black bull's-eye. Maggie Smith, a thin woman with a strong chin and a ski cap covering a crop of dark hair, looked up from the targets and shrugged. "Looks like JoBob gets the oysters again," she said. It was the third time JoBob Fagundes, a local merchant, had won. The men standing around her grunted and moved off.

Beside Smith was a twelve-gauge shotgun and a box of shells. She is Mac Midgett's sister, and she seemed at ease chatting with a half-dozen local men who stood on the fringe of the group. "C'mon," she coaxed. "Who's next? Three bucks for a shot at a half-bushel of Stumpy Point oysters, the best oysters around."

I walked around the community center to where two men—both Midgetts—were stringing fishing net around a patio and stoking an oversized roaster with charcoal and wood. The roaster had been fashioned from a rusty oil drum cut in half and hinged on one side. Long tables with rough plywood tops had been placed around it. As bushels of oysters finished roasting, the men would shovel them onto the tables for the crowd to shuck and eat. The coals would not be ready for a half-hour, and I wandered inside.

The tiny dance hall had begun to fill, and the instruments for a bluegrass band were set on stage. The dancing would come later; now was the time for visiting. At the door Louell Midgett, an Ocracoke native who lives in Rodanthe with her husband, collected money and hugged friends as they entered. She saw many of them several times a month, but it was Old Christmas, after all. I rounded a corner to the building's small kitchen and was enveloped by Virginia O'Neal, the postmistress, before I even saw her. "Merry Old Christmas," she beamed, hugging me tighter. She wore a Christmas-red skirt and jacket, with a holly-green pin on her lapel. Her face shone with a gracious, happy beauty. Around were her friends from the Fairhaven Methodist Church—older women named Midgett, O'Neal, Hooper, and Gray—all in holiday clothes with festival smiles on their bright-red lips.

At a string of tables just off the kitchen, several women supervised a group of young children. These were the wives of the fishermen who congregated in a corner of the dance hall, smoking and leaning back, their crossed arms resting on ample bellies. I scanned the hall, finding scores of faces I did not recognize. It seemed many people had come from towns on the southern part of the cape. I waved to Mac Midgett and pushed my way toward the patio door. As I did, a stout women with a wide face and large, stylish glasses caught my arm. "Jan." I looked at her blankly. "I'm Joyce Rucker."

Ersie Midgett's only daughter. I pumped her hand and smiled. As a young girl she had slept in the upstairs bedroom I would later use as an office. At the age of twelve she had huddled inside the yellow frame house as a brutal wind wrenched it from its foundation. Standing behind her were her brothers, Stockton and Anderson, dressed nattily in plaid slacks. "I'm surprised to see you here," I said. It had not occurred to me that Ersie's children would attend Old Christmas.

"We wouldn't miss it for the world," Rucker said. "This is still home in some ways. But my, it's changed. Every year there are more strangers. There's no way to stop more people from coming here. The island's growing, and in many ways it's good that we have the kinds of amenities we have now. It was hard to live the way we did, with no electricity or roads. We have a movie theater in Avon now. I never thought I would live to see a movie theater open in Avon."

A few minutes later I left her to get some oysters. Ersie's children were among the wealthiest and most controversial figures on Hatteras Island. They had made a substantial portion of their money by selling land. Tonight they would rub elbows with fishermen who were slowly losing their livelihoods to pollution and powerful sportfishing lobbies. During the past ten years the people of Hatteras have divided themselves into two bitter camps, one that wants to preserve the cape's rugged desolation and a second that is working to build a string of glitzy resorts. Among the crowd in the community center were people who had grown up as cordial neighbors, and who now were entangled in disputes over the boundaries of their land. The real estate speculators were winning the fight—or at least were making the most money and gaining the most political clout. But the development of Hatteras was not to be a topic of discussion. Not here, not on Old Christmas.

Outside, a batch of Oysters had just finished cooking. A wiry man with curly, brown hair opened the lid of the roaster. Steam cascaded into the night. "Who wants oysters?" he hollered. "You want oysters, you got to make some noise."

A few of us whooped.

"Pretty slack," he said, spreading the oysters across the table in front of me. I picked one up, twisted an oyster knife to pop open the gritty shell, and sucked down the tender flesh. I downed a dozen more and went inside, where the band had begun to play.

The dance floor was filling with people of all ages and physiques, some twisting, some dancing a jerky version of the fox trot. A fisherman with the build of a concrete block held up an arm to twirl his wife, who in her forties still had the figure and toothy smile of a debutante. A thick-bodied elderly couple waltzed in the middle of the floor, bumping buttocks with the people around them. On the sidelines, women leaned their heads close together to talk above the music, and teenage girls shyly watched the dancers. I picked my way through to the other side and halted near Louell Midgett, who was still standing guard at the door. "Interesting party, isn't it?" I said.

"We usually have a good bit of fun," she said smiling. "If I were you I'd stand back against the wall a bit. Old Buck's getting ready to come in."

Old Buck is a kind of Old Christmas Santa Claus, a mythical wild bull. It is said that many years ago Old Buck impregnated every cow in Buxton Woods and terrorized local farmers until a hunter finally shot him. His spirit lives in the marshes and hammocks of Rodanthe. I had expected him to be personified by a mounted cow head, but the creature that stomped through the door had no eyes, nose, or mouth, just two horns and a piece of cowhide mounted on top of some long, sturdy object, probably a piece of wood. His lumpy back was covered by a green Army blanket, beneath which protruded two sets of legs in blue jeans and men's boots. People crowded into the smoky hall, yelling and clapping, stomping their feet.

A red-faced and jovial man led the cow into the room with a tether. "Look out, Old Buck's wild," he yelled in a gravelly voice. "He's wild tonight."

I pressed myself against the wall as the four legs beneath the blanket kicked and clomped past me. Old Buck was not only wild, he was bent on knocking down as many people as he could. The crowd screamed with laughter and scrambled for cover, some people jumping into the laps of friends who had managed to find seats on the edge of the dance floor. As one man crouched down for a picture, the bull hit him broadside and sent him reeling across stage. Fifteen seconds later Old Buck had jostled his way outside and vanished for another year.

Seldom had I laughed so hard. The crowd caught its breath as the band swung into "Truck Driving Man" for the third time. The celebration had peaked. People drifted outside, calling good-byes into the crisp night air. I had begun searching for my coat when the wiry man who had tended the oysters grabbed a microphone from the band. "Okay, I want the children cleared out of here," he said, "because this is an adult's night. And us adults are gonna fight."

"No we're not," said a large fisherman standing next to me.

I did not stay around to hear the shouting match that followed. Later I learned that the man had been calmed by friends and that violence had been avoided for another year. Barring hangovers, the town awoke the next day in good spirits. The only apparent casualty was a red pickup that had somehow missed the road and landed on its side in a muck-lined drainage ditch.

By spring I was able to move back to Hatteras Island, back into Miss Ersie's yellow house, which still creaks and moans like an old wooden boat in high winds. In summer the sea oats explode with tawny seeds, the black skimmers glide over Pamlico Sound, the loggerheads heave themselves ashore on silent nights. In fall my neighbors meet in the post office and remark on the weather, the fishing, the hurricanes that may or may not come spinning through.

In a very real sense, Hatteras Island will remain as it has for centuries, a malleable finger of land in a moody, hostile sea. In another sense, just as real and more distressing, its essence vanished with the opening twenty-five years ago of the Oregon Inlet bridge. By moving to the area and settling down with the hope to stay, I myself have chipped a piece from its core. There is a feeling that the island's charm has eroded beyond repair, and that it will only get worse in years to come. To me, Hatteras still seems pristine, yet pockets of shoddy development have so marred it that lifelong residents talk of selling their land and leaving. In Avon and Buxton developers draw up plans for golf courses and exclusive garden homes, to be built as soon as they can find the means to pump enough water and dispose of enough sewage. Such expensive housing would attract a different clientele to Hatteras Island, people with sleek clothes and elegant tastes. Whether or not the developers carry out their plans, Hatteras Island is in the process of being "discovered." Its new popularity is bound to drive up the cost of living and the dearness of land.

In a decade Cape Hatteras may well resemble every other East Coast seaside resort, not only physically but demographically. It is my fear that the independence and self-reliance—the very spirit that has enabled people here to survive storms and shipwrecks and centuries of isolation—will virtually cease to exist. What little spirit remains will be relegated to the rather demeaning category of "colorful" or "quaint." The concept of island time will become one more relic of a discarded past, in league with hurricane oil lamps, hand-woven fishing nets, and bags of yaupon tea.

Jan DeBlieu

During the months I was in Atlanta, I lived in a house surrounded on all sides by spreading dogwoods, sweet gums, and loblolly pines. In that sheltered setting I became introspective; I grew oblivious to the direction of the wind, the rise and fall of the earth, the scattering of plants and trees. The light that filtered through my curtains was more white than yellow, the light of an un-reflected sun. To soothe my homesickness for Hatteras, I conjured up memories of a fall afternoon I had spent watching birds on the beach north of town. Those images return to me even now, like a recurring dream that is sweet with beauty yet bitter with a fleeting, fragile feel.

I am walking north before sunset. The air is calm, though a short while ago the wind lifted plumes of sand and hurled them against my legs and arms with tiny, painful pricks. Sea oats spill halfway down the dunes and end in crumbling cliffs. Below, the sand is smooth but for tiny mounds of sediment pushed up by burrowing ghost crabs. The beach juts thirty yards to the east, flat as a table, then drops sharply and disappears in sky-blue, shimmering surf. Marbled waves sweep beneath my feet, like clouds sliding against a mountain.

The shorebird migration has reached its height. In front of me sanderlings, turnstones, and at least two types of sandpipers work the beach, chasing mole crabs that fizzle to the surface with receding waves. The birds are in their pale winter plumage; to tell one species from another will take a studious, unwavering eye. Moving carefully, I inch my way closer; I step ten feet toward a flock, bring my binoculars to my eyes, and freeze as the birds skitter a few steps away. They move in and out with the surf, never stopping, the clouds of their numbers dovetailing with the waves. I will never capture everything I want from them, never consume enough to be sated.

The sand is a deep buff, the color of brushed suede. Salty wind blows in my eyes, and I feel the skin on my face tighten from sun. In front of me small white birds startle, fly over the surf in an arc, and light to feed. They spook and again take wing, and again, luminous and white, like handfuls of glitter tossed in the wind.

Choosing the Coast

Working along the Shorelines

By the time Kali and I reach Ditch Plains, most of the surfers are already out of the water, taking a break from the morning's wave activity. The beach is crowded with surfers and their boards, small children running around (some in bathing suits and some completely bare), and the many others who come to watch the surfers' morning show. Kali finds herself surrounded by a pack of friendly dogs, and while she is occupied in dog social activities, I wander up to the Ditch Witch to say hello to Lil. Lil runs a small business selling breakfast, lunch, snacks, and drinks from her Wagon, as it is known. She also takes messages for the surfers, helps sell the books of local authors, is a font of information about surfing and good literature, and is, in general, a fixture on this beach. She is one of those women who successfully manages to make her living working along the shoreline, living where she wants and in the manner she wants. After saying hello and thanking her for her latest reading suggestion, I go in search of Kali and think about Lil's role in the Montauk coastal community.

Work along the shoreline inevitably calls for workers to understand and engage the ocean, powerful and calm, dangerous and full of offerings of sustenance. The authors included in this section of the anthology look at the experiences of those whose livelihoods often depend on the coastal environment and their ability to cope with the rapid changes of coastal conditions.

Lucille Clifton and Nancy Lord remind us that the ocean feeds us, but hard work, long hours, and years of knowledge go into catching the fish, crabs, or clams for our tables, while Joan Didion writes about two men, Dick Haddock and Amado Vazquez, whose career choices lead them on different paths—one a lifeguard, the other a breeder and grower of orchids—although they share the same fragile landscape, subject to ocean storms and coastal wildfires. Working coastal waters, as Tess Gallagher reminds us, may tire the body, but, there is fulfillment in this kind of work, satisfying and difficult to put into the past. While many of these authors focus their attention on male characters and their struggles to work the coast, Nancy Lord tells a more modern tale of a woman who works the Alaskan coastline alongside her husband. She is clearly his partner in fishing, yet as she reflects on her role as a fisherwoman, she realizes her comfort in returning to land, to staying on the edge and settling into a coastal world rather than a world dominated by water. All of these authors raise our awareness of the role women play working along the shores.

Kali and I have rested long enough. If we are to reach our final destination today, we had better leave this lively and friendly section of the beach and march forward. Before continuing east, however, we take a few moments to watch one surfing old-timer on his long board. We see him get into position, and, in a breathless moment, he is up and riding like a lone dancer on the waves, graceful and weightless. As the surfer and the wave move shoreward, Kali and I turn and walk toward the lighthouse, our final destination.

Ruth Moore

· ·

From *The Weir*

From his usual point of observation on Crab Point, Hardy watched the ugliness of the gathering storm. The tide was on the ebb, about half out. At any time now he could begin to drop his weir nets. But he stood for a while watching for weather signs in the curdled clouds that came driving in over the islands from the open sea.

Suppose he took the nets down now and by sunset it cleared off? It often did, this time of year. He could imagine what people would say. He could imagine Jasper and Cack having it over and Cack telling it all around the town. "Somebody broke wind and Hardy dropped his nets down."

The wind blowing in fitful gusts tugged at his sou'wester and sent a slap of rain off its brim into his eyes. Hardy fished for his handkerchief and wiped them dry. The weather signs were all bad. Wind coming in gusts, sea making up fast on the ebb tide, clouds black and roily-looking over Canvasback Island. Well, they had been last time too. He'd wait a little while longer.

Maybe in an hour or so it would either begin to clear or get worse enough so he could tell. So many times he'd taken precautions for nothing. And so many times he'd taken precautions and something had happened. Twenty years ago he could have told in a minute just what he wanted to do and when he was going to do it. Twenty years ago he'd have dropped them or left them up and wouldn't have given a hang. Now the problem nagging at him left him feeling foggy, so that the sense of wind and weather he had always depended on didn't seem to tell him anything.

People said that Hardy Turner could smell a storm three days away, and he'd always thought he could. Now, with the clouds rolling out over Canvasback and the combers beginning to put up their heads so you could see them over the outer ledges, the *feeling* of storm eluded him. He felt storm in the air these days whenever a cloud blew up on a bright day, or the wind in its ceaseless searching around the points of the compass blew for an hour or so from any of the danger spots between east and south.

He stood uncertainly, a little stooped and weary in the drooping lines of his loose wet oilskins, trying to convince himself of the signs which now bewildered him.

A scrambling on the rocks made him turn. Mildred, in raincoat and rubbers, was climbing up to him, agile as a monkey over the slippery boulders.

"Pa," she shrilled, "Ma wants to know shall she put away dinner or are you comin up to eat?"

Her bright eyes slid past him to the gray-green water, spotted here and there now with white rags of foam, then returned to fasten on his face with enjoyment and a kind of inquisitive malice.

Hell, thought Hardy. Even the kids. Even my own kid. "I'm comin home to dinner," he said aloud, more loudly than he needed to. "How'd you and your mother happen to run of an idea I wasn't?" He began stalking down the rocks slipping a little as he went.

"What's it goin to do, Pa?" Mildred came lightly down behind him, racing on ahead when he went too slowly. "Ain't it goin to be a bad storm?"

"Oh, I don't think so," said Hardy firmly. He thrust out his chest and looked grandly up at the sky. "It'll clear off before night. Don't look to me like no more'n a whisper."

    ❅   ❅   ❅

At three o'clock Leonard and Morris and Joe, in Morris's boat, came in from outside along the lee of the islands and shot up to the mooring in the Pool. It had been too nasty to drag fish, with promise of being a good deal nastier, and then they had given up the trip.

Morris made it clear on Sunday night that he expected Joe and Leonard to finish out the fishing season with him or at least go dragging until their own boat was finished, and Joe had persuaded Leonard to do it.

"After all," he said, "we do own thirds on the drag and we'd lose the rest of the season if we didn't."

"It's up to you, Joe," Leonard conceded. "As long as Morris acts human, I'll go."

Morris had acted very human—in fact, for him he had been almost pleasant. He had wanted to stay outside longer, even in the teeth of the rising weather, but he had given in with good grace when he saw that both Joe and Leonard thought it was best to come in. He hadn't, either by word or raised eyebrow, implied that they might be just a little white-livered for wanting to quit.

Ordinarily he would have suggested something of the sort, Leonard thought, although Morris knew as well as anybody that the thing to do was to quit and come inshore when the wind and sea started to kick up like this.

Working along the Shorelines

Now, as they rowed ashore from the mooring, bending their heads against the rain that slashed across the Pool, Joe suddenly said, "Godsake, Len, what's the matter with your old man? He ain't got his nets down."

"He ain't!" Leonard half stood up to look out at the weir, rocking the punt precariously as he did so. A bucket or so of water splashed over the side and Morris let out a yell.

"Hey! Maybe you know how to swim. I don't, and I don't care about the idea."

Leonard looked at him startled, and Morris glared back at him. "Rockin a boat like that!" he said. "Damn fool!"

"Ain't but five-six feet of water this far inshore," said Leonard. "What's the matter with you?"

"I said, I can't swim," said Morris, in his usual bland voice.

"Maybe Hardy's sick or somethin," interposed Joe. "He sure ought to have his nets down."

"He must be," said Leonard, with concern. "Look, Joe, if you don't mind, I'll let you do my share of the stowin away, while I hop up to the house and see where he is."

"Sure," said Joe. "Look, if ya need any help, let me know."

"Thanks," said Leonard.

At the house nothing seemed to be amiss. Grammy made a face at him through the window, and Josie was sitting at the sewing machine placidly stitching.

"Wher'n hell's Pa?" Said Leonard breathlessly.

"Out whitewashin the tie-up," said Josie. "Why, what's the matter, Leonard? Somethin wrong?"

Leonard dumped his dinner bucket in the sink and started for the wood-shed door. "He ought to be down droppin his nets, that's all," he fired back over his shoulder. "It's hellish outside, and blowin on every minute."

Hardy was in the tie-up, methodically working whitewash on to a beam with an old broom. Leonard was taken aback by his unruffled calm.

"Hello!" Hardy said, glancing at him briefly. "Have engine trouble or somethin?"

Leonard sat down on a barrel, wiping the sweat off his forehead with his handkerchief. Seeing his father all right made him feel better. "Too rough outside to drag," he said. "Thought maybe I'd get in in time to help you drop the nets."

"Why," said Hardy, dipping his broom in the bucket, "I don't believe it's bad enough for that, is it?"

"My God, Pa," Leonard burst out, "the spray's comin in over Ram Island Head in sheets! It's flood tide now, and if we don't hurry we won't get em down. You crazy?"

"No, I ain't!" snapped Hardy. "I ain't goin to drop em, that's all!"

"You'll lose em," said Leonard desperately. "This looks to me like the worst summer storm in years."

"Well, it ain't. I guess I know weather signs. I watched off the Point awhile before dinner, and it didn't look so bad to me."

"Well . . ." said Leonard. "Well . . ." He didn't know what to say or what to make of his father not being worried, not even bothering to go and look at the weather for three hours. "You . . . you ain't sick, are you, Pa?"

Hardy whirled around so sharply that the whitewash from his broom spattered on Leonard's pants. "Sick? Sick, hell! Your ma and you 'rangue the daylights out a me when I do drop them nets and now you're startin in on me cause I don't. Get to hell on out a here and let me alone!"

Leonard stared at him open-mouthed. "Look, I'll go drop em for you—"

"You touch them nets and I'll warm the hide off you. I can do it, too. I've had the hell'n enough of people tellin me what to do."

Leonard backed out of the tie-up and stamped into the house. All right, by God, he muttered to himself, if that's the way he feels.

He had not noticed in the dim light of the barn that his father's hands on the broom were shaking, and his face was set and strained and white as a sheet.

The weir must have started to go sometime in the early part of the night, probably around high tide, at nine o'clock. As darkness came on, the storm grew worse instead of showing any signs of the clearing that Hardy had promised himself. He ate his supper without saying much to anyone, and when he had finished, he left the others eating, put on his hat, and went out of the house.

"Maybe I ought to go with him," Leonard said morosely, as soon as the door had shut behind Hardy. "But I don't feel much like it, the goin-over he gi' me this afternoon."

"I don't know what's got into him," said Josie. "I never knew him to act this way before. Most always he wants people to give him advice and tell him what to do, but all day he ain't listened to one word I've said." She got up and went to the window, peering after Hardy's retreating figure as it dimmed in the dusk coming down over the island.

"He's just guessed wrong again," announced Mildred, looking up with her mouth full from her swiftly emptying plate. "He told me today it wan't goin to be a bad storm atall."

"Oh, you shut up!" Haral suddenly leaned across the table and gave her a stinging slap on one bulging cheek. The charged atmosphere of the last few hours had been a little too much for his nerves, already frayed by the weekend's sobering experience.

Mildred's mouth opened wide in a shattering roar, disclosing various objects of food lying unresolved on her tongue.

"Oh, God," said Haral, closing his eyes.

"Haral!" burst out Josie. "You go straight upstairs to bed. That was uncalled for."

"I don't think so," said Leonard. "I don't much like the way that kid talks about Pa. She's done it two-three times lately, right in front of him."

Mildred's yells, which had died down somewhat while she observed what punishment Haral was going to get, burst out again, redoubled.

"Somebody shut that blasted little sireen up," snorted Grammy. "I'm goin crazy!"

Leonard reached out and put a big hand over Mildred's mouth. "Tell her to stop, Ma, and I'll let her go."

Josie reached out and took Mildred by the arm. "Mildred," she said, "you ain't hurt. Now stop it, or upstairs you go to bed."

Leonard experimentally took his hand away, then clapped it back firmly. He picked Mildred up and carried her upstairs. "Now, look," he said. "You get undressed and into bed. You show downstairs again tonight and I'll beat a pickle out of you."

She stopped obediently, her breath catching in pitiful gasps. Leonard stood uncertainly a moment, then reached in his pocket and pulled out a quarter. "Look, you can have this," he said, and fled from the room.

"I don't know's I should 'low it," he heard Grammy say as he came back into the kitchen. "She never said no more'n any of us know is so. Hardy Turner never had no mind in his life. He—"

Leonard let out a roar. "You lay off Pa!" he shouted furiously. "If he can't make up his mind, it's because you womenfolks have picked at him till he's half out of it! You say any more, Gram, and you'll go to bed, too!"

He dragged on his sou'wester and oilcoat and slammed out of the house after Hardy.

"My!" said Grammy, wagging her head. "If that didn't sound like his grandfather!"

Hardy stood for a while in the quickly thickening darkness, watching for as long as he could see the malignant heads of the big combers rear up over the ledges and go crashing down through the weir. So far as he could tell in the dim light, nothing had carried away yet, but his sense, clear now as glass, told him that it was only a question of time. Growing in him was a feeling of relief, strong and warm as a long drink of whisky. The thing he had been afraid of for so long was happening at last. He stood quietly watching until it was too dark to see, then he walked home, bending his head against the rain that cracked like bullets against his stiff oiled hat and jacket.

Halfway up the hill he met Leonard coming down to meet him. Leonard said nothing, but swung around and fell into step with him.

"Anything we can do?" Leonard asked, as they stepped up on the porch.

"Just go to bed," said Hardy quietly. "That's where I'm headed now."

※　　※　　※

At four-thirty in the morning it was light enough to see what damage had been done. The storm had not eased off in the night, even on the ebb tide. At low water, big breakers were still curling across the channel from shore to shore, shattering on the shallows, and turning the usually still water around the weir into a weltering tumult. The wind came pouring in steadily from the southeast, carrying rain that cut the skin almost like sleet. All around the islands to the east the water was steel-gray slashed with white, and the ledges on Canvasback were buried under tons of green and white water. The spray form the crashing combers shot fifty feet into the air, falling among the flecked branches of the spruce trees a hundred yards back from the shore.

As Hardy walked along the eastern side of the beach, his boots went out of sight well over the knee in dirty yellowish foam that had blown off the combers and lay like a soiled meringue burying the beach rocks above high-water mark.

He felt at peace this morning for the first time in months. The weir, so far, was not gone, but a gap had been smashed out of one side of it, and so far as he could see from the shore, all the nets had carried away. Even as he looked now, his shoulders squared against the push of the wind and braced against his hands driven deep into his pockets, he saw a denuded pole piling shoot into the air and fall over, buried under the top of a big comber.

"Jeezus, Hardy," said a voice at his shoulder, "how come you didn't drop them nets down yistiddy, boy?"

It was old Jarvis Willow, staring blearily past him at the wreckage.

"Wouldn't a done no good if I had," said Hardy composedly. "Carried away a little slower, maybe, but it would a gone all the same."

"If you don't beat hell!" Jarv eyed him curiously. "Here I thought you'd be flat on your belly this mornin, the way you've worried about that weir. And you don't act as if you cared a hoot in hell, Hardy."

Hardy grinned. "Oh, I care," he said. "Ayeh, Jeezus, I care, Jarv."

He went along the beach past the New York House and down to the shore of the Pool where his weir dory was hauled up. The dory was half full of water, and Hardy tipped it out, puffing as he turned the heavy boat on its side.

"Hi, Hardy." Perley Higgins had spied him from the fishhouse door and had followed him down across the flats.

"Hi, Perley."

Perley's whole face drooped with unmitigated melancholy. Even his ragged mustache, wet, with the drops rolling off the ends of it, was depressed. He shifted from one rubber boot to the other, waiting for Hardy to say something, turning his eyes sidelong toward the weir. He wanted to let on to Hardy that he was sorry for him, but even a man of words like Perley couldn't seem to think of anything to say.

"Gi'me a hand haulin the dory down, will you, Perley?"

"Haul her down? Jeezus, you ain't goin off there now, are ya, Hardy?"

"The's a few nets driftin around I didn't know but I might haul aboard."

Perley looked out at the white harbor, then back to the dory. His face, twisted with unexpressed sympathy, twisted still further with relief that here was a way of showing Hardy he was sorry without talking about it. He grabbed hold of the bow of the dory and put his back into hauling her down into water deep enough to float her. Then he piled in, taking the rowing thwart and setting the tholepins into their sockets.

Hardy acknowledged his offer of assistance by saying nothing. If Perley wanted to come, he was glad to have him. He'd need someone to handle the boat while he hauled in the nets. Some of them were drifting around out there in the breakers around the weir. How many he didn't know.

Joe Comey and Leonard, walking down the road to the Pool, were electrified to see the dory heading out into the harbor.

"Hey!" said Joe. "Your old man must be goin after nets."

The boys broke into a run. The other dory was turned bottom up for safe-keeping a few hundred feet up the beach. They rolled her over and took her down the sand at a run.

Old Jarv Willow, with battle in his eye, stuck his head in at the end door of the New York House. His voice, coarsened and roughened by years of hollering two-masters from Nova Scotia to Boston, had not weakened any with his age. "Hi!" he roared. "Who's comin off with me and help Hardy pick up his nets?"

Josie, happening to look out of the window a few minutes later, was horrified to see the four or five dories heading out of the Pool. Hardy, she thought, with a cold lump of apprehension at the back of her throat. He hadn't been acting right. Had he done something foolish now? She cast a look at Grammy, trying to hide the fear in her face, but Grammy had left the west window already and was furling her heavy woolen outdoor shawl over her head and around her shoulders.

Other women in the village had already seen the dories, Josie realized, hurrying down the hill. Cack Comey, in one of Eddy's old pea jackets and her head bare, was waddling down the road ahead as fast as her flesh-impeded thighs could travel. A bunch of kids was already climbing the rocks on Crab Point. Josie only half wondered, with a worry in the back of her mind, if Mildred was among them. Haral went past her on a dead run, headed for the shore, and she heard the rising volume of voices, excited and shrill, as women and girls came out of the houses and down the path behind her. Grammy, outdistanced, screamed at the top of her cracked voice for Josie to wait, but Josie was running.

She passed Cack, and Cack called out after her, "What is it, for God's sake, Josie? Who's drownded?"

"Nobody's I know of," Josie tossed back. "You know as much as I do."

She saw soon enough, when she reached the shore, what the men were doing. A dory with Jap Comey and Morris in it was tossing only a hundred feet or so off the rocks. Jap was handling the oars, his big shoulders bent with the effort of holding the boat into the wind, while Morris, his feet astride the thwart as if it were a saddle, was fighting a big weir net in over the side. The net twisted and sucked away from him like something alive, and even as she looked, a gust of wind turned the dory half around in spite of all Jap could do. Morris let go of the net and it slithered away into the water out of reach, while he helped Jap shove on the oars and turn the dory back into the wind.

"My Lord in the landlocked heaven, look at Morris!" wheezed Cack, suddenly beside her. "What's he doin out there with a white shirt on?"

Josie located Hardy at last. He was in a dory with Perley Higgins, inside the gaping brush sections of what had been the wall of the weir. The dory was deep in the water, whether from salvaged nets or from water, Josie couldn't tell.

Leonard! She thought, her eyes hunting swiftly through the crews of the scattered dories. Yes, there he was. He and Joe Comey. She was glad he was with Joe. What Hardy had been thinking of, going off there in a dory with that fool of a Perley Higgins, she didn't know. But Hardy's dory was headed inshore now, both he and Perley pulling at the oars, and Josie saw as they came nearer that the dory was indeed loaded with nets.

"My Lord!" said Cack. "Hardy must think an awful lot of his property, lettin people risk their lives gittin drownded to save it."

May Higgins, Perley's wife, swung around on her, her eyes darkening. "It ain't property they're doin it for, as you well know, Cack Comey," she said.

Cack reddened. She started to say something, then thought better of it.

May means they're doing it for Hardy, Josie thought. Something inside her chest suddenly warmed and spread outward and she stood with tears running down her cheeks looking at the plunging dories, the harbor white and murderous, the wrecked weir against which the combers poured unceasingly.

Joan Didion

Quiet Days in Malibu

1

In a way it seems the most idiosyncratic of beach communities, twenty-seven miles of coastline with no hotel, no passable restaurant, nothing to attract the traveler's dollar. It is not a resort. No one "vacations" or "holidays," as those words are conventionally understood, at Malibu. Its principal residential street, the Pacific Coast Highway, is quite literally a highway, California 1, which runs from the Mexican border to the Oregon line and brings Greyhound buses and refrigerated produce trucks and sixteen-wheel gasoline tankers hurtling past the front windows of houses frequently bought and sold for over a million dollars. The water off Malibu is neither as clear nor as tropically colored as the water off La Jolla. The beaches at Malibu are neither as white nor as wide as the beach at Carmel. The hills are scrubby and barren, infested with bikers and rattlesnakes, scarred with cuts and old burns and new R.V. parks. For these and other reasons Malibu tends to astonish and disappoint those who have never seen it, and yet its very name remains, in the imagination of people all over the world, a kind of shorthand for the easy life. I had not before 1971 and will probably not again live in a place with a Chevrolet named after it.

2

Dick Haddock, a family man, a man twenty-six years in the same line of work, a man who has on the telephone and in his office the crisp and easy manner of technological middle management, is in many respects the prototypical Southern California solid citizen. He lives in a San Fernando Valley subdivision near a freshwater marina and a good shopping plaza. His son is a high-school swimmer. His daughter is "into tennis." He drives thirty miles to and from work, puts in a forty-hour week, regularly takes courses to maintain his professional skills, keeps in shape and looks it. When he discusses his career he talks, in a kind of politely impersonal second person, about how "you would want like any other individual to advance yourself," about "improving your rating" and "being more of an asset to your department," about "really knowing your business." Dick Haddock's business for all these twenty-six years has been that of a professional lifeguard for the Los Angeles County Department of Beaches, and his office is a $190,000 lookout on Zuma Beach in northern Malibu.

It was Thanksgiving morning, 1975. A Santa Ana wind was just dying after blowing in off the Mojave for three weeks and setting 69,000 acres of Los Angeles County on fire. Squadrons of planes had been dropping chemicals on the fires to no effect. Querulous interviews with bummed-out householders had become a fixed element of the six o'clock news. Smoke from the fires had that week stretched a hundred miles out over the Pacific and darkened the days and lit the nights and by Thanksgiving morning there was the sense all over Southern California of living in some grave solar dislocation. It was one of those weeks when Los Angeles seemed most perilously and breathtakingly itself, a cartoon of natural disaster, and it was a peculiar week in which to spend the day with Dick Haddock and the rest of the Zuma headquarters crew.

Actually I had wanted to meet the lifeguards ever since I moved to Malibu. I would drive past Zuma some cold winter mornings and see a few of them making their mandatory daily half-mile swims in open ocean. I would drive past Zuma some late foggy nights and see others moving around behind the lookout's lighted windows, the only other souls awake in all of northern Malibu. It seemed to me a curious, almost beatified career choice, electing to save those in peril upon the sea forty hours a week, and as the soot drifted down around the Zuma lookout on that Thanksgiving morning the laconic routines and paramilitary rankings of these civil servants in red trunks took on a devotionary and dreamlike inevitability. There was the "captain," John McFarlane, a man who had already taken his daily half-mile run and his daily half-mile swim and was putting on his glasses to catch up on paperwork. Had the water been below 56 degrees he would have been allowed to swim in a wet suit, but the water was not below 56 degrees and so he had swum as usual in his red trunks. The water was 58 degrees. John McFarlane is 48. There was the "lieutenant," Dick Haddock, telling me about how each of the Department's 125 permanent lifeguards (there are also 600 part-time or "recurrent" life-guards) learns crowd control at the Los Angeles County Sheriff's Academy, learns emergency driving techniques at the California Highway Patrol Academy, learns medical procedures at the U.S.C. Medical Center, and, besides running the daily half-mile and swimming the daily half-mile, does a monthly 500-meter paddle and a monthly pier jump. A "pier jump" is just what it sounds like, and its purpose is to gain practice around pilings in heavy surf. There was as well the man out on patrol.

There were as well the "call-car personnel," two trained divers and cliff-climbers "ready to roll at any time" in what was always referred to as "a Code 3 vehicle with red light and siren," two men not rolling this Thanksgiving morning but sitting around the lookout, listening to the Los Angeles Rams beat the Detroit Lions on the radio, watching the gray horizon and waiting for a call.

No call came. The radios and the telephones crackled occasionally with reports from the other "operations" supervised by the Zuma crew: the "rescue-boat operation" at Paradise Cove, the "beach operations" at Leo Carrillo, Nicholas, Point Dume, Corral, Malibu Surfrider, Malibu Lagoon, Las Tunas, Topanga North and Topanga South. Those happen to be the names of some Malibu public beaches but in the Zuma lookout that day the names took on the sound of battle stations during a doubtful cease-fire. All quiet at Leo. Situation normal at Surfrider.

The lifeguards seemed most comfortable when they were talking about "operations" and "situations," as in "a phone-watch situation" or "a riptide situation." They also talked easily about "functions," as in "the function of maintaining a secure position on the beach." Like other men at war they had charts, forms, logs, counts kept current to within twelve hours: *1405 surf res-cues off Zuma between 12:01 A.M. January 1, 1975 and 11:59 P.M. Thanksgiv-ing Eve 1975. As well as: 36,120 prevention rescues, 872 first aids, 176 beach emergency calls, 12 resuscitations, 8 boat distress calls, 107 boat warnings, 438 lost-and-found children, and 0 deaths.* Zero. No body count. When he had oc-casion to use the word "body" Dick Haddock would hesitate and glance away.

On the whole the lifeguards favored a diction as flat and finally poetic as that of Houston Control. Everything that morning was "real fine." The head-quarters crew was "feeling good." The day was "looking good." Malibu surf was "two feet and shape is poor." Earlier that morning there had been a hun-dred or so surfers in the water, a hundred or so of those bleached children of indeterminate age and sex who bob off Zuma and appear to exist exclusively on packaged beef jerky, but by ten they had all pocketed their Thanksgiving jerky and moved on to some better break. "It heats up, we could use some more personnel," Dick Haddock said about noon, assessing the empty guard towers. "That happened, we might move on a decision to open Towers One and Eleven, I'd call and say we need two recurrents at Zuma, plus I might put an extra man at Leo."

It did not heat up. Instead it began to rain, and on the radio the morning N.F.L. game gave way to the afternoon N.F.L. game, and after a while I drove with one of the call-car men to Paradise Cove, where the rescue-boat crew needed a diver. They did not need a diver to bring up a body, or a murder weapon, or a crate of stolen ammo, or any of the things Department divers sometimes get their names in the paper for bringing up. They needed a diver, with scuba gear and a wet suit, because they had been removing the propeller from the rescue boat and had dropped a metal part the size of a dime in twenty feet of water. I had the distinct impression that they particularly needed a diver in a wet suit because nobody on the boat crew wanted to go back in the water in his trunks to replace the propeller, but there seemed to be some tacit agreement that the lost part was to be considered the point of the dive.

"I guess you know it's fifty-eight down there," the diver said.

"Don't need to tell me how cold it is," the boat lieutenant said. His name was Leonard McKinley and he had "gone permanent" in 1942 and he was of an age to refer to Zuma as a "bathing" beach. "After you find that little thing you could put the propeller back on for us, you wanted. As long as you're in the water anyway? In your suit?"

"I had a feeling you'd say that."

Leonard McKinley and I stood on the boat and watched the diver disappear. In the morning soot from the fires had coated the surface but now the wind was up and the soot was clouding the water. Kelp fronds undulated on the surface. The boat rocked. The radio sputtered with reports of a yacht named *Ursula* in distress.

"One of the other boats is going for it," Leonard McKinley said. "We're not. Some days we just sit here like firemen. Other days, a day with rips, I been out ten hours straight. You get your big rips in the summer, swells coming up from Mexico. A Santa Ana, you get your capsized boats, we got one the other day, it was overdue out of Santa Monica, they were about drowned when we picked them up."

I tried to keep my eyes on the green-glass water but could not. I had been sick on boats in the Catalina Channel and in the Gulf of California and even in San Francisco Bay, and now I seemed to be getting sick on a boat still moored at the end of the Paradise Cove pier. The radio reported the *Ursula* under tow to Marina del Rey. I concentrated on the pilings.

"He gets the propeller on," Leonard McKinley said, "you want to go out?" I said I thought not.

"You come back another day," Leonard McKinley said, and I said that I would, and although I have not gone back there is no day when I do not think of Leonard McKinley and Dick Haddock and what they are doing, what situations they face, what operations, what green-glass water. The water today is 56 degrees.

3

Amado Vazquez is a Mexican national who has lived in Los Angeles County as a resident alien since 1947. Like many Mexicans who have lived for a long time around Los Angeles he speaks of Mexico as "over there," remains more comfortable in Spanish than in English, and transmits, in his every movement, a kind of "different" propriety, a correctness, a cultural reserve. He is in no sense a Chicano. He is rather what California-born Mexicans sometimes call "Mexican from-Mexico," pronounced as one word and used to suggest precisely that difference, that rectitude, that personal conservatism. He was born in Ahualulco, Jalisco. He was trained as a barber at the age of ten. Since the age of twenty-seven, when he came north to visit his brother and find new work for himself, he has married, fathered two children, and become, to the limited number of people who know and understand the rather special work he found for himself in California, a kind of legend. Amado Vazquez was, at the time I first met him, head grower at Arthur Freed Orchids, a commercial nursery in Malibu founded by the late motion-picture producer Arthur Freed, and he is one of a handful of truly great orchid breeders in the world.

In the beginning I met Amado Vazquez not because I knew about orchids but because I liked greenhouses. All I knew about orchids was that back in a canyon near my house someone was growing them *in greenhouses*. All I knew about Amado Vazquez was that he was the man who would let me spend time alone in these greenhouses. To understand how extraordinary this seemed to me you would need to have craved the particular light and silence of greenhouses as I did: all my life I had been trying to spend time in one greenhouse or another, and all my life the person in charge of one greenhouse or another had been trying to hustle me out. When I was nine I would deliberately miss the school bus in order to walk home, because by walking I could pass a greenhouse. I recall being told at that particular greenhouse that the purchase of a nickel pansy did not entitle me to "spend the day," and at another that my breathing was "using up the air."

And yet back in this canyon near my house twenty-five years later were what seemed to me the most beautiful greenhouses in the world—the most aqueous filtered light, the softest tropical air, the most silent clouds of flowers—and the person in charge, Amado Vazquez, seemed willing to take only the most benign notice of my presence. He seemed to assume that I had my own reasons for being there. He would speak only to offer a nut he had just cracked, or a flower cut from a plant he was pruning. Occasionally Arthur Freed's brother Hugo, who was then running the business, would come into the greenhouse with real customers, serious men in dark suits who appeared to have flown in from Taipei or Durban and who spoke in hushed voices, as if they had come to inspect medieval enamels, or uncut diamonds.

But then the buyers from Taipei or Durban would go into the office to make their deal and the silence in the greenhouse would again be total. The temperature was always 72 degrees. The humidity was always 60 per cent. Great arcs of white phalaenopsis trembled overhead. I learned the names of the crosses by studying labels there in the greenhouse, the exotic names whose value I did not then understand. *Amabilis* x *Rimestadiana = Elisabethae. Aphrodite* x *Rimestadiana = Gilles Gratiot. Amabilis* x *Gilles Gratiot = Katherine Siegwart* and *Katherine Siegwart* x *Elisabethae = Doris. Doris* after Doris Duke. *Doris* which first flowered at Duke Farms in 1940. At least once each visit I would remember the nickel pansy and find Amado Vazquez and show him a plant I wanted to buy, but he would only smile and shake his head. "For breeding," he would say, or "not for sale today." And then he would lift the spray of flowers and show me some point I would not have noticed, some marginal difference in the substance of the petal or the shape of the blossom. "Very beautiful," he would say. "Very nice you like it." What he would not say was that these plants he was letting me handle, these plants "for breeding" or "not for sale today," were stud plants, and that the value of such a plant at Arthur Freed could range from ten thousand to more than three-quarters of a million dollars.

I suppose the day I realized this was the day I stopped using the Arthur Freed greenhouses as a place to eat my lunch, but I made a point of going up one day in 1976 to see Amado Vazquez and to talk to Marvin Saltzman, who took over the business in 1973 and is married to Arthur Freed's daughter Barbara. (As in *Phal. Barbara Freed Saltzman* "Jean McPherson," *Phal. Barbara Freed Saltzman* "Zuma Canyon," and *Phal. Barbara Freed Saltzman* "Malibu Queen," three plants "not for sale today" at Arthur Freed.) It was peculiar talking to Marvin Saltzman because I had never before been in the office at Arthur Freed, never seen the walls lined with dulled silver awards, never seen the genealogical charts on the famous Freed hybrids, never known anything at all about the actual business of orchids.

"Frankly it's an expensive business to get into," Marvin Saltzman said. He was turning the pages of *Sander's List*, the standard orchid studbook, published every several years and showing the parentage of every hybrid registered with the Royal Horticultural Society, and he seemed oblivious to the primeval silence of the greenhouse beyond the office window. He had shown me how Amado Vazquez places the pollen from one plant into the ovary of a flower on another. He had explained that the best times to do this are at full moon and high tide, because phalaenopsis plants are more fertile then. He had explained that a phalaenopsis is more fertile at full moon because in nature it must be pollinated by a night-flying moth, and over sixty-five million years of evolution its period of highest fertility began to coincide with its period of highest visibility. He had explained that a phalaenopsis is more fertile at high tide because the moisture content of every plant responds to tidal movement. It was all an old story to Marvin Saltzman. I could not take my eyes from the window.

"You bring back five thousand seedlings from the jungle and you wait three years for them to flower," Marvin Saltzman said. "You find two you like and you throw out the other four thousand nine hundred ninety-eight and you try to breed the two. Maybe the pollenization takes, eighty-five per cent of the time it doesn't. Say you're lucky, it takes, you'll still wait another four years before you see a flower. Meanwhile you've got a big capital investment. An Arthur Freed could take $400,000 a year from M-G-M and put $100,000 of it into getting this place started, but not many people could. You see a lot of what we call backyard nurseries—people who have fifty or a hundred plants, maybe they have two they think are exceptional, they decide to breed them—but you talk about major nurseries, there are maybe only ten in the United States, another ten in Europe. That's about it. Twenty."

Twenty is also about how many head growers there are, which is part of what lends Amado Vazquez his legendary aspect, and after a while I left the office and went out to see him in the greenhouse. There in the greenhouse everything was operating as usual to approximate that particular level of a Malaysian rain forest—not on the ground but perhaps a hundred feet up—where epiphytic orchids grow wild. In the rain forest these orchids get broken by wind and rain. They get pollinated randomly and rarely by insects. Their seedlings are crushed by screaming monkeys and tree boas and the orchids live unseen and die young. There in the greenhouse nothing would break the orchids and they would be pollinated at full moon and high tide by Amado Vazquez, and their seedlings would be tended in a sterile box with sterile gloves and sterile tools by Amado Vazquez's wife, Maria, and the orchids would not seem to die at all. "We don't know how long they'll live," Marvin Saltzman told me. "They haven't been bred under protected conditions that long. The botanists estimate a hundred and fifty, two hundred years, but we don't know. All we know is that a plant a hundred years old will show no signs of senility."

It was very peaceful there in the greenhouse with Amado Vazquez and the plants that would outlive us both. "We grew in osmunda then," he said suddenly. Osmunda is a potting medium. Amado Vazquez talks exclusively in terms of how the orchids grow. He had been talking about the years when he first came to this country and got a job with his brother tending a private orchid collection in San Marino, and he had fallen silent. "I didn't know orchids then, now they're like my children. You wait for the first bloom like you wait for a baby to come. Sometimes you wait four years and it opens and it isn't what you expected, maybe your heart wants to break, but you love it. You never say, 'that one was prettier.' You just love them. My whole life is orchids."

And in fact it was. Amado Vazquez's wife, Maria (as in *Phal. Maria Vasquez* "Malibu," the spelling of Vazquez being mysteriously altered by everyone at Arthur Freed except the Vazquezes themselves), worked in the laboratory at Arthur Freed. His son, George (as in *Phal. George Vasquez* "Malibu"), was the sales manager at Arthur Freed. His daughter, Linda (as in *Phal. Linda Mia* "Innocence"), worked at Arthur Freed before her marriage. Amado Vazquez will often get up in the night to check a heater, adjust a light, hold a seed pod in his hand and try to sense if morning will be time enough to sow the seeds in the sterile flask. When Amado and Maria Vazquez go to Central or South America, they go to look for orchids. When Amado and Maria Vazquez went for the first time to Europe a few years ago, they looked for orchids. "I asked all over Madrid for orchids," Amado Vazquez recalled. "Finally they tell me about this one place. I go there, I knock. The woman finally lets me in. She agrees to let me see the orchids. She takes me into a house and . . ."

Amado Vazquez broke off, laughing.

"She has three orchids," he finally managed to say. "Three. One of them dead. All three from Oregon."

We were standing in a sea of orchids, an extravagance of orchids, and he had given me an armful of blossoms from his own cattleyas to take to my child, more blossoms maybe than in all of Madrid. It seemed to me that day that I had never talked to anyone so direct and unembarrassed about the things he loved. He had told me earlier that he had never become a United States citizen because he had an image in his mind which he knew to be false but could not shake: the image was that of standing before a judge and stamping on the flag of Mexico. "And I love my country," he had said. Amado Vazquez loved his country. Amado Vazquez loved his family. Amado Vazquez loved orchids. "You want to know how I feel about the plants," he said as I was leaving. "I'll tell you. I will die in orchids."

4

In the part of Malibu where I lived from January of 1971 until quite recently we all knew one another's cars, and watched for them on the highway and at the Trancas Market and at the Point Dume Gulf station. We exchanged information at the Trancas Market. We left packages and messages for one another at the Gulf station. We called one another in times of wind and fire and rain, we knew when one another's septic tanks needed pumping, we watched for ambulances on the highway and helicopters on the beach and worried about one another's dogs and horses and children and corral gates and Coastal Commission permits. An accident on the highway was likely to involve someone we knew. A rattlesnake in my driveway meant its mate in yours. A stranger's campfire on your beach meant fire on both our slopes.

In fact this was a way of life I had not expected to find in Malibu. When I first moved in 1971 from Hollywood to a house on the Pacific Coast Highway I had accepted the conventional notion that Malibu meant the easy life, had worried that we would be cut off from "the real world," by which I believe I meant daily exposure to the Sunset Strip. By the time we left Malibu, seven years later, I had come to see the spirit of the place as one of shared isolation and adversity, and I think now that I never loved the house on the Pacific Coast Highway more than on those many days when it was impossible to leave it, when fire or flood had in fact closed the highway. We moved to this house on the highway in the year of our daughter's fifth birthday. In the year of her twelfth it rained until the highway collapsed, and one of her friends drowned at Zuma Beach, a casualty of Quaaludes.

One morning during the fire season of 1978, some months after we had sold the house on the Pacific Coast Highway, a brush fire caught in Agoura, in the San Fernando Valley. Within two hours a Santa Ana wind had pushed this fire across 25,000 acres and thirteen miles to the coast, where it jumped the Pacific Coast Highway as a half-mile fire storm generating winds of 100 miles per hour and temperatures up to 2500 degrees Fahrenheit. Refugees huddled on Zuma Beach. Horses caught fire and were shot on the beach, birds exploded in the air. Houses did not explode but imploded, as in a nuclear strike. By the time this fire storm had passed 197 houses had vanished into ash, many of them houses which belonged or had belonged to people we knew. A few days after the highway reopened I drove out to Malibu to see Amado Vazquez, who had, some months before, bought from the Freed estate all the stock at Arthur Freed Orchids, and had been in the process of moving it a half-mile down the canyon to his own new nursery, Zuma Canyon Orchids. I found him in the main greenhouse at what had been Arthur Freed Orchids. The place was now a range not of orchids but of shattered glass and melted metal and the imploded shards of the thousands of chemical beakers that had held the Freed seedlings, the new crosses. "I lost three years," Amado Vazquez said, and for an instant I thought we would both cry. "You want today to see flowers," he said then, "we go down to the other place." I did not want that day to see flowers. After I said goodbye to Amado Vazquez my husband and daughter and I went to look at the house on the Pacific Coast Highway in which we had lived for seven years. The fire had come to within 125 feet of the property, then stopped or turned or been beaten back, it was hard to tell which. In any case it was no longer our house.

1976–1978

3 A.M. Kitchen: My Father Talking

For years it was land working me, oil fields,
cotton fields, then I got some land. I
worked it. Them days you could just about
make a living. I was logging.

Then I sent to Missouri. Momma
come out. We got married.
We got some kids. Five kids.
That kept us going.

We bought some land near the water.
It was cheap then. The water
was right there. You just looked out
the window. It never left the window.

I bought a boat. Fourteen footer.
There was fish out there then.
You remember, we used to catch
six, eight fish, clean them right
out in the yard. I could of fished to China.

I quit the woods. One day just
walked out, took off my corks, said that's
it. I went to the docks.
I was driving winch. You had to watch
to see nothing fell out of the sling. If
you killed somebody you'd
never forget it. All
those years I was just working
I was on edge, every day. Just working.

You kids. I could tell you
a lot. But I won't.

It's winter. I play a lot of cards
down at the tavern. Your mother.
I have to think of excuses
to get out of the house. You're
wasting your time, she says. You're wasting
your money.

You don't have no idea, Threasie.
I run out of things
to work for. Hell, why shouldn't I
play cards? Threasie,
some days now I just don't know.

Boat Ride

for Galway

Since my girlhood, in that small boat
we had gone together for salmon
with the town still sleeping and the wake
a white groove in the black water, black
as it is when the gulls are just stirring and
the ships in the harbor are sparked with lights
like the casinos of Lucerne.
That morning my friend had driven an hour
in darkness to go with us, my father
and me. There'd been an all-night party.
My friend's face so tired I thought, *Eskimo-eyes*.
He sighed, as if stretched out
on a couch at the back of his mind.

Getting the bait and tackle. What
about breakfast? No breakfast.
Bad luck to eat breakfast before fishing, but
good luck to take smoked salmon to eat
on the water in full sun. Was my friend's coat

Working along the Shorelines

warm enough? The wind can come up.
Loaning him my brothers plaid jacket.

Being early on the water, like getting first
to heaven and looking back through memory
and longing at the town. Talking little, and
with the low, tender part
of our voices; not sentences but
friendlier, as in nodding to one who already
knows what you mean.

Father in his rain-slicker—seaweed green over
his coat, over blue work shirt, over cream-
colored thermal underwear that makes a white V
at his neck. His mouth open so the breath
doesn't know if it's coming or going—like any
other wave without a shore. His mind
in the no-thought of guiding the boat.
I stare into the water folding
along the bow, *gentian*—the blue with darkness
engraved into its name, so the sound
petals open with mystery.

Motor-sound, a low burbling with a chuckle
revolving in the *smack smack* of the bow
spanking water. *You hear me, but you don't
hear me,* the motor says
to the fish. A few stars
over the mountains above the town.
I think *pigtails,* and that the water under us
is at least as high as those mountains, deep
as the word *cello* whispered under water—
cello, cello until it frees a greeting.

We pass the Coast Guard station, its tower
flashing cranky white lights beside
the barracks where the seamen sleep in
long rows. Past the buoy, its sullen red bell
tilting above water. All this time
without fishing—important to get out of
the harbor before letting the lines

down, not time wasted but time
preparing, which includes invitation and
forgetting, so the self is occupied freely
in idleness.

"Just a boat ride," my father says, squinting
where sun has edged the sky toward Dungeness
a hazy mix of violet and pink. "Boat ride?"
I say. "But we want salmon."
"I'll take cod, halibut, old shoes, anything
that's going," says my friend. "And you'll get
dogfish," my father says. "There's enough
dogfish down there to feed all Japan."
He's baiting up, pushing the double hooks
through the herring. He watches us
let the lines out. "That's plenty," he says,
like it's plain this won't come
to much.

Sitting then, nothing to say for a while,
poles nodding slightly. My friend, slipping
a little toward sleep, closes his eyes.
Car lights easing along Ediz Hook, some
movement in the town, Port of the Angels,
the angels turning on kitchen lights,
wood smoke stumbling among scattered hemlock,
burning up questions, the angels telling
their children to get up, planning the future
that is one day long.

"Hand me that coffee bottle, Sis," my father
says. "Cup of coffee always makes the fish
bite." Sure enough, as he lifts the cup,
my pole hesitates, then dips. I brace
and reel. "Damned dogfish!" my father says,
throwing his cigarette into the water. "How
does he know?" my friend asks. "No fight,"
I say. "They swallow the hook down
their gullets. You have to cut
the leader."

Working along the Shorelines

No sun-flash on silver scales when it
breaks water, but thin-bellied brown, shark-
like, and the yellow-eyed insignia
that says: *there will be more of us.*
Dogfish. Swallower of hooks, waster of hopes
and tackle. My father grabs the line, yanks
the fish toward the knife, slashes twice,
gashing the throat and underbelly so
the blood spills over his hand.
"there's one that won't come back," he says.

My friend witnesses without comment or
judgment the death and mutilation
of the dogfish. The sun is up. My friend
is wide awake now. We are all wide
awake. The dogfish floats away, and a tenderness
for my father wells up in me, my father
whom I want my friend to love and who intends,
if he must, as he will, to humor us, to keep
fishing, to be recorded in the annals
of dogfish as a scourge on the nation of
dogfish which has fouled his line, which is
unworthy and which he will single-handedly
wipe out.

When the next fish hits my friend's line
and the reel won't sing, I take out my
Instamatic camera: "That's a beautiful
dogfish!" I say. "I'll tell them in New York
it's a marlin," my friend says. I snap
his picture, the fish held like
a trophy. My father leans out of
the frame, then cuts the line.

In a lull I get him to tell stories,
the one where he's a coal miner in Ottumwa,
Iowa, during the Depression and the boss
tries to send the men into a mine where
a shaft collapsed the day before. "You'll
go down there or I'll run you out of

this town," the boss says. "You don't
have to run me. I'm not just leaving
your town, I'm leaving your whole goddamned
state!" my father says, and he turns
and heads on foot out of the town, some
of the miners with him, hitching from there
to the next work in the next state.

My father knows he was free
back there in 1935 in Ottumwa, Iowa, and he
means you to know you don't have to risk
your life for pay if you can tell the boss to
go to hell and turn your heel. What
he doesn't tell is thirty years on the docks,
not a day missed—working, raising
a family.

I unwrap smoked salmon sandwiches and we bite
into them. It is the last fishing trip
I will have with my father. He
is ready to tell the one about the time
he nearly robbed the Seminole Bank in
Seminole, Oklahoma, but got drunk
instead and fell asleep.
He is going to kill five more dogfish
without remorse; and I am going to
carry a chair outside for him
onto the lawn of the Evergreen Radiation
Center where he will sit and smoke
and neither of us feels like talking, just
his—"The sun feels good."
After treatments, after going back
to my sister's where he plays with her baby—
"There's my gal! Is the Kiss Bank
open?"—in the night, rising up in the dream
of his going to say, "Get my billfold," as if
even his belongings might be pulled into
the vortex of what would come.

We won't catch a single salmon that day.
No strikes even. My friend and I
will share a beer and reminisce in advance
about the wonderful dogfishing we had.
My father wipes blood from his knife
across his knee and doesn't
look up. He believes nothing
will survive of his spirit or body. His god
takes everything and will not be
satisfied, will not be assuaged by the hopes, by
the pitiful half-measures of the living.
If he is remembered, that too
will pass.

It is good then,
to eat salmon on the water, to bait the hook
again, even for dogfish, to stare back at
the shore as one who withholds nothing, who,
in the last of himself, cannot put together
that meaning, and need not, but yields in thought
so peacefully to the stubborn brightness of
light and water: we are awake with him
as if we lay asleep. Good memory,
if you are such a boat, tell me
we did not falter in the vastness
when we walked ashore.

Tess Gallagher

Nancy Lord

· ·

Putting Up Boat

At the end of the season, the fireweed blossoms are closed clear to their last spiky tops, and geese straggle into overhead vees. Mornings and evenings, unless there's a good wind, the gnats come out; they chew at the skin on my wrists and along my hairline. Ken and I catch the only not-too-rough tide in several days to beach our skiff, and then we crank it up over a berm and pull its drain plug for the winter.

Every year when we do this, I think of our neighbor Charlotte Hayden. When we first came to the beach, she confided in me that this was her favorite time of the year—when the boat was put up. Each fall I understand a little more what she meant. We survived another season. Nobody on the beach drowned. No boats were lost; all potential disasters were averted. I will no longer need to strain my eyes to check our moored skiff at first light or to worry as I lose sight of it behind the big fall-storm swells. We are out of the water, and we are indeed lucky in this world.

Charlotte's been dead for ten years, but in some ways I feel closer to her each year, almost as though I were becoming her. These neighbors of ours— George and Charlotte Hayden—have acted as elders to Ken and me, teaching us the ways of the beach, and although we haven't always wanted to do things *their* way, we have perhaps become more like them than we ever intended.

As usual, this year we're the last ones on the beach—Ken and me and George. George's two-man hired crew is gone, and his visitors, too, and the bum knee that's bothered him all summer goes back and forth between just hurting and not working at all. Together, we pick a day to put up his boat.

The aluminum dory's already on the beach when we get to George's camp, a mile and a half away. The tide had still been coming in, and sloppy, when George beached the boat, and he'd taken waves up through the motor well. The stern sits awash, and everything he'd pulled from the boat—gas tanks, oars, his traveling tarp, a tote of raingear and boots, anchor, mooring buoy—

lies on the beach. The gas tanks were swamped before he unloaded them, and his two outboards might have taken a couple of wave-overs, too.

We go to work. The task is simple, really. We have a puller that's like a heavy-duty come-along, and we attach its cable to the boat's bow and then crank, swinging the handle back and forth, back and forth. The boat, far larger and heavier than our own, advances bit by slow bit up the beach.

It all takes time. The boat needs to be lined up with the dock beside the cabin, and this means pulling from one point and then another and shoving the boat sideways with poles we jam under it. It needs to be on rollers, which we cut from beach logs, but it's so heavy it presses the rollers into the sand, and we shovel out the sand that builds up as berms. The boat's weight cracks to splinters one dry cottonwood roller and then another, and we cut larger, sturdier ones from spruce. We move rocks out of the path. We set up a come-along to pull the stern to one side. Ken cranks and then I crank, and then Ken cranks again. George limps around, fetching lines and shovels and putting things away. We talk and joke, loud so George can hear. We take off the smaller outboard to lighten the load. We place another roller under the bow and keep cranking. We stop to watch a landslide of dusty dirt fall down the bank on the far side of the creek.

I think of the times I've crossed the inlet in George's boats, catching a ride back from town or going with him for groceries and parts. Once on a clear day, from the middle of the inlet, we exclaimed over Denali towering on the horizon a hundred seventy-five miles away. Usually we were beaten with spray, and always we had to negotiate the rips—those areas where the currents bang together in sharp, pitching waves that can swallow a smaller boat and where submerged logs and other scrap collect.

We bully and crank the dory some more, and I consider the business of getting around. Back when their only propulsion was legs and strong paddling arms, and later, when outboards were all of nines horsepower, people traveled the inlet and its beaches more than they do today. The first time our southside neighbor, Gladys Elvaas, came back here in 1939, she and her husband were long-distance boating from the southern inlet to Anchorage with a load of beaver and muskrat pelts; later, she would walk ten miles or more to exchange *Redbook* and *Good Housekeeping* magazines with the other women on the beach.

Overhead, another de Havilland Beaver drones. These big planes, from flying services across the inlet, have become a fixture of the summer's airspace, crossing back and forth all daylight long. They carry sport fishermen to inland lakes full of sockeyes and, now, to upriver sections of the Kustatan, where their paying passengers sit in lawn chairs at the river's edge and hurl lures at silver salmon. The "sports," as George calls them, fly in and out the same day, each hauling home the limit of salmon. They cover distances without, I think, really traveling. They are transported.

George's dory slides forward another inch. I'm getting to know each grain of sand along its path.

Like watching for fish to hit a net, like net mending, like filling buckets with beach coal, putting up boats is not only a ritual of the beach, but an act of *kairós*[sacred]-time contemplation. Clouds move slowly across the sky; waves beat at the shoreline; George's wind sock flutters. A lone glaucous-winged gull glides past. I peel off my sweatshirt and feel the air on my arms. I know this ritual. It has history and purpose, a way of doing and a way of being. It's part of what we do here, one of the many neighborly conditions of living in this place. My mind moves back and forth through space and time. I think about splashing through rips, about Charlotte and Gladys, and about Doris, before our time, who used to winter up beyond the lake and periodically snowshoe or sled down to Gladys's camp to bake bread in her large oven. When Gladys returned in the spring, she'd find socks stuffed around her windows where Doris had tried to block the frame-rattling winds.

Putting up boat was how we began, after all, the first time we came to the beach, in 1978.

We came once by chartered plane and stayed for about an hour, looking over the camp and the beach. Although it was still only August, the fisherman whose place it was had left for the year, and we didn't see anyone else. We went home and bought the cabin, the fishing locations, the necessary permit, a dinky wooden boat, and a pile of wet nets. What we knew about fishing Ken had learned in a week of helping friends at their camp farther down the inlet; I knew fish only from working at a salmon hatchery and kayaking among the seine boats that fished an adjacent lagoon.

Still, we'd moved to Alaska five years earlier with fishing in mind. From our college rooms on the East Coast, we'd studied maps of the state, narrowing our choices to coastal towns, to coastal towns we could drive to, to towns where commercial fishing was a main industry, to coastal fishing towns that were small but not too small. I was the one who was determined to move to Alaska; I had, I think, always known I would, but ever since my visit to the state's interior two years earlier, my resolve had been absolute. Ken was less monomaniacal about our relocation or its permanence, but since we wanted to be together, the only issue was exactly where we'd land. Ken, in particular, thought he'd like to fish, while I was most committed to finding a community where the landscape would stun my eyes every single day. We picked two towns that seemed to meet our criteria and wrote for their weekly newspapers and to their chambers of commerce. We got a nice note back from one of the chamber secretaries, full of small-town pride but warning us that there really wasn't any work to be found there. We bought a no-frills pickup truck and built a camper on the back, and when school was out we drove straight to that town in ten days.

It turned out to be the right place for us. When we're not at fishcamp, we live there still.

There weren't many jobs—that much was true. We didn't become fishermen but did whatever we could that would allow us to stay where we wanted to be. For me, that meant cracking crab legs and sorting shrimp at the cannery, and then cleaning rooms in a hotel, and then trying to stay awake nights at the weather service, where I filed hourly temperature and wind reports. Ken helped out at a fledgling sports shop and changed the recordings at a volcano-monitoring station. Nights, he worked the desk at another hotel. At first we lived in our truck; then we house-sat at an off-road homestead. Eventually we bought the sports shop business and then its building and lot, and then we built a new, larger building. We ran that business, without employees or pay, six days a week for five years, in addition to always working, between us, at least a couple of other jobs. Finally we made our grubstake.

We worked hard in those early years, but we were young and we expected to. Ken and I had in common, as well, stubborn beliefs in our own capabilities—we were certain we could do just about anything we wanted to, if we just did it. Neither of us suffered any concerns about "career paths"; that was not what we were up to in stitching together our lives.

There were, of course, moments when I stood behind our store counter and wondered why I was there instead of out in the Alaska I'd come for, putting to use the boots and skis we sold. There were moments in our partnership, too, when Ken and I infuriated each other. We were still so young; in some ways we were still being formed—tempered, maybe—by our environment and by each other.

So it was that we finally came to fishing. We chose setnetting because it was something we could do together, and we chose the west side of Cook Inlet because it was somewhere we could get to but still far enough away, in roadless Alaska. We returned to the beach in September, shortly after our initial look, to dry the nets we'd just bought and figure out what we'd need for the next season. On our first day, we walked north on the beach to a substantial red-and-white building with a plume of chimney smoke and met George and Charlotte. They were the last fishermen on the beach that year.

George is a big man, and he was wearing what we would come to recognize as his trademark white dress shirt, slightly frayed, which set off the bronze of his face and forearms. Thick, white hair curled onto his forehead, which—from being shaded by his hat—was paler than the rest of his face, and his eyes were a watery, seagoing gray. He was, I thought, an icon of a fisherman, and it was clear from his first handshake that he belonged to his life, to the beach and the fishing. Charlotte might have been anyone's kindly grandmother—a little thin, a little stooped in the shoulders, content to let George talk while she heated water and gazed from the window at their dory bucking on its mooring.

We had tea and cookies with them and learned a first few things about our fishing sites and what we could expect from them. They'd been George and Charlotte's sites before they'd sold them, and when they were theirs, George told us, they were the best producers on all their long beach. (Only later would we learn they were also the hardest to fish because of the current and rocks and that George referred to our beach as a "young man's beach.")

George took us into the back part of the building—a workshop stuffed with old leadlines, wooden corks and kegs, and tools I couldn't even imagine a use for—and showed us a huge pressure-canning retort. Their camp was a former cannery where, in the 1940s, they'd put up in hand-packed cans the catch from a dozen nets fished six days a week, day and night. Back in the kitchen, George told us a story about a fisherman who, when asked what he'd do if he had a million dollars, said he guessed he'd just keep fishing until it was all gone. Charlotte looked slightly pained—whether from hearing the story so many times or from knowing the truth in it, I couldn't guess.

They were finished fishing for the year, and we agreed to come back on a calm day later in the week and help put up their boat. When we left, George handed us a package of smoked salmon wrapped neatly in newspaper and said, "Welcome to the beach," words that seemed at the time to be both a vow of friendship and a sort of blessing. They were in fact both, and over the years George and Charlotte and their children and grandchildren and, later, George's second wife, Lorraine, have all been good to us, and so has the beach.

And so it was that our first act as new fishermen was helping to put up George's old wooden dory, the *Running W*.

The *Running W* was old even then, and heavy. George had built her of his own design, which was, like many of George's efforts, unique. Her thirty-foot hull was shaped like a W, made to cut through the water like the usual V shapes but offering greater stability. Floorboards fit in to make a flat working surface, but openings on the sides allowed fish to fall under the boards, where they'd be stored until delivery time. Another feature was a pipe hole in its center, normally kept sealed. George used large rocks as offshore anchors for his nets, and he moved these with a winch he braced across the boat gunnels, over the hole. The line to an eyebolt screwed into the rock was passed through the hole and pipe, and the rock—sometimes as big as a washing machine— was winched off the bottom and slowly motored to its location.

George had an equally ingenious way of bringing in the *Running W* for winter storage. Using a come-along and log rollers, we cranked it partway up the beach. Then we turned it over, blocked it up, slid a huge cylindrical metal buoy—one of George's scavengings—under it, and winched and rolled that up the beach, then up the ramp to the top of the dock.

That first year the whole operation, which took an entire day, was a mystery to me. I never grasped the mechanics of what we were doing, never anticipated the next step so I could be truly helpful. George would get a roller. Ken would tie a line. One of them would crank on the come-along. George would get a block for under the boat. He'd shovel. He'd get a pole and lever the boat sideways. Ken would attach another come-along and pull from another direction. They'd wrap a line around the boat. Charlotte watched nervously from the window, cigarette to her lips.

I felt caught in a male rite, something I decided must be linked to male chromosomes or hormones, something begun with Tinkertoys and Erector sets for which I had no natural ability and that I had failed to learn along the way of wanting to be a fisherman. It occurred to me that there were simple and essential things I didn't know and I would need to learn, things that might be hard to learn, even things about fishing I might never be able to master.

I went in to visit with Charlotte in the kitchen. She told me to sit, not to bother about the men; I didn't need to help. We talked about family and where we were from, about baking bread in peanut butter cans. I liked Charlotte and I liked what we talked about, but I was also keenly aware that her life in the kitchen was not what I expected, or wanted, for *my* life.

I went back out and tried again to help. The big boat turned gently over, with lines pulling it every which way, and it lifted as it was levered onto stacked wood blocks and gas drums until the cylinder, with paddle-shaped arms attached to its axle, fit beneath it. I was in awe of what time and a few physical laws, a few lines and sticks of wood, could do. I helped clear away the blocks and poles and rollers.

Charlotte fixed us lunch and dinner that day—meals she and George called dinner and supper. We ate like farmers, piling our plates with chicken casserole, bread and jam, green beans, peaches, watermelon pickles, and cake. The food was all home-canned, brought with them from Nebraska, where they wintered. Every year they traded, case for case, their vanload of canned salmon for Nebraska's best.

This fall day all these years later, we crank up the *Proud Bow* inch by inch. From the first time we met him, George disdained what he called "tin boats" and said he wouldn't have one, but soon after we traded up from our shattered fiberglass model to a tough twenty-three-foot aluminum skiff, he did the same, only bigger. The boatbuilder he hired didn't have a lot of experience, though, and he apparently ran into trouble with George's design. It's an unhandy boat for fishing, with a bow so far off the water that George's helpers can barely lift nets over it. This year one of his crew went home with a ruined back before the season even got started.

We don't turn this boat over, and the puller we're using is a lot easier than a come-along, but it still takes time to bring the *Proud Bow* up the beach. The three of us do it together, although roles have changed. Ken's in charge, setting up the lines, cutting rollers, deciding when and how much to swing the stern. He does most of the cranking. I at least understand what we're doing and can anticipate the steps. I place the next roller where the bow will slide onto it check the one that's about to spin out from under the stern. I get the shovel and dig away berms that build up under the rollers, and I clear away rocks. George makes suggestions, but he's comfortable letting us do most of the actual work, just as we're comfortable doing it. I tell him to be sure to see a doctor about his knee over the winter, and he says he might see a sports specialist.

George cooks us spaghetti and garlic toast, although he forgets the toast is in the oven when he comes out again to help and it burns black. He apologizes to Ken for not having any watermelon pickles and opens a fresh jar of homemade dills instead. We sit at the table with lowered heads while he says his grace:

Grant us Thy grace, O Lord.
Whether we eat or drink or whatsoever we do,
May we do it in Thy name and to Thy glory.
Amen.

George's voice is soft and melodic, and the simple words rise and fall with a canonical resonance. George never varies this saying of grace; it's part of the pattern of his life, and of ours when we eat with him. Although my own spiritual life doesn't involve any sort of prayer, these familiar lines of George's never fail to remind me how fortunate we are to gather again at his table.

In the corner of the room, over the old rolltop desk and beside a clipboard of pink fish tickets, hangs a photograph of a small, sturdy, fair-haired boy—perhaps two years old—kneeling over a net on the beach. He grips a mending needle firmly and enthusiastically in hand and wears a look that's at once determined and angelic. This picture, which has hung in that spot at least as long as we've been coming to the beach and probably more than twice that long, has always spoken to me about the good fit of life on the beach. Here, the photograph says, is a place that interlocks family and work and play, imagination and environment, learning by hands and learning by minds. At the same time, the picture always saddens me. The child is George's son, Buck, and although Buck loves the beach in his own way, he was also a slave to it all his youth. By the time Buck finished and paid for college, he was also finished with fishing. A few years back, when he was between jobs, he and his wife and two of his children came back to try fishing once more, but there was no money in it, and his father was still the driven and driving skipper.

Same old story, I guess. The kid who grows up on the farm leaves for the city lights, and the city kid wants only to try living on the land. Had I grown up in this life, I really have no idea what I'd be doing today. I have a strong suspicion I would not be here. Buck has an older sister with even less attachment to this place.

While we eat, George keeps glancing out the window, watching for Grandpa, an old white-headed eagle that he's befriended over the years. The bird typically roosts on a snag just outside the kitchen window and will practically feed from George's hand. We've sat many times at George's table when he's leaped up at the sight of Grandpa and run out to throw a fish head on the beach.

This mealtime, Grandpa doesn't show.

The next day, we finish putting up George's boat. It takes pulling from one side and another to get it lined up for the ramp, and a lot of hard cranking. Ken moves behind the dock to pull from a monument of old cannery machinery, but when the boat's partway up the ramp, the old pile begins to creak and lean. We need to go farther back behind the camp, to anchor to a sturdier deadman, a boulder that won't move.

George thinks cable will be better than line, so he and I go off in his jitney to pick up a coil at Nick's, the cabin halfway between his place and ours where his help usually stays.

We bounce along in the skeletal, balloon-tired jitney, which has lost so much body to rust it's barely more than a seat on wheels, its exposed drive chain coated with sand. The last time I'd ridden with George was early in the season, when I went with him toward our camp to look for an anchor he wanted to borrow.

That time, as we had rounded a rocky corner, I spotted an enormous brown bear directly in our path, some distance away but headed toward us. I couldn't believe that it wouldn't have heard us coming and hightailed away long before either one of us caught sight of the other. I leaned close to George and shouted, "Bear!" At the same instant we both saw the second bear, a smaller one just behind the first, and George slowed the jitney. "I think we should turn back," I said, not sure that George would have the same idea. He began to circle through the rocks.

When I looked behind us, the large bear was still coming our way. In fact, it was gaining on us. We hit clear sand and picked up speed, and George waited another day to borrow our anchor. Later, when Ken and I looked at the tracks, it was clear the sow had bluff-charged just long enough for her cub to climb the bank.

Today, our ride to Nick's is uneventful. George and I fetch the cable and head back. At Hightowers, where the cottonwood trees grow, George points up the bluff. An eagle sits at the peak of a spruce, its white head brilliant against a patch of blue sky.

"Come on down, Grandpa!" George yells. He slows the jitney and makes a sweeping motion with his arm, toward the old cannery. "COME ON DOWN!"

The bird tilts its head, one old white-top regarding another.

Finally the big aluminum boat reaches its balance point and tips forward onto the dock. It's up against the *Running W*, and we have to squeeze and shift to work it farther without knocking the old dory off its blocks or pushing it too hard against the cannery wall.

After our two days of intimate contact with the hard, gray aluminum of the newer boat, the *Running W* looks parched and tired. It's almost surely seen the end of its fishing days, maybe even had its final taste of salt. The last years he fished it, George treated it as though it were eggshell. He kept off the rocks and trained his crew to jump out in chestwaders to keep the boat from bumping shore. It got to be hard work; nets caught on its old shoes and splintering un-

Working along the Shorelines

derbelly. But it's a beauty still—the long curves, gunnels worn to a rich, buttery shine. I think of all the nets that have crossed that bow, all the hands that have gripped its rail, the loads of fish it's held. In the old days, George said, they used to catch a thousand king salmon in a season, and ten thousand "small fish." I remember the last time the *Running W* was painted—George's grandson Cade, Buck's son, was here on the dock, stroking it a bright, bright, blindingly bright orange.

I can't recall what year that was, only the image of a young Cade, all legs and hair, and the bright paint. The past for me is already starting to blur, one year and decade into another. Cade is a grown man living in Hawaii, and I feel a little creakier all the time in my knees and shoulders. I know better, too, than to ask George about dates. Five or ten or forty years all compute in his remembrances to "a few years back." Ken has taken to teasing him by doing the same thing. "That dock we built a couple years ago" refers to the only dock we ever built, our first summer, that was taken out by storms the same year.

We wouldn't build such a dock again because we learned that one won't stay in such a place. George knew that, of course, but he never advised against our effort. We might not have listened, and he probably wanted us to learn for ourselves and to find out, himself, if we had the mettle and the salt to lose docks and boats and whole seasons to the sea, to suffer the life of fishermen and not be defeated by it.

It's struck me recently that Ken has started telling stories like an old-timer, much like George, and that he tinkers with camp projects in a similarly relaxed way. They're different stories and different projects, to be sure, but there's more resemblance than I would have expected. I've noticed, too, that both Ken and George, big men, can move surprisingly fast when they need to, grabbing a net or hopping in or out of a boat. Ken is starting to lose a little of his hearing, an occupational hazard of spending so much time around motors; he will one day, I suppose, be as deaf as George. When I imagine us as an old couple, it's with me shouting to be heard, the same way both of us shout when we're with George, the way Charlotte shouted.

Watching George and Ken together, it comes to me that the source of any resemblances is nature more than nurture. We've learned from George, but more than that, we've stayed on this beach because the place fits us, just as it's fit George for fifty years. Ken's inborn nature agrees with the place and the life and is satisfied with what they offer. A more aggressive or desperate fisherman would have moved on; a slower or weaker one, or one with limited imagination, would not have survived. This is a place for using muscles, for tinkering, for scheming out new ways to fish a net. Each of the three of us made matches here; we agreed to live with the beach's rhythms and with its birds and bears and the neighbors we are. And then, of course, after the beach became home, the place itself continued to shape each of us, just as the sea rounds the edges of all rocks that roll into it.

I imagine Charlotte in the window, watching us winch the boat its final distance. In fall, her hair would be flattened under a kerchief, her permanent long ago grown out. My fingers go to my bandanna, which keeps my own overgrown hair out of my eyes. I know that behind Charlotte the next meal would be steaming on the stove. Very likely the canner would be knocking its way through yet another case of fish to take back to Nebraska. Charlotte would know by the cooker's sound, without even looking at the gauge, that the pressure was holding at ten pounds.

Charlotte, of course, lived in a different and more restricted age from mine, her life circumscribed by closely defined roles as mother, cook, and caregiver. She never fished as I fish but maintained the warm and well-fed home life of fishcamp. On stormy days in her younger years, she walked the beach and released nets from their inside ends, allowing the men to pick them up without coming ashore. Rarely, though, did we ever see her outside the kitchen, where she organized meal after meal, cookies after cake, washing and cleaning after sweeping.

Still, when I imagine her face in the window I see the tension it so often wore begin to dissolve, and I understand, as I never could have that first fall visit or for many years after, what that means. As much as I love fishing, there's something particularly satisfying about putting up boats. Waves can smack rocks now, and I won't need to look. I can sleep at night without fearing frayed lines, rainwater to be bailed, the next day's weather. I can turn away from the sea.

Such concern about boats and boat safety, I know now, belongs to women. Men sleep at night—quickly, soundly, deeply. Deaf men don't even hear the surf. But women hear every change in the weather, just as they hear the faintest cries of children. Charlotte worried. I worry. That's our nature. If she were here today, we would look at each other and not need to say a word. Or we might. She might say, "This is my favorite time of year." Or I might. I might be the first to say it.

Ken cranks on the *Proud Bow* while I stand to one side. Aluminum presses wood and the wood squeaks, a shrill, yielding protest. George tells us it's good; the boat is far enough back. A little more shifting and blocking, and at last we've got everything right.

Lucille Clifton

blessing the boats

(at St. Mary's)

may the tide
that is entering even now
the lip of our understanding
carry you out
beyond the face of fear
may you kiss
the wind then turn from it
certain that it will
love your back   may you
open your eyes to water
water wavering forever
and may you in your innocence
sail through this to that

crabbing

(the poet crab speaks)

pulling
into their pots
our wives
our hapless children.
crabbing
they smile, meaning us
i imagine,
though our name
is our best secret.

this forward moving
fingered thing
inedible
even to itself,
how can it understand
the sweet sacred meat
of others?

On the Edge

Madness, Illness,
Seeking, and Healing

The stretch of beach east of Ditch Plains is one of the least traveled and most sparsely inhabited portions of Montauk. As Kali and I wander along, picking our way over slippery rocks and driftwood, we can look at the homes of the very wealthy tucked into the landscape, each occupying its own bluff. The first house to catch my attention once belonged to Andy Warhol; I recall reading that he did not like coming out to Montauk and instead preferred to lend the house to friends. The house is isolated, lovely, but perhaps its location at the edge of the world feels just a bit lonely. There are a few more architecturally stunning homes to see as we walk along, but eventually the beach and bluffs empty out, and there is nothing but sky, wind, water, and shoreline.

I wonder why someone would take the trouble to build a lone house on a bluff and then shy away from spending time there, or why others who have no home by the beach would stay in tiny thin-walled hotel rooms just to be close to the water. We will find one explanation in this section of the anthology, which concerns itself with forms of sorrow and paths to overcome that sorrow.

Death is a recurring theme in women's coastal literature. As the poets Marianne Moore and Edna St. Vincent Millay tell us, the sea is a grave, a fact that coastal dwellers are well aware. And while some of the writers in this section mourn their losses as they look out at the ocean or walk along the shore, others seek out the coast to heal from their grieving. The writers in this section present readers with characters who choose to be alone, who, whether they struggle with physical illness, mental illness, or death and loss, hope that their time at the coast will provide peace. In some instances, the peace they find, as in Kate Chopin's *The Awakening*, is eternal.

Kali nudges me along, and after taking a second look at the Warhol house, now surrounded by Nature Conservancy lands, we continue our walk. We have come this far and we are determined to walk to the very end of Long Island.

Kate Chopin

Chapter 39, *The Awakening*

Victor, with hammer and nails and scraps of scantling, was patching a corner of one of the galleries. Mariequita sat near by, dangling her legs, watching him work, and handing him nails from the tool-box. The sun was beating down upon them. The girl had covered her head with her apron folded into a square pad. They had been talking for an hour or more. She was never tired of hearing Victor describe the dinner at Mrs. Pontellier's. He exaggerated every detail, making it appear a veritable Lucullean feast. The flowers were in tubs, he said. The champagne was quaffed from huge golden goblets. Venus rising from the foam could have presented no more entrancing a spectacle than Mrs. Pontellier, blazing with beauty and diamonds at the head of the board, while the other women were all of them youthful houris, possessed of incomparable charms.

She got it into her head that Victor was in love with Mrs. Pontellier, and he gave her evasive answers, framed so as to confirm her belief. She grew sullen and cried a little, threatening to go off and leave him to his fine ladies. There were a dozen men crazy about her at the *Chênière;* and since it was the fashion to be in love with married people, why, she could run away any time she liked to New Orleans with Célina's husband.

Célina's husband was a fool, a coward, and a pig, and to prove it to her, Victor intended to hammer his head into a jelly the next time he encountered him. This assurance was very consoling to Mariequita. She dried her eyes, and grew cheerful at the prospect.

They were still talking of the dinner and the allurements of city life when Mrs. Pontellier herself slipped around the corner of the house. The two youngsters stared dumb with amazement before what they considered to be an apparition. But it was really she in flesh and blood, looking tired and a little travel-stained.

"I walked up from the wharf," she said, "and heard the hammering. I supposed it was you, mending the porch. It's a good thing. I was always tripping over those loose planks last summer. How dreary and deserted everything looks!"

It took Victor some little time to comprehend that she had come in Beaudelet's lugger, that she had come alone, and for no purpose but to rest.

"There's nothing fixed up yet, you see. I'll give you my room; it's the only place."

"Any corner will do," she assured him.

"And if you can stand Philomel's cooking," he went on, "though I might try to get her mother while you are here. Do you think she would come?" turning to Mariequita.

Mariequita thought that perhaps Philomel's mother might come for a few days, and money enough.

Beholding Mrs. Pontellier make her appearance, the girl at once suspected a lovers' rendezvous. But Victor's astonishment was so genuine, and Mrs. Pontellier's indifference so apparent, that the disturbing notion did not lodge long in her brain. She contemplated with the greatest of interest this woman who gave the most sumptuous dinners in America, and who had all the men in New Orleans at her feet.

"What time will you have dinner?" asked Edna. "I'm very hungry; but don't get anything extra."

"I'll have it ready in little or no time," he said bustling and packing away his tools. "You may go to my room to brush up and rest yourself. Mariequita will show you."

"Thank you," said Edna "But, do you know, I have a notion to go down to the beach and take a good wash and even a little swim, before dinner?"

"The water is too cold!" they both exclaimed. "Don't think of it."

"Well, I might go down and try—dip my toes in. Why, it seems to me the sun is hot enough to have warmed the very depths of the ocean. Could you get me a couple of towels? I'd better go right away, so as to be back in time. It would be a little too chilly if I waited till this afternoon."

Mariequita ran over to Victor's room, and returned with some towels, which she gave to Edna.

"I hope you have fish for dinner," said Edna, as she started to walk away; "but don't do anything extra if you haven't."

"Run and find Philomel's mother," Victor instructed the girl. "I'll go to the kitchen and see what I can do. By Gimminy! Women have no consideration! She might have sent me word."

Edna walked on down to the beach rather mechanically, not noticing anything special except that the sun was hot. She was not dwelling upon any particular train of thought. She had done all the thinking which was necessary after Robert went away, when she lay awake upon the sofa till morning.

She had said over and over to herself: "To-day it is Arobin; to-morrow it will be some one else. It makes no difference to me, it doesn't matter about Léonce Pontellier—but Raoul and Etienne!" She understood now clearly what she had meant long ago when she said to Adèle Ratignolle that she would give up the unessential, but she would never sacrifice herself for her children.

Despondency had come upon her there in the wakeful night, and had never lifted. There was no one thing in the world she desired. There was no human being whom she wanted near her except Robert; and she even realized that the day could come when he, too, and the thought of him would melt out of her existence, leaving her alone. The children appeared before her like antagonists who had overcome her; who had overpowered and sought to drag her into the soul's slavery for the rest of her days. But she knew a way to elude them. She was not thinking of these things when she walked down to the beach.

The water of the Gulf stretched out before her, gleaming with the million lights of the sun. The voice of the sea is seductive, never ceasing, whispering, clamoring, murmuring, inviting the soul to wander in abysses of solitude. All along the white beach, up and down, there was no living thing in sight. A bird with a broken wing was beating the air above, reeling, fluttering, circling disabled down, down to the water.

Edna had found her old bathing suit still hanging, faded, upon it accustomed peg.

She put it on, leaving her clothing in the bath-house. But when she was there beside the sea, absolutely alone, she cast the unpleasant pricking garments from her, and for the first time in her life she stood naked in the open air, at the mercy of the sun, the breeze that beat upon her, and the waves that invited her.

How strange and awful it seemed to stand naked under the sky! how delicious! She felt like some new-born creature, opening its eyes in a familiar world that it had never known.

The foamy wavelets curled up to her white feet, and coiled like serpents about her ankles. She walked out. The water was chill, but she walked on. The water was deep, but she lifted her white body and reached out with a long, sweeping stroke. The touch of the sea is sensuous, enfolding the body in its soft, close embrace.

She went on and on. She remembered the night she swam far out, and recalled the terror that seized her at the fear of being unable to regain the shore. She did not look back now, but went on and on, thinking about the blue-grass meadow that she had traversed when a little child, believing that it had no beginning and no end.

Her arms and legs were growing tired.

She thought of Léonce and the children. They were a part of her life. But they need not have thought they could possess her, body and soul. How Mademoiselle Reisz would have laughed, perhaps sneered, if she knew! "And you call yourself an artist! What pretensions, Madame! The artist must possess the courageous soul that dares and defies."

Exhaustion was pressing upon and overpowering her.

"Good-by—because I love you." He did not know; he did not understand. He would never understand. Perhaps Doctor Mandelet would have understood if she had seen him—but it was too late; the shore was far behind her, and her strength was gone.

She looked into the distance, and the old terror flamed up for an instant, then sank again. Edna heard her father's voice and her sister Margaret's. She heard the barking of an old dog that was chained to the sycamore tree. The spurs of the cavalry officer clanged as he walked across the porch. There was the hum of bees, and the musky odor of pinks filled the air.

Sara Teasdale

. . . .

On the Dunes

If there is any life when death is over,
    These tawny beaches will know much of me,
I shall come back, as constant and as changeful
    As the unchanging, many colored sea.

If life was small, if it has made me scornful,
    Forgive me; I shall straighten like a flame
In the great calm of death, and if you want me
    Stand on the sea-ward dunes and call my name

To the Sea

Bitter and beautiful, sing no more;
Scarf of spindrift strewn on the shore,
Burn no more in the noon-day light,
Let there be night for me, let there be night.

On the restless beaches I used to range
The two that I loved have walked with me—
I saw them change and my own heart change—
I cannot face the unchanging sea.

Edna St. Vincent Millay

. . . .

Exiled

Searching my heart for its true sorrow,
    This is the thing I find to be:
That I am weary of words and people,
    Sick of the city, wanting the sea;

Wanting the sticky, salty sweetness
    Of the strong wind and shattered spray;
Wanting the loud sound and the soft sound
    Of the big surf that breaks all day.

Always before about my dooryard,
    Marking the reach of the winter sea,
Rooted in sand and dragging drift-wood,
    Straggled the purple wild sweet-pea;

Always I climbed the wave at morning,
    Shook the sand from my shoes at night,
That now am caught beneath great buildings,
    Stricken with noise, confused with light.

Edna St. Vincent Millay

If I could hear the green piles groaning
    Under the windy wooden piers,
See once again the bobbing barrels,
    And the black sticks that fence the weirs,

If I could see the weedy mussels
    Crusting the wrecked and rotting hulls,
Hear once again the hungry crying
    Overhead, of the wheeling gulls,

Feel once again the shanty straining
    Under the turning of the tide,
Fear once again the rising freshet,
    Dread the bell in the fog outside,

I should be happy!—that was happy
    All day long on the coast of Maine;
I have a need to hold and handle
    Shells and anchors and ships again!

I should be happy . . . that am happy
    Never at all since I came here.
I am too long away from water.
    I have a need of water near.

Burial

Mine is a body that should die at sea!
    And have for a grave, instead of a grave
Six feet deep and the length of me,
    All the water that is under the wave!

And terrible fishes to seize my flesh,
    Such as a living man might fear,
And eat me while I am firm and fresh,—
    Not wait till I've been dead for a year!

Low-Tide

These wet rocks where the tide has been,
    Barnacles white and weeded brown
And slimed beneath to a beautiful green,
    These wet rocks where the tide went down
Will show again when the tide is high
    Faint and perilous, far from shore,
No place to dream, but a place to die:
    The bottom of the sea once more.

There was a child that wandered through
    A giant's empty house all day,—
House full of wonderful things and new,
    But no fit place for a child to play!

Marianne Moore

The Fish

wade
through black jade.
    Of the crow-blue mussel-shells, one keeps
    adjusting the ash-heaps;
        opening and shutting itself like

an
injured fan.
    The barnacles which encrust the side
    of the wave, cannot hide
        there for the submerged shafts of the

sun,
split like spun
    glass, move themselves with spotlight swiftness
    into the crevices—
        in and out, illuminating

the
turquoise sea
    of bodies. The water drives a wedge
    of iron through the iron edge
        of the cliff; whereupon the stars,

pink
rice-grains, ink-
    bespattered jelly-fish, crabs like green
    lilies, and submarine
        toadstools, slide each on the other.

All
external
    marks of abuse are present on this
    defiant edifice—
        all the physical features of

ac-
cident—lack
    of cornice, dynamite grooves, burns, and
    hatchet strokes, these things stand
    out on it; the chasm-side is

dead.
Repeated
    evidence has proved that it can live
    on what can not revive
        its youth. The sea grows old in it.

A Grave

Man looking into the sea,
taking the view from those who have as much right to it as
                                  you have to it yourself,
it is human nature to stand in the middle of a thing,
but you cannot stand in the middle of this;
the sea has nothing to give but a well excavated grave.
The firs stand in a procession, each with an emerald turkey-
                                  foot at the top,
reserved as their contours, saying nothing;
repression, however, is not the most obvious characteristic of
                                  the sea;
the sea is a collector, quick to return a rapacious look.
There are others besides you who have worn that look—
whose expression is no longer a protest; the fish no longer
                                  investigate them
for their bones have not lasted:
men lower nets, unconscious of the fact that they are
                                  desecrating a grave,
and row quickly away—the blades of the oars
moving together like the feet of water-spiders as if there were
                                  no such thing as death.
The wrinkles progress among themselves in a phalanx—
                                  beautiful under networks of foam,
and fade breathlessly while the sea rustles in and out of the
                                  seaweed;
the birds swim through the air at top speed, emitting cat-calls
                                  as heretofore—
the tortoise-shell scourges about the feet of the cliffs, in motion
                                  beneath them;
and the ocean, under the pulsation of lighthouses and noise of
                                  bell-buoys,
advances as usual, looking as if it were not that ocean in which
                                  dropped things are bound to sink—
in which if they turn and twist, it is neither with volition nor
                                  consciousness.

May Sarton

Preface, *The House by the Sea*

When I moved to this house by the sea in May of '73 I had it in mind to keep a journal, to record the first impressions, the fresh imprint of a major change in my life, but for a year and a half the impulse to be silent and live into this new place before speaking about it remained very strong. For months the sea was such a tranquilizer that I sometimes wondered whether I had made a fatal mistake and would never be able to write again. The *Journal of a Solitude* had been a way of dealing with anguish; was it that happiness is harder to communicate, or that when one is happy enough there is little incentive even to try to sort out daily experience as it happens? I became haunted by something I read years ago to the effect that when the Japanese were in a period of peace they painted only fans.

Why, then, had I made the move, left Nelson and my friends there, left village life that had taught me so much, left "the hills of home," the only house I shall ever own, the garden I had created with so much labor over fifteen years? Why move into a much larger house at a time in my life when it might have seemed sensible to pull in my horns?

Such major decisions are made on instinct rather than reason, and in them chance plays a part . . . after all, it had been quite by chance that I landed in Nelson in the first place, for fifteen years ago I had looked in vain for a house by the sea—houses by the sea with any privacy, with any considerable land, were beyond my means. As I think it over now, I realize that the decision to leave Nelson had been ripening in me for over a year. I knew it was time to go, time for radical change.

Of course there were reasons. My house was right on the village green, too exposed; too many strangers in the last years found their way to my door. At the end I began to feel I lived in a museum and had become a target for public curiosity—flattering perhaps, but hard to handle. If I turned such visitors away I felt guilty, and if I asked them in I felt invaded. Another reason was that both Quig and Perley Cole had died and, with them, two of the major friendships born of that place. But the most imperative reason was that I had been through a traumatic personal experience in Nelson in the last two years there, and the house itself felt contaminated by pain.

Nevertheless I might have stayed on had it not been for an extraordinary act of chance, and an extraordinary act of friendship that made major change as easy as the opening of a door. Had the guardian angel been at work? It did seem so when my friends Mary-Leigh Smart and Beverly Hallam came over from Ogunquit, Maine on April 9, 1971, to pick up a monotype of Bev's for her retrospective show. They were full of excitement as they had just bought an old estate on the coast near York and were in the midst of making plans to build a modern house right on the rocks. They described vividly the combination of open fields, rocky beaches, ponds, a swamp, and the big woods at the back, and showed me photographs, and I listened. Later in the day I told them of my depression and that I seemed to be at a dead end in my own life. Then Beverly, with a twinkle in her eye, said, "Take another look at the old house." I still did not understand what she was suggesting. They had mentioned that there was a house on the place, but I had not really paid attention so I looked again at the photograph of a shingled, many-windowed house set back on a knoll against big trees, looking down to the sea across a long field.

"Why don't you come and live there, rent it from us, and settle in?"

It was a staggering moment. Now that I might be able to move, would I dare? How could I leave Nelson, after all? Did I really want to?

I arranged to go over and have a look. And once I had stood on the wide flagstone terrace and looked out over that immensely gentle field to a shining, still, blue expanse, the decision was taken out of my hands. I had to come. The landscape, not the house at first, was the magnet . . . after all, Mrs. Stevens, a character in a novel of mine who bears some resemblance to me, felt that the sea was her final muse.

I had two years in which to dream myself into the change, sell Nelson, and pull up roots. And before the next year was out I had sold to Nancy and Mark Stretch, whom I felt at once would be the right people for the village—young, determined to live a country life and bring up the children they hoped to have in just such a village. Mark was then an apprentice to a cabinetmaker and would make the barn into a workshop.

Meanwhile I went back and forth to Wild Knoll, measuring walls for bookcases, closing off one big porch to make wall space for the old Belgian furniture, laying a yellow rug in the library (to remind me of the yellow floor at Nelson), choosing colors for the rather dark kitchen, feeling my way into large spaces. Eleanor Blair suggested that I make one large bay window into a plant window, and that has worked better than I could have dreamed. It is really like a small greenhouse, filled with flowering plants all year long. My one anxiety when I first walked through the empty rooms, so large and full of light, was where to find the shelter I need for my work. And when I finally climbed to the third floor, there it was—a room paneled in soft beige-colored pine, under the eaves, the small windows looking down on the grassy path to the sea on one side and into the treetops on the other, for the house stands high on a knoll.

"The grassy path . . ."

If there is one irresistible piece of magic here among many others, it is the slightly curving path down to the sea that begins in flagstones on the lawn, cuts through two huge junipers, and proceeds, winding its way down to Surf Point, through the wooded lilies in June, to tall grasses in summer, the golden-rod and asters in September, leading the eye on, creating the atmosphere of a fairy tale, something open yet mysterious that every single person who comes here is led to explore. It is the signature of the place, and also perhaps of its former owner, Anne Robert.

It was she who came here and turned a rather modest house into a lordly "summer cottage" by building out on each side the wings of enclosed porches, by laying the great terrace and its stone wall, and enclosing the formal garden with flowering bushes and trees. It was she, no doubt, who installed casement windows and had built the curving fence, a bower of purple and white clematis in June; she perhaps who planted the big pine trees, spruce, hemlock, and oaks at the back, so the house stands against, and is sheltered by, a small forest.

I feel her presence everywhere and it is a wholly beneficent one. I like to think she would be glad to know that someone is working in her garden again, planting bulbs and tree peonies and azaleas, keeping it alive. She loved this place and her love of it and happiness in it have been contagious.

I knew from the first moment, in May of '73, a few days after the move that "I have slipped into these wide spaces, this atmosphere of salt and amplitude, this amazing piece of natural Heaven and haven, like a ship slipping into her berth." But it was a year and a half later when I felt ready to start a journal. It was designed to be the record of my happiness here. But a journal cannot be planned ahead, written as it is on the pulse of the moment. I could not know that in 1974–75 I was to lose three of my oldest friends, nor that in the spring of '75 I would be nearly incapacitated by a long siege of virus infection in my throat. So what began in joy ended by being shot through by grief and illness, although the leitmotif is still the sea, and the house by the sea, and the garden by the sea.

When I first decided to come, I also made the very important decision to bring a dog with me, my first dog . . . this house is far more isolated than the house in Nelson. I was to be here alone for the first year while Mary-Leigh and Bev's house was a-building, and a dog, I felt, would be just the companion I needed. Also, I had fallen in love with Pixie, a Sheltie belonging to the Frenches up the road in Nelson, and had begged them to let me have a puppy when she had her first litter. In this way Tamas came into my life, Tamas Sea Island March Wind, to give him his full name. At three months of age he began to live with me, sleeping beside me at night and playing in a playpen by my desk while I worked. When he was six months old, he and I went to school together, so that by the time we moved into this big house, he was a very gentlemanly well-behaved dog.

I was totally ignorant about dogs. I had fallen in love with one special dog, Tamas' mother, but knew nothing about the breed except that they were sensitive and beautiful. But luckily for me Shelties (Shetland shepherds) are by nature guarders not hunters, so Tamas can be let out safely at all times, even when I go away for half a day, and will never run off. He also shepherds Bramble, the last of the wild cats, whom I had tamed at Nelson. For her, his arrival as a small barky puppy was traumatic. For three weeks she wouldn't come up on my bed and stayed out most of the time. But Tamas learned, learned not to bark—how moving it was that afternoon when he approached Bramble, sitting beside me on the couch, and swallowed his bark! I saw him do it, saw the impulse come, and then be quelled. And for a while that day they sat side by side, and then, little by little, became fast friends.

Everyday we set out together in the late morning after the stint at my desk is done, and walk through the woods making a large circle on dirt roads, around the swamp and home again. They both sleep on my bed at night, Bramble coming in through the window when she wants to and often leaving before dawn. Solitude shared with animals has a special quality and rarely turns into loneliness. Bramble and Tamas have brought me comfort and joy.

There is another member of the family who comes here for a day or so every month, Judith Matlack, with whom I shared a house in Cambridge for many years, and who is now in a nursing home in Concord, Massachusetts. For thirty years or more she had been the closest thing to family in my life. Without her presence, even though her mind is failing and she has no memory of all our journeys to Europe together and all our summers in Nelson, there would be no Christmas and no Thanksgiving, and I would feel like an orphan. This journal is a partial record of what it is like to experience senility close to home.

In the years at Wild Knoll my life has expanded rather than narrowed. Not only is this house larger and more comfortable than the Nelson house, but my life inside it has changed. I find myself nourished by the visits of many friends, friends of the work who have written me for years and finally turn up from South Dakota, or Ohio, new friends, old friends who are passing by, for everyone comes to Maine sooner or later! I try to see them one at a time. I mean every encounter here to be more than superficial, to be a real exchange of lives, and this is more easily accomplished one to one than in a group. But the continuity is solitude. Without long periods here alone, especially in winter when visits are rare, I would have nothing to give, and would be less open to the gifts offered me. Solitude has replaced the single intense relationship, the passionate love that even at Nelson focused all the rest. Solitude, like a long love, deepens with time, and, I trust, will not fail me if my own powers of creation diminish. For growing into solitude is one way of growing to the end.

Wild Knoll
October 1976

Tuesday, October 7th, *The House by the Sea*

A long hiatus because these are such great days, and so full, between the garden (I planted fifty tulips day before yesterday) and the rising pressure on the book. I have been working all this week on revising the portrait of my mother that I first wrote ten years ago; yesterday, while trying to find a letter I might use, I came on a snap taken in 1920 at Pemaquid Point. I was eight and I am standing on a rock in bare feet, very straight, solemn, my mouth open, and clearly singing loudly. On the back my mother wrote, "May chantant à la mer—elle a aussi dansé frénétiquement!—La mer par moments l'excite—Elle a dansé et crié la première fois qu'elle a été à une plage (en 1916) vraiment comme une petite folle." I have no memory of this; my memories of the summer at Pemaquid Point are of gloomy and dark woods, mushrooms, a long walk to get water every day, and my mother depressed. I remember my terror at the surf on the rocks because a woman had been drowned there, sucked down by a wave, then battered. A place of real fear for me. So it is strange to come upon this totally different picture, and it gave me heart. For, clearly, the sea was a powerful emotional force. So perhaps my dream that it might be the final muse and bring me back to poetry may not be mad after all.

On the Edge

But this photo also made me realize again for the thousandth time since I began *A World of Light* how tricky memory is. And in how many ways the same experience may be seen, even by the person himself. Yesterday at two P.M., when I was fast asleep, trying to quiet down after a harrowing morning of work and be ready for David Michaud, who was coming at three for a short visit, the front door bell pinged. I got up and staggered down in my stocking feet, thinking it must be a delivery. Instead, an elegant middle-aged woman stood there and said, "I'm from La Jolla and couldn't resist coming to see you to tell you how much I admire . . . et cetera" I was cold with anger, flurried, and said, "Please give me a moment to put on some shoes . . . I was resting." It's strange how very perturbed and jangled I felt, but so far no one has arrived here unannounced, and I hoped it would never happen. I couldn't shake the anger, and told her and her daughter whom she went to fetch (the daughter had stayed in the car) that I felt it was an imposition, and would they knock on Anne Lindbergh's door unannounced? "I should have written her a note to ask," said the woman, "but there was no time since we are just passing through." All summer I have been badgered by people who have come to see me at *their* convenience, because they are in the region, and I've done hardly any good work as a result. I suppose that is why I felt outraged. These last days have been or felt like "my real life" again . . . the autumn so beautiful, the dark blue sea, and time to myself . . . it all got ripped to pieces by "a person from Porlock" yesterday.

I slept badly, a night of flotsam and jetsam moving around in my head. At one point I had such a clear vision of Rosalind that it is still vivid. I was really too tired after David left . . . all I could manage was to pick a few flowers (any night now we'll have the killing frost).

It is not that I work all day; it is that the work needs space around it. Hurry and flurry break into the deep still place where I can remember and sort out what I want to say about my mother. And this is a rather hard time, because it is still hard to write about her, so I was more than usually vulnerable and exposed.

Ursula K. Le Guin

Texts

Messages came, Johanna thought, usually years too late, or years before one could crack their code or had even learned the language they were in. Yet they came increasingly often and were so urgent, so compelling in their demand that she read them, that she do something, as to force her at last to take refuge from them. She rented, for the month of January, a little house with no telephone in a seaside town that had no mail delivery. She had stayed in Klatsand several times in summer; winter, as she had hoped, was even quieter than summer. A whole day would go by without her hearing or speaking a word. She did not buy the paper or turn on the television, and the one morning she thought she ought to find some news on the radio she got a program in Finnish from Astoria. But the messages still came. Words were everywhere.

Literate clothing was no real problem. She remembered the first print dress she had ever seen, years ago, a genuine *print* dress with typography involved in the design—green on white, suitcases and hibiscus and the names *Riviera* and *Capri* and *Paris* occurring rather blobbily from the shoulder seam to hem, sometimes right side up, sometimes upside down. Then it had been, as the saleswoman said, very unusual. Now it was hard to find a T-shirt that did not urge political action, or quote lengthily from a dead physicist, or at least mention the town it was for sale in. All this she had coped with, she had even worn. But too many things were becoming legible.

She had noticed in earlier years that the lines of foam left by waves on the sand after stormy weather lay sometimes in curves that looked like handwriting, cursive lines broken by spaces, as if in words; but it was not until she had been alone for over a fortnight and had walked many times down to Wreck Point and back that she found she could read the writing. It was a mild day, nearly windless, so that she did not have to march briskly but could mosey along between the foam-lines and the water's edge where the sand reflected the sky. Every now and then a quiet winter breaker driving up and up the beach would drive her and a few gulls ahead of it onto the drier sand; then as the wave receded she and the gulls would follow it back. There was not another soul on the long beach. The sand lay as firm and even as a pad of pale brown paper, and on it a recent wave at this high mark had left a complicated series of curves and bits of foam. The ribbons and loops and lengths of white looked so much like handwriting in chalk that she stopped, the way she should stop, half willingly, to read what people scratched in the sand in summer. Usually it was "Jason + Karen" or paired initials in a heart; once, mysteriously and memorably, three initials and the dates 1973–1984, the only such inscription that spoke of a promise not made but broken. Whatever those eleven years had been, the length of a marriage? a child's life? they were gone, and the letters and numbers also were gone when she came back by where they had been, with the tide rising. She had wondered then if the person who wrote them had written them to be erased. But these foam words lying on the brown sand now had been written by the erasing sea itself. If she could read them they might tell her a wisdom a good deal deeper and bitterer than she could possibly swallow. Do I want to know what the sea writes? she thought, but at the same time she was already reading the foam, which though in vaguely cuneiform blobs rather than letters of any alphabet was perfectly legible as she walked along beside it. "Yes," it read, "esse hes hetu tokye to' ossusess ekyes. Seham hut' u." (When she wrote it down later she used the apostrophe to represent a kind of stop or click like the last sound in "Yep!") As she read it over, backing up some yards to do so, it continued to say the same thing, so she walked up and down it several times and memorized it. Presently, as bubbles burst and the blobs began to shrink, it changed here and there to read, "Yes, e hes etu kye to' ossusess kye. ham te u." She felt that this was not significant change but mere loss, and kept the original text in mind. The water of the foam sank into the sand and the bubbles dried away till the marks and lines lessened into a faint lacework of dots and scraps, half legible. It looked enough like delicate bits of fancywork that she wondered if one could also read lace or crochet.

When she got home she wrote down the foam words so that she would not have to keep repeating them to remember them, and then she looked at the machine-made Quaker lace tablecloth on the little round dining table. It was not hard to read but was, as one might expect, rather dull. She made out the first line inside the border as "pith wot pith wot pith wot" interminably, with a "dub" every thirty stitches where the border pattern interrupted.

But the lace collar she had picked up at a secondhand clothing store in Portland was a different matter entirely. It was handmade, handwritten. The script was small and very even. Like the Spencerian hand she had been taught fifty years ago in the first grade, it was ornate but surprisingly easy to read. "My soul must go," was the border, repeated many times, "my soul must go, my soul must go," and the fragile webs leading inward read, "sister, sister, sister, light the light." And she did not know what she was to do, or how she was to do it.

Susan Kenney

Sailing

The Indian Cove boatyard takes up almost the whole wharf, with its floating dock and boat slips, its lobster shack, its chandlery and sail loft, the boat brokerage office around the back. The graveled drive edges over the hill toward the water, but Phil parks the car behind the office and he and Sara walk down to the dock. It's warm for late October; even so he wears corduroy pants and a crewneck sweater over a flannel shirt, a down vest over that. He's felt slightly cold ever since they sent him home from the hospital last month, something to do with altered metabolism, the doctors say, or maybe it's just the loss of weight. Skinny people seem to feel the cold more. He's not skinny, at least not yet, but he does get cold.

The air is so warm now it's hard to believe it's no longer midsummer. But all around them as they've driven from yard to yard looking at boats, the trees have been flagged with autumn colors, the leaves so bright they seem to flicker and change before his eyes and he feels pulled along by the pressure of their turning. He has found that if he stares closely enough he can freeze that burning look into an image as still and permanent as a painting done on glass. As he stares now across the bay at the surrounding hills and islands, the landscape takes on that flatness, that brittle luminous clarity of detail. He blinks. The sharpness dissolves; the truth is, the foliage is already past its peak. The scarlet maples are mere remnants, the colors have faded, so that far away the land on the horizon lies curled around the water like a rusty chain.

He senses a movement next to him, a stirring of the air. Sara has walked off and is pacing up and down the wharf, hands stuffed into the pockets of her jeans, looking down at the sailboats bobbing in their slips. It's a couple of hours past low tide, but the boats are still a good five feet below the dock. Phil watches her as she comes back toward him, feeling more removed from her than he is in actual distance; this is the way it's been ever since he got out of the hospital more than a month ago.

He walks down the hall toward the long Chippendale mirror, peering at his reflection, half-expecting it to disappear. The mirror is old and makes him look more blue and fragile than he really is. The truth is, he looks no different now, a little thinner perhaps, but really very much the same. He has lost no weight to speak of, only five pounds or so, is still strong, but there is a pallor to his complexion, as though someone had powdered his face with chalk and then blown all but a bare residue away. He feels this paleness as a thin layer of ice water just beneath his skin.

He is still examining himself in the mirror when he sees Sara come and stand behind him. As his reflection's eyes catch hers he says casually, lightly, "Now I ask you, do I look like a dying man?"

Sara blinks, goes ghostly pale herself. Before she turns away she says quite calmly, her voice as precise and level as the glass, "No, as a matter of fact you don't." But he is sorry that he asked.

Sara walks down onto the dock and stands next to him, looking at him with an air of expectancy, as if to say, "Now what?" This is the third time they've been to this particular boatyard in the past month, because Phil has seen a boat here that he likes more than any of the others they have looked at this fall. It's one of the boatyard's charter fleet, a twenty-odd-feet long full-keel fiberglass sloop with a small cabin and lots of wood trim, fairly new sails including a big deck-sweeping genoa, and an outboard motor in a well in the aft compartment. Phil likes the idea of the full keel, the sleek look of the upswept stern, the quaint extravagance of the cabin, even though he can't imagine ever using it; the idea of sleeping in anything that narrow and confined gives him the creeps.

The boat is a little bigger than they had in mind—also older, twenty years old, in fact—but in very good condition. "A real classic, Alberg design, don't build 'em like that anymore," the used-boat broker told them the last time they were here. "Hey, man, this boat will take you anywhere you want to go." A real bargain, too: the yard is going out of the charter business, so they've put all the rental boats up for sale. Big as it is, the broker was careful to point out, it only draws three and a half feet. "Fix yourself up with a heavy-duty trailer, you can haul her right home and sail her in one of those big lakes," he told them. The boat is sitting in the water below them right now. Phil can see it tugging at its mooring lines, moving up and down with the swell.

"What do you want to do?" Sara asks.

Phil shrugs. "I thought we could just walk around, look at the boats, talk to the broker, do what we always do . . ."

Sara turns away. After a moment she says over her shoulder, "I don't see why you want to keep looking at boats all the time if you think we can't buy one."

For an instant Sara reminds him of the boat, tugging at the lines, impatient to get on with it. Phil feels no need to get on with anything; he is perfectly content to stay as he is. "I like to look at boats," he answers. "I love boats. Besides, it's not so much the boats themselves as the idea of boats. You know that."

Sara shakes her head slightly, but she does know, Phil is certain of that. After all, she is the real sailor. It was her tales of sailing in her youth—Comets, Lightnings, Bantams, Stars, white flags rampant across a field of blue—that had gotten him started on this so late in life in the first place. He hadn't learned to sail until after that bloody mess of an operation that almost killed him two years ago, at Sara's suggestion, in a boat borrowed from friends. It had come upon him as something of a revelation, and his only regret was that he had waited until he was thirty-five years old even to try. They had been looking for a boat of their own before he got sick again, and they are still looking, more as a way to pass the time than anything else. It is not so much the boat itself, or even the sailing, as the idea of it. There is something so complex yet pure about the relation of wind and sail, so absorbing about the need to balance conflicting forces, that he finds sailing is all he thinks about, or tries to, and it is more than just a way to pass the time. Who had ever thought to harness the wind with little more than a bedsheet, two sticks, and twenty yards of rope? His sailing manuals have little to say about this, other than it was inevitable that the earliest seafarers should find a way to use the free power of the wind. That seems obvious enough. But who were those early seafarers? Aborigines? Indians? Phil imagines a birchbark canoe, a buffalo skin hoisted on a spear, a lone Indian with feathers in his hair being blown before the wind down Gitchee-Gumee, down the shining Big-Sea Water. But he knows this is wrong; it was not the Indians but the grave Tyrians—Phoenicians—who first ventured into open ocean under sail, or so the story goes. Still, as he looks out across the water he sees the sailboats making a temporary encampment in light air, their sails like wigwams against the ragged trees.

"Besides," he says by way of conversation, "it's too late in the season to buy a sailboat. We'd never use it."

There is a slight pause. Finally Sara says, "We could buy it for next year."

This is a sticking point, of course; everything always comes back to this, the question of next year. Phil says nothing, hoping she will drop it, sorry he even brought it up. But she goes on.

"We've spent all this time looking, and we know what we want, so why don't we just buy it? We've got the money. We can trail it home, store it over the winter, and put it in the lake next spring." She gestures at the boat below them, the *Loon*. All the charter boats have bird names stenciled on their transoms: *Osprey, Eagle, Tern, Teal, Loon, Petrel*. Phil glances down at the *Loon*. He likes it well enough, but he'd just as soon go right on looking. Sara likes to have things settled, nothing left up in the air. Phil is sympathetic to her need for certainty, her impatience; he just doesn't share it.

"That way we'll have it," she persists. "We won't have to waste time looking next spring. We can start in at the beginning of the season."

Phil sighs. It is clear she is not going to drop it. He does not want to be cruel, but there are times when he wishes she would get over these dogged forays into the future. They make him uncomfortable. "I may not be here next spring," he says. He hears her quick intake of breath.

"Don't say that."

"Why not? You know it's true."

"You don't know that. Nobody knows that."

"It doesn't really matter," Phil says. "I just don't think it's worth the risk. What are you going to do with it if I'm not here?"

"Sail it myself," she says sharply and walks away. Behind him he can hear the gravel crunching, but he does not turn to see where she is going. He steps to the edge of the dock and looks down, sees far below a shadow of himself only a little darker than the murky, oil-slicked water, undulating strangely with the moving tide.

When Sara returns to the dock she has Wally Perkins, the yacht broker, in tow. "Hi. How's things? Your wife says you two might be interested in going sailing. The *Loon*'s available, if you want to take her out. We're pulling all the boats out first of the week, so now's your chance. No charge. I'll even throw in the gas for the outboard."

Phil hesitates, looks from one to the other. He hasn't thought about actually going sailing, it's so late in the season.

"How long have you got?"

Phil blinks, stares at him.

"Most of the day," Sara answers quickly. "I told the baby-sitter we'd be back by the kids' bedtime. It's about a three-hour drive, if we leave by five . . ."

"Oh, that's plenty of time," Wally says. "You can get a real feel for a boat in an afternoon. No problem."

Sara and Wally Perkins stand on either side of him, waiting for him to decide. Phil looks at Sara. This is her idea. Still, he understands it as a gesture, an alternative to looking that isn't buying, in fact a compromise. It's a nice day, the air is warm, and they have lots of time. He smiles to himself, then nods.

"Sure, why not?" he says. "What have we got to lose?"

Lying in his hospital bed, he cannot see all the way down the corridor, but Sara can. He sees her stiffen. "Here he comes," she says quietly, her fork resting in the macaroni and cheese she is supposed to be eating for lunch. Phil lies back against the pillows, a layer of ice water spreading under his skin. The arteriogram was done on Wednesday; it's past noon on Thursday now and still they haven't heard. He has told Sara that this means bad news; good news travels fast in a hospital and no news is bad news, but Sara, meliorist as always, has insisted that the doctor is very busy, that they finished the test late, that it is all very complicated, that it doesn't mean a thing; at worst it means a puzzle. But Phil knows what it means. He watches Sara lift her fork to her mouth, glad that she is eating. He hasn't felt much like eating lately himself. First it was all the tests, and now the hospital food seems to turn his stomach. Maybe he's just gotten out of the habit of eating. When he gets home, Sara says, she will feed him up.

Now he can see the doctor coming toward his room. He certainly looks grim enough, Phil thinks, his brow furrowed, his mouth drawn up in a tight pucker of what could be either disgust or resignation. He's as pale as Phil feels. His hands are behind his back as he walks along, but as he comes through the door he brings them forward, holding Phil's chart in one hand. He pulls up a chair, sits down, flips open the chart, and studies it. Oh, hell, Phil thinks. He doesn't know a thing. The doctor looks up, nods at Sara, then fixes his eyes on Phil.

"Hi, Phil. How're you feeling?"

"Fine." It's a lie, of course, he has a headache, his nose is stuffed up, and his stomach is bothering him. But one of the rituals of hospital behavior is that you don't complain.

"Good" the doctor says, and looks back down at the chart, flipping over pages again. Phil glances at Sara, who is chewing macaroni and cheese in slow motion, as though she's forgotten what she's doing. Her eyes are riveted on the chart, and Phil knows that she is busy trying to read it upside down, an old trick of hers. But the doctor is flipping the pages over too fast, not even looking at them himself. He knows what's there. Finally Sara swallows, and pushes the fork around in the small casserole, but does not take another mouthful.

"Hey, Sam," she says. "How come you always show up at lunchtime?"

Sam's face creases into a smile; for a moment he looks like an amiable troll. "Is it any good?" he asks, peering over at Sara's dish.

"I couldn't tell you," Sara says, and puts her fork down. She waits, watching Sam's face, sitting on the end of Phil's bed with her hands folded in her lap, looking, Phil thinks in admiration, perfectly composed.

"Well," Sam says, and shuffles the chart once more. Then he shuts the hinged cover with a snap, crosses his legs, folds his hands casually, and stares out the window. He takes a deep breath. Here we go, thinks Phil. "The arteriogram demonstrates conclusively a large mass, presumably tumor, in the right retroperitoneal space, surrounding the kidney. That's what's causing your extreme high blood pressure, which is what caused those bad headaches, nausea, dizziness, all those other symptoms. The reason I'm late," he inclines his head at Sara, "is that I've been on the phone to Lahey, the head kidney man at Mass General. We talked quite a long time about you, Phil." Sam darts a look at Phil, clears his throat, and sits in silence.

Phil lies back against the pillows, feeling suddenly exhausted. His mouth is dry and he is short of breath. Side effects of the drugs, he thinks, looking up at the ceiling. He concentrates on slowing down his breathing, the pounding of his heart.

"And?" Sara asks.

Sam shifts in the chair. "His conclusion is that whatever can be done can be done here."

"Phil feels relieved. He won't have to leave home, go to another hospital for more tests, not see Sara and the kids every day. Maybe he can go home soon, spend some time outside while the weather is still nice, see if he can borrow the Lanes's boat again, and do a little sailing. Maybe he can even go back to work.

"What's that?" Sara asks. "What can be done here?"

Sam clears his throat again; he must have a cold too, Phil thinks, poor bastard.

"That's what I want to discuss with you. The options." He glances at Phil. "You've taken medical leave, haven't you?" Phil shakes his head. "AWOL, huh? Well, you better do that. The college will just have to do without you for a while." Phil nods, resigned. He hadn't wanted to stop work in the first place, but things got out of hand, and now he's stuck with it. Still it's probably better to step out early in the semester, before they all get too used to having him around.

"Then what?" Sara asks. "More surgery?"

Oh my God, Phil thinks. Not another operation; the last one damn near killed me. I'm not doing that again. He shuts his eyes tight, wishing he were somewhere else. Sam's and Sara's voices echo, then grow smaller, as if they were leaving the room, but when he opens his eyes a slit he can see that they are still sitting right where they were.

"It's clearly inoperable," Sam says. "That means . . ."

"Why?" Sara interrupts him. "Why can't you operate?"

Sam shuts his eyes, then opens them. "The mass is too large, and spread all over the retroperitoneum," he says, as if this were perfectly self-evident.

But Sara doesn't give up. "Didn't you say it was on the right side?"

"Right, left, left, right," Sam says crossly. "What difference does it make? It's all over him." Phil opens his eyes wide, sees Sam wave his hand dismissively at Sara, as though she were a pesky insect. He's getting impatient, wants to get this whole thing over with. Phil thinks how much alike Sam and Sara are, a matched pair of bulldogs on either end of a rag. Sara wants to know everything, and she wants to know it now. Sam wants to get out of here. Sara, inexplicably, is stuffing forkfuls of macaroni into her mouth, chewing and swallowing. The thought makes him sick; he can't believe she's still eating. Then he is overtaken by an awful thought; he sits up and leans forward on one elbow, addressing Sam.

"Not chemotherapy?"

Sam glances at him, startled. His eyelids flutter closed and he dips his head, but Phil can't tell whether the movement means agreement or dissent.

"Chemotherapy and radiation have been demonstrated to have no effect on this kind of tumor," Sam says.

Phil lies back, once again relieved. No chemo, no radiation, no operation. No getting sick, no losing his hair. David and Linnie will not have to watch his retching, vomiting, getting bald. But Sara's voice breaks in on his relief.

"What kind of tumor? Couldn't it be something else?

Phil can't understand why she is so persistent. What more is there to know. His mind is swaddled in a kind of pleasant fog, his grandmother's crazy-quilt stuffed into all the nooks and crannies that were echoing so strangely a few minutes ago. He feels sleepy. He wishes Sam would leave, that Sara would let him go.

Sam's voice drones on. "Same as before. Renal cell carcinoma. Metastatic kidney cancer. It's not good, Sara." His patience is elaborate now, his politeness palpable. Phil can feel it stretched thin, twanging in the air.

"That's not what Sloan-Kettering said."

Sam rolls his eyes to the ceiling. "It's the diagnosis of record," he says.

"They said it was some sort of ganglioma. Not renal cell," Sara says doggedly. Phil can hear the desperation edging into her voice. That was over two years ago, that other opinion. Still, he's got to hand it to her, remembering all that stuff, keeping it in her head all this time. He feels sorry for her, left holding the bag like this. He feels as though he has behaved badly, let everybody down.

"It doesn't matter," Sam says curtly, standing up. "It's all the same, six of one, half-a-dozen of the other." He tucks Phil's chart under his arm, "Any more questions?" He looks at Phil, carefully avoiding Sara.

"Yes, I've got a question," Sara says clearly. "If it's not surgery, and it's not radiation or chemotherapy, then just what the hell is it that can be done here?"

Sam pauses in the doorway, his face inscrutable. There is a long silence. Then he looks directly at Phil.

"If it were me, I would do nothing," he says, turns abruptly and walks away.

They both stare after him for a moment, then Sara flings down her fork and jumps up, runs out the door and down the hall. It isn't until she returns a few moments later, saying through the doorway, "I'll be right back, I've got to talk to Sam," that he realizes he thought she'd run away.

The sailboat's wake leaves a corridor of calm behind them as the wind pulls them forward. Not a lot of wind, just enough. Phil leans back against the cockpit coaming, elbows resting on the deck, watching Sara at the helm. He smiles at her. "How does it feel?" he asks.

"Fine," she answers, stooping slightly to peer under the boom, checking the set of the jib. The near feather is fluttering wildly. Phil pulls the jib sheet in. The feathers flutter, then lie flat against the sail as though they had been pasted on. "It's a great day for sailing. Who wants to look at boats when you can sail one?" She pulls the mainsheet in slightly so that both sails are close-hauled, their curves parallel. The boat heels slightly. Phil moves to windward, sits next to her. They sit for a while, not talking. Phil's arm lies along the coaming, just touching her back, so that she can lean against it if she wants, the way the sail leans against the air behind it.

He looks up to where the mast prods the sky in small half-circles. The sky goes on forever, uniform, clear, vast. Far up, very small, a red kite flutters and swings against the air, scooting back and forth, captive on its string. No, too far out, Phil thinks; it must be loose, blowing out to sea. As he watches, it loses the wind, begins to fall, slowly drifting down a zigzag path. Phil stares up at it, mesmerized by the precision and predictability of its movement, the balance of conflicting forces. Back and forth, back and forth, a fast swoop, then slow recovery, friction overcoming gravity, each time a little lower down. He feels himself drawn up, and for a moment he is riding the kite, high above, looking at himself and Sara in the sailboat. He sees the white triangle from above, as bright and angular as a gull's wing. But he is also in the boat, watching the kite's red diamond swoop closer, falling toward them, bringing him with it. He nudges Sara. "Look," he says. "A lost kite."

Sara glances upward. "That's not a kite," she says casually. "That's a red maple leaf."

With an odd jerk, Phil's sense of size and distance contracts. It is indeed a leaf. Phil watches it flutter past, fall into the water and float there. The scalded, curled-up edges catch the wind, and the leaf skims away. The wind is coming up. Phil can see it on the water, roughened patches of darker blue scattered here and there, moving closer. "Look out," he says, "Here comes a puff."

Sara pushes the tiller away slightly, reaches over to release the mainsheet, but it's too late; the boat leans, then heels sharply as the wind gusts into the sails. Like a giant hand the wind presses the sails down toward the water, then just as abruptly lets them up. The boat tilts wildly. Water rushes up and foams along the rail. Suddenly the deck is perpendicular, and they are standing nearly upright, their feet braced against the opposite seat. A second wave sluices over the rail. Sara hangs onto the tiller for a moment longer, then says, "Here, you take it," as she turns and claws her way onto the deck, instinctively throwing her weight out over the rail to bring the boat back down, even though with a full-keel boat this size it won't do any good.

Phil grabs the flailing tiller. The *Loon* is wallowing, trying to round up into the wind, the sails banging and snapping. He's just as glad they decided not to fly the genoa, this boat is so responsive to the wind. He takes the mainsheet from Sara, eases off slightly, lets the main out, then holds the tack, studying the telltales, adjusting and correcting until once more the feathers lie flat against the sail. The boat heels over smoothly, not too far, and runs through the waves. The water foams and hisses as the boat pushes it aside.

"I couldn't hold it," Sara says from the deck above him.

That's all right," Phil says absently, already caught up in the business of sailing. He looks backward over his shoulder and without turning his head adjusts the tiller so they are on a beam reach. The boat seems to lift up and leap ahead. "That's it," he says. "That's perfect."

He's talking to Spencer, the head man at Boston Institute for Cancer Research and Treatment. Sara is hovering somewhere in the background. It was her idea to call, to try to find out what's taking so long. It's been almost a month since Phil got out of the local hospital, more than that since all his records were sent down. There are some things he would rather not know right now, but Sara is insistent, insisting they should know whatever there is to know, even if it's nothing.

"Ah, yes. Mr. . . . Ah. Why yes. What can I do for you?" He's very courteous, with a small, neat, finicky voice. Phil wonders what he looks like in real life, if he is a small, neat, finicky person.

"I called to see if you knew anything yet." Already he feels at a disadvantage. The Institute gets hundreds of referrals every month; probably Spencer doesn't even know who he is. He hears the sound of papers being shuffled on the other end.

"Ah yes. Here we are. Well, as a matter of fact, things are getting on quite nicely. We've sent your slides all over the city. Interesting case." Phil imagines a fleet of taxicabs with his slides and X-rays riding in the back seat crisscrossing the streets of Boston. "We've got a pretty good idea," Spencer goes on, "but we're still waiting for a definitive answer. One more country to be heard from."

Oh, Christ, another country? Phil thinks, then realizes Spencer is speaking metaphorically. At least he hopes he is. Anyway, as far as Phil's concerned it's all another country. He feels strangely breathless. Sara is standing at his side, looking anxious.

"Ask him," she urges. "Ask him."

"Do you have any better idea what it might be?"

"Well. We have to use special dyes, a very complicated procedure, but yes, most of the reports have come back. Yes, here it is. Probably paraganglioma or pheochromocytoma. It's quite rare. A difficult diagnosis."

"Para-gang-glioma," Phil repeats. The word means nothing to him. He can't even pronounce the other one.

"Not renal cell?" Sara says, grabbing on to his arm. "Ask him to spell it." He doesn't understand why she gets so excited. They are only words.

"Not renal cell carcinoma?" he repeats to Spencer.

"No, oh no. Who told you that?"

"It's something different," he says to Sara.

"I beg your pardon?" Spencer's polite voice says faintly over the line. Sara has turned away. Phil cannot see her face.

"I'm sorry. I was talking to my wife. We were told up here that it was renal cell carcinoma."

"Oh, I see. No, it looks like paraganglioma all right." There is a silence; the phone hums. "Did you have any other questions?" Spencer asks finally.

"Ask him what they're planning to do," Sara says.

"What's going to be done? I mean, can you give us an idea of what's going to happen next, when they're . . . when you're . . ."

"Yes, well." The voice seems to shrink and fade inside the telephone. "I think we'd better get you down here for a consultation, anyway. Possibly, no, make it probably, an operation, but we can't tell at this point. We'll need more tests. But we'll definitely want to see you. And your wife, of course."

"How long," Sara says. "Find out how long."

"When?"

"Ah well. I think we might as well wait until the last report is in." He sounds so tentative. Phil wonders briefly if he is being evasive. But then the voice come on much louder. Maybe it's the connection. "Quite probably right after the weekend," Spencer says. "As soon as we get a free bed. Then we'll want to get more pictures of that left side . . ."

"Left? Phil asks. Why the left?"

There is a puzzled silence. "That's where the tumor is." Pause. "Isn't it?"

Phil holds the phone away from his ear, stares at it. Sara comes back and stands close to him.

"I thought it was on the right," Phil says finally. "That's what they told us up here."

"Oh, well, that could be. But we'll find out," Spencer says cheerfully. "Don't worry, we'll get it sorted out. You'll be hearing from us. Goodbye now," He breaks the connection, leaving Phil holding the empty phone.

He turns to Sara, shaking his head.

"I give up," he says.

Sailing is not so much a science as an art, and thus demands complete attention, Phil thinks, turning his head now toward the mainsail to check the luff, now toward the water to look for cat's-paws, feeling the steady pressure of the tiller under his hand. There are so many variables, wind strength and direction, tide changes, rocks and shoals, so much to watch for. And then there are matters of discretion, whether to sail closer to the wind to gain distance at the expense of speed, or to lay off to gain the fastest point of sail. In sailing you don't always get exactly where you meant to go. It's a question of balancing forces that are constantly changing, possibilities that continually transmute. Still there is that moment always hoped for, when everything conjoins and the boat leaps forward, creating its own wind, apparent wind exceeding true wind, drawing the boat onward. Looking at his own tautened sail, he wonders who ever imagined that wind blowing sideways would make a boat go forward, that the fastest point of sail is a beam reach, the wind at your back blowing over the rail, the sails almost perpendicular to the direction of the wind.

"Aren't you hungry?" Sara asks, breaking into his concentration. He looks at his watch. They have been sailing for almost three hours, threading their way in and out among the coastal islands as far as the mouth of the main bay. It's long past lunchtime, but Phil shakes his head, twitches the mainsheet, adjusts the tiller. He's not thinking about lunch. The boat's speed increases almost imperceptibly. Ah, good, he thinks. He pulls the sail in more; they are sailing close-hauled, to gain distance to windward. But not at the expense of speed.

"We should start thinking about getting back," Sara says after a while. "Even if we're not hungry, it's still a long drive home."

Phil nods absently, watching the configuration of the sail, the arrow line of telltale pointing out the wind direction. "I could stay out here forever," he says without thinking.

Without even looking at her he can feel her stiffen, feels it almost as a change in wind direction, her sense of outrage at the lack of forever, or even next year. He wishes he had said something else.

"Be that as it may," Sara says calmly, "I think we should be getting back while there's still wind. Who wants to chug all the way in with that disgusting thing?" she finishes, gesturing toward where the clunky old engine hangs down through its well inside the stern compartment. Phil has forgotten it existed, but there it is, their insurance against the failure of the wind. No, they would not want to go back that way, with all the noise and smell and commotion.

"All right," he says, and pushes the tiller across the coaming. The boat begins to swing around, then stalls, its sails flapping aimlessly, as limp and fragile as a closed eyelid. The water has lost its ruffled quality, and between them and the shoreline the surface lies as flat and slippery-looking as a pool of oil. The boat coasts for a few feet, then settles back into the water like a roosting bird. The wind has simply blown itself away.

"Well, how do you like that?" Phil says, leaning back against the deck. The tiller nudges his hand, and he slaps it away. "Wouldn't you know? You can't trust anybody." He looks back toward where they came from; they must be at least three miles out. He can't even make out the boatyard from here. "Isn't this just our luck?" He hasn't meant to sound so resentful, but the annoyance wells up from someplace deep inside and surprises even him. He stares around at the surface of the water, looking for any sign of wind.

There is a silence. Then Sara says, "Do you want to talk about it now?"

"Shhh," Phil mouths, shaking his head and waving her to silence. Not twenty feet away a black faucet has appeared above the surface of the water. Sara looks bewildered; he puts a hand on her head and directs her gaze toward the loon. The faucet-like head swivels, showing a white neck patch, flashes a startled red eye at them, then with a quick looping dive shoots under the water, a dark torpedo speeding out of range. Birdmarines, his son calls them. Often they float with their bodies almost submerged, only their heads and necks showing, turning silently, intelligently, like periscopes, precise, mechanical.

"I didn't know they came out this far," Sara whispers, her head swiveling in an odd imitation of the bird. "Where is it?" Silently they watch the smooth surface for the loon's reappearance. Phil is grateful for the distraction. The sails hang loosely, the boom sways back and forth in the slight swell, and the only sound is the clink of halyards swinging against the mast. Phil misses the sound of the wind; the air seems empty now.

The loon does not reappear. Sara stands up, her hand shielding her eyes, and looks all around. "Do you suppose we frightened it?" she asks, her attention focused on the loon, or lack of it. Phil can't take his eyes off her now; he stares at her, seeing her anxious for once about something else but him, the intensity of her concern. He knows that she is willing the loon to reappear, drawing it toward the surface with her vigil. Then he realizes that he is holding his breath, watching her. Carefully he lets it out, not wanting to startle her. He jumps as he hears overhead the sudden raucous cheer of gulls, sees them flung across the sky like so many bits of torn-up paper. They wheel and turn, jeering, squabbling. He wonders if the loon can hear them. A few white feathers float down, settle on the water and seem to stick, motionless, in a pool of tar. The silence lengthens, and Sara does not move.

"Don't worry," he says at last. "They can stay down as long as fifteen minutes."

She turns and looks at him, bemused. "How do you know that?"

Phil shrugs. "I read it in an article. Loons are an endangered species."

"Well, this one isn't," Sara says, pointing behind him. Far away the black

On the Edge

crescent head sticks up above the surface, flicks around, spots them, and quickly sinks out of sight again. Another disembodied head appears, or is it the same one? No, there are two; Phil has read that they travel in pairs, and usually mate for life. For several minutes he and Sara watch the loons work their way in and out under the still water, relieved of the necessity to talk. They just sit, listening to the halyards clank like cowbells. The water is as still as glass. Phil looks up into the shrouds, sees the telltales hanging limp and motionless. He reads this as defeat, stands up, lifts the cover of the engine compartment and reaches for the starter handle of the motor.

"Phil, wait." Sara's voice startles him. "Can't we talk a minute before you start that thing?" Even without looking he knows she is regarding him across the cockpit; he feels like a skewered butterfly. He knows what she is leading up to, and he feels the resistance stiffening, pressing upward. She want to talk, but what good does talking do? What is there to say? He turns, stares past her to study the meager motion of the telltale on the shroud. The little bit of thread twitches, then falls limp again. There is no hope of wind. There is no escape, though talking is the last thing he wants to do.

"Phil, we've got to talk sometime. You may be leaving in three days." Her voice goes on, relentless, to its real point. "If we bought the boat then we wouldn't have to keep borrowing. You could sail it any time you wanted and not worry. And we would have it . . ." She does not say the words "for next year"; she will not make that mistake again. "It'll give you something to think about when you're down in Boston. Something to look forward to."

Phil finally looks at her, he knows she feels his silence as a rebuke. She looks so pretty, sitting there with her cheeks reddened by the wind, her hair blown around in wisps, a fuzzy halo around her face, her hands clasped in her lap. She is staring at him earnestly, intently, and suddenly he recalls all the stories she has told him about her father sailing in an old crock of a boat those summers on the lake where she grew up, her father gay and smiling in the pictures, dead long before Phil met her. He realizes in this instant that if they buy this boat and sail it on the lake near them Sara will have recreated nearly all the elements of her childhood and early youth. He knows that this is not her motive, that she is not even aware of it, but he feels this knowledge as his own guilt, thinking of her father dead so young, the loss he knows she still feels so acutely, and accepts the knowledge, standing helpless in the rocking boat, that this is the worst thing he could have done to her, this dying of his own.

"I don't want to talk," he says, as gently as he can. "I just want to sail."

"I know that," she says and starts to cry.

He starts to reach out for her, but hesitates; there is really nothing he can do for her, not now. Instead he reaches for the starter cord. He grabs hold, cocks his shoulder, is about to yank when he feels Sara's hand on his arm. He turns, and she points wordlessly at the horizon. He hears, inside the silence, a regular lapping noise, gurgling, percolating as though the boat were moving. Little ripples appear along the surface of the water. But when he glances at the shrouds the thread is limp.

"The tide is turning," Sara says. "That means there'll be wind."

"Oh, sure," Phil snorts. "Wind from where?" He waves her off and leans toward the engine. "That's an old salt's tale."

"It's true," Sara insists. "Something about the movement of great masses of water all at once. Stirs up the air. The wind dies down, then comes back from the opposite direction. I read it in one of your books." She sticks a wet finger up, sitting there almost primly, like a schoolteacher making one last point to an unruly class. "You just wait, we'll be able to run all the way back."

"So now you can predict the future," Phil says, smiling at her prim certainty.

"You bet," she says.

Sure enough, standing upright in the cockpit, Phil feels a slight wind grope across his face, pluck at his hair. He squints across the water, sees far off tiny ripples starting as the wind frays the water into little raveled skeins of white. The sea resembles a worn and crumpled garment someone has spread out and tried to smooth. As he watches, it buckles, flaps, then frays to foam, changing color as a line of darker blue flies toward them.

"Here it comes!" Phil barely has time to shout, as he sits down and grabs for the tiller and the mainsheet. Suddenly the wind is all around them, waves splashing against the hull, shooting up like whitewater. Farther away, the surface breaks as though it were flowing over a series of obstructions, but there are no rocks or shoals out here; it is the wind driving the water back against the tide. The wind frets the chops to miniature fountains, and blows their spray to smithereens. Phil heads the boat around, and the wind knocks them forward, swings the main far out to one side. The jib whips back and forth around the forestay. Sara grabs a long wooden pole from down below, leaps up on deck, moves forward swiftly. She captures the flailing jib, inserts the end of the pole, angles the pole into the mast and stretches the sail out the side opposite the main. "Hey, what are you doing?" Phil shouts, impressed by her agility.

"Setting the jib for wing and wing," she answers breathlessly, hopping back down into the cockpit with a jib sheet in her hand. The boat moves forward, gaining speed, scooting along over the waves. Now they are sailing and there is no more time to talk.

There is something so complex yet pure about the relation of wind and sail, Phil thinks, as he stands on the dock watching the yardman strip down the *Loon* and tie it to. Sara is standing next to him, and he can tell that she is not watching the boats. He hears a motor start up and looks out through the multitude of bobbing masts to where one is moving, a sailboat gliding through the channel in the chop, its sail fluttering. Someone starting out even this late in the day. Phil wishes he were with him. But it is almost time to start for home. He feels rather than sees Sara contemplating him. She reaches up and puts a hand against his cheek. It feels like a patch of sunlight warm across his skin.

"You look wonderful, you know. Your color's better, not so chalky. This is good for you," she says.

All around him the yellow birch leaves turn into the hardness of brass and rattle in the wind. He looks at Sara, silhouetted against the leaves, her yellow windbreaker the same color, her face ruddy and hopeful from the sun and wind, the long day's sail. It is a matter of balancing conflicting forces. He looks all around him, at the trees, the masts, the sea, the sky, pale and fathomless overhead. The wind blows, the landscape moves, but it does not stare back. Hard, indifferent, the leaves of brass, of copper, of bronze, the vast unbroken mirror of the sky, the water shards broken glass glittering in the sun, have nothing more to say to him, nothing at all. He feels this silence hardening inside him. Sailing close hauled means gaining distance, sometimes at the expense of speed. Even in sailing, you can't always get exactly where you want to go.

"I wish that I had died during that first operation," he says. "Then you would be used to it by now."

Sara stares at him for an instant, then turns and runs, the wind behind her spinning hard discs of leaves across her path. He watches as she runs down the dock, across the wharf, up the little graveled drive and out of sight, going nowhere, anywhere, Phil thinks, as long as it's away.

When she comes back, he is still standing on the dock, staring out across the bay. Sara stands close to him, slides her hand between his arm and side. He doesn't speak, doesn't look at her. After a while she withdraws her arm, and they stand side by side, not touching, staring at the water. The wind is gentler now, the waves no longer frayed with white.

"I bought the boat," Sara says finally.

Phil nods. It is not sailing so much as the idea of sailing, not boats, but the idea of boats. He looks at Sara curiously, as if from far away. He wonders if she has acted out of knowledge, faith, or sheer bravado. He wonders what, if anything, she knows, and how she knows it. But then it hardly matters; she has already said that she will sail it herself. Life will go on without him after all.

Across the bay the sunlight falls obliquely on the water, turning the ripples into tiny bright dagger points of light, and for a moment, as he watches, each one becomes a minute triangle of sail, dashing one after another, hundreds of sails dancing, scooting, rushing persistently across his line of sight. But then his vision clears, and once again he sees only ripples touched with light. Far down the bay another triangle of sail, real this time, heads up into the wind, shivers momentarily, then tightens to a plume. Standing there, Phil sees his whole life compassed in this passage of one feathered sail across a sea of jagged glass.

"You can always sail it yourself," he says.

"You'll be here," Sara answers.

Carolyn Kizer

· · · · · · · · · · · · · · · · · · · ·

The Great Blue Heron

M.A.K., September, 1880–September, 1955

As I wandered on the beach
I saw the heron standing
Sunk in the tattered wings
He wore as a hunchback's coat.
Shadow without a shadow,
Hung on invisible wires
From the top of a canvas day,
What scissors cut him out?
Superimposed on a poster
Of summer by the strand

Of a long-decayed resort,
Poised in the dusty light
Some fifteen summers ago;
I wondered, an empty child,
"Heron, whose ghost are you?"

I stood on the beach alone,
In the sudden chill of the burned.
My thought raced up the path.
Pursuing it, I ran
To my mother in the house
And led her to the scene.
The spectral bird was gone.

But her quick eyes saw him drifting
Over the highest pines
On vast, unmoving wings.
Could they be those ashen things,
So grounded, unwieldy, ragged,
A pair of broken arms
That were not made for flight?
In the middle of my loss
I realized she knew:
My mother knew what he was.

O great blue heron, now
That the summer house has burned
So many rockets ago,
So many smokes and fires
And beach-lights and water-glow
Reflecting pin-wheel and flare:
The old logs hauled away,
The pines and driftwood cleared
From that bare strip of shore
Where dozens of children play;
Now there is only you
Heavy upon my eye.
Why have you followed me here,
Heavy and far away?
You have stood there patiently
For fifteen summers and snows,

Denser than my repose,
Bleaker than any dream,
Waiting upon the day
When, like gray smoke, a vapor
Floating into the sky,
A handful of paper ashes,
My mother would drift away.

Elizabeth Spencer

. . . .

From *The Salt Line*

"I'm just an old brown locust shell, stuck on a tree, Lex," Arnie Carrington announced next morning down on a pier in the small craft harbor. Lex had arrived at the appointed time, in tan cotton slacks looking way too new and a knotted silk scarf, dark blue, tucked into his shirt. Nothing if not well-dressed. Mackintosh and sweater, drawn from the back seat of his shimmering car, hung over his arm. "Oh, it's a great life in store for you, Lex."

Carrington vaulted into his boat, a fat-bellied old shrimper with the net masts removed, the gunnels painted red. Rocking from his weight, she made the water she rested in wash with a soft sigh. She lay as comfortably in the warm winter sun as an old dog might on a rug in a sunlit room. To Lex, watching like a child in a kitchen where he didn't know what to do, this timeless sense came easily. (Dangerous, he thought, and stiffened.)

"Next thing you know," Arnie was shouting, and postponed the sentence to kneel in the bow, coil ropes into standing rings, return to lift down from the pier a Styrofoam cooler heavy with ice and beer, a canvas bag encasing the oddments of travel. He unlocked the narrow door that led to the pilothouse and kicked it free of the jamb. Then he was looking up and there was something coming between him and Lex, leaning down toward the boat from the pier, handing down a basket, a woman. Lex had not heard her come. She wore a loosely cut blouse, sandals, a peasant skirt, and her dark hair swung down curtainlike, blocking from his sight not only her face but Arnie's also, so that

Lex saw only the hands and arms, hers to extend a basket, his to take. Pre-arranged. She straightened, flung her hair aside, and was, as Lex now saw instead of guessing, good-looking, sexy, what Arnie would have. Her name and his were being exchanged, but he couldn't make the words out. She said hello and left, with a wave to them both, her sandals slapping fast on the wood of the pier.

"Friend of mine. Mavis. Brought some lunch for us." Arnie held the boat close to the pier for Lex to vault in. "As I was saying, you'll next be boarding your own fine little twin-engined launch at the yacht club docks. But for now, you must suffer with this down-at-the-heels but strong and worthy character." He slapped the side of the pilothouse affectionately, like the flank of a horse. An old tan sweater, faded blue work shirt, worn chino trousers, frayed canvas shoes—what did Arnie care? "It's a great life in store for you, the way I see it. First, department head—you're in line for it, I would imagine. Then a year or so of a high administrative post, rector, vice-chancellor, something or other, then retirement. And there will be your beautiful house, waiting just for you and Dorothy and your girl, your mansion by the sea."

"As if I thought in terms like that." Lex felt the heat of anger, a tiny beginning flame which he quickly put out. Playing cool was the method.

"I'm carried away," growled Carrington and slapped his shoulder. "See my island and you'll know why. My little properties salvaged from the ruins. My heart is in them, Lex! You'll hear it all."

By then he was leaping about the boat like a jumping jack. He lifted the anchor clear on its winch, let gas into the starter mix, yanked the motor to life, and cut speech off entirely. He scurried out, cast the last rope from the pier, mounted back to the cabin, nudged the motor into a slow reversal, and steered the craft down the watery aisle between ranked rows of boats moored along the piers. Solemnly as a march, they sputtered down the distance to the end, then with a spurt of speed, a flourish of the wheel, they swung toward the open channel. The old boat seemed to feel her freedom recurring and to have for a moment what the sailboat knows even better, a single impulse with water and current, air and wind all worked to its own purpose.

Lex's busy anxieties went mercifully dead for the moment. He felt the thrill of their opening motion, saw the sweep of the wake like the parabola of a gull's flight, and thought of a skating mark on ice such as television shows often held him with, or, from a campus path in the afternoon, the sight of a jet plane rising on the wide curve of its stream. Even seediness could come to life was what he had to admit, and from its unlikely bosom he chose his moment to look back toward the shore's curve, to seek the white rise of his new home.

Barrel-chested, short-legged, looking taller than he was, Carrington stood at the wheel with his mouth working full blast, singing, it was to be supposed. It was like watching a movie before the advent of sound. Then the motor lost its sputter, cut down to a steady purr as they took direction and put on speed. Now, streaming from the pilothouse, came the loud warbling of Carrington's baritone: "You Are My Sunshine," "Home on the Range," "Basin Street Blues" . . . . The pursuing gulls no doubt heard the cadence, and flapped their wings in time to it, thought Lex, and looked outward to where the winter water lay flat and rippleless, slightly hazy, sunwarmed, a dim cottony mist just above it a few yards distant, which vanished as the prow cut the peaceful surface.

Islands were rising now, at first like indentations of the horizon, then assuming individual shape and character. The gulls, hovering high, knew the islands, closing or opening distances as they chose. A string of pelicans, in configuration like the tail of a kite, beat steadily toward a knoll of land and banked, curving in unison to settle in on fishing territory, chose a given moment for folding wings. Pouches hung from their bills to dump their catch in, old ladies with their reticules. Nature's jokes, thought Lex, included Arnie Carrington, now warbling "Harvest Moon" in broad daylight. Among oyster shells on a scant slope of beach, part of an islet, a tall white heron, awkwardly alert for fish, leaned into the wind on fragile legs like ill-set bean poles. She looked up as if she knew them, saw them pass. Winter, in her pale look against the wind, recalled itself.

For now shore breath had fallen behind and they moved through the pure Gulf itself; outlines stripped by the season stood sharply visible, the water flashed up in higher play against their hull. A distant fishing boat appeared, the first in a time, two figures hunched at either end. Far off, a beach showed the remains of a picnic: beer cans and a charred splotch left from fire.

"Where are the shrimpers?" Lex shouted.

"Far out," Arnie waved to indicate. "Out and to the west." Then, an hour later, it was to the southwest that he was excitedly pointing. "There she is!" He had seen his island.

The island now rapidly drawing them toward it was like the others only larger than most, and seemed, in the shift of light caused perhaps by Carrington's swing to the left, to lie under a haze of blue. Arnie cut the motor down to a sputter, and white sand gradually extended itself before them to make a small horizon. A deep notch appeared on their right, around a forward spit of beach where some scrappy oaks had grown to make a little wood, tough fighters used to wind and wreckage. The boat rounded the point and, barely powered now, moved into a natural harbor.

Hearing surf as the motor died, Lex stood up eagerly, but almost toppled as the boat swayed. Carrington passed insect repellent; from beyond the trees the surf withdrew, fading.

A tapestry of mosquitoes drifted forward to meet them. Carrington made the boat fast to a short pier. Soon they were standing on it, carrying cooler, basket, and canvas bag, and faced toward the island.

They had started at ten; it was now past noon. The sun from its winter angle warmed them. The stubby oaks at this end of the island looked dense enough to call a wood. A great sand dune, rising up from a midpoint of the land, looked over the wood. Lex had seen it, a landmark, on their approach, and seen how the reach of island to the east was sandy, bare, shell-strewn, fleeced with long grass. They were to move through wood to beach, he guessed, by a path, but the weeds just before them looked squashy with wet, perennially green, the ground black and treacherous. Arnie went ahead, stepping into weeds that nodded forward over a little-used path. He was suddenly to the waist in weeds. Lex followed. Conquistadores.

The path turned, approaching the oaks. The ground was not so spongy here. I will be taller than these trees, thought Lex, and saw their twisted branches, gray, the size of children's limbs. But they were above him, in low command, and ahead he heard, when the surf drew back, the rustle of a stream, and heard the ground suck again when Arnie stepped. "A spring?" he asked. There it came across the path, an indentation lined with rocks and shells, the rush of clear water. His eye followed it up toward the island's center, quickly lost to the sight among reeds and tree roots, up toward a space suggested at its turning, where yellow flowers slanted, dry, left from autumn in this shelter, but boldly colored still. Sun was reaching in to touch them. He stopped still, head among the treetops. He saw gnats dance in the sunlight, a black fist of motion. Arnie went down, sloshed through the stream and up the opposite bank, while Lex stood listening to the withdrawal of the surf so he could hear again the hidden spring. "Yes, a spring," said Arnie, looking back. "Everything's here," he added, and the surf rushed back, over his words. But it was the smell of something crushed, a wild plant stem or fungus, that pierced through the insect oil, and made Lex think of women, girls especially, their nudging odor, and that not of his present household but cousins he used to visit as a child, way out in the country, the other side of nowhere, his father said, and a spring had been there, too. His little cousin had been with him when they went to find the spring, the blond one with a cast in one blue eye, the one who had said, "When I bend over, don't look up my dress, now." "I'll turn my back," he'd said, the way his mother had told him, but then she laughed over her shoulder, "Oh, I don't *rilly* care." Face dripping with the fresh water cold as a silver knife blade, she'd tickled him and giggled, and wanted him to play a game she could teach him, but by what rules? He thought with fear of all the things they'd told him not to do.

"If you take a long enough step," Arnie was saying, "you'll clear it." The stream murmured between them. His attention returned and he smiled. When had there been a smile like that—easy, natural? Long ago, he had reached out with good faith to Arnie and Evelyn Carrington. There had been a possibility of love. He had followed it with faithful tread. How was it lost? Lex jumped toward Arnie. The canvas bag, holding a snakebite kit, a collapsible casting rod in an aluminum tube—what else?—banged against his thigh. He half slipped; Arnie caught him. They went on.

They came from the wood on a path, which now skirted the foot of the great lopsided dune. A myriad dazzle of butterflies, brown and gold, swarmed up out of nowhere. They danced around Lex's head. He saw light through them, a world of translucent amber, the dazzle of deep dimension, pulsing to its own notion. The very wings were now beating his face, soft and multiple, his cheeks, brow, even eyelids. One was wading knee-deep in his hair. When they dipped and rose, moving away as one, he was gasping. "I saw them!" Carrington was crying. "All around your head!" Lex rubbed his hand to his face as though emerging from a trance. All together, they had been like separate parts of one creature. Cousins . . . angels . . . he seldom thought such things. But still the pressure of the wings on his flesh kept beating like a noise. They came past the dune together and walked toward the island's eastward reach, bare of trees, land risen to sun its back, whales hump, haired with long pale grass. The surf, withdrawing, left a hush behind it, and a light, still dryness came up from the thin crust of soil, holding its own against the sea breeze. Along the slope of earth before them, the cement foundations of a building could be seen, with a curving shell walk toward it.

"There was a chapel here," said Carrington, waving his hand. "The place was run by some nuns. They were building a retreat when the storm came. Gave it up afterward. We can sit here." He had reached the old foundations and sat down on a length of broken wall. He set the basket and Styrofoam bucket down between them; the bucket lid came off with a squeak. "It's not the school cafeteria, all the better." He snapped the lid from a can of beer and passed it. "God Almighty with his powerful winds was no respecter of his servants. The nuns would make their day trips here by the boatload, I reckon, clustering around on the sand like big black birds, filing like missionaries through the wood. The Holy Ghost is a swarm of butterflies." He snapped a second can. "Happy times for the sisters. Now, swept away. After the big blow, they got discouraged. Other reasons, too. Fewer going into orders, so I've heard. Women getting less and less spiritual. Evelyn loved it here. She had a remission after the storm. A fantasy we had: the wind had drawn her trouble out, blown it clear away. No use in that. But we would come out here, middle-aged, doomed, happy, full of empty plans. All done now, no use to remember. Now I want to put a fishing lodge here. There's a natural harbor. I can rent it out. An architect—friend of mine—is drawing up the plans. A Mafia guy wants to buy. Not the deal I'd like." He pointed eastward. "Once out on that beach, a big sea turtle came up. I climbed aboard its back, Lex. I rode the bastard out to sea. I was alone, Evelyn gone. 'Take me to the deep,' I ordered and he did. Swam right out from under me." Having described a suicide attempt that failed, he drew sandwiches from the basket, bit into chicken salad, offered ham to Lex, lifted out a Thermos of coffee.

"I was sorry to hear about Evelyn," said Lex. Arnie did not reply, and he felt his own sincerity fall back upon himself. He remembered the innocence of the spring, light through the beating wings. The world, at least partly, is what we make it. He ventured further. "I want us to be friends again." The butterflies.

"Friends?" Arnie repeated, with a sudden, appraising turn of his shaggy head—unkempt and older; a wild outcast found wandering here alone might have looked the same. "So do I, Lex!" He leaped up, grasped Lex's hand and shook it, eyes flaming their strange yellow light. His grasp was rough, callused, with cracked skin. "You must understand the opportunities!" He had to shout over breaking surf.

"To hell with opportunities," said Lex, and hoped for a tidal force of understanding. "I was so lonely as a boy, and what's important now? My daughter's a treasure, but pretty girls don't stay around forever and I—" He raised shy eyes and met avidity in the yellow gaze. He was being heard, all right, his words drunk as if by a sponge, but as information only, he saw, and withdrew at once—sensible, sensitive—into silent caution. He perceived Arnie as enemy, a wearisome presence. But, in the absence of evidence to the contrary. . . .

"So you and Dorothy," said Arnie, "you never really worked it out?"

The next step, of course, had been that one. Should he go right on with it, get in up to his neck, say: Maybe she was happier with you? But there was darkness there; he had a right, at least, to normal clarity. The sea withdrew, hissing softly.

"It's peaceful here," Lex said. "Something mysterious about it. Did the nuns give it that?"

"All islands are mysterious, I guess," said Carrington. He glanced about him as though someone might be there with them. The next wave trod softly in. "Oh, to get you in on my interests here, Lex. We'd both be the better for it. Call the past shredded, ripped apart, hurricane-blasted: your choice of metaphor. We both know there was a tangle back there. But the knack of going forward from now, that's the survival route. If you retreat, even up to your ears in money, retired and neat and elegant as hell, your daughter married and moved to Kalamazoo—why, that's misery, Lex. You best involve yourself. I always had a gift for that, at least; nobody ever suggested differently. I can point to what's the vital spot like a bird dog. The mystery you mentioned—I won't hide it from you. It's Evelyn. She's out here. In spirit. Nothing sinister. Friendly as hell."

They sat eating sandwiches. A gull sailed close and tilted over them, head bent to search out what they had. It screamed. Action, Lex knew, was being pointed out, pled for. Decision, activity. He would sooner have lingered with emotions, feelings, longings he had just begun to find words for. Arnie, God knew, took feeling so for granted dozens of cousins might have gone down on their backs for him, and he would have enjoyed, forgotten them every one. In sunlight, the wind blew chill. It was, after all, winter.

In the winter light, on a ruined wall on a Gulf island, Lex Graham sat tall and silent, looking out. To someone coming on the scene, he might have appeared to be controlling here—an island king. "You're asking," he said at last, "to give what I have to keep your projects going. But the ideas here, they all are yours."

"Oh, yours would be welcome. I wouldn't dictate. Working together is the only way."

"My life," said Lex, "all that's in it, or that it could ever be, cradle to grave—to you it's nothing but an episode. Why care about it? Why pretend to care?"

Arnie did not relpy.

"I came all the way out here to tell you the one answer to anything you could ever ask of me. I came all this way so you'd hear me plainly, because, to tell the truth, I don't think you've ever heard me, ever really listened to what I said. I won't help you in any way. It's final."

Arnie presently got up and walked away.

Lex sat listening to the surf. The water itself, its rush and retreat, seemed to give back the hot screaming of the sixties decade, all that had made him feel out of it. So he had been true to what he felt last night, high in the motel room, overlooking the water.

Carrington sat down some distance away on a log half sunk in the sand, his head bent, his gaze gone out to sea. He seemed to have grown into the log. The shagginess of the head and moustache were intricate growth: weeds, shells, driftwood, and dishevelment of sand. The tone was altogether earth, myriad, unfathomable. He moved once, to scratch his leg, then pulverized small chips of sandy bark form the log's back. The gesture brought life to what it touched and made that life his own. Lex, in estrangement, looked away to the east where, to his surprise, a proud silent fishing schooner, blue and dazzling white, was passing in a furrow of white foam. When he looked back, the log was empty. Did eyes play tricks? He got up and shook himself.

Lex assumed that Arnie's absence was due to nature. He went, himself, behind a wall, then strolled as far as he could to the eastern reach, saw the proud boat, a dot now, disappear, the thin trail of churned water dissolve to nothing. Alone, then: had Arnie left him there, vengeance for his refusal? The idea, which he did not really believe, nevertheless set up a groaning within him, such as one hears within a tree trunk. Dully, he noted the return of what had been absent since all the money had come to him: psychic pain. He walked inland and circled the tall dune, really only a packed drift of sand against a once-commanding tree, probably blown there by the hurricane. Branches and driftwood were laced in it, and what looked to be the side of a refrigerator, probably from a wrecked boat's galley, and the splinters of a chair. By the dune's foot, he re-entered the wood of small trees. He followed what seemed to be a path, hoping it would bring him back to the spring, which he now remembered fondly, like something out of a long-ago dream. He immediately lost direction in the thick growth. Once he stumbled over a rotted tree stump, pulverized to dust by hordes of ants, and again sank to his ankles in soggy ground, layered with thick moss and fringed with ferns. On firmer ground, he was clawed across the face by briars, and vines clung about one leg, removing his shoe which he was at some trouble to find. Then he saw what seemed to be the path again and at a little distance, just at a turning place, a naked woman with her back toward him, unmistakably his wife. "Oh, Dorothy!" He cried it at once, knowing the sight to be merely a trick of shadow, or the way a feathery bush was growing by the trail, swelling out to shape a shadow. He took the whole impression into him, even while knowing it false. A sense of her having just swum the Gulf and now sheltering to dry herself with a towel, fit back into clothes. He saw the gleam of her thick hair, with its cosmetic streaking, the long sunken line of her spine, and again said, "Oh!" and, stepping forward (even as the configuration turned into itself only), he stumbled and fell forward, his arms stretched out.

It was difficult to scramble up. His leg at first was numb, and he was never clear whether the numbness was already occurring and had caused the fall, for it had already begun to sting like crazy, itch like fire, he couldn't tell why, but heard a scraping noise a few feet from him, to the left, and parting some tall grass, found there before him an open sunlit space with Arnie Carrington hard at work in it, clearing growth back from a flat rectangular marble slab which lay before a formal pedestal. It was astonishingly gardenlike, and Arnie's motions in clearing back what would soon obliterate it had the quality of a monkish kind of devotion, of the person who leaves off manuscript illumination of Scriptural translation in order to do his patient chores. For Evelyn? He'd said she was here—did he mean literally?

"Oh, there you are," said Arnie, looking up. "You know what this was? A shrine to St. Francis. Evelyn liked it. The statue blew away and couldn't be found. The patron saint of birds went shooting off on the wind." He dumped an armload of weeds and vines, out into the wood's edge. There went the stream Lex had sought, winding through the foot of this little civilized plot. "I thought I saw Dorothy," he said. "It was just an optical illusion."

Arnie scrubbed a sleeve across his sweating brow. "So we're all four here, you might judge," he remarked.

His work was finished. They walked back to gather up their gear, finding an easy way along the beach. But Arnie noticed that Lex looked like the wrath of God, must have wandered off into a jungle, and Lex at last admitted, limping painfully behind as they approached the boat, that something had bitten or stung or in some way attacked him when he fell—he remembered no hiss or squeak or snarl, or any animal motion, but his leg went numb and then it hurt and now the hurt was growing stronger. Arnie turned back. Lex pulled up his trouser leg. There was swelling already and a curdled mass of color— purplish-red—had commenced. Arnie knelt to look for evidence of snakebite, but found no marks of fangs. The injury simply sat there, as evident as a toad, getting worse. Lex let out a plaintive moan. His face had gone white and small, distant with strain. "Let me help you," Arnie said.

So they came painfully into the boat together. Arnie, leaned against so heavily, remembered other rescues—the soldier in Korea, the son in Colorado, episodes of other days. Well, Lex had said the truth maybe: he, too, was an episode. How much did Arnie care? Still, he was doing his best for him.

In the cabin below the pilothouse, he made Lex comfortable, put blankets around him, settled him on a bunk, soothed him with aspirin and whiskey.

But what could it have been? It was as though the island itself had left its stinger in him, a venomous refusal of the Graham presence. What was this about seeing Dorothy? Evelyn was the name he mentioned now. "She's buried there—I know it," Lex mysteriously announced to him, delirious maybe. "Why not admit you've put her out there? That was her grave and you know it."

"There now," said Arnie, moving from one task to the other, mounting now to steer. The boat backed slowly off and nosed toward open water. A day not quite like any other in his life, or Lex's either, Arnie reflected, was ending in this strange way. "You'll be home soon—at the most, two hours. Poor old Lex!"

At that, the motor roared.

Diane P. Freedman

. . . .

A Whale of a Different Color—Melville and the Movies: The Great White Whale and *Free Willy*

Because One Did Survive the Wreck

Whenever it's a damp, drizzly November in my soul, my "hypos" getting the upper hand of me, salt water spouts from my eyes, and I take to the sea, as Melville's Ishmael claimed to need to. But this sea-son, my seas are drifting memories, mostly hardby pond or page. I've had the blues all my life, and proximity to water, too, but the two coalesced most intensely with the mater-nal-professional crisis I had upon moving to a new home for a new job with my three-month-old son in tow. My husband loved being a father, loved the overpriced beat up house on the pond in New Hampshire. But I felt a tremen-dous (and, unfortunately, familiar) loss of faith, felt swallowed up by a whale, or by wails of a different pitch. But I get ahead of myself.

Diane P. Freedman

Wide-Sweeping White Whale

I first read *Moby-Dick* my sophomore year of college, when Dan McCall assigned the mammoth book in Early American Novels. As he spoke, his hands and voice shook; he reminded me of a drunken sailor gone to the dt's. I loved the overall size of the novel, drew bold outlines of whales in the margins of my spiral notebook, although I skipped over the sensuous spermaceti chapter and some of the reference-book ones as well. (Perhaps I was looking for action in all the wrong places.) I remembered seeing paintings of whales and fishermen and seabirds in art galleries in Cold Spring Harbor, Long Island. My parents would tire us out in weathered galleries, then take us to lunch in Neptune's Cave. We kids ate burgers surrounded by gray plastic walls we loved because they made the restaurant look like the Flintstones' house. Our parents ordered drinks. We gave ourselves the willies staring at tanks full of the live lobsters my parents would sometimes order boiled and buttered, but which we never touched. Then, sleepy, we'd whine to go home.

Some weekends, I'd sleep over at my friend Linda's house and we'd go on our own outings instead of our families'. Once we took the train to New York City to see the Central Park Zoo, including its Children's Zoo. We climbed in and out of Cinderella's castle and walked into the mouth of a gargantuan gray whale whose jaws were big enough to sink their teeth forever into my memory. The whale had a water tank stuck in its throat: its mouth opened to a huge aquarium of tiny live fish. My memory isn't as clear about the rest of the whale's body; I think we could walk inside it through a hole in the side, and I was sorry it wasn't white—this before I'd ever read *Moby-Dick*.

Pilgrim at Mill Pond

I grew up on Long Island, not far from the ocean on the south shore and the whaling museum on the north shore, where my father fascinated my sisters and me with the wide-ribbed skeleton preserved there—as he'd fascinated us with the brontosaurus reconstructed in the Museum of Natural History in New York City. Once my father brought home from the whaling museum a beautiful scrimshaw pendant and sent it to me for a gift at college. None of my younger siblings had wanted carved and colored whalebone to wear on sueded rawhide. I wore it constantly, until I lost it, as I'd lost the little gold horse charm my mother gave me and the charm bracelet she'd given me before that to dangle other (now also lost) charms from. College was a place for losing things.

I attended college in Ithaca, New York, where I once wrote a local newspaper article beginning "Cayuga crooks its finger" and where I wrote many poems, one of which commented, "everything is flooded with blue." Upon graduating, I lived a brief time in Boston near the Chestnut Hill Reservoir (where I slipped through the fence to jog and let my college dog swim until a police car, lights flashing, bullhorn blaring, gave us chase and chastisements); then, Odysseus-like, I moved back to Ithaca. I moved back to Boston suburbs and again to Ithaca before moving farther west.

In Seattle, Washington, I lived within biking distance of Lake Washington and Puget Sound, not to mention the university that was my reason for being there before moving east again, where I lived and taught in Saratoga Springs, a town where the lake was frustratingly privatized and inaccessible but where sprang hope and mineral springs eternal, and thence to Durham, New Hampshire, where I live by Mill Pond my new dog mucks about in and herons choose as their convention site each spring.

Just yesterday, after several hours of fishing, six herons took flight, one after another, just outside my study window. (As I write, I see another heron float by.) Other days I see a range of other water creatures: kingfishers, cormorants, osprey, painted turtles—their hatchlings toddling from their egg site right in our garden, frogs and beavers splashing off as I walk by with my dog, Dusty. A neighbor catches white perch on a line cast from his green canoe. Toads in our garden hop after and dragonflies and bats swoop around after mosquitoes. At different times of day and night, we hear bullfrogs and owls, mourning doves, chickadees, scarlet tanagers, cardinals, Baltimore orioles, blue jays, grosbeaks, hairy woodpeckers, and goldfinches. We have purple finches nesting on a floodlight, phoebes building their skyscraper nests above a garage door. Swans and mallard families parade by, wood ducks flapping up into the trees when Dusty and I surprise them in their nest in a neighbor's lowlands. Yesterday, a river otter tottered on a log not twenty-five yards from the kitchen window.

At present, I teach Twentieth-century American literature by women at the University of New Hampshire. In Saratoga, I'd taught American romanticism at Skidmore College as well. Now I don't read or teach the American romantics or Nineteenth-century figures so much as contemporary women poets and essayists. But I do take in a good deal of whale imagery in watching over and over, in bootleg home-video format (with a stripe across the middle and rarely in its entirety), the popular film *Free Willy*.

When I'm feeling down and blue, I write, out of the blue. Out of the deeps. To out them. Motherhood has so far been for me the greatest lost-at-sea space

for me, full of thoughts too deep for words (so I can only list them here tele-
graphically—guilt at delivering by Caesarian section/not nursing/paying
sitters so we could pack to move/subjecting Abraham to construction noise,
dust, fumes/paying nannies so I could work at a job that got in the way of my
work, writing, mothering/pushing my child aside so I could read but not read,
write only in fragments). I've slowly come to a kind of peace with not getting
things done, with no longer working nights or weekends. I've slowly come to
accept a house by a pond that turns mucky (and my dog ever muddy) in
summer; a perennial garden plagued by Japanese beetles, asiatic beetles, root
weevils, moles, ants, aphids—woolly and not—grasshoppers, mud-daubers,
blackflies, leafminers, spider mites, powdery mildew, black spot, and crown
vetch; a house in need of constant repair and renovation (earlier, didn't I describe the setting almost as a magical place?). I've accepted too a marriage similarly in need of constant repair and renovation and the installment mode that
is sleeping, writing, teaching, reading, thinking, gardening, playing, renovat-
ing, and video viewing with a one- then two- now three-year-old in the house.

Abraham is obsessed with the film *Free Willy*, whose twin protagonists—
for those who have not seen it—are a young orphaned boy named Jesse and
the black orca, or killer whale, Willy, he ends up training at a sorry-looking
aquarium somewhere in the Pacific Northwest. Jesse apparently was abandoned by his mother when he was four or five, and he has lived on the streets
or in foster care ever since. Both Jesse and Willy are separated from family that
the action of the film helps them each to find or form. My son has renamed his
security blanket Jesse, pretends he carries with him another "downstairs" invisible Jesse as well, and asks his father, my husband, to play Glen the Jesse
character's foster father, and asks me to play Annie, the Jesse character's foster
mother. When *he's* Jesse, there are three in his, in our, arms. (But like Jesse and
his new family and new friends, we're none of us completely comfortable as
yet, still singing, as Jesse plays nightly on his harmonica, the nostalgia or
postpartum blues that perhaps only nature can simultaneously assuage and
augment.)

The Great White Whale and Willy

I'm taken by the idea that I was steeped in Melville and nostalgic for New
England while I studied American literature in Seattle and that I'm now
accidentally obsessed with a Northwest whale of another color while teaching
American literature in the New Hampshire seacoast area not far from the
whaling capital of the New World. One life rewrites the other. In Seattle, I

longed for Walden Pond and the Atlantic, for Thoreau's wild apples rather than Washington State's watery Delicious cultivars; in Durham, I hang the arcing Orcas of Nootka and Kwakiutal art on my walls (I almost typed whales). I'm intrigued that the whale of a different color is no longer Ahab's great white— as the kind of literature I no longer read and teach is by "great" whites or the big white whales. Compared with Moby-Dick, Willy is black with some white swatches and is smaller and friendly to a small boy, who, together with a Haida Indian native to the Northwest, works to free him. It further intrigues me that I cannot "read" even a film uninterruptedly or in chronological order now that I'm a mother, and that the film is visually resonant with Northwest art just as Melville's novel is textually resonant with literature in English.

The movie's opening vignettes are nearly sepia-toned scenes of modern whalers/wild poachers (called later by the hired keeper "slimeball whale catchers") who look and sound much like their nineteenth-century counterparts, especially off in the dusky distance at sea—in a wooden boat with the name *Pequod*, in fact, painted in yellow on its white and red bow. Rather than a sperm or right whale, this whale is an orca, or "killer" whale, but both Moby-Dick and his alleged historical counterpart Mocha-Dick were killer whales, the historical and literary records show. The problem isn't an Ahab monomania but the orca whale–owner Diehl's monetary hopes and greed. This time, the whale is not harpooned (although whales are still killed around the world—as the opening and follow-up movie advertisements for adopting a whale reveal), but is captured (and later almost killed—for insurance money). In both stories, the danger of closeness to the whale is invoked. In *Moby-Dick,* that dangerous closeness might symbolize many things, according to various scholars. In *Free Willy,* Jesse fears closeness to the whale and his foster parents who may hurt or leave him or whom he will have to leave. As in Melville's novel, there is a friendly, "heathen" native, or person of color, but Randall is a friend of the whale not the whaler and a native of the whaling grounds rather than a tattooed cannibal hailing from far away. Like Melville's Queequeg, however, Randolph reverences un-Christian idols and beliefs. He reads quietly to Jesse from an old story of a Haida boy rescued by an orca, then he says a prayer over him, the "coolness" and mysteriousness of which Jesse shares with his foster mother later that night, when he reads the story to her and shows her the orca carving Randolph has given him.

Free Willy revolves around the whale Willy; Randolph, the Haida aquarium caretaker, Ray; a female marine biologist working as the overseeing trainer; and Jesse, a young vandal performing community service by working at the aquarium. They work together to free Willy, first through trying to get him to perform, Sea World–style, in the hopes that he will be rewarded with a bigger tank, and, later, by hauling him out of his tank and towing him to the sea in a trailer pulled by a truck Jesse has temporarily stolen from his foster father. Four marginalized characters—the native, the female, the young/criminal (an orphan, even), and an animal—ask viewers to imagine a new order has come or is coming, one that respects nature and ways and traditions not the White Man's own.

The outlaw culture is set at outlawing culture, outsmarting marine technology and harbors, all the while celebrating the safe harbor of a nuclear family (such as the quartet resembles and that Jesse finds finally with the sympathetic foster parents, who provide the final props for freeing Willy—truck and winch and commitment) over silent businessmen who would have suffocated Willy in his tank for the insurance money once they realized Willy was too old or shy or outlaw to perform obligingly for the popcorn crowd.

I remember that although Melville has occasionally been heaped with other dead white male authors and even heaved out of the contemporary classroom as exclusionary, presenting a world without women, and a violent racist, monomaniacal world at that, his characters were nonetheless outlaws and loving it, not part of the patriarchy per se or the privileged (Ishmael celebrates going to sea as a simple sailor not as a passenger with a purse who grows seasick nor as "a Commodore, or a Captain, or a Cook," since he abominates "all honorable respectable toils, trials, and tribulations of every kind whatsoever"). Even Melville was not part of the privileged, and elsewhere, as in his stories "The Paradise of Bachelors and the Tarturus of Maids," he showed how acutely sensitive he was to gender and class inequities. Jesse, too, a juvenile offender several times over (as the movie begins, Jesse is shown stealing food from a restaurant and a caterer's truck, running with peers from a police car in pursuit, then spray-painting the observation deck of Willy's tank at the aquarium, where he's caught) is shown to be an honorable dishonorable, as it were.

Once Jesse is installed at his foster parents' house, with its beautiful view of the ocean, he still suffers attacks of the blues that make him yearn to be closer to Willy and water. This yearning may also be a pre-Oedipal longing for his mother (consider the French pun of *mer* [sea] as *mere* [mother]). Jesse climbs out his window and slides down a drainpipe and heads for Willy's tank. There, he plays his harmonica blues. One evening, saying good-bye to Willy, as he later explains it (it is the last day of his required community service), Jesse slips into the tank and is rescued by the orca (Randolph calls him lucky that the whale didn't eat him up), as he was earlier partially rescued by Dwight, his African American probation officer, and by Randolph and Ray and Annie and

Glen. Jesse seems to feel that since Willy most overtly saved his life, Jesse owes this whale, whom Randolph claims has eyes "that can look into a man's soul." Such language is reminiscent of the "maudlin sentimentalism, tragi-comic bubble and squeak" with which William Harrison Ainsworth long ago identified Melville. Later, Ray tells Jesse that "Orcas love to be touched and hugged," and Willy, who stays at the aquarium a while longer before he's freed, allows Jesse touches, hugs, and rides—things one might say he remembers or misses from his absent mother.

In *Free Willy*, the outlaws are not "simple sailors," the whale catchers, but are those landlubbers or lovers who would free the captive and a part of themselves, and us, of course, as we roil with pleasure watching a prologue of free whales at the beginning of the movie and Willy rolling and gamboling later in the waves (while orca-stra music sounds, Abe reminds me, and the credits roll). The whale that was Ahab's enemy was white and deadly and the whale that is Abraham's and Jesse's friend is black and white, capable of bringing together various outlaw and minority persons. The whale's escape is literally uplifting—he leaps to freedom over a rocky promenatory separating him from the ocean—and spiritually uplifting, of course—Jesse is reconciled to his losses and to his new family. As the music reaches crescendo and the Whale breaches, so am I uplifted and reconciled.

Here's some more of what I wanted to say before the mast. My work gets in the way of my work, my writing. My child gets in the way of my reading, writing, traveling, but he enhances my daydreaming, and I enhance his as we play at his cast of characters. I walk with him imaginatively down the aquariums of my youth and discuss the virtues of pet turtles (safety, sure food, fungus fought, clean water for them: we have a Malaysian box turtle and a Chinese "roof" turtle) and free ones (a life in a pond as bumps on a log, as possible prey for the fisher birds and owls, maybe raccoons: we see painted turtles and snappers lay eggs in our yard for hatchings but see few hatchlings each year). Life can tip this way and death that. That's what Melville and the movies teach. I count my blessings. Sometimes the whale that swallows you whole spits you back up, saved. And you live to tell the tale.

Beyond

Our final stop is the old Montauk Lighthouse on Turtle Hill. Commissioned in 1795 by George Washington, it has long been a famous destination. Originally, the lighthouse was intended to serve as a landfall light for ships bound from Europe to New York, and, while there have been some famous wrecks in these waters, for over two hundred years the lighthouse has more often protected those who sail these difficult waters and inspired those who have walked along its shore. Kali and I sit on the jetty just below the light, watching the converging tides of the Atlantic Ocean and the Block Island Sound: both of us look out beyond the end of Long Island.

While most of this anthology is dedicated to those women who write from the perspective of the shoreline, the authors in this section write about their own experiences venturing beyond the coast or their characters' adventures at sea. The central figures found in this last section of the anthology have spent enough time on the shore to know that they must go beyond, but unlike the typical maritime stories by and about men, women's coastal literature shows a constant connection to the shore, a look backwards. The early adventurer Mary Brewster recorded her 1847 trip to Maui. After marrying Captain William E. Brewster and after being left on shore for more than three years, she determined that she would no longer stay at home but instead travel with her husband on his whaling voyages. Dorothy Balano, Nancy Allen, and Sena Jeter Naslund also write of women who leave the comfort and the solidity of the land to venture out to sea. Naslund's heroine disguises herself as a cabin boy and takes to the sea as she imagines a typical young man seeking his fortune and place in the world. What the women find is that they have the skills and courage to become assets aboard ocean-going vessels. These women (authors and characters alike) are new adventurers in both maritime literature and maritime experience. However, when they go beyond the shore, they take with them an intimate understanding of and connection to the coast. As Emily Dickinson wrote, they carry with them "an inland soul to sea."

Kali and I sit on the jetty behind the lighthouse watching the waves sweep up against the rocks. I look for ships in the distance, but the horizon remains an unbroken line of sky against water. A few least terns and some gulls stitch their way across my view, but mostly I look out on the vast expanse of ocean before me and contemplate what is beyond my jetty seat—mystery and adventure, I think. But still, there is comfort in sitting on a great flat rock at the foot of the lighthouse tucked up against the shore.

Mary Brewster

. . . .

A Season on Maui

Wednesday June 30th [1847]

Had a very wakeful and restless night. The house was near the sea and the surf roared with such a noise I could not sleep which with the incidents of the day was sufficient to keep us awake a great part of the time. The morning proved showery with considerable winds. We took breakfast midst a swarm of natives who had heard of our arrival and who dropped in one after another till I begun to think we should be stiffled as the houses are made without windows and of course there is no chance for the air to circulate freely. this house was the best one I had seen—having two doors which were opposite. The occupants seemed like good people—I was quite surprised when—the old man informed us he was about to attend to family prayer and wished our attention. I could understand but few words of his prayer tho' I listened with pleasure and felt deeply interested relative to the occurance. It was arranged that a canoe should be procured and we sail round the *palais* as there were some eight or ten more, all of them similar to those we had passed. by sailing we could go much faster and easy in comparison to walking. The horses were all sent over by land, Simon to take care of them—the natives took the baggage over and all was to meet us at Hamakuapoko. They started some two hours before us as it would take them much longer—

We got everything ready and went down to the shore to start and were obliged to go back on account of a rain squall—after waiting some time we concluded to start as the rain was light, which we did not mind, but the weather was anything but flattering—the canoe was large as could be got. in looking at it I could not contrive where we could all sit, as it was very narrow so that once in the room was filled, but my feelings were greatly cleared when I saw natives putting the cot or manele across the top which was all secured by ropes and made a far more comfortable seat than I had expected. Mrs. Winslow self and 3 children our feet and legs all doubled up, the little ones tied on as they were on the top and a sudden roll or movement would pitch them overboard, Doctor and Charles seated on a piece of board in the middle, two natives in each end and one in the middle and so we started—

It was very rough and a bad swell, the waves heavy and high, the wind at times blowing hard and our little canoe danced merrily up and down on the billows very deeply laden, the outrigger almost the whole time under water. We had but just got round the point when a wave struck our tiny bark and wet one half of us through and was just pleasing ourselves with the notion that one side was dry, when in came a wave from the other side which wet us completely through. the canvas to the cot was so thick much of the water remained and was soaked up in our clothes. here we was, wet through and had not gone more than a mile, but go we must. I soon began to feel the motion and was so sick in a few moments I could not keep my head up—and it was not long before all were in the same condition and vomiting. When I could look up I cast my eyes towards the Doctor who sat pale and looked mournful. I could not even provoke a smile. Nothing of the scenery was seen which must have been very fine, only occasionally as I looked up, We were about half a mile from the shore which was perpendicular and covered with verdure to the edge—numerous waterfalls pouring down from the mountains with the deep ravines would if sickness had not prevented been enjoyed very much by all of us. One hard shower which served to wet us still more was all we had—

The natives found it would be impossible to round another point which would have taken us to the place where we wished to stop, as it was very rugged and the weather unfavorable—so they began to make in towards the land—as we neared I could see no place where we could land, the passage was between two rocks which was so narrow that the canoe could but just get in, the waves had increased and were rolling in with great force and it was with the greatest difficulty we could land. a native man was down on the rocks and beckoned to us to come here. The surf was so high that it was as much as they could do to manage the canoe. I expected to see it dashed to pieces at each successive wave against the rocks—and wondered so frail a bark could live in a sea—One of the men jumped out on to the rock, one overboard at each end to hold it. Doct. was the first one to leave and by taking a favorable time and watching the sea as it receded they got the children out. The canoe by this time had got some ways out and was again fetched up. a native took Mrs. Winslow and after a short time I was safely landed to my great joy—not so much on account of the danger as sea-sickness. I did not feel able to hold my head up—By climbing up the rocks we at length reached the shore and found we were in a valley between two mountains, one of them we knew we must climb up. we sat down on the rocks whilst the natives got our baggage, took off our wet shoes, and spread them out, hoping they would dry a little, got rested some when it began to rain hard, but spreading the umbrellas, we were protected dome from the shower.

The men who brought up was obliged to leave and take their canoe to a more safe place, so we remained till they returned—they then took the children and we commenced our march and more deplorable looking objects are seldom seen, the females in particular, wet as water could make us, in our stocking feet as we had only one pair of shoes and they were so wet we could not walk in them, weary from being in the boat so long and our sickness had lent us no additional strength—luckily for us the mountain was not as bad as some we had travelled—

We had gone but a little ways before I felt as though I could go no farther, my clothes so wet and heavy. I stopped and tried wringing which did for little while but we were thickly clad, knowing we should need more on the water. I at length halted and took off most of my underclothing which was unnecessary—and then took a fresh start. I never felt so tired, and had it not been for this—I knew I must go—I should have remained a long while behind to rest. After much panting and short breathing we got up and met a native who had carried one of the girls up. he was going down to the shore after some of our things. we stopped to see him go—which was no ways slow. he jumped and bounded like a deer and scarcely stopped a second till he reached the valley—and in all was only a few minutes whilst it had taken us all an hour to get up.

Happily for us we had not to descend this mountain, the road was some ways back in the interior. After traveling two miles we reached a native village and were accommodated in the house of one of the head men who was absent. Upon query we found Simon had been here and gone on, report said so had the natives. such was not so as we soon saw them coming. A messenger was immediately dispatched after Simon and another for the shore after the things we had left there.

This occupied full 2 hours before they got back—all this time we sat in our wet clothes. At length the long wished for calabashes arrived. We changed our apparel as well as we could, which was scant as our most useful things we had not seen since they were put on board of the boat. we had got all the wet articles spread out to dry on the bushes expecting to remain here through the night when Simon came with the horses—he had been waiting two hours a few miles from this place where he expected we should land. At this last arrival word was given *to march on, pack up and start.* as the Doctor thought we could reach Macawao by night and there we should be comfortable. hastily all things were bundled up and carriers sent on ahead—whilst we were taking a cold bite—and then mounted our steeds and rode on. I had no shoes save the pair which was wringing wet so went without. We had gone a few miles when night began to overtake up—as it was much later than we supposed when we started—

A place was looked for to pitch our tent where we could pass the night. A valley was chosen where it would be good pasturage for the horses and the grass was thick and soft for our bones, for bodies we felt were amongst the missing. By this time it was nearly dark—and the tent but half up when there came a hard shower wetting the grass, blankets and nearly all the articles we wished to sleep on. At length the tent was fitted and we went in, the grass was high and the water stood in large drops on it. My stockings soaking wet, riding dress and all our outside clothing.

We spread down all we could, first to soak up the rain, then went down blankets and bedding. took a mouthful of bread and butter and then stretched our limbs for the night, not the least depressed in spirits but all laughing and joking about the moisture which our *Physician* said would be as good as a steam bath and we should be completely steamed before the morning— but not with me, for I felt as though heat was and would be for the night a stranger to us all.

Emily Dickinson

On this wondrous sea

On this wondrous sea
Sailing silently,
Ho! Pilot, ho!
Knowest thou the shore
Where no breakers roar—
Where the storm is o'er?

In the peaceful west
Many the sails at rest—
The anchors fast—
Thither I pilot *thee*—
Land Ho! Eternity!
Ashore at last!

Exultation is the going

Exultation is the going
Of an inland soul to sea,
Past the houses—past the headlands—
Into deep Eternity—

Bred as we, among the mountains,
Can the sailor understand
The divine intoxication
Of the first league out from land?

Dorothy Balano

· ·

December 11, 1912. (At home in Herring Gut, known to the better element as Port Clyde.)

Eva Boyden came with us to Maine, and she was such a rock to lean on through all the trials we've had since that entry I made when sailing away from Puerto Rico. There's been so much to write about but no time to write. Now as I get well from my long siege there's finally time, and, as Doctor North forbids me any activity, I can find time to read and write by the fireplace, which I love and over which there is a large and lovely painting of my Hopkins.

Captain J.W. was shot on board his schooner while at Martinique. He died there, and the body was shipped home for burial on the Ridge. From what I gather he and the ship's engineer, one Cook who Fred said was never any good and who, Fred said, should have been strangled at the time Fred had his hands on Cook's throat, went ashore to deliver some revolvers requested by a local Frenchman from a past trip. The Frenchman refused the guns. Captain Will went back to the ship, but the engineer went to a rum shop. When he returned on board he was crazed and went aft to where Captain J.W. was sleeping in his hammock and shot him. Captain Will's last words, heard by the mate and several crew members, were, "Everything goes to Fred." My poor boy is now saddled with not only going out to Martinique at the Consul's request for the trial of Cook, but he also has to tend the local Balano interests, the water company, the tenements, the wood business, and the sale of the Wawendnock to the Harrises, who have never paid all the bills regarding the purchase of that lovely place which should never have been sold. I'd love to live there.

I was confined for weeks at Knox Hospital, my baby boy having been the first baby born there. James Wilfred, named for his grandfather who would have loved him but whom he will never see, is a dear, precious little darling son, born on September 2, his father's birthday. He's now just over three months and had to be put on a bottle, poor little chap, because his mother didn't take care of herself on her rovings and drink enough milk with the salt mackerel.

Was just interrupted by Isaiah Balano, delivering the wood for my winter fireplace fire. He also dumped off a load for the schoolhouse and the roar woke Wilfred. I told Isaiah about his brother's death and let him read Fred's letter from Martinique. The jurymen of the murder were twelve French-speaking blacks. Fred is going from Martinique down to Barbados and thence home on the mail steamer to New York. I wrote to find out his arrival date and shall go to New York to meet him no matter what Doctor North says against my trip. The poor boy needs me now more than ever. And just to think that a year ago we were so happily entering lovely Rio. And I was hurt because Fred was giving me a gangway instead of a baby. Now I have both, however, and can't wait to see Wilfred creeping up the gangway, bound for Rio, all three of us.

Friday, December 13, 1912.

I told Dr. North, a wonderful physician, to go back to Bowdoin College and study some psychology in order to learn that the best cure for a woman is to go and meet her husband. He laughed and said he guessed Captain Fred could find his way home without my navigation. So I read *Daddy Longlegs* by the lovely fire, about a girl who wrote letters to a man she didn't know but later married. Very bright but quite dangerous for her.

A letter from Puerto Rico tells me that my good old friend, Mr. Benedict of Hatillo, has passed away, leaving a pregnant widow who has gone to her brother's in Mississippi. Little Bernard has been shipped off to his sister, Mabel, my old teaching comrade at Utuado, who now lives in Oneonta, N.Y., and whom I shall visit if I can make the trip to meet Fred at the dock in New York City. But Dr. North says my convalescence still needs inactivity for a month of Sundays. No news from the *Hopkins*, temporarily commanded by another, or from Fred or from the Royal Mail about the ship on which Fred is supposed to arrive from Barbados. I'd convalesce faster if Jim Wilson and his rushing horses would get me something in the mail instead of magazines, advertisements, and bills. Why doesn't Fred telegraph me? Why doesn't he take the French steamer from Fort-de-France? Has he the typically English and American distaste and distrust of French ships? I'd love wine with my meals and a dish of bouillabaisse before my filet mignon and crepes suzettes to top it off, with a bit of Camembert to boot. It would be a welcome and far cry from Mother B's menu of cold porridge for breakfast, stale ham for lunch, and crackers with milk, sour milk at that, for supper. Her penny-pinching affects my health also, with the lack of heat. Captain J.W. installed a hot-water system for heating, radiators and a new coal-burning furnace, but she won't use it because the price of coal is greater than the cost of cutting wood from her own woodlots. That would be reasonable, I suppose, if she allowed the cutters to cut more than what is needed for her kitchen stove and a bit for the fireplace, but she doesn't. The radiators must be frozen because there's no heat in the up-stairs bedrooms. To keep from freezing, I must nap by the fireplace. Although some days she's not so vexing as usual, I do wait for Fred to straighten her out. Childbirth was not the cure-all for me that she claims it was for her (why did she have just the one child?), and I am in pain so often that I can't fight, especially in her own home.

To escape for a short while, I attended the Sewing Circle at the Advent Church and tonight will go to the annual sale at Mrs. Marshall's Bazaar. Shall have the Tibbetts girl in to care for Wilfred. She is so attentive and sweet with him and would never let him come to any harm.

At Mrs. Marshall's, I bought little Dutch bonnets made by Lena Harris. They are so fetching and make lovely presents. The center part is blue and pink muslin with white embroidery in matching colors. I shall send one to Eva Boy-den, who is spending the year at Fajardo in a splendid position as principal. Awfully glad for the wondrous girl. Must get baby's photos from Rockland. Must get together a group interested in having a village library. There's so much to do that I shouldn't let Mother B. bother me. How I do miss Fred, who has been twice as gentle to me since his father died, not nearly so cross. It will be five weeks tomorrow that the poor boy has been gone on his fruitless er-rand. The jury acquitted the murderer, and the Consul wrote me privately that he believes it was due to the blacks being so scared of white Frenchmen having guns. They ignored the murder and ganged up against gun-running. I do find some sympathy with them, I must admit, and wasn't it a shame that Captain J.W. should get involved in such foolishness, but, as the Consul wrote, every skipper visiting Martinique is requested to bring in guns. The situation, he says, is such that the whites, a tiny minority, feel threatened every hour of the day and night and must protect themselves or flee their island.

I got word of Fred's arrival date and telegraphed cousin Roscoe to meet him. Shall try to get shiftless Roy Hupper, he who mismanages the water works, to drive me in the machine to Thomaston when Fred's train arrives.

December 16, 1912.

Hurrah! Hurrah! Came a telegram this morning from Fred. He arrived in New York and is coming home at once. I am so glad. He'll get the furnace going and rub my back and play with his little son. Wilfred laughed so coyly at me when I told him his Daddy was coming home. You'd think he almost understood. He is a perfect dear and more fun than a basket of monkeys.

December 17, 1912.

Fred came home on the *SS Monhegan* today. I had made fudge and stuffed dates for him. I had also decorated our room and embroidered pillows for his homecoming. I should have known better. All the thanks I got was, "Where in hell have you hidden Nellie's pillow?" Also. I purposely gave up an invitation to meet with my library group because Fred was coming home, and damned if he didn't go out and spend the whole evening with nasty Perce Hupper, his bastard cousin. I do get so everlastingly weary of being the only one to do the square thing. And how my poor back does ache from doing all those things for his arrival. I'd better get him away from his mother soon. Shall we go to sea in the *Hopkins* or in Father J.W.'s *Margaret Thomas?* I don't care, just so long as we go.

December 22, 1912.

Uptown to Rockland today after the bad storm yesterday. Had to go on the mail carriage with Jim Wilson's racing horses, because the snow was too deep for the Regal to manage. We got stuck three times before we got out of the village. Bought Christmas cards and many goodies at Fuller, Cobbs. Tried condensed milk for Wilfred, so he can get used to it before going shipboard. Used some this evening instead of sending young Alton up to Leonard Seavey's house for fresh milk [Editor's note: Leonard Seavey lived up Horse Point Road, in the house later taken over by N. C. Wyeth, where Andrew Wyeth spent his summers].

Have received many packages from friends but shall not open them until Christmas morning. Sent sister Nettie a bracelet from Rio and sister Myra a check for $25 to help out at the University. Must thank Fred for being able to do so much more than I ever used to be able to do about giving presents. Much of what I wrote about his stinginess in the first part of these diaries should be deleted. He has a native generosity which, sometimes, allows him to overcome his mother's training toward making every penny holler for mercy.

December 23, 1912.

Took Granma Balano her Christmas presents, baby's photo, and a white woolen vest. Mailed cousin Marjorie's and Aunt Mary's presents, also from Rio; also went into the woods and selected Wilfred's Christmas tree, baked Indian pudding, and trotted down cellar for raspberry sauce to top it with. Did a thousand things to keep busy. Wilfred seems to thrive on condensed milk, and that makes me happy because he will soon go to sea where that is all we can supply him with.

Now Mr. Diary, here's a proposition for you, or a riddle to solve. It is about living with Fred's mother. Fred never did stay at home evenings and never will. He is the prima donna in that lowlife Perce's store, glorying in being admired by the lobstermen, the factory workers, and the coastal sailors. How do I manage to move into the little house across from the chapel right away, so that when we return from our trips at sea I shall have my own home? Fred merely sleeps at his mother's and can't stand being there during waking hours. Do I tell him that I can't stand it, either? He should understand, but will he? I doubt it. But if I were to spend my evenings out, as he does, where would I go? I certainly don't want to listen to the women's gossip every evening. And I don't dare talk to anyone here of anything besides who is sleeping with whom. Shall I just walk out and startle him? Think it over, diary, and I'll be waiting.

January 2, 1913.

Son Billy is four months old today and a dear little fellow, too. He has sported short clothes since his Daddy got the furnace going and weighs 15 pounds. His foolish mama wheeled him all the way over to Watson Balano's today to see his greatgrandmother and *resultamente* his mama has a furious backache.

Letters from Myro and Aunt Sue. Heard today that the *SS Savannah* was lost on Frying Pan Shoals, and Captain Giles's schooner was lost off Sandy Hook. I became a member of the Eastern Star, although I don't want to be a "joiner." The Masonic order is very strong in St. George what with so many descendants of Scots and Scotch-Irish protestants. The members see to it that their lodge brothers are selectmen and tax assessors and sheriffs. Woebetide a catholic who enters here, although he'd never know what he was up against until it hit him. Huey Dunn, he of legend, was a catholic. 'Tis said of him that he jumped overboard in Halifax harbor, escaping with a fellow Irishman from a British frigate, back in the seventies. In the icy waters, Huey said he was cold and his mate told him to turn up his coat collar. He wore it ever afterwards turned up, but he changed his religion soon after finding out that he couldn't get a job in any of the local factories. After that he prospered.

After Fred's bout with Mother B. about the price of coal, he now talks of building a coal shed on the shore and dealing in coal. However, it seems as if that dream is on the level with buying a farm out west, because when a report came today that the *Hopkins* had been reported off Montauk, Fred told me to get ready to leave with him to join her. Am worried about Billy getting along on condensed milk, but I must go and take him with me. The lamp has gone out here in this gloomy, gloomy house, and I want no more of this sadness. As Dawsie would say, "I done got de miseries." And Fred just won't stay at home. Once away at sea I shall recover quickly, I know, and Billy will be alright. I shall consult every doctor at Harvard about getting the right formula for his health. Then, when we return to Herring Gut, I shall have my own place, and, as Fred said en route to Rio, it will have a fireplace, a good bath, a furnace, and something he didn't add, a full library.

January 6, 1913.

At sea, glory be, and it's Three King's Day too.

What a wonderful present from The Three Kings, *Los Tres Reyes Magicos*. We are loaded to the gunwales with a full cargo for enchanting England. I wonder, did Mr. and Mrs. Lykes have anything to do with this? Maybe, because we have scores of long masts as deck load. On deck last night, my diamond sparkled in the starlight and so did I, Fred said. Our baby turned in his little hammock and sighed. The nanny goat recommended by the Harvard professors blatted a protest about being milked by the old steward for Billy's midnight milk, and the little kitten Fred got for Billy came purring at my feet for protection against the cold, which I don't feel because I am all warm inside. I am speaking Spanish as well as English to our son and, for myself, learning French. We shall do England before crossing over to Bordeaux to load wine for Boston. Selah!

Nancy Allen

· ·

Back in the U.S.A.

January 5

As a welcome-home gift, the Port of Long Beach presents us with a postcard day. Mid-70s, blue sky spotted with cottony clouds, diamond facets scattered across the sea. Outside the harbor, dozens of sailboats have come out to play, darting around Endurance's *hull. I wave down, the sailors wave back. My perspective has definitely changed from my old boating days: I am the superior high up on this black hull.*

Oddly, the M/V Endurance *is the only containership pointed toward the port. One of the shipping magazines in the lounge had me convinced we'd be only one fish in a big school of commercial vessels:*

> The Port of Long Beach is the busiest containerport in the U.S., with over 2,000 containerships calling in 1994. Upcoming years will bring greater cargo volume, as trans-Pacific shipping companies bring into their fleets new, larger containerships capable of hauling 5,000 TEUs (a 25% larger carrying capacity than current ones possess).

Keith pops out of the radio room to join me on the bridge-wing. "Some sight, huh?" he says, pointing to starboard. "Those landmarks signal 'This way to Long Beach.'" The three poppy-red and black smokestacks of the *Queen Mary* are distinctive navigational aids. I watch the luxury liner, launched in 1936 and once the undisputed queen of the sea, come closer. I think of her heroism during World War II, when she ferried divisions of U.S. soldiers to Europe. She was able to evade all of Hitler's U-boats, with a $250,000 price on her head, only to become a Long Beach tourist attraction.

I've heard that it took eight tugboats to maneuver the *Queen Mary*—159 feet longer than we are—into port. And here are two tugs twirling our ship around in a turning basin, then backing her into the dock as if she were floating on a cushion of air.

Even before *Endurance*'s mooring lines tighten around the bollards, several cars approach with determination down the dock. Significant others emerge, some with small children in tow, and search aloft. All they find is my face as everyone else is still working, and I receive some uncertain stares. I feel I should shout down, "Don't worry . . . I'm legal."

Standing out from a fleet of Sea-Land trucks, two well-polished CUSTOMS and IMMIGRATION cars glide up to the gangway. The Chief Mate had warned me, "Have your passport and customs declaration ready. Please don't embarrass me by disappearing into the workout room. Everyone had to be checked off before the ship is cleared."

So I'm sitting dutifully at my desk, waiting to be called, when Bob storms in. "I can't believe the bastard, I wonder where his brains live, assuming he has any," he sputters. "Louis. Just walked off, said he was looking for a phone to rent a car, then sauntered back. The Immigration folks are furious; they're threatening to retaliate and hold up the whole ship."

"Well I don't know why you're surprised," I answer. "Louis is a video vampire: he's devoured every film on the ship and is desperate for a fresh fix." The Chief Mate does not think the Supernumerary is either amusing or in order.

While Bob and the crew placated the powers that be, I observed something called "bunkering." I'd heard rumors we were going to do this in Long Beach and asked Jim the First what it meant. He answered, "It's what recreational boaters call refueling. *Endurance* can fill her tanks in California and carry enough bunkers—fuel—for the entire voyage. Or she can shop the Far East market and bunker with cheaper fuel over there. This voyage, we bunkered at the beginning and ran so low, we came in on sludge this morning. Had to rev down to 95 rpms.

"Now if we do use foreign fuel, we try to get it tested up front. Bad fuel not only stops you dead in the water but can ruin engine parts. We try to keep bunkers from different ports separate because mixed fuel often waxes up."

"When the fuel barge pulls alongside, she disgorges 3200 tons of heavy fuel oil into *Endurance*'s tanks. The ship's diesel engine burns about ninety tons of this stuff on a good day, more when the seas are rough, the currents strong, the bottom dirty, and the cargo or ballast heavy."

The two-hundred-foot barge tied up alongside. A small crane rigged on *Endurance*'s 02 deck hauled up a long reinforced neoprene hose. A flange at the end of the hose was mated with its partner on the ship's fuel manifold with half a dozen bolts. With the flanges held securely in place, the fuel flowed from barge to ship. The whole procedure could take up to twelve hours, depending on the temperature of the fuel. Pity the poor engineers stuck in the engine room, staring at the gauges and directing the fuel flow into eight pairs of port and starboard tanks.

At lunch, everyone at the table seems all steamed up. Bob declares, "It's not been the greatest morning of my life. I had the whole deck department practically standing at attention for the Coast Guard inspection, and they were an hour late. That screwed up discharging the crew and signing the new ones on. Then one of the fire hoses sprang a leak. That got written up. But here's the last straw. The 'Medical Officer' on the last voyage was supposed to check the dates on all our meds; he forgot. So the Coast Guard found that we've got a bunch of expired drugs and won't let us sail until we replace 'em."

January 6

Somehow I'd forgotten that the alarm was set for 0600—wishful thinking, I guess, that our next-to-last day together might start with love in the morning. For after we'd sailed up the coast to Oakland, I would have to get off. Sea-Land's policy limits the Spouse to one voyage in a calendar year. But Bob is gone and only returns to get me for breakfast. The tension in his face breaks my reverie about togetherness aboard the Queen. *"Is it worse today than usual?" I sympathize.*

"Just the same old you-know-what," he answers. "I always have a headache on departure day from Long Beach. Getting the ship out on time is like conducting. All the musicians must finish on the same note. The longshoremen can screw up without consequence, but if a Chief Mate delays a sailing, he's in danger of getting fired. If there's one thing the company can't tolerate, it's a ship leaving late.

"What's really hard," he says, pocketing the aspirin bottle, "is knowing I'm going back out to do this all over again. I just want to go home with you. . . ." *Reluctant to show more emotion, he turns away.*

At breakfast, the Chief Mate was up/down/back/forth like a wind-up toy as he gave the Bosun instructions about jury-rigging the lifeboat wires. The wrong ones had been delivered. He instructed the cadet to stow the medications, which had finally arrived. He rounded up one of the new ABs with big muscles and explained, "We need a strong arm to free up the stacking frame in #4 hatch. The company keeps pestering us to paint the twistlocks yellow, to help the crane operators get their bearings, but the paint got in between the peckerheads, freezing the locking mechanisms."

By some Act of Providence, the Second Mate noticed that the ship was down at the head. It's an old superstition—never proven—that this makes the wheel unresponsive. There was a mad rush to trim the ship: the C/M rang the engine room and ordered immediate deballasting of the forward tank. All seven hundred tons. By sailing time minus three hours, the final cargo plan still hadn't been delivered, and the C/M had to ask the Captain to call the Marine Office.

Finally, when the Chief Mate checked the container securing, he had to fix a couple of unsecured ones himself. He commented, "All the cargo will be double-checked again before we head out from Oakland. I'm always thinking worst-case scenario."

Let me out of here. In the distance, the skyscrapers of Long Beach, like a group of distinguished guests at a party, beckon me. I step around the mountains of dirty laundry waiting to be offloaded, and onto the Sea-Land shuttle bus. After the security gate, I walk alongside a phalanx of trucks lined up to take our cargo, and down to a Port Authority building where The City of Long Beach kindly provides a free bus to downtown.

I've been dropped back into Civilization. The bus and the streets are clean, immaculate really, around a new convention center. All the signs are in English. The atmosphere is clear as Windexed glass. No surgical masks or kamikaze motorbikes. No piles of rubble, squatting on sidewalks, or snake soup. It's all so agreeable, so American, but strangely, a little boring. I'm able to get a haircut, buy the New York Times, *a rosy lipstick, and a bottle of Napa Valley merlot. But once the necessities are out of the way,* Endurance *pulls me back. I'm in plenty of time for cast-off.*

I open the merlot and pour it to the top of a juice glass I'd stolen from the galley. When I look out the porthole, I remember Bob's orchestra metaphor about everything coming together at once. As the last truck drives off, diesel smoke is already shooting up from Endurance's *two tugboats. The fore and aft lines are cast off from shore and reeled aboard the ship. M/V* Endurance *is bound for sea once more.*

As we glide out to the channel, I look back toward the Queen Mary. *From a different angle and a new perspective, the Sea-Land terminal stands between us and her; and slowly her hull disappears behind a mountain of containers until all I can see is her superstructure and smokestacks. The poor old* Queen: *even with her endearing beauty, as a sea creature, she's functionally obsolete.*

Instead of pampered human passengers, chemicals, "chicken paws" and plastic casters sail the oceans now.

I wonder again how many more years Endurance *has left under her keel. Sea-Land is already anticipating the decline of the D-9's, like the C-4's before them, by ordering a new generation of containerships: longer, faster, designed to carry larger boxes. And if* Endurance *is able to survive another fifteen years or so, what flag will flutter from her stern pole?*

My emotions run as strong as the tide that thrusts us through the Santa Barbara Channel:

I feel sad for all the scrapped, mothballed or permanently tethered vessels, each of which was once a "she" with a real identity and purpose.

I'm proud of the M/V Endurance *which, true to her name, has once again delivered, in spite of icy winds, menacing seas and human discord. Of her officers and crew who, shorthanded, weary, deprived, still band together to keep U.S. commerce rolling. And of Sea-Land; it invented a better way to transport cargo and its vessels still ply the coasts and circle the globe. Whatever happens to American shipping in the future, Sea-Land has had an impressive past.*

I'm grateful that I was able to step inside a working ship and explore her from stem to stern, engine room to bridge. Though I entered the world of merchant shipping unbaptized like Dana, I'm leaving it with respect for those who make their living battling the sea.

Like my hero, I will walk down the gangway to resume a landlubber's life. And like him, "I bade farewell—yes, I do not doubt forever—to those scenes which, however changed or unchanged, must always possess an ineffable interest for me." A ship's lighted bridge will always make me wonder, and remember. I know I can always return in my mind to that place where sky and water meet.

The Cabin Boy

Never while I was at the Sea-Fancy did I sit down at the table with my sisters. I feared hearing more stories, uniquely female, uniquely painful. I wanted shed of such stories.

I wanted my own life. And I wanted it to be different.

Choice lies in the purse. In mine, a denim bag with a drawstring, I had had the foresight to place, besides the money, my needle and thread, for those implements, for a woman, can be transformed into money, or as good as money. And I had in my purse also the dried petals of Giles's rose, but they were coins of the heart. The money intended for hiring the *Camel* to ferry Mother and me to the Island I quickly spent on coarse clothing and a larger needle at a shop near the wharf. And I bought one gold-plated earring.

Then back to the Sea-Fancy. Scissors I borrowed from Mrs. Swain for cutting my hair, which I stuffed into the kitchen garbage under some potato peels. I also used the scissors to cut two other pairs of trousers and their linings, using the bought ones as a pattern, from my navy dress. Lightweight, for the tropics, I thought. How my needle flew up and down those flat-felled seams; men's britches must be firmly stitched. A loose jacket, with warmth, was a necessity—and that afternoon I found one at a pawnshop, cheap, because both sleeves were partly torn away from the armholes, but again my sewing skill prevailed. With the large needle I pierced one earlobe, and then inserted the golden hoop.

Then I told, or rather wrote, the necessary lies. To Uncle and Aunt and Frannie I conveyed the news of the miscarriage and claimed that I had gone to Kentucky. To Mother I wrote that I had returned to the Island. The fall supply boat would leave tomorrow for the island, and it would be months more before any news would pass among my family. When I was safely at sea, I would send back a letter with more truth in it. Since Mrs. Swain had read the letter from my mother telling me not to come to Kentucky, I left on the receiving desk a note saying I had gone back to the Island. And should Giles Bonebright or Kit Sparrow call for me, to tell them I had gone home!

A loosely filled duffel sagging on my shoulder, I strode all-boyish under the elliptical sign, *Mrs. Rebekkah Swain, Proprietress—The Sea-Fancy—Hotel for Ladies,* and set out for the wharf, to see what job I could procure. Suppose, having done so much, no ship would have me? I posed the question as I descended the street toward the boats, my feet shod in men's shoes, for which I had swapped my button boots. Would I ship with whatever vessel would take me? Yes. Yes, I would.

I found a red cap in the street, with a dusty footprint on one side, but I took it as a good omen, brushed it off, and put it on my head. How light and free it is to have short hair! My neck felt bare, and longer, as though it had grown up out of my shoulders.

How full of scurry had been the taking of definitive action! But when I reached the wharf and looked up at the *Sussex,* I stopped as though a stick had been stuck among the spokes of my wheel. I saw standing on the deck the very picture of what I myself would be: a cabin boy. His hair, too, was dark and curly, and he was as pretty a chap as any girl. I judged him to be about ten years old. His jacket fit tightly while mine was loose, but aside from that, we were almost the mirror image of each other.

"Hi, there," I shouted, with all the confidence of an older boy. How much older? I decided to be thirteen and a half.

"Hi, yourself," he said. "Come aboard." He spoke as though he were the captain. Later I learned that this was his usual manner of speaking, and for this much of the crew disliked him, since, of course, no captain was he; but he was the captain's son, Chester Fry.

He rightly divined that I was looking for a berth, and I found out from him that the *Sussex* was due to embark on the morrow. How little time Giles and Kit had allotted for me! I was angry at them both.

The *Sussex* was British-made and christened, I learned, but now she flew an American flag. I had never walked the deck of a big ship before, let alone a whaler. There were the brick furnaces for trying out! Cold, of course, now.

When I asked the boy how he liked serving the ship, he said it was boring. I laughed at him. "I've never been bored in my life," I told him.

This surprised him. At once, he took me for an inventive, entertaining chap—a valuable one to have at sea. He ushered me directly to his father, a man with kindly eyes and somewhat older than I would have expected. Before I could open my mouth to account for myself (in the tradition of lies I had newly taken up), the boy explained that I wished to be a cabin boy, second to himself!

The captain inquiring my name, on the spot I took my father's: "Ulysses

Spenser." The captain said he really had no need of a second cabin boy, but his son would be happier for a companion, and what else could I do? Quickly I said that I could be cook's help as well and could mend as well as a girl. On the last, I felt particularly audacious.

Captain Fry replied that all sailors sewed well and would this be my first voyage.

I readily admitted my greenness.

"But what can you do for a whaler?" he said. His manner was so sweet and meditative, his tone so conversational and eschewing of authoritativeness, that I thought of Giles. Just such a quiet captain could he make!
I told the captain I had remarkable eyes.

"But can you climb the rigging? The height might make you sick."

Then I said that I could stand a hundred feet high and not be sick, for I was a lighthouse boy, but that I would have to learn to go up the ropes.

"A hundred feet? What lighthouse, Ulysses?"

Here I was in trouble, for I did not want to name my own. I could not say Alexandria or Cordouan or Eddystone—historical and foreign! I knew but one at all likely and named it: "Sandy Neck. The light at Sandy Neck across from Barnstable."

"Sandy Neck is scarcely a hundred feet, boy."

I said that was true, but I *could* stand at a hundred feet.

"Then you must show me," he said. "But take your time climbing, I'll not have you splattered on the deck."

Chester hugged his dad as though he were a child of six, and the captain's gnarled hand rested lovingly on the boy's curls. I saw why the boy was aboard; his father could not bear to part with him. I wondered if Chester did any work at all.

"What do you see, Ulysses, that you stare so at us? mMy captain asked.

Ah, he was quick as Torchy had been, when I first met him, to read my face for my thoughts, or, at least, for their shadow.

"Would there not be, Captain Fry, quite enough of the usual cabin boy work to spread out between the two of us?"

The captain glanced up the mast as though to check its height.

"You are afraid?" he said.

With that I turned to the lower footings and began my ascent of the rigging. I went willingly, for I was not afraid and he misquestioned me there, but I was careful.

"Sailors go faster, Ulysses," Chester called to me.

Promptly his father called up an amendment: "Take your care. As you are."

Beyond

Thus instructed by my captain, I climbed with a light heart, for surely I was a girl who could climb. Now I remembered climbing white pine trees in Kentucky, for the mast of a ship reminded me more naturally of a tree trunk than the innards of my old friend the Giant. After climbing the standing rigging, I passed the lower of the furled sails and looked sternward to the mainmast and beyond that to the timber pole of our third mast. Beyond that I looked into the rigging and masts of other ships, and the horizon of the waterline began to be perceived at a different angle. I could see down into the whaleboats hoisted on the davits of the whalers, and the aspects of items left on their decks were now a matter of an above-perspective. From this height, a coil of rope looked like a button with a spiral design, and a bundle of lances, standing like a shock of wheat, were seen mostly as their bright tips, the rest of the head and their staffs being foreshortened. Here was the wind! Here was the sense of sky and air, and this I recognized from standing on the platform of the Giant more than being among the white pine, for in the woods the view was obstructed. The rigging seemed like cobwebs before my eyes that I would brush aside because I was used to the view of utter clarity the Giant afforded.

Now my body spoke to me—my arms trembled. To climb rigging, the legs are not enough, and my arms were all weak and unpracticed in comparison. Yet my legs were so extra-strong that they compensated without complaint. It was more for balance that I wished my arms to be stronger, and I vowed to exercise them till they were the fit companions for my wonderful legs.

Legs like springs! I would glance down at the tops of my shoes occasionally to be sure that I purchased the rope at the ball of my foot and did not work dangerously toward inserting only the toe into the rigging. Though these shoe soles were thick and less sensitive than button boots would have been, still I could feel the sagged rope of the ratlines underfoot. Below my toes, I saw once or twice the upturned faces of Captain Fry and Chester, and how their bodies disappeared so that they were only faces floating like face-fishes some yard or two above the planking of the deck. Surprised fish, they. But with kindly eyes and smiling mouths. Excitement on Chester's face, that I could do such a thing. Pleasure on the captain's face, caused by the same reason. Then I climbed higher.

Up and up! How to tell you about it? You have looked from the edge of a cliff? Climbed your own trees? Those efforts suggest a whiff of rigging-climbing—as the volatile oil from an orange peel suggests the full flavor of its ecstatic juice.

Think of a kite. You know the pleasure in that, I am sure. It is you who are up there dancing, riding the wind. Yes, those who really love to fly the kite no longer have two feet planted firmly on earth. Though there is pleasure in the horselike, alive-seeming pull on that elongated rein of kite string, if you soar airborne with the kite, then perhaps you rejoice with me in the eagerness and liberty of my sky-climbing.

I hope so, for this physical thrill—as wise Wordsworth knew—is but prelude to the symphony of soaring that I would show you and share with you before this tale is done, for it is of the spirit.

I reached my goal—the palms of my hands imprinted with the twisted and tarred hemp. I threaded my body through the opening that is the eye of that tall, upright needle of the mast. And immediately, I began to use my eyes, for of what use is a lookout if she can only climb? There must be some advantage for the ship; it must profit. I looked to sea.

Ah, training of the eye! How many ships had I spotted from the Island? High in my tower at home had I not seen specks in the air and come to know them as the precursors of birds? I could tell by the shape of the speck, the proportion of horizontal dash to vertical depth, by the flying habit of dipping or curving, by its very speed of approach, whether I was looking at a gull or sea eagle or tern or puffin or lone goose blown off course. Likewise the distant bodies of whales strung on the line where water meets sky; that shape was long known to my eye and distinctive as to species. Take the plumes they made— well, that had been my ocean–fashion show, a parade of parasols, and as surely as some girls might say "made in Paris" or "domed up in the English manner" of city sunshades so could I say, noting the distant promenade of whale spouts, "a finback" (whose origin I knew—having asked—from Uncle to be the Azores) or "a right whale" (swum up from Cape Horn). If the beast was a humpback sounding, I knew it by its flukes, and the sperm whale by its gigantic battering-ram head.

(But more of that last quality anon—and doubly more of that, and tragically. How the excitement comes upon me to tell it all! In the quest of writing, the heart can speed up with anticipation—as it does, indeed, during the chase itself of whales. I can swear it, having done both, and I will tell *you* though other writers may not. My heart is beating fast; I am in pursuit; I want my victory—that you should see and hear and above all feel the reality behind these words. For they are but a mask. Not the mask that conceals, not a mask that I would have you strike through as mere appearance, or, worse, deceitful appearance. Words need not be that kind of mask, but a mask such as the ancient Greek actors wore, a mask that expresses rather than conceals the inner drama.)

(But do you know me? Una? You have shipped long with me in the boat that is this book. Let me assure you and tell you that I know you, even something of your pain and joy, for you are much like me. The contract of writing and reading requires that we know each other. Did you know that I try on your mask from time to time? I become a reader, too, reading over what I have just written. If I am your shipbuilder and captain, from time to time I am also your comrade. Feel me now, standing beside you, just behind your shoulder?)

When I reached the crow's nest, I heard a faint "Bravo" waft up. A strong, good, male voice: Captain Fry extending congratulations. But I could not let myself be distracted by that.

My well-trained eyes swept past the harbor—there was someone, manning the masthead of our sister ship the *Essex*, for what reason I didn't stop to imagine—and my gaze roved out to sea and on to the horizon. But stop. Back up. Well before the horizon, just three eyesteps out to sea—say, three thousand feet—what was that submerged shadow? Did I see a treacherous rock waiting to scrape out the hull of some harbor-bound ship? No, it moved. There it was again. A dark gliding. Rapid.

I looked down to aim my voice at my captain. "Whale, ahoy!" I sang out. All triumphant now.

But his words climbed slowly up: "Not possible, boy."

I doubted not my vision, or my judgment, but I looked again to make it more precise. "Killer whale, sir!" "If you see a whale," he shouted, pausing, "shout 'There she blows!'"

"There she blows!" I yelled with all my heart to all the world, and pointed. And at that moment, the lookout on the *Essex* who had happened to be aloft turned like a surprised automaton, and the whale breached.

"There she blows," the *Essex* shouted, as though his cry were echo of my own.

The whale was elegantly patterned all black and white, as neat as a penguin. Its black glistened in the sun, and its white flagged pennantlike. It arched skyward, birdlike, but hefty, wet and sleek, with so much power in his curve that it took your breath. And then it landed, spray flying as though a palm had smacked water, and the sound of smacking, too, and then tucked itself back into the deep.

"There she leaps!" I yelled. And then the killer whale emerged again, farther away. "There she flies! There she runs! There she sails!"

Suddenly the decks of all the whalers and some of the merchant ships were alive. Up their rigging they scrambled, till every masthead as manned, and the harbor rang with their cries like a disorderly choir—"There she blows!" They could not quit, but repeated my origal cry compulsively, as a cluster of hills will announce in many rebounds the first shout.

She was not spouting, but sewing the water with her body, headed for the open sea. The lookouts strained forward in their perches, but, course, the boats could not give chase. Sails were furled, anchors were down. The ships were like tethered dogs, penned up and scrambling at the gate to race after prey that has innocently crossed their yard. The lookouts could only look. The rhythm of her breaching and diving proved regular and ordered the cries of the men (and myself) so that we did begin to sing in unison; and there was a kind of harmony, too, for our voices were at different pitches.

I ceased in my shouting.

Noble Woman, I silently apostrophized the killer whale. I leaned my breasts forward, as though I, too, were breasting the water. Why did I call her Noble, when her name was Killer? I muttered, *She kills no more than any creature of the sea.* Her nobility lay in her freedom.

Gradually, all the voices grew quiet. The last one, like the last pitch in a game of horseshoes, sailed out, clanked down. I watched the other sailors descend one by one. Some nimbly; some carefully; some sliding down, their feet cupped outside the lines. In the mastheads, they had like bright birds, now flown down out of sight, songs silenced. Still I stood and looked to sea.

"Ulysses!" it was Captain Fry. "Stay there."

Then he began to climb, with little Chester climbing, too, in front of him but with the captain's body providing a kind of movable cradle in that Chester climbed within the captain's hands and body and feet. They climbed very slowly, and I could see by his glances and conjecture from his moving mouth that the captain was gently encouraging his boy.

I began to be cold, exposed as I was to the September air, as I waited for them. No doubt little Chester had insisted that he, too, as superior cabin boy, must go aloft. I was sorry I had not bought a regular pea jacket, for I felt I would freeze in a wintry sea. Yet I trusted my ingenuity to provide when need arrived. I would quilt a lining from sailors' scraps.

At length, first Chester, who reached up for my hand, and then the captain threaded into the loop. Some whalers do not have this safety device, but just a tiny open platform to stand on. It was typical of good Captain Fry that he provided safety insofar as it was mortally possible to do so. Ah! the limits of mortality. But that comes later. If only writing were like music with many strands in many layers progressing at once! Da Vinci was said to be able to write different messages simultaneously with each hand! But can anyone read that way? Da Vinci himself, I suppose.

Standing all three together, Fry said to me, "Now, boy, let me look at your eyes."

Obligingly, I looked straight into his, and we commenced to read each other shamelessly.

"So these are eyes that can see under water?" he asked.

"There was a shadow. A moving shadow. Moving at the speed of small whales."

"Looking into your eyes, I do not know what I am seeing," he mused. "But I know that I have never seen it before."

Nor I, sir," I answered somewhat shakily. For the first time, I felt a little afraid. Here was an impertinence, as is any utterance from the heart.

"Can you teach me to see so keen?" Chester asked.

I looked at the father to see his wish.

"Yes," I said. "Partly, at least. I'll teach you from the deck."

But we three stood some time longer in the masthead, and both the captain and I pointed out boats and currents and clouds to Chester.

After a few moments the captain said kindly, "You're cold, Ulysses. Your cheek is flushed. We should go down."

I went first, and they followed after. We all moved slowly, like crippled ants. As children try to tell their pet cats, climbing down is harder than climbing up. But I vowed to practice.

I was assured my berth on the *Sussex*. There was no need to talk further of that. I felt most unusual, most lucky.

That night in my hammock, slung next to Chester's in the stateroom which opened into the captain's cabin, I thought of the three of us aloft in the crow's nest, with volumes of air about us. The present chamber spoke confidingly of close wooden walls, white-painted, a low wooden ceiling. My breath seemed enclosed. I was hung all netted up like a leg of mutton in a string sack. I felt feverish from too much wind. Beyond his closed door, I could hear the captain snoring. A homey sound. The wind had all but blown through me when I was aloft. Did I inhabit wind, or the wind inhabit me?

I thought of my searching in Captain Fry's blue eyes—steady, penetrant. Kind. What had I thought I saw? All reflective in my hammock, I knew at once. I had seen the eyes of a true father.

Notes on Authors

JENNIFER ACKERMAN (b. 1959) studied literature at Yale College and has worked as a contributing writer and editor for the *New York Times* and *National Geographic Magazine*. She was the editor-in-chief of *The Curious Naturalist*, a collection of essays about North American ecosystems, and she was a fellow in creative nonfiction at the Bunting Institute of Radcliffe College. *Notes from the Shore* (1995) is her first book.

NANCY ALLEN (b. 1937) was raised in Pittsburgh, Pennsylvania, and she graduated from Brown University, in Providence, Rhode Island. She has been a contributing editor to *Motor Boat and Sailing* magazine and a field editor for *Motor Boat* magazine.

GLORIA ANZALDÚA (b. 1942) was born to sharecropper parents in the Rio Grande Valley of South Texas. She earned her B.A. from Pan American University and her M.A. from the University of Texas. A Chicana poet, writer, and theorist, she has won numerous awards for her work: Lambda Lesbian Small Book Press Award, NEA Fiction Award, Before Columbus Foundation American Book Award, and Sappho Award of Distinction. Her works include *Borderlands/La frontera: The New Mestiza* (1987) and *Friends from the Other Side/Amigos del otro lado* (1993), and she is the editor of *Making Face, Making Soul/Haciendo caras: Creative and Critical Perspectives by Women of Color* (1990).

KERRY NEVILLE BAKKEN (b. 1972) was born and raised on Long Island, New York. She has published her short stories in the following journals: *Story Quarterly, Cimarron Review, Hampton Shorts,* and *Gulf Coast.* She has been awarded the following prizes: Pushcart Prize Honorable Mention, Associated Writing Intro Journals Award in Fiction, Donald Barthelme Fellowship in Fiction, and the Henfield/Transatlantic Review Fellowship in Fiction.

DOROTHY BALANO (1882–?) was born in Yellow Medicine County, Minnesota, and attended the University of Minnesota. She had a lifelong dedication to keeping journals, and she wrote the most extensive entries in her diary from 1908 until 1913, just before World War I interfered with her life. *The Log of the Skipper's Wife* (1979) was edited and published by her son James W. Balano.

ANDREA BARRETT (b. 1965) is the author of five novels and two collections of short stories: *Lucid Stars* (1988), *Secret Harmonies* (1989), *The Middle Kingdom* (1991), *The Forms of Water* (1993), and *Ship Fever and Other Stories* (1996), and *Voyage of the Narwhal* (1998) and *Servants of the Map: Stories* (2002). She has also been awarded the Distinguished Story Citation from Best American Short Stories for "The Littoral Zone" (1995) and a National Book Award for *Ship Fever and Other Stories* (1996).

DORIS BETTS (b. 1932) is the Alumni Distinguished Professor of English at the University of North Carolina. Among her many awards are an American Academy of Art and Letters Medal and the 1995 Southern Book Critics Award for Fiction for *Souls Raised from the Dead*. She is a writer of both short stories and novels, and her works include *The Gentle Insurrection* (1954), *The Astronomer and Other Stories* (1965), *The River to Pickle Beach* (1972), *The Beasts of the Southern Wild and Other Stories* (1973), *Heading West* (1981), and *Souls Raised from the Dead* (1994).

KATE BRAVERMAN (b. 1950) has been a freelance writer since 1971. She was born in Philadelphia, Pennsylvania, and educated at the University of California, Berkeley. She has published *Milk Run* (1977), *Lithium for Medea* (1979), and *Poems* (1979); and she has edited two anthologies, *Cameos* (1978) and *Ten Los Angeles Poets* (1978).

MARY LOUISA BURTCH BREWSTER (1822–1878) was the daughter of Nancy Maria Chesebrough and Billing Burtch Jr., a successful captain of the whaling vessels *Corvo* and *Charles Phelps*. She married Captain William E. Brewster in 1841 and after being married for four years—separated for more than three—she decided to accompany her husband on his whaling voyages. Mary was a dedicated journal keeper. Her journals have been preserved at Mystic Seaport's G. W. Blunt White Library, and her journals from the years 1845–1851 have been carefully edited by Joan Druett in *"She Was a Sister Sailor": The Whaling Journals of Mary Brewster, 1845–1851* (1992).

MARY PARKER BUCKLES is the author of several natural history books, including *Animals of the World* (1978), *The Flowers around Us* (1985), and *Margins: A Naturalist Meets Long Island Sound* (1997). She was also an editor at the National Audubon Society.

RACHEL L. CARSON (1907–1964) is most well known for her ecological studies. Her works include *Under the Sea Wind: A Naturalist's Picture of Ocean Life* (1941), "Food from the Sea: Fish and Shellfish of New England" (monograph, 1943), "Food from the Sea: Fish and Shellfish of the South Atlantic (monograph, 1944), *The Sea around Us* (1951), *The Edge of the Sea* (1955), and *Silent Spring* (1962). She has won an impressive list of awards: George Westinghouse Science Writing Award (1950), National Book Award (1951), Guggenheim Fellowship (1951–1952), Henry

G. Bryant Gold Medal (1952), Book Award from the National Council of Women in the United States. (1956), Achievement Award from American Association of University Women (1956), New England Outdoor Writers Association Award (1963), and Conservationist of the Year Award from the National Wildlife Federation (1963).

KATE CHOPIN (1851–1904) was born in St. Louis, Missouri. She is most widely known for her novel *The Awakening* (1899), but her other works include *At Fault* (1890), *A Vocation and a Voice: Stories* (1891), and *Bayou Folk* (1894).

AMY CLAMPITT (1920–1994) was born in the small town of New Providence, Iowa. She spent most of her adult writing life working in obscurity, publishing her first book of poems when she was sixty-three years old. Her works include *The Kingfisher* (1983), *What the Light Was Like* (1985), *Archaic Figure* (1987), *Westward* (1990), *A Silence Opens* (1994).

LUCILLE SAYLES CLIFTON (b. 1936) was born in Depew, New York. In 1969 she won the YW-YMHA Poetry Center Discovery Award and with it the publication of her first volume of poems, *Good Times.* Clifton served as poet laureate of Maryland from 1979 to 1982. Her achievements also include fellowships and honorary degrees from Fisk University, George Washington University, Trinity College, and other institutions; two grants from the National Endowment for the Arts; and an Emmy Award from the American Academy of Television Arts and Sciences. Clifton is Distinguished Professor of Humanities at St. Mary's College in Maryland. Her works include *The Black BC's* (1970); *Some of the Days of Everett Anderson* (1970), fourteen works of juvenile fiction she published between 1970 and 1984 (in this series, *Everett Anderson's Goodbye* [1983] received the Coretta Scott King Award in 1984); *Good News about the Earth* (1972), *An Ordinary Woman* (1974), *Generations: A Memoir* (1976), *Two-Headed Woman* (1980), *Next: New Poems* (1987), and *The Book of Light* (1993).

WANDA COLEMAN (b. 1946) is the author of *Imagoes* (1983), *Heavy Daughter Blues: Poems and Stories, 1968–1986* (1987), *A War of Eyes and Other Stories* (1988), *Sleeping Sickness* (1990), *Hand Dance* (1993), *Native in a Strange Land: Trials and Tremors* (1996), *Bathwater Wine* (1998), *Mambo Hips and Make Believe: A Novel* (1999), and *Mercurochrome: New Poems* (2001).

REBECCA BLAINE HARDING DAVIS (1831–1910) was born in Washington, Pennsylvania. In 1861 her long story "Life in the Iron Mills" was accepted by the *Atlantic Monthly.* In the following years she published *Margaret Howth: A Story of Today* (1862), *Waiting for the Verdict* (1868), "In the Market" (1868), *John Andross* (1874), and *Bits of Gossip* (1904). In her lifetime she published ten novels and more than one hundred short works of fiction and nonfiction prose.

JAN DEBLIEU (b. 1955), a journalist, has written for the *Wilmington Delaware News-Journal*, the *Eugene (Oregon) Register-Guard, Newsweek, Emory Magazine, Smithsonian*, the *New York Times Magazine, Southern Living*, and *Orion*. Her works include *Hatteras Journal* (1987), *Meant to Be Wild: The Struggle to Save Endangered Species through Captive Breeding* (1991), and *Wind: How the Flow of Air Has Shaped Life, Myth, and the Land* (1998).

EMILY DICKINSON (1830–1886) was born in Amherst, Massachusetts, and she attended the Amherst Academy and the South Hadley Female Seminary (now Mount Holyoke College). She wrote nearly two thousand poems, of which only a dozen were published during her lifetime. In 1955 Thomas Johnson published her complete works in a form true to her original intent.

JOAN DIDION (b. 1934) is a native of the Sacramento Valley. Her works include *Run River* (1963), *Slouching towards Bethlehem* (1968), *Play It As It Lays* (1970), *A Book of Common Prayer* (1977), *The White Album* (1979), *Salvador* (1983), *Democracy* (1984), *Miami* (1987), and *The Last Thing He Wanted* (1996).

ANNIE DILLARD (b. 1945) was born in Pittsburgh, Pennsylvania. Her works include *Pilgrim at Tinker Creek* (1974), for which she received a Pulitzer Prize; *Tickets for a Prayer Wheel* (1974), *Holy the Firm* (1977), *Teaching a Stone to Talk: Expeditions and Encounters* (1982), *Living by Fiction* (1982), *An American Childhood* (1987), *The Living* (1992), and *Mornings Like This: Found Poems* (1995).

GRETEL EHRLICH (b. 1946) grew up in Santa Barbara, California. Her works include *To Touch the Water* (1981), *The Solace of Open Spaces* (1985), *Heart Mountain* (1988), *Islands, the Universe, Home* (1991), *Arctic Heart: A Poem Cycle* (1992), and *A Match to the Heart: One Woman's Story of Being Struck by Lightning* (1994). She has been honored by the American Academy and Institute of Arts and Letters and has also been the recipient of a Whiting Foundation grant.

ANITA ENDREZZE (b. 1952) is a Yaqui artist and writer who was raised in California, Hawaii, Washington, and Oregon. She earned her M.A. in creative writing from Eastern Washington University in 1975. Her work has been published in a number of magazines and books, and in 1983 she published two chapbooks, *Burning the Fields* and *The North Country*. In 1992 she published *at the helm of twilight*. In addition, her artwork has been used to illustrate a number of books on American Indian writing, including the cover art for *Harper's Anthology of Twentieth-Century Native American Poetry*.

DIANE P. FREEDMAN (b. 1955), who grew up on Long Island, has published poems, essays, and literary criticism in journals and collections such as *Wind, Sou'wester, Ascent, Bucknell Review, ISLE, College Literature, Anxious Power, Constructing and Reconstructing Gender*, and *Personal Effects*. She is the author of *An Alchemy of Genres: Cross-Genre Writing by American Feminist Poet-Critics* (1992); coeditor of *The Teacher's Body: Embodiment, Identity, and Authority in the Academy* (2002) and *The Intimate Critique: Autobiographical Literary Criticism* (1993); and editor of *Millay at 100: A Critical Reappraisal* (1995).

Tᴇss Gᴀʟʟᴀɢʜᴇʀ (b. 1943) was born in Port Angeles, Washington. She has published poems, essays, stories, a recording, and a screenplay written with her husband, Raymond Carver. Her poetry includes *Stepping Outside* (1974), *Instructions to the Double* (1976), *Under Stars* (1978), *Portable Kisses* (1978), *On Your Own* (1978), *Willingly* (1984), *Amplitude: New and Selected Poems* (1987), *Moon Crossing Bridge* (1992), *Owl-Spirit Dwelling* (1988), and *My Black Horse: New and Selected Poems* (1995). Her other writings include *Some with Wings, Some with Manes* (1982), *Dostoevsky: A Screenplay* (1985), *A Concert of Tenses: Essays on Poetry* (1986), *The Lover of Horses and Other Stories* (1987), *Across the Bridge* (1994), and *At the Owl Woman Saloon* (1997). She is also the winner of awards from the National Endowment for the Arts (1976 and 1981), a CAPS grant from the New York State Arts Council, the Elliston Award, Voertman Award, a 1978–1979 fellowship from the Guggenheim Foundation, a Governor's Award from the State of Washington in 1984, 1986, and 1987, a New York State Arts grant, and a Maxine Cushing Gray Foundation Award.

Sᴜsᴀɴ Gʟᴀsᴘᴇʟʟ (1876–1948), born and raised in Davenport, Iowa, attended Drake University and began her writing career as a journalist for the *Des Moines Daily News*. Glaspell, a noted dramatist and fiction writer, was a cofounder of the Provincetown Players, a group of experimental actors who performed one-act plays in a wharf theater. She won a Pulitzer Prize for *Alison's House: A Play in Three Acts* (1930). Her works include *Trifles* (1916), *A Jury of Her Peers* (1916), *The Outsiders* (1916), *Inheritors: A Play in Three Acts* (1921), *The Verge: A Play in Three Acts* (1922), *The Road to the Temple* (1927), *The Comic Artist: A Play in Three Acts* (1927), and *The Morning Is Near Us* (a novel) (1940).

Mᴀʀʏ Hᴏᴏᴅ (b. 1946) was born in Brunswick, Georgia, and has always had a deep interest in natural history, ornithology, and wildflower gardening. Her books include *How Far She Went* (1984), *And Venus Is Blue* (1986), and *Familiar Heat* (1995). She has contributed short stories and essays to *Georgia Review, Kenyon Review, Ohio Review, North American Review, Yankee, Harper's Magazine, Art and Antiques,* and *Southern Magazine.* She has won the Flannery O'Connor Award for short fiction and Southern Review/Louisiana State University Short Fiction Award for *How Far She Went.* She has also won the National Magazine Award in fiction for the short story "Something Good for Ginnie" (1986) and the Townsend Prize for Fiction (1988) for *And Venus Is Blue.*

Cʏɴᴛʜɪᴀ Hᴜɴᴛɪɴɢᴛᴏɴ has received grants from the New Hampshire State Council on the Arts, The Fine Arts Work Center in Provincetown, and the Massachusetts Cutlural Council, as well as two fellowships from the National Endowment for the

Arts. Other awards include the Robert Frost Prize from the Frost Place in Franconia, New Hampshire; the Jane Kenyon Award in Poetry, the Emily Clark Balch Prize, and the Levis Prize. Her works include three books of poetry, *The Fish-Wife* (1986), *We Have Gone to the Beach* (1996), and *The Radiant* (2003), and a prose memoir, *The Salt House* (1999).

SARAH ORNE JEWETT (1849–1909) (born Theodora Sarah Orne) grew up and lived her entire life in South Berwick, Maine, in the house her shipbuilding grandfather bought. Her first stories were published under the pseudonym A. C. Eliot in the *Atlantic Monthly* and the *Riverside Magazine for Young People*. Published under the name Sarah Orne Jewett were *Deephaven* (1877), *A Country Doctor* (1884), *A White Heron and Other Stories* (1886), and *The Country of Pointed Firs* (1896).

MARY KARR (b. 1954), the daughter of J. P., an oil refinery worker, and Charlie Marie, an artist and business owner, was born in East Texas, where she grew up in a small coastal town. She has written two collections of poetry, *Abacus* (1987) and *The Devil's Tour* (1993), as well as *The Liars' Club: A Memoir* (1995) and *Cherry: A Memoir* (2000).

SUSAN KENNEY (b. 1941) won the first annual New Voices Literary Award from the Quality Paperback Book Club for *In Another Country: A Novel* (1984). She won the 1982 O. Henry Award for her short story "Facing Front." Her other works include *Garden of Malice* (1983), *Graves in Academe* (1986), *Sailing* (1988), and *One Fell Sloop* (1990).

CAROLYN KIZER (b. 1925) was born in Spokane, Washington. Kizer studied with Theodore Roethke and traveled widely through China and Japan. In 1985 she won a Pulitzer Prize for *Yin* (1984). Her other works include *The Ungrateful Garden* (1961), *Knock upon Silence* (1965), *Midnight Was My Cry* (1971), *Mermaids in the Basement* (1984), *The Nearness of You* (1986), and *Proses: On Poems and Poets* (1993).

URSULA K. LE GUIN (b. 1929) was born in Berkeley, California, and she studied at Radcliffe College and Columbia University. Known primarily as a science fiction writer, she is a prolific author who has also written essays, short stories, novels, poetry, and children's literature. Her works include *Rocannon's World* (1966); *The Left Hand of Darkness* (1969); and the *Earth Sea* trilogy: *A Wizard of Earthsea* (1968), *The Tombs of Atuan* (1971), and *The Farthest Shore* (1972). Some of her other works are *The Dispossessed* (1974), *Always Coming Home* (1985), *Catwings* (1988), *Wild Oats and Firewood* (1988), *Catwings Return* (1989), *Fire and Stone* (1989), *Dancing at the Edge of the World* (1989), *Tehanu* (1990), *Searoad* (1991), and *Going Out with Peacocks* (1994). She has won the Hugo and Nebula Awards from the Science Fiction Writers of America, and, in addition to receiving a National Book Award in 1991, she was honored by the American Academy and Institute of Arts and Letters with the Harold D. Vursell Memorial Award.

DENISE LEVERTOV (b. 1923), although born in Essex, England, has become known as an American poet. Levertov emigrated to the United States in 1948 and became an American citizen in 1955. Her works include *The Double Image* (1946), *The Jacob's Ladder* (1961), *O Taste and See* (1964), *The Sorrow Dance* (1967), *Relearning the Alphabet* (1970), *The Poet in the World* (1973), *The Freeing of the Dust* (1975), *Light Up the Cave* (1981), *Candles in Babylon* (1982), *Breathing the Water* (1987), *Evening Train* (1992) and *Tesserae: Memories and Suppositions* (1995).

ANNE MORROW LINDBERGH (1906–2001) was born in Englewood, New Jersey, and is most widely known for her environmental and autobiographical writings. Her works include *North to the Orient* (1935), *Listen! The Wind* (1938), *The Wave of the Future* (1940), *The Steep Ascent* (1944), *Gift from the Sea* (1955), *The Unicorn and Other Poems* (1956), *Dearly Beloved* (1962), *Earth Shine* (1969), and *Christmas in Mexico, 1927* (1971), as well as diaries and letters collected in *Bring Me a Unicorn Lindbergh* (1972), *Hour of Gold, Hour of Lead* (1973), *Locked Rooms and Open Doors* (1974), *The Flower and the Nettle* (1976), and *War Within and Without* (1980).

NANCY LORD has lived in Alaska since 1973, fished commercially for salmon, and written and taught at the University of Alaska. She is the author of *The Compass Inside Ourselves* (1984), *Survival* (1991), *Fishcamp* (1997), *Green Alaska: Dreams from the Far Coast* (1999), and *The Man Who Swam with Beavers* (2001).

SANDRA MCPHERSON (b. 1943) was born in San Jose, California, and attended San Jose State College and the University of Washington. Her work is widely anthologized, and she has published ten poetry collections: *Radiation* (1973), *The Year of Our Birth* (1978), *Sensing* (1980), *Patron Happiness* (1983), *Floralia* (1985), *Streamers* (1988), *Designating Duet* (1989), *The God of Indeterminacy* (1993), *Edge Effect: Trails and Portrayals* (1996), and *The Spaces between Birds: Mother/Daughter Poems, 1967–1995* (1996).

EDNA ST. VINCENT MILLAY (1892–1950), born in Rockland, Maine, began her writing career as an adolescent. At the age of twenty, she entered "Renascence" into a poetry contest and won fourth place. She attended Vassar College, where she wrote *Ballad of the Harp-Weaver and Other Poems*, for which she received a Pulitzer Prize in 1923. Her other works include three verse plays, *Aria da Capo* (1920), *The Lamp and the Bell* (1921), and *Two Slatterns and a King* (1921); she later published *Collected Sonnets* (1941) and *Collected Lyrics* (1943).

MARIANNE MOORE (1887–1972) was born in Kirkwood, Missouri, but grew up in Carlisle, Pennsylvania. She attended Bryn Mawr College. *Observations* was published in 1924, and in 1925 she became the editor of the *Dial*. In 1935 *Selected Poems*, with an introduction by T. S. Eliot, brought her greater public attention. She was awarded a Bollingen Prize, a National Book Award for Poetry, and a Pulitzer Prize.

RUTH MOORE (1903–1989) was born on Gotts Island, Maine. She attended the New York State Teachers College at Albany, and after college she worked for the NAACP. Eventually, she returned to Bass Harbor, Maine, where she wrote fourteen novels and three books of verse. Some of her works include *The Weir* (1943), *Candlemas Bay* (1950), *Speak to the Winds* (1956), and *Lizzie and Caroline: A Novel* (1972).

SENA JETER NASLUND was born in Birmingham, attended Norwood Elementary School, Phillips High School, and Birmingham-Southern College. She holds a Ph.D. from the University of Iowa Writers' Workshop. She has received grants from the National Endowment for the Arts, the Kentucky Arts Council, and the Kentucky Foundation for Women. Naslund, the recipient of the Harper Lee Award and chosen Alabama Writer of the Year 2001, is the author of *Ice Skating at the North Pole* (1989), *The Animal Way to Love* (1993), *Sherlock in Love* (1993), *The Disobedience of Water* (1999), and *Ahab's Wife: Or, The Star-Gazer* (1999).

GLORIA NAYLOR (b. 1950) was born in New York City. She received her B.A. from Brooklyn College and her M.A. from Yale University. She has published *The Women of Brewster Place* (1982), *Linden Hills* (1985), *Mama Day* (1988), and *Bailey's Café* (1992). She has received the following awards and fellowships: American Book Award for Best First Novel, Distinguished Writer Award, Mid-Atlantic Writer's Association, National Endowment for the Arts fellowship, Candace Award of the National Coalition of One Hundred Black Women, Guggenheim fellowship, and Lillian Smith Award.

MARY OLIVER (b. 1935) was born in Maple Heights, Ohio. She is the author of ten volumes of poetry, including *American Primitive* (1983), for which she won a Pulitzer Prize; *House of Light* (1990), which won the Christopher Award and the L. L. Winship/PEN New England Award; *New and Selected Poems* (1992), which won the National Book Award; *White Pine* (1994); *West Wind* (1997); and *Winter Hours: Prose, Prose Poems, and Poems* (1999). She has also written three books of prose: *A Poetry Handbook* (1994), *Blue Pastures* (1995), and *Rules for the Dance: A Handbook for Writing and Reading Metrical Verse* (1998).

ELIZABETH STUART PHELPS (1844–1911) was the author of fifty-seven volumes of fiction, poetry, and essays. Some of her works include *The Gates Ajar* (1868), *The Silent Partner* (1871), *The Story of Avis* (1877), *Doctor Zay* (1882), *A Singular Life* (1895), and *Chapters from a Life*, her autobiography (1896).

E. ANNIE PROULX (b. 1935) won the 1994 Pulitzer Prize in fiction, the National Book Award for Fiction, and the Irish Times International Fiction prize for *The Shipping News* (1993). She is also the author of *Postcards* (1992), winner of the 1993 PEN/Faulkner Award; *Accordion Crimes* (1996), and two collections of short stories, *Heart Songs and Other Stories* (1988) and *Close Range* (1999).

MAY SARTON (1912–1995) was born in Belgium but raised in Cambridge, Massachusetts, and attended schools in both Cambridge and Brussels. Her works include *The Single Hound* (1938), *A Shower of Summer Days* (1952), *The Small Room* (1961), *Joanna and Ulysses* (1963), *Mrs. Stevens Hears the Mermaids Singing* (1965), *Kinds of Love* (1970), *As We Are Now* (1973), *Journal of a Solitude* (1973), *The House by the Sea* (1977), *The Magnificent Spinster* (1985), *After the Stroke* (1988), *The Education of Harriet Hatfield* (1989), *Encore: A Journal of the Eightieth Year* (1993), and *Collected Poems 1930–1993* (1993).

ELIZABETH SPENCER (b. 1921) has written novels, short stories, a play and a memoir. Her works include *Fire in the Morning* (1948), *The Crooked Way* (1952), *The Voice at the Back Door* (1956), *The Light in the Piazza* (1960), *Knights and Dragons* (1965), *Ship Island and Other stories* (1968), *The Snare* (1972), *Marilee* (1981), *The Salt Line* (1984), *Jack of Diamonds and Other Stories* (1988), *The Night Travellers* (1991), *On the Gulf* (1991), and *Landscapes of the Heart: A Memoir* (1998).

HARRIET BEECHER STOWE (1811–1896) grew up in Litchfield, Connecticut, later lived with her family in Cincinnati, Ohio, and then settled in Maine. She was best known for her novel *Uncle Tom's Cabin: Or, Life among the Lowly* (1851). Some of her other works include *Sunny Memories of Foreign Lands* (1854), *Dred* (1856), *The Minister's Wooing* (1859), *The Pearl of Orr's Island* (1862), *Oldtown Folks* (1869), *Oldtown Fireside Stories* (1871), and *Poganuc People* (1878).

MAY SWENSON (1913–1989) was born in Logan, Utah, and she died in Ocean View, Delaware. In her lifetime she worked as a journalist, an editor, a ghostwriter, and a poet. She published eleven volumes of poems and received numerous awards, including Brandeis University Creative Arts Award; Rockefeller, Guggenheim, and Ford fellowships; the Bollingen Prize for Poetry; a grant from the National Endowment for the Arts; an honorary doctorate from Utah State University; and a MacArthur Fellowship. She was a member of the American Academy and Institute of Arts and Letters and a chancellor of the Academy of American Poets. Her works include *Another Animal* (1954), *A Cage of Spines* (1958), *To Mix with Time* (1963), *Poems to Solve* (1966), *Half Sun, Half Sleep* (1967), *Iconographs* (1970), *More Poems to Solve* (1971), *The Guess and Spell Coloring Book* (1976), *New and Selected Things Taking Place* (1978), *In Other Words* (1987), *The Love Poems* (1991), *The Complete Poems to Solve* (1993), and *Nature: Poems Old and New* (1994).

SARA TEASDALE (1884–1933) was born in St. Louis, Missouri. She won the Columbia University Society Prize (which later became the Pulitzer Prize in poetry). She also won a Poetry Society Prize. Her works include *Sonnets to Duse, and Other Poems* (1907), *Helen of Troy and Other Poems* (1911: rev. 1922), *Rivers to the Sea* (1915), *Love Songs* (1917), *The Answering Voice: One Hundred Love Lyrics by Women* (1917), *Flame and Shadow* (1920; rev. 1924), *Dark of the Moon* (1926), *A Country House* (1932), and *The Collected Poems* (1937).

CELIA THAXTER (1835–1894) grew up on White Island, one of the nine islands comprising the Isles of Shoals, a group of small islands off the coast of Maine and New Hampshire. Her father, Thomas Laighton, was the keeper of the lighthouse. Her works include *Among the Isles of Shoals* (1873), *Ballads of Home* (1876), *Blackberry Bush* (1878), *Driftwood* (1878), and *An Island Garden* (1894).

Acknowledgments

· ·

The editor and the publisher are grateful for permission to include the following copyrighted material in this collection:

Jennifer Ackerman: "Prologue" and "Osprey" from *Notes from the Shore* by Jennifer Ackerman, copyright © 1995 by Jennifer Ackerman. Used by permission of Viking Penguin, a division of Penguin Putnam Inc.

Nancy Allen: Chapter 22, "Back in the U.S.A.," from *Fair Seafarer: A Honeymoon Adventure with the Merchant Marine,* by Nancy Allen. Copyright © 1999. Reprinted by permission of Bridge Works Publishing Co.

Gloria Anzaldúa: "El otro México" from *Borderlands/La frontera: The New Mestiza.* Copyright © 1987, 1999 by Gloria Anzaldúa. Reprinted by permission of Aunt Lute Books.

Kerry Neville Bakken: "Vigil" from *Hampton Shorts.* Reprinted by permission of the author.

Dorothy Balano: Selection from *The Log of the Skipper's Wife* by James W. Balano, reprinted courtesy of Down East Books.

Andrea Barrett: "The Littoral Zone" from *Ship Fever and Other Stories* by Andrea Barrett. Copyright © 1996 by Andrea Barrett. Used by permission of W. W. Norton & Company, Inc.

Doris Betts: Selection from *The River to Pickle Beach* by Doris Betts. Copyright © 1972 by Doris Betts. Reprinted with the permission of Scribner, an imprint of Simon & Schuster Adult Publishing Group.

Kate Braverman: Selection from *Small Craft Warnings* by Kate Braverman. Copyright © 1995 by Kate Braverman. Reprinted with the permission of the University of Nevada Press.

Mary Brewster: Selection from *"She Was a Sister Sailor": The Whaling Journals of Mary Brewster, 1845–1851.* Copyright © Mystic Seaport, Manuscript Collection.

389

Mary Parker Buckles: "Intertidal Zone" and "The Shore" from *Margins: A Naturalist Meets Long Island Sound* by Mary Parker Buckles. Copyright © 1997 by Mary Parker Buckles. Reprinted by permission of Farrar, Straus and Giroux, LLC.

Rachel Carson: "The Marginal World" from *The Edge of the Sea* by Rachel Carson. Copyright © 1955 by Rachel L. Carson, renewed 1983 by Roger Christie. Reprinted by permission of Houghton Mifflin Company. All rights reserved.

Amy Clampitt: "Beach Glass" and "The Outer Bar" from *The Collected Poems of Amy Clampitt* by Amy Clampitt, copyright © 1997 by the Estate of Amy Clampitt. Used by permission of Alfred A. Knopf, a division of Random House, Inc.

Lucille Clifton: "blessing the boats" and "crabbing" © 2000 by Lucille Clifton. Reprinted from *Blessing the Boats: New and Selected Poems, 1988–2000*, with permission of BOA Editions, Ltd.

Wanda Coleman: "Woman on Sand" copyright © 1987 by Wanda Coleman. Reprinted from *Heavy Daughter Blues* with permission of the author.

Jan DeBlieu: "Old Christmas" with permission from *Hatteras Journal*, by Jan DeBlieu. © 1987 Fulcrum Publishing, Golden, Colorado. All rights reserved.

Joan Didion: "Quiet Days in Malibu" from *The White Album* by Joan Didion. Copyright © 1979 by Joan Didion. Reprinted by permission of Farrar, Straus and Giroux, LLC.

Annie Dillard: Selection from *The Living* by Annie Dillard. Copyright © 1992 by Annie Dillard. Reprinted by permission of HarperCollins Publishers Inc.

Gretel Ehrlich: "Santa Rosa" from the July/August issue of *ISLANDS Magazine*. Copyright © 1996 by ISLANDS Media. Reprinted by permission.

Anita Endrezze: "The Mapmaker's Daughter" from *At the Helm of Twilight*. Copyright © 1992 by Anita Endrezze. Reprinted by permission of the author.

Diane P. Freedman: "A Whale of a Different Color" reprinted with permission from *ISLE* 4.2.

Tess Gallagher: "The Woman Who Raised Goats," "3 A.M. Kitchen: My Father Talking," and "Boat Ride" © 1987 by Tess Gallagher. Reprinted from *Amplitude: New and Selected Poems* with the permission of Graywolf Press, Saint Paul, Minnesota.

Mary Hood: "First Things First" from *Familiar Heat* by Mary Hood, copyright © 1995 by Mary Hood. Used by permission of Alfred Knopf, a division of Random House, Inc.

Cynthia Huntington: "The Edge" from *The Salt House: A Summer on the Dune of Cape Cod*, © 1999 by Cynthia Huntington. Reprinted by permission of University Press of New England.

Mary Karr: Chapter 5 from *The Liars' Club* by Mary Karr, copyright © 1995 by Mary Karr. Used by permission of Viking Penguin, a division of Penguin Putnam, Inc.

Susan Kenney: "Sailing," from *Sailing* by Susan Kenney, copyright © 1988 by Susan Kenney. Used by permission of Viking Penguin, a division of Penguin Putnam Inc.

Carolyn Kizer: "The Great Blue Heron" from *Mermaids in the Basement: Poems for Women*. Copyright © 1984 by Carolyn Kizer. Reprinted with the permission of Copper Canyon Press, P.O. Box 271, Port Townsend, WA 98368-0271.

Ursula K. Le Guin: "Texts" copyright © 1990 by Ursula K. LeGuin; first appeared in *American Short Fiction* as part of the American Syndicated Fiction; reprinted by permission of the author and the author's agents, the Virginia Kidd Agency, Inc.

Denise Levertov: Selections from *Sands of the Well,* copyright © 1996 by Denise Levertov. Reprinted by permission of New Directions Publishing Corp.

Anne Morrow Lindbergh: "Channelled Whelk" from *Gift from the Sea* by Anne Morrow Lindbergh, copyright © 1955, 1975, renewed 1983 by Anne Morrow Lindbergh. Used by permission of Pantheon Books, a division of Random House, Inc.

Nancy Lord: "Putting Up Boat" from *Fishcamp: Life on an Alaskan Shore.* Copyright © Nancy Lord 1997. Reprinted by permission of Counterpoint Press, a member of Perseus Books, LLC. Used by permission of Nancy Lord.

Sandra McPherson: "Edge Effect" and "Ocean Water Absorbs Red, Orange and Yellow Light" from *Edge Effect: Trails and Portrayals* by Sandra McPherson. Copyright © Sandra McPherson 1996. Used by permission of Wesleyan University Press.

Marianne Moore: Poems reprinted with the permission of Scribner, an imprint of Simon & Schuster Adult Publishing Group, from *The Collected Poems of Marianne Moore* by Marianne Moore. Copyright © by Marianne Moore; copyright renewed © 1963 by Marianne Moore and T. S. Eliot.

Ruth Moore: Selection from *The Weir*, copyright © 1943 by Ruth Moore. Thank you to the family of Ruth Moore for providing permission to reprint material from *The Weir*.

Sena Jeter Naslund: "The Cabin Boy" (pp. 142–51) from *Ahab's Wife* by Sena Jeter Naslund. Copyright © 1999 by Sena Jeter Naslund. Reprinted by permission of HarperCollins Publishers Inc.

Gloria Naylor: Selection from *Mama Day* by Gloria Naylor. Copyright © 1988 Gloria Naylor. Reprinted by permission of Houghton Mifflin Company. All rights reserved.

Acknowledgments